Beginning ASP.NET MVC 1.0

Beginning
ASP.NET MVC 1.0

Beginning
ASP.NET MVC 1.0

Simone Chiaretta
Keyvan Nayyeri

WILEY

Wiley Publishing, Inc.

Beginning ASP.NET MVC 1.0

Published by
Wiley Publishing, Inc.
10475 Crosspoint Boulevard
Indianapolis, IN 46256
www.wiley.com

For my wife, Daniela, and for the friends who supported me.
—Simone Chiaretta

For all Iranians around the world.
—Keyvan Nayyeri

About the Author

Simone Chiaretta (Milan, Italy) is a software architect and developer who enjoys sharing his development experience and more than 10 years' worth of knowledge on Web development with ASP.NET and other Web technologies.

He is currently working as a senior solution developer for Avanade, an international consulting company jointly owned by Accenture and Microsoft. Before working for Avanade, he worked for eight years as a Web developer and all-round developer for Esperia, a Web agency based in Milan, Italy, where he developed a CMS that still powers the AC Milan Web site. Then he decided to go to the place that is farthest from Milan: Wellington, New Zealand, where he worked for one year as chief software architect for Calcium Software Ltd.

He is a Microsoft MVP in ASP.NET, and he has been involved in many open source projects, but now he focuses only on SubText to try to take it to the next level. He is also an active member of the Italian .NET User Group, cofounder of the UGIALT.NET user group, the Italian chapter of the ALT.NET movement, and a frequent speaker for community events throughout Italy.

Simone loves sharing his thoughts and knowledge on his blog at `http://codeclimber.net.nz` and, if you can read Italian, also at `http://blogs.ugidotnet.org/piyo`.

When not working or playing with technology, Simone tries to spend time with his wife, Daniela, climbing various kind of walls: ice-climbing, free-climbing, and alpine and mountain climbing. Additionally, he just started training to take part in triathlons.

Keyvan Nayyeri (Tehran, Iran) is a software architect and developer who has a bachelor of science degree in applied mathematics. He was born in Kermanshah, Kurdistan, in 1984.

Keyvan's main focus is on Microsoft development technologies and their related technologies. He's also experienced in practices and enjoys them very much. Keyvan has a serious passion for community activities and open source software. As a result, he is an author for some famous .NET communities and has published various articles and tutorials on them. He is also a team leader and developer of some famous .NET open source projects, where he tries to learn many things through writing code for special purposes. Keyvan also has received a number of awards and recognition from Microsoft, its partners, and online communities. Some major highlights include Microsoft VSX Insider and Telligent Community Server MVP.

Before writing this book, Keyvan worked on other Wrox titles as an author and technical editor, including *Professional Visual Studio Extensibility* (ISBN: 978-0-470-23084-8), *Professional Community Server* (ISBN: 978-0-470-10828-4), and *Professional Visual Studio 2008* (ISBN: 978-0-470-22988-0).

You can check out his blog, which contains his thoughts about technical and personal views, at `http://www.nayyeri.net`.

About the Technical Editors

Eilon Lipton: Starting out with Turbo Pascal and assembly language, Eilon used to work on underground "demo" graphics animations while in high school. He graduated from Boston University in 2002 with a dual degree in Computer Science and Math. In the past six years, Eilon has worked at Microsoft on the ASP.NET team on data source controls, control designers, and the UpdatePanel control. Eilon is currently a senior development lead and works on the ASP.NET MVC framework.

Ivan Porto Carrero is a freelance consultant on .NET and Ruby. He has six years of experience with C# and three years with Ruby. Ivan has been developing Web sites with Castle/Monorail for three years and has contributed to the Castle project and various JavaScript libraries. Ivan also contributed the XSLT View engine in the mvccontrib project. Ivan's background is primarily on the Internet, where he has been active for the biggest part of the last 10 years. Ivan is also active in the community and started the .NET user group chapter in New Plymouth, New Zealand. Later he started an architect's lunch meeting in Wellington, New Zealand before moving back to Belgium.

Credits

Acquisitions Editor
Katie Mohr

Development Editors
Kelly Talbot
Sydney Jones

Technical Editors
Eilon Lipton
Ivan Porto Carrero

Production Editor
Kathleen Wisor

Copy Editor
Kim Cofer

Editorial Manager
Mary Beth Wakefield

Production Manager
Tim Tate

Vice President and Executive Group Publisher
Richard Swadley

Vice President and Executive Publisher
Barry Pruett

Associate Publisher
Jim Minatel

Project Coordinator, Cover
Lynsey Stanford

Compositors
Jeffrey Wilson
Kate Kaminski,
Happenstance Type-O-Rama

Proofreader
Nancy Carrasco

Indexer
Robert Swanson

Acknowledgments

We have to start by thanking God for being such a great support in all steps in our life, including this book. Doubtlessly, we would have been unable to make it without the power that He granted to us.

We also should thank our family members and friends for their continued help and for believing in us. We both owe them for our achievements.

Besides that, we should thank the editorial group for the book. Katie Mohr (Acquisitions Editor) helped us to get started and address all the problems that rose during the long process of writing. Kelly Talbot and Sydney Jones (Development Editors) did a great job copyediting our material and improving the language while they took care of schedules and communications between authors and other editors. Eilon Lipton and Ivan Porto Carrero (Technical Editors) helped us catch our technical flaws and add helpful content to our chapters, so they have had an important influence on the quality of the book.

We should thank all these editors for their hard work and close collaboration on this book. Most of the content was being written for early builds of ASP.NET MVC, and we had to apply major changes as we moved on in several stages. It took a lot of time and effort from both us and these editors to keep up with the latest changes given our tight schedule, and our busy personal and career lives.

We also give credit to Jim Minatel (Associate Publisher) for his early help and for putting us in touch with Katie Mohr.

But this book was not possible without the great help and support outside Wiley as well. We got help from Microsoft ASP.NET MVC team members, especially Phil Haack (Program Manager), who kept us synchronized with the upcoming changes and addressed our questions. We should also thank this team for the creation of the great technology that we have in hand.

We also received great acclaim from the community, which pushed us forward and encouraged us to work on this book in difficult circumstances. We are proud of this community and proud to have such friends.

We also want to thank some individuals who, with their suggestions, helped us make the book better: Gian Maria Ricci, for his help and suggestions about unit testing concepts; Roberto Valenti, for pairing with us for the sample about Test Driven Development; Nate Kohari for reviewing the parts related to Ninject, the DI/IoC framework he wrote, and its integration with ASP.NET MVC; Louis DeJardin, for helping out with the Spark alternative view engine; and Andrew Peters, who helped with NHaml, the view engine he wrote.

Finally, a big thanks goes to Simone's coworkers and managers at Avanade for their support.

Contents

Contents

Contents

Contents

Contents

Contents

Contents

Foreword

In 2007 I was visiting the Redmond campus for a conference and happened to be walking the halls of building 42 when I ran into Scott Guthrie, corporate VP of the .NET Developer Platform (he was General Manager at the time). He is probably better known by his alias, ScottGu, or by his nickname, "The Gu". He was rushing off to a meeting but asked me to swing by his office later as he had something "interesting" to show me. If you know Scott, you know when he has something interesting to show, it's going to be good.

That interesting thing of course was the nascent design of ASP.NET MVC. As he started drawing the conventions and code patterns in use for this new framework, my only response was, "I want to work on that." Though it wasn't intended to be a recruiting pitch (as far as I know), it was the best one I've ever received. I ended up moving to Microsoft to be a part of this product.

What excites me about ASP.NET MVC? In many ways it represents a lot of firsts for Microsoft in its approach to product design. We've released previews early and often complete with source code which allowed modifications very early in the process. In doing so, we've received unprecedented amounts of feedback from the community and even made significant design improvements in response. Increased transparency and community involvement was a key goal of this project.

ASP.NET MVC is also the first product from Microsoft to include a third party open source library, jQuery "in the box". This is a great JavaScript library widely regarded in the community and is a great complement to the Microsoft Ajax libraries.

And the source code for ASP.NET MVC is itself licensed under the Ms-PL license, an OSI certified license, something I'm particularly happy about as an open source community member and someone who sees the benefit in increased openness.

Of course, it's not just the nature of the project that excites me about ASP.NET MVC, it's the code and tooling itself. ASP.NET MVC really focuses on solid principles such as Separation of Concerns to provide a framework that is extremely extensible and testable. While it's possible to change the source as you see fit, our goal was to make sure that the framework was open for extension without needing to change the source.

Of course, the most fun part of this project has been the vibrant community that has arisen around ASP.NET MVC. These developers are extremely passionate about their craft and really keep us on our toes. Keyvan and Simone are two of these community members who have channeled their passion and enthusiasm for the framework into this book. In this book, they've written about the basics of software development using ASP.NET MVC as the backdrop for learning how to build web applications. I hope you enjoy the book and share in their passion for building web applications. Happy coding!

Phil Haack
Senior Program Manager, Microsoft Corporation

Introduction

No one can deny the fact that Microsoft is a giant in the software industry, and this large company has been continuously trying to extend its market in different areas related to software, hardware, networking, gaming, and entertainment.

One of the primary areas of Microsoft's focus is in the field of software development technologies. It tries to provide development technologies that enable the extension of other products and the building of solutions for business scenarios specifically for Microsoft platforms and operating systems (Windows, Windows Server, and Windows Mobile). Web development has been a very rapidly growing and highly demanded aspect of software development, and it has been the one of the most frequently used software development approaches in the past decade.

Microsoft has responded to the high demand for Web development technologies with two products: traditional *Active Server Pages* (ASP classic) and ASP.NET (which is a part of the .NET Framework). The latter technology is currently being used widely by developers. Its high level of integration and consistency with other parts of the .NET Framework has allowed many developers, regardless of their background, to use it in a short time. The main advantages of ASP.NET are the speed and ease of development, which allow you to build a Web application in a shorter time in comparison with other Web development technologies.

However, software development is one of the most progressive fields of science. New inventions and the advent of new techniques force software vendors and developers to adapt to the most recent changes in their works. In the past few years, the *Model-View-Controller* (MVC) pattern in software development has been revived by the great success of Ruby on Rails, and this has compelled Microsoft to think about its market. Besides this, it realized that its initial implementation of ASP.NET (that is now is referred to as ASP.NET WebForms) had some weaknesses in certain circumstances.

Therefore, in 2007 Microsoft started working on alternative solutions for ASP.NET WebForms. The main alternative was a new product named ASP.NET MVC. It applies the ASP.NET core API with its own implementations of some fundamental classes and provides a completely different model of software development using the MVC pattern with a great level of separation of concerns.

ASP.NET MVC works fine with modern inventions in software development by Microsoft. It also integrates well with today's Web development tools such as the popular jQuery library (a JavaScript library that simplifies the code model for JavaScript developers and adds cool features with ease of development).

Besides this, ASP.NET MVC opens new doors to developers by offering a lower level of access to APIs and full control over all elements of the application, such as the output HTML code. It also simplifies unit-testing capabilities to help you build projects with higher quality.

The Philosophy of the Book

Every book has a story behind it, and this one is no different. A very short while after the first public release of the preview build of ASP.NET MVC by Microsoft, we (the authors) started writing an article series for two prominent .NET communities, with a pragmatic approach, that could become rich resources about the product at that time. We knew each other from the past from the .NET community, blogosphere, and open source projects. We realized that we could extend our article series, take the articles to the next level, and write a book about ASP.NET MVC. At that time, there were few books being written in this area, and we found that they all targeted professionals.

Therefore, after some conversations with each other and with Wiley editors, we decided to start writing a book in the Beginning series for Wrox Press. Some of the main reasons for our decision to address the beginner level are outlined here:

❑   First, ASP.NET MVC is supposed to be an alternative approach to Web development for ASP.NET developers, so it's worth having an independent learning process as much as possible. A Beginning book helps with this learning process.

❑   Second, ASP.NET MVC implements the MVC pattern, and unlike ASP.NET WebForms, it relies heavily on some principles and practices that are mandatory for the implementation of a standard ASP.NET MVC application. ASP.NET WebForms applies a very classical form of development with some drag and drops and wizards that don't necessarily require in-depth knowledge of principles. Unfortunately, we found that many ASP.NET developers lacked this background, and having a Beginning book that relies on these concepts looked like a good idea to us.

❑   Third, our articles and blog posts relied heavily on a practical approach with examples, so it was appropriate for us to work on a Beginning series book with its predefined guidelines.

Hence, we should strongly encourage you to go over this introduction section and read it carefully before reading the rest of the book, or even buying it. Based on our experience with other titles, and seeing controversial reader reviews of other books, we realized that many readers choose the wrong title to read, which gives them a bad impression of that book, although it's great for its proposed audience. The helpfulness of a technical title varies from person to person, and knowing the level, structure, and audience of a book can help you choose the best book to read.

Why C#?

The primary programming language for this book is C#, which is one of the .NET programming languages and has become very popular in recent years. But why did we use C# for this book?

First, over the years we've seen that .NET developers are able to read and understand code in both Visual Basic and C#, so writing in two languages would waste time and paper.

Second, C# is getting more popular every day. The .NET community is going to accept it as the first programming language for .NET, and most code samples are provided in C#.

Third, we believe that most of the developers who are motivated to use ASP.NET MVC are those who have a level of experience with .NET programming in which they can read and understand sample code in both C# and Visual Basic, so it's not so important to have code in two languages.

Even though we chose C# as the main language, Visual Basic developers should be able to benefit from the content without any problems because all the code samples are very simple and readable, so a VB developer can read and understand them pretty easily.

Who This Book Is For

The audience of this book is Web developers who have a background in core ASP.NET APIs (whether from their existing knowledge in ASP.NET WebForms or their independent studies) and are seeking knowledge in ASP.NET MVC.

This book tries to teach a newbie in the field of ASP.NET MVC the principles, concepts, and methods to help him develop ASP.NET MVC skills so he can fulfill real-world responsibilities.

Having this general goal, we expect our readers to have some background information in certain fields as a prerequisite for reading this book. Although the first few requirements are absolutes, the latter requirements are negotiable in some circumstances because we have provided some background information in the text. If you don't have enough background in the solid requirements, we strongly recommend that, before reading this book, you try reading other books to improve your knowledge.

❑   The first and most important nonnegotiable prerequisite for this book is the capability to read and understand simple C# code samples. No matter whether you are a C# developer or VB developer, you should be able to read and understand simple code samples in this book. Of course, the code samples come with descriptions, but some rudimentary points aren't explained. LINQ expressions and generic types are commonly used in this book, so you need to know them as a part of your programming knowledge.

❑   The second important requirement is a good level of knowledge of the development model and principles of ASP.NET WebForms (not the whole thing, of course) and how an ASP.NET WebForms application is built. This book is about ASP.NET MVC, but based on experience, we believe that knowledge of ASP.NET WebForms provides some information that is very helpful when working with MVC as a beginner, so you can compare two technologies and extract some important differences.

❑   Besides this, you also need to have a good background in ASP.NET core APIs, whether from your WebForms knowledge or from other studies. Specifically, you need to know about caching, authentication, authorization, different providers (membership and role providers), and core objects (`HttpContext`, `Server`, `Request`, and `Response`).

❑   As a vital aspect of Web development, you need to know HTML and the basics of Cascading Style Sheets (CSS) and more specifically JavaScript in order to understand code samples in our chapters. Having a background in AJAX, ASP.NET AJAX, and jQuery would be an advantage.

❑   Throughout the book, we have also applied different storage systems to demonstrate concepts and showcase theories, so you need to have some familiarity with data storage technologies.

You have to know at least one from among SQL Server, ADO.NET database objects, LINQ to SQL, and the ADO.NET Entity Framework, at least at a basic level. Of course, we have tried to provide some background information about these technologies that can help you, but you certainly need to be fairly well-versed in at least some data storage technologies to succeed in your career.

❑ As the last requirement, you also may need to know XML syntax and how to use XML APIs in .NET (specifically LINQ to XML APIs).

What This Book Covers

This book covers all the introductory concepts, principles, methods, and development strategies that you need to know in order to build ASP.NET MVC applications up to a medium scale.

We first give you a background in the core principles of the MVC pattern and then show how they are implemented in ASP.NET MVC and contrast it with ASP.NET WebForms. In the main body of the book, we talk about the major elements of ASP.NET MVC to show you how to develop your applications. We use a pragmatic approach with basic but key examples to demonstrate concepts. In addition, we compare the highlights of ASP.NET WebForms to ASP.NET MVC and point out differences between the two to help you on your development path.

In the final two chapters, we offer two real-world case studies that complement the basic theoretical discussions in the book to help you learn the development process and prepare for real-world projects.

This book emphasizes concepts, principles, and simple examples with a pragmatic approach. Naturally, many more advanced details and techniques extend beyond these core fundamentals. As you become more proficient with ASP.NET MVC, you might want to expand your knowledge with a book like Conery's *Professional ASP.NET MVC 1.0* (978-0-470-38461-9), also available from Wrox.

How This Book Is Structured

This book is organized into 19 chapters and 2 appendixes. Chapters are written in a way that covers independent topics, but in many cases it's necessary to know the information in preceding chapters in order to read the new chapter and get the most out of it. Most of the chapters offer exercises that can help you specialize in the area of the discussion covered by that chapter or master a part of it.

Chapters 1 through 3 give you some initial information about the MVC pattern, how MVC is implemented in ASP.NET MVC, and how the concepts of ASP.NET, ASP.NET WebForms, and ASP.NET MVC all relate to each other.

Chapters 4 through 11 go over the main elements and methods in ASP.NET MVC development and cover topics that are new in and specific to ASP.NET MVC.

Chapters 12 through 17 extend the discussion with more specific topics and apply some core ASP.NET features as well as ASP.NET WebForms features in ASP.NET MVC to let you implement some common Web development scenarios in your MVC applications.

Finally, Chapters 18 and 19 offer two case studies that can enhance your practical knowledge in the field of ASP.NET MVC and supplement other chapters of the book.

Appendix A is a list of additional resources for further reading in the area of ASP.NET MVC and related technologies. It includes a list of books, communities, blogs, and open source projects that can help you.

Possible solutions to exercises are provided in Appendix B. We strongly recommend that you work on the solutions and then compare your answers with those provided.

What You Need to Use This Book

You need to meet some software and hardware requirements in order to be able to use ASP.NET MVC and the sample code in this book.

First of all, you need to have hardware that can run your Windows operating system and development environment as well as a working installation of Microsoft Windows. You can use Windows XP, 2003 Server, Vista, 2008 Server, or Windows 7; however, we have used Windows Vista throughout this book.

Obviously, you need to have a development environment to be able to build your ASP.NET MVC applications. You can use any commercial edition of Visual Studio 2008 or free edition of Visual Web Developer Express 2008. Note that you need to install Service Pack 1 of Visual Studio 2008 as well. Visual Studio 2008 Team Suite Service Pack 1 is what we used to write the book. The installation of your development environment resolves another requirement, which is the installation of .NET Framework 3.5 Service Pack 1. Note that Service Pack 1 is only necessary for a few parts of the book, so you can benefit from most of the content without this Service Pack as well.

Some chapters use SQL Server databases, so you need to have an installation of a commercial edition of SQL Server 2005 or 2008 or SQL Server Express 2005 or 2008 to use our sample code. For SQL Server 2005, you need to install Service Pack 2 as well.

Besides that, you need to have a working installation of the final version of ASP.NET MVC Framework 1.0 on your machine, which installs necessary assemblies and registers them to the GAC, and adds appropriate project templates to your Visual Studio IDE.

Conventions

To help you get the most from the text and keep track of what's happening, we've used a number of conventions throughout the book.

> **Boxes like this one hold important, not-to-be forgotten information that is directly relevant to the surrounding text.**

Notes, tips, hints, tricks, and asides to the current discussion are offset and placed in italics like this.

As for styles in the text:

- ❏ We *highlight* new terms and important words when we introduce them.
- ❏ We show keyboard strokes like this: Ctrl+A.
- ❏ We show file names, URLs, and code within the text like this: `persistence.properties`.
- ❏ We present code in two different ways:

```
We use a monofont type with no highlighting for most code examples.
We use gray highlighting to emphasize code that's particularly important in the
present context.
```

Source Code

As you work through the examples in this book, you may choose either to type in all the code manually or to use the source code files that accompany the book. All of the source code used in this book is available for download at `http://www.wrox.com`. Once at the site, simply locate the book's title (either by using the Search box or by using one of the title lists), and click the Download Code link on the book's detail page to obtain all the source code for the book.

Because many books have similar titles, you may find it easiest to search by ISBN; this book's ISBN is 978-0-470-43399-7.

Once you download the code, just decompress it with your favorite compression tool. Alternatively, you can go to the main Wrox code download page at `http://www.wrox.com/dynamic/books/download .aspx` to see the code available for this book and all other Wrox books.

Errata

We make every effort to ensure that there are no errors in the text or in the code. However, no one is perfect, and mistakes do occur. If you find an error in one of our books, such as a spelling mistake or faulty piece of code, we would be very grateful for your feedback. By sending in errata you may save another reader hours of frustration and at the same time you will be helping us provide even higher-quality information.

To find the errata page for this book, go to `http://www.wrox.com` and locate the title using the Search box or one of the title lists. Then, on the book details page, click the Book Errata link. On this page you can view all errata that has been submitted for this book and posted by Wrox editors. A complete book list, including links to each book's errata is also available at `www.wrox.com/misc-pages/booklist.shtml`.

If you don't spot "your" error on the Book Errata page, go to `www.wrox.com/contact/techsupport .shtml` and complete the form there to send us the error you have found. We'll check the information and, if appropriate, post a message to the book's errata page and fix the problem in subsequent editions of the book.

p2p.wrox.com

For author and peer discussion, join the P2P forums at p2p.wrox.com. The forums are a Web-based system for you to post messages relating to Wrox books and related technologies and interact with other readers and technology users. The forums offer a subscription feature to e-mail you topics of interest of your choosing when new posts are made to the forums. Wrox authors, editors, other industry experts, and your fellow readers are present on these forums.

At http://p2p.wrox.com you will find a number of different forums that will help you not only as you read this book but also as you develop your own applications. To join the forums, just follow these steps:

1. Go to p2p.wrox.com and click the Register link.
2. Read the terms of use and click Agree.
3. Complete the required information to join as well as any optional information you wish to provide and click Submit.
4. You will receive an e-mail with information describing how to verify your account and complete the joining process.

   You can read messages in the forums without joining P2P, but in order to post your own messages, you must join.

Once you join, you can post new messages and respond to messages other users post. You can read messages at any time on the Web. If you would like to have new messages from a particular forum e-mailed to you, click the Subscribe to this Forum icon by the forum name in the forum listing.

For more information about how to use the Wrox P2P, be sure to read the P2P FAQs for answers to questions about how the forum software works as well as many common questions specific to P2P and Wrox books. To read the FAQs, click the FAQ link on any P2P page.

The Model-View-Controller Pattern

The first three chapters of this book give you the foundation on which you will build up your knowledge about the ASP.NET MVC framework.

The ASP.NET MVC framework, unlike traditional ASP.NET programming, incorporates the usage of the Model-View-Controller (MVC) pattern. So, before you look at how the framework works, it's critical that you understand how the pattern on which it's based works. Then, in the following chapters, you learn how Microsoft implements that pattern in its library and how to write your first ASP.NET MVC Web application.

In this chapter you learn:

- ❑ The principles behind this pattern
- ❑ How the MVC pattern works
- ❑ The other advantages that it provides

The History of MVC

The Model-View-Controller (MVC) pattern, even if it gained popularity only recently, mainly thanks to Ruby on Rails and to the ASP.NET MVC framework, is not new. It was invented back in the 1970s by Trygve Reenskaug, a Norwegian computer scientist. The original pattern, named Thing-Model-View-Editor, was invented to solve a problem of the shipbuilding industry in Norway. They had the need to build information systems that could easily fit into existing organizations and be adapted for their continual development.

The pattern was later renamed to Model-View-Controller when Trygve worked with the SmallTalk group at Xerox PARC. A year later other researchers at Xerox PARC implemented a version of MVC and included it into the Smalltalk-80 class library, thus making Smalltalk the first programming language with native support for MVC.

Later, many other GUI frameworks took inspiration from the SmallTalk implementation, the most notable of which is Cocoa, the main application programming environment for Apple Mac OS X, which is based on its precursors OpenStep and NextStep, both of which encouraged the use of the MVC pattern.

On the Web application side, the first framework based on MVC was Apache Struts, a framework for building Java Enterprise Edition Web applications. Then came Ruby on Rails and the many other MVC-based application frameworks.

The Principles of MVC

Web applications based on ASP.NET that use the WebForm approach sometimes commingle database code, page design code, and control flow code. In practice, what happens is that, unless these elements are separated, larger applications become difficult to maintain.

One way to separate elements in a software application is to use the Model-View-Controller pattern. This paradigm is based on breaking an application into three parts, loosely related to the three usual tiers of a three-tier application:

❑   **Model** — The model is the part of the application that is responsible for retrieving data from the database, converting it to objects, and applying domain-specific elaboration to it.

❑   **Controller** — The controller orchestrates the operations. It's responsible for handling and validating user input, calling the model, choosing which view to render, and handing it the data to be displayed to the user.

❑   **View** — The view is the front end of the application. It shows to the user the results of the operation and the data retrieved.

Separating the application in loosely coupled components brings many advantages that help in managing applications that need to evolve to keep up with the quick change of requirements typical of today's IT projects.

At this point you might be wondering why the pattern is named "MVC" but the components were explained here (and will be throughout the book) in the order of Model-Controller-View. The reason is simple: The most logical way to explain how the components work is by starting from the model, then going through the controller, and finally reaching the view. And "MCV" would not have been nearly as appealing a name to the ear as "MVC."

But before looking at which specific advantages this pattern brings, in the next section you learn about the flow of an application based on MVC.

How the MVC Pattern Flows

As you already know, the core principle of the MVC pattern is a strict separation of concerns among the parts of the application. Figure 1-1 represents the MVC pattern as applied to Web applications.

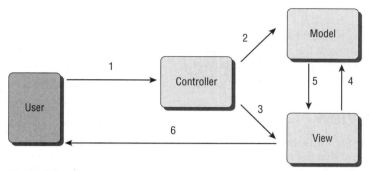

Figure 1-1

This implementation is also referred to as Front Controller or Model 2, from the name given to the first widespread implementation of this pattern in Apache Struts.

The name is Model 2 as opposed to Model 1, which refers to the old-style development of Web applications, where the page handled everything from the validation of the user input, to the data retrieval, to the rendering of the markup sent to the browser. Model 1 is pretty much how most of the Web applications developed using the WebForm paradigm.

Model 2 and Model 1 are names of different flavors of the Model-View-Controller pattern; they are not different types of models used within the pattern. Outside of this section that discusses the flavors of Model-View-Controller, you will generally see the term "model" used to refer to the model within the Model-View-Controller pattern.

The flow of the request follows this path:

1. The user interacts with the browser, typing a URL in the address bar or clicking a link or a button on a Web page. This starts the request (Step 1 in Figure 1-1).

2. The request hits the controller, which performs some validations on the user input ("Is the user ID a valid one? Is it a number or has someone passed in a string?") and delegates the execution of the request to the model (Step 2 in Figure 1-1).

3. Based on the results returned by the model, the controller goes on orchestrating the processing. It chooses the correct view that needs to be rendered to the user and calls it (Step 3 in Figure 1-1). For example, if the model says that the product the user wants to buy is not available, the view rendered will be different from the one that will be sent back if the product was available.

4. The view then calls the model that has been selected by the controller and asks it for the data needed to populate the page (Steps 4 and 5 in Figure 1-1). During this phase no logic or processing decision operations are performed, only data retrieval.

5. As the last step, the view receives the data needed, formats it in the appropriate manner, and sends the response back to the user (Step 6 in Figure 1-1).

Each part of the application performs well-defined tasks and communicates with the other components only to pass the results of their operations.

Reading on blogs, you might have heard about the Routing component. This component is responsible for routing the requests to the appropriate controller. This component is not part of the MVC pattern itself, but it's one of the implementation details of ASP.NET MVC. You read a little about it in Chapter 2, and get a detailed explanation in Chapter 7.

The Passive View

Some people started to think that separation of concerns can be pushed even further than in the Front Controller model and that the dependency of the view on the model can be removed. Doing this makes the three parts of the application completely independent and reduces the number of operations on the data storage during the rendering phase of the view.

This operational flow is depicted in Figure 1-2.

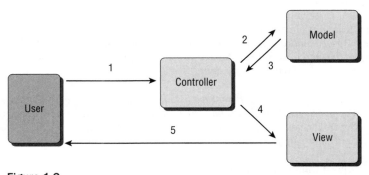

Figure 1-2

In this flavor of MVC, the process flow is the same as the traditional MVC for the first two steps, but then it changes radically:

1. As before, the user, interacting with the browser, starts the request (Step 1 in Figure 1-2).

2. The controller receives the request, validates it, and delegates the execution to the model (Step 2 in Figure 1-2).

3. The model hits the database and returns the data retrieved back to the controller (Step 3 in Figure 1-2).

4. At this point the controller selects the view and passes to it the data previously retrieved by the model. Actually, it doesn't pass exactly the same data, but it rearranges the data in a way that is better suited for the view (Step 4 in Figure 1-2).

5. As the last step, the view renders the output and sends it back to the user (Step 5 in Figure 1-2).

The main difference between the two flavors is that, whereas in the traditional MVC the view interacts with the model to get the data and then reformats it to render the Web page, in this flavor the model sends all the data to the controller, which then, again with the help of the model, reformats it and sends it to the view, whose only role is to render the data in the output sent to the user. Because of this passive role of the view, this flavor of MVC is called "Passive View."

The Presentation Model

Later, in Chapter 4, you learn about the model part and the Presentation Model in detail, but to help you better understand the differences between the two flavors of MVC and why the Passive View is usually a better option, this section gives you a quick introduction of the Presentation Model.

The model is an interface to the objects stored in the database. The graph in which these object are organized represents the connections that they have in real life: A customer places many orders, and each order is made up of many items, each with its name and quantity (see Figure 1-3).

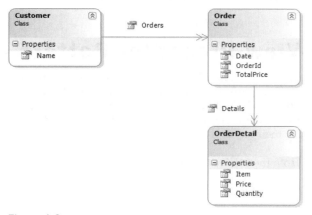

Figure 1-3

Imagine that you want to display on a Web page the list of customers who ordered a long-sleeved shirt last week. If the view retrieves the data organized in the hierarchy of Figure 1-3, it must know how to navigate the object graph to reformat the data in a plan table. But this means that the view has to know about how the data is organized inside the model. This is not good because it means that if the organization of the model changes, the view has to change as well, and this is something you want to avoid when using the MVC pattern. (One of the reasons for using MVC in the first place is to separate these responsibilities so that you can increase maintainability by managing these matters separately.)

When using the Passive View flavor of MVC, the controller reformats the data with the help of the Presentation Model. The Presentation Model is the only part of the application that knows how to transform the hierarchical object graph in the plan object (see Figure 1-4) needed to display a list of customers with the shirts they ordered.

Figure 1-4

> The view must only consume data, eventually formatting it, but the view should never generate (retrieve or transform) new data.

The Model-View-Controller is not the only pattern that tries to split the responsibilities across different parts of the application. Before explaining what the advantages of using the MVC pattern are, the next section quickly introduces the Model-View-Presenter pattern.

The Model-View-Presenter Pattern

The other pattern that has gained a lot of popularity in recent years is the Model-View-Presenter (MVP) pattern. As the name itself suggests, the MVP pattern is quite similar to MVC. In fact, some developers joke about that, saying that the only difference between the MVC and the MVP pattern is the letter P instead of the C. And to an extent, they are right. The first noticeable difference between the controller and the presenter is only their name.

The MVP also differs from the MVC pattern in two other ways:

❑ Where the requests hit the system

❑ How the parts are wired up together

The flow of processing is also different from the one you saw in the previous section:

1. The user interacts directly with the view (Step 1 in Figure 1-5).

2. The view, raising an event, notifies the presenter that something happened (Step 2), and then the presenter accesses the properties that the view exposes through its interface Iview (Step 3 in Figure 1-5). These properties are wrappers to the actual UI elements of the view.

3. The presenter then calls the model (Step 4), which then returns the results (Step 5).

4. The presenter transforms the data and then sets the values in the UI, always through the IView interface (Step 6 in Figure 1-5).

5. The output is the returned to the user (Step 7).

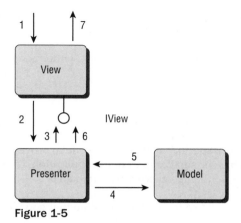

Figure 1-5

In the Model-View-Presenter pattern the view is even more "passive" than the one in the MVC. The view raises events, but it is up to the presenter to read and set the values of the UI elements. In fact, this pattern has been designed as an enhancement over the MVC, to try and make the view even dumber to make it easier to swap views.

So why did Microsoft decide to built its new Web application framework based on the MVC pattern and not based on MVP? The problem with MVP is that the wiring of the view and the presenter is more complicated than in MVC. Every view has its own interface, and because it is specific to the contents of the page, its creation cannot be easily delegated to the framework, but must be created by the developer.

The Web Client Software Factory, developed by the Pattern & Practices team at Microsoft, addresses the problem of automatically creating all the components needed to implement the MVP pattern. It's a graphical tool that allows the developer to design the interactions and the UI elements that need to be handled by the presenter. But this is a development helper, not a full-blown framework, and the kind of developer that the MVC framework has been mainly designed for prefers simpler solutions that can be managed with "stylistically nice" code over more complicated solutions that need the aid of a tool to be implemented.

Now that you understand what the pattern is and how it works, in the following sections you learn the advantages of using the Model-View-Controller pattern over the traditional WebForm approach.

Advantages of MVC over Traditional Web Development

The MVC paradigm, because of the great emphasis it puts on separating responsibilities, brings several advantages to Web development: Unit testing and test driven development are probably the most important advantages, and probably the factors that drove the creation of the ASP.NET MVC framework. It also enables an approach called *Interface First*, a design methodology that advocates the design of the UI before the business logic and data access.

The next section gives a quick overview of why the MVC pattern enables these three scenarios.

Unit Testing

The first and most important practice that is facilitated by MVC is unit testing. You read more about unit testing in Chapter 8, but here you get a quick introduction to what it is and why it is important. Unit testing is about isolating a specific "unit" of your code to prove its correctness. In object-oriented programming, a unit, which is the smallest part of the application, is a method. Each test case must be autonomous and repeatable, so that it can be easily automated.

Why is isolating a specific "unit" so important? Imagine that you want to prove the correctness of a method that renders a list of all the customers who live in a certain city and who ordered a specific kind of shirt. This method hits the database to retrieve the list based on the city, then filters out all the ones who didn't buy the shirt, orders the results, and formats the output. This test can fail because the filtering part, which is the code you want to test, went wrong. But it can also fail for external reasons that are out of the control of the method you want to test. The data access layer might have some problem, the database administrator might have dropped a stored procedure by mistake, or there even could have been a network problem that prevented the communication with the database.

With traditional Web application development, it can be difficult to isolate single parts of an application because, most of the time, the code that accesses the data repository is not formally separated from the code that transforms that data or that manages the process flow.

With the MVC pattern, you can replace the real implementation of the model with an implementation made on purpose for the test, for example with a fake model that always returns 10 customers. This model will never fail, so the only reason for the preceding test to fail is that the filtering algorithm fails.

Furthermore, with the WebForm paradigm, the request processing is tightly tied to the Web server runtime. With MVC, instead, the parts that are doing most of the job, the controller and the model, don't interact directly with the Web server runtime, allowing tests also to be executed outside the Web server container.

Another reason why this isolation and repeatability is important is that all test cases need to run automatically, as a way to ensure that the code still works even after major changes, and that the implementation of new features doesn't break the ones that have already been implemented and tested.

The loose coupling and the strict separation of concerns also makes it easier to adopt practices coming from the Agile world such as test driven development or the UI First approach. In the following sections, you learn about these practices.

Test Driven Development

The name test driven development, even if it contains the word "test," is not a testing methodology but a design and development methodology. It consists of writing a test case that covers the feature that you want to implement and then writing the code necessary for the feature to pass the test.

When adopting this development methodology, you tend to run the entire automated suite of tests a lot of times, and unit testing will save you precious time. Restoring the database to a known state and hitting the database for each test case (could be thousands of times) is much more time-consuming than using fake models that return predefined sets of data (as you do with unit testing).

If you like this approach, you can read about it in more detail in Chapters 8 and 9.

The Interface First Approach

Another design methodology that can benefit from the use of the MVC pattern is the one proposed by the book *Getting Real*, written by the software company called 37signals, the creators of some popular Web 2.0 project management applications like Basecamp and Campfire, and of the Web application framework that probably started all this interest around MVC: Ruby on Rails.

They found that using a top-down approach works better for Web applications than the usual bottom-up approach. Starting from the database and then going up to the user interface adds too much inertia to your development process. When you show the UI to the end users, your application has already been developed, and even small changes in the requirements can raise the costs of development a lot.

Starting from the UI and going down instead allows you to show the end users the application and to gather immediate feedback. Changing a requirement at this stage of the process is just a matter of changing some HTML and some code in the controller. This is possible because the complex and expensive parts of the applications are all in the model, which at this stage is not implemented yet, but only loosely sketched out.

Instead of starting from the model or the controller and then going up to the view as in other usual methodologies, with the Interface First approach you first design the view, then work on the controller, and finally, you design and develop the (Domain) model of your application.

We won't talk about this development methodology, because it's not as formalized and widespread as the previous two. If you are interested in this kind of approach, I encourage you to visit the *Getting Real* Web site (`http://gettingreal.37signals.com`) and buy the book or read it online.

Summary

The Model-View-Controller is a pattern that encourages loose coupling and separation of duties to make the design of the application flexible and quickly adaptable to changes and to facilitate the usage of the methodologies typical of the Agile world.

In this chapter you learned:

- ❏ That the Model-View-Controller pattern was created in the late 1970s with SmallTalk and gained popularity in the new century thanks to Struts and Ruby on Rails
- ❏ That Model-View-Controller splits the application into three components:
    - ❏ Model, which encapsulates the operation with the database

❏ View, which is responsible for the rendering of the final output

❏ Controller, which orchestrates all the operations

❏ What the process flow of the MVC pattern is and how the traditional implementation differs from the Passive View one

❏ How to use a Presentation Model

❏ How the MVC compares to the Model-View-Presenter pattern

❏ That the MVC pattern facilitates the adoption of Agile practices like unit testing, test driven development, and the Interface First approach

With the knowledge acquired about MVC, in the next chapter you learn more specifically how the MVC pattern works using the ASP.NET MVC framework, but before moving on try to answer to the following questions.

Exercises

1. Can you list the three components of the MVC pattern and the roles of each of them?

2. What's the role of the Presentation Model?

3. What are the differences between the MVC and the MVP patterns?

ASP.NET WebForms vs. ASP.NET MVC

The first chapter of the book presented a short overview of the Model-View-Controller (MVC) pattern and introduced the main components involved in this popular software development pattern. You read about the model as the component responsible for data operations and business logic implementation, the view as the component to display the output, and the controller as the component to connect your model to the view. You also read about the pros and cons of the MVC pattern and how it can resolve common issues raised in today's development scenarios.

Here in Chapter 2 you are given a general background about the way that the MVC pattern is implemented in ASP.NET MVC. You also take a step forward and connect the theoretical concepts in the first chapter to your existing knowledge of ASP.NET, specifically ASP.NET WebForms and the main elements that contribute to the runtime workflow of an ASP.NET MVC application. In addition, this chapter discusses the pros and cons of ASP.NET MVC and contrasts its implementation with ASP.NET WebForms to show the main differences between the two. These topics are discussed in more detail throughout the book, but this chapter should ground you in some important core concepts.

Before stepping into the details, look at the main topics covered in this chapter:

- ❑ An overview of the history of ASP.NET WebForms and ASP.NET MVC and the process that led ASP.NET MVC to come into being
- ❑ The advantages and disadvantages of ASP.NET WebForms contrasted with ASP.NET MVC
- ❑ The programming model of the ASP.NET WebForms and ASP.NET MVC applications
- ❑ The main elements in the ASP.NET development
- ❑ How ASP.NET, ASP.NET WebForms, and ASP.NET MVC relate
- ❑ How MVC pattern is implemented in ASP.NET MVC

An important point that you need to be aware of is that many commonalities exist between ASP.NET WebForms and ASP.NET MVC. Many of the concepts and classes are constant between the two. Many other concepts and classes act in a similar way, with their difference being in their internal workings. Therefore, having a solid background in ASP.NET WebForms development can help you succeed with ASP.NET MVC.

Overview

Back in 2002 Microsoft released the first version of the .NET Framework including several technologies. The most notable technology in this stack was ASP.NET, the new generation of Microsoft Web development technology that came after its popular *Active Server Pages* (ASP). ASP.NET proved to be a great technology and quickly became popular among developers.

After several successor releases of this technology and testing it for various circumstances on different scales, Microsoft realized that ASP.NET had some weaknesses and some areas that needed improvement. However, not all of these improvements could be achieved within the standard ASP.NET implementation and some of them required fundamental changes of approach. In addition, new development patterns and technologies had become common, and Microsoft saw an opportunity to adopt them into existing technologies.

Therefore, Microsoft thought about alternatives to the original implementation of ASP.NET and worked on two new products and revisited the architecture of the ASP.NET technology. The first step was taken after the release of the .NET Framework 2.0 by building rich ASP.NET 2.0 WebForms, but the real action was taken in late 2007 with ASP.NET MVC.

We elaborate the changes and distinction between these new derivations and the original ASP.NET implementation later in this chapter, but for now keep in mind that before 2008 the term ASP.NET was referring to a single technology, and that technology included what is now known as ASP.NET WebForms. Since 2008, you need to consider the distinction between ASP.NET as the parent of the stack that contains both ASP.NET WebForms and ASP.NET MVC. You read more about this distinction in this chapter.

Contrasting ASP.NET WebForms with ASP.NET MVC

As stated in the previous section, after a few years of ASP.NET existence, Microsoft understood the necessity for some fundamental changes. Naturally, it saw an opportunity to strengthen its market share, but it also saw some technical opportunities as well. Here our main focus is on the technical reasons.

In this section we point out some weaknesses with ASP.NET (ASP.NET WebForms) that convinced Microsoft to revisit its ASP.NET technology structure. Right after that, we contrast these problems with ASP.NET MVC and how it goes about resolving them.

Problems with ASP.NET WebForms

ASP.NET WebForms is a great technology with many advantages of its own. For many circumstances, the issues we discuss in the following sections may be advantages, and for many of the circumstances these advantages outweigh the disadvantages. Therefore, it's critical to know that ASP.NET WebForms is a great solution for many problems in its own right.

One of ASP.NET WebForms' biggest advantages is that it offers a classical form of development that accelerates and simplifies the process of development. It even allows very inexperienced developers to be able to write basic applications. It also provides a development practice very similar to Windows desktop application development, so desktop developers can start building Web applications with the least amount of extra learning necessary.

However, as you read next, ASP.NET WebForms may exhibit some weaknesses, specifically when it comes to the more professional level of development and advanced scenarios.

The Dependency on Environment Parameters

The infrastructure of ASP.NET WebForms is based on some objects that are tied to environment properties such as those provided by the operating system, Web server, client, request, and response. This dependency on environment parameters can provide some problems for developers when they try to build professional Web applications.

Generally, in today's software development practices, it's strongly recommended that you write code with the least possible dependency on other components and environment parameters. As you see in the next few sections, this dependency can become a crucial issue when you're trying to unit test or maintain your applications.

The Level of Control on Rendering Code

The classic form of Web development with ASP.NET WebForms is accomplished with the usage of ASP.NET server controls that encapsulate the functionality that you need for common scenarios. Most of these controls provide a set of properties to let you manipulate the rendering of HTML code, but even in their best form, they still have many limitations and are not very compliant with Web standards.

This has been one of the major problems with ASP.NET WebForms that the ASP.NET team has been trying to resolve in each new version with some new features, but the nature of encapsulation in server controls doesn't give much space for improvements.

Abundant Repetitions

The development model of ASP.NET WebForms applications (which is discussed later in this chapter) mandates you to distribute your code in code-behind files or `.aspx` files. In either case, you usually end up with the repetition of a piece of code in several places that makes it difficult to develop and maintain the project.

Obviously, this is a bad practice that is not recommended, but the structure of WebForms compels you to do precisely that.

The Level of Testability

Test driven development and unit testing have become very common parts of modern software development. They are used to evaluate the quality of the written code using some formal methods.

One of the principles of unit testing is *mocking*, where you simulate the behavior of an object. To successfully mock an object, it must have as few dependencies as possible on other objects and environment parameters. As you read in the previous sections, ASP.NET WebForms is very dependent on environment objects, which turns out to be a major obstruction confronting developers who want to unit test.

Chapter 8 discusses unit testing concepts in detail and Chapter 9 shows you how to unit test your ASP.NET MVC applications.

State Management

The other commonplace task in Web development technologies is the management of state and its persistence between clients and servers for several pages. Each technology implements this task in its own way. Some technologies have a built-in mechanism to save their developers work, and others ask developers to do this manually.

ASP.NET WebForms offers such a built-in mechanism using the concept of `ViewState`, which is actually a hidden field that appears in the HTML code of the page and keeps the encrypted value of form values. This `ViewState` is a part of the page and as long as it grows, it affects the speed of your site.

`ViewState` can be both a good and a bad tool. For several circumstances the simplicity of state management is something that developers love to have, and for some other circumstances they dislike this value because it can be very large for some pages.

Adaption to Modern Development Patterns

Software development technologies are usually built in a way that allows developers to adapt development techniques and patterns easily. ASP.NET WebForms has some weaknesses in this area as well because its classical form of development along with the programming model restricts developers from being able to adapt modern development patterns, or it at least makes it difficult to accomplish this.

The MVC pattern (which was introduced in Chapter 1) is one of those popular development patterns that was difficult to use with ASP.NET WebForms applications.

How ASP.NET MVC Resolves Issues with ASP.NET WebForms

Speaking of ASP.NET WebForms' weaknesses and the issues that you may face when developing applications with this technology, now it's time to contrast these issues with ASP.NET MVC and see how it comes to resolve these issues.

In ASP.NET MVC fundamental objects are rewritten to be independent from the server, request, response, and other environment parameters, so ASP.NET MVC resolves the issue of dependency on environment parameters. Likewise, ASP.NET MVC offers a lower level of control for rendering HTML code, which allows you to manipulate the output code to be compliant with Web standards. Because

ASP.NET MVC implements the MVC pattern for ASP.NET developers, it resolves the issue of repetition in code in a Web application. Moreover, the independence of ASP.NET MVC fundamental objects from other objects and parameters improves the level of testability and makes it the most suitable implementation of ASP.NET for unit testing purposes. State management is not managed by ASP.NET MVC by default, and it's left to developers to handle it themselves; therefore, it's a good technology for those who have problems with state management and ViewState in ASP.NET WebForms. Finally, ASP.NET MVC is written to implement the MVC pattern for developers. This pattern is one of the most common and popular technologies among Web developers today, and it can be used by ASP.NET developers who are seeking to use this pattern in their applications.

Although these are great improvements for ASP.NET developers working with ASP.NET MVC, it's important to note that the implementation of ASP.NET MVC may make some tasks harder and more time-consuming for developers. The new method of user interface manipulation that drops the usage of server controls can be an advantage, but it usually forces developers to do more work in order to build their user interface. Some common tasks (such as validation) in ASP.NET WebForms that could be achieved without writing lines of code are also made harder in ASP.NET MVC.

All in all, it's not easy to choose between ASP.NET WebForms and ASP.NET MVC to identify either one as the better option for all circumstances. The appropriateness of these technologies varies significantly from project to project. Throughout this book we try to show you all the aspects of ASP.NET MVC development so you can contrast them with their corresponding implementation in ASP.NET WebForms and apply your existing knowledge and experience to choose what works best for you.

The Programming Model

The ASP.NET programming model is completely different in ASP.NET MVC. This section first reviews the programming model for ASP.NET WebForms, and then looks at the ASP.NET MVC programming model so you can see how it compares.

The ASP.NET WebForms Programming Model

The programming model for use with ASP.NET WebForms has several aspects. In general, you deal with master pages, ASPX Web pages, user controls, and server controls:

❑   A master page is a parent file that holds the general layout of the site and is constant among various Web pages. You can define a single master page and share it among multiple ASPX Web pages to save you time, instead of adding the same code and user interface to both pages.

❑   An ASPX Web page is the main element in ASP.NET, and it will be requested by clients through the browser. It represents a single page of a site and can be associated with a master page. You can add user controls and server controls to your ASPX page in order to split its functionality and organize it.

❑   A user control is a component that can hold a part of an ASPX Web page. As with a master page, it's a good way to share a common user interface element among multiple pages, and it's also helpful in organizing the business logic and user interface of a Web page.

❑   Server controls (built-in ASP.NET controls or third-party controls) are basic elements of the user interface that can be inserted in a master page, Web page, or user control to accomplish a goal. For example, a textbox can act like an HTML input element that gets user input.

Master pages, Web pages, user controls, and server controls have events associated with them. For example, one common event is the load event, which fires when the component is being loaded. Likewise, server controls have a set of events associated with them. For instance, a button control has a click event that will be fired when the end user clicks it. When developing an ASP.NET WebForms application, you need to handle these events and implement your business logic in order to respond to the request by the user.

Usually master pages, ASPX Web pages, and user controls have business code associated with them, which is a programming class with a specific structure. You have two options for developing a master page, Web page, or user control:

❑   **Code inline** — With this approach, you add your programming code directly to the master page, ASPX file, or user control where you also add your server controls and HTML markup. This is usually used for elements that have simple and short code; otherwise, this can create a mess of your files and damage the organized code structure.

❑   **Code-behind** — With this approach, you implement your event handlers in a separate class that is called a code-behind file. This is more common than code inline because it's organized and easier to maintain.

One of the drawbacks of both these methods is the way that they end up with many files in different locations, which results in maintenance being difficult for larger projects. Likewise, they result in the repetition of code in many places in your application, which also increases maintenance headaches.

The ASP.NET MVC Programming Model

Now let's contrast the programming model in ASP.NET WebForms with the new programming model in ASP.NET MVC to see how it helps in improving the quality of software development and project organization.

One of the biggest differences is that ASP.NET MVC implements the MVC pattern for ASP.NET, so one of the main principles is splitting your programming structure into three components.

ASP.NET MVC doesn't have any server controls. Instead, it uses helper methods to render user interface elements. (You read more about helper methods in Chapter 6.) Because there aren't any server controls, you need to use basic HTML elements in your views to render user interface elements, which gives you more control over these elements.

ASP.NET MVC also doesn't have any events and event handlers. Instead, it offers action methods as a mechanism to respond to requests. The main advantage of this change is the reduction in the repetition in your code compared with ASP.NET WebForms.

In ASP.NET MVC you implement the main business logic of your application in the model component, and you use controllers to receive requests and connect your model to the view (and thus the user interface).

When developing view files, you may write some programming code and may notice the similarities between this model and what you may have seen in classic ASP, but don't forget that in ASP.NET MVC you only write programming code in views in order to get the data items and display them. You don't have any business logic associated with them within the actual views.

The Main Elements of ASP.NET Development

Some classes play key roles in ASP.NET development and are commonly used in all the ASP.NET applications. These classes are brought to ASP.NET from classic ASP but with a completely different implementation and internal workings. These elements play the same key role in the ASP.NET MVC as well, but they also have a different implementation behind the scenes.

Here, you walk through these main elements and see their purpose. You use them frequently later in this book, so you need to understand how they work. A vast majority of the properties and information provided by these objects directly or indirectly relate to HTTP request and response headers, and there may be circumstances when you need to debug your application and monitor these values. In such cases, you can use some tools like Firebug to access the information you need.

❏   `HttpApplication` — This class represents an ASP.NET application with some properties, methods, and events. This class is a good source to find information related to your ASP.NET application. `HttpApplication` also has some methods related to the main events in the ASP.NET request life cycle.

❏   `HttpServerUtility` — This class provides a set of helper methods and a few properties that will assist you with some operations that you frequently need to run. `HttpServerUtility` provides a variety of methods related to the server side of your Web application.

❏   `HttpContext` — This class is one of the fundamental classes and encapsulates some information related to an HTTP request, your server, and its response by clients. `HttpContext` contains several properties and methods that all provide information about the current HTTP request and response and help you accomplish operations with them.

❏   `HttpRequest` — As its name suggests, this class represents an HTTP request on the server and provides information and operations related to this request. Like `HttpContext`, the `HttpRequest` class is a very common and important class in ASP.NET development.

❏   `HttpResponse` — The last class is `HttpResponse`, which is very important (like `HttpContext` and `HttpRequest`). This class does the same job as `HttpRequest` for the server response, so it represents the response from the server to the client. It provides some properties and methods to assist a developer in working with the response and manipulating it.

How ASP.NET, ASP.NET WebForms, and ASP.NET MVC Relate

If you are coming to ASP.NET MVC with a lower level of experience in ASP.NET WebForms, you might have some confusion about how ASP.NET, ASP.NET WebForms, and ASP.NET MVC relate. Many developers mistakenly think that ASP.NET MVC is a replacement for ASP.NET WebForms. Likewise, some developers think that ASP.NET is identical to ASP.NET WebForms, which is also wrong!

What's the truth? Such an understanding of the distinction between these technologies might have been correct in 2002–2006, but after that, Microsoft worked out new technologies and derivations that proved that ASP.NET is something bigger than ASP.NET WebForms, ASP.NET MVC, or other lesser-known technologies.

ASP.NET is the name of a major portion of the .NET Framework that consists of a set of *Base Class Library* (BCL) classes that are mainly responsible for Web development scenarios. ASP.NET is also the most popular and commonly used applied technology in the .NET Framework by developers.

In the early days of the .NET Framework existence, there was only one implementation of ASP.NET, which is now known as ASP.NET WebForms, and almost all developers considered these two to be identical technologies. In those days, no one could have predicted that there would be new derivations of ASP.NET in the coming years.

But in 2006, Microsoft started to provide new implementations of ASP.NET as alternatives for ASP.NET WebForms with new features and capabilities for other problems and development patterns. This was a starting point for the confusion of some developers.

However, as time progressed, Microsoft clarified that ASP.NET is an infrastructure that consists of several core APIs that can be used to build different derivations of Web development technologies. Microsoft itself built ASP.NET Dynamic Data and ASP.NET MVC along with ASP.NET WebForms in the past few years.

Therefore, ASP.NET is a set of smaller portions of technologies such as core infrastructure, ASP.NET WebForms, ASP.NET AJAX, ASP.NET Dynamic Data, and ASP.NET MVC. This is shown in a schematic view in Figure 2-1.

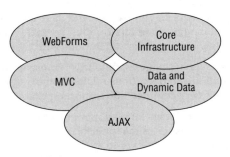

Figure 2-1

Having this background, you now know that ASP.NET refers to a major portion of the .NET Framework that consists of smaller parts, including ASP.NET WebForms, ASP.NET AJAX, ASP.NET MVC, and ASP.NET Dynamic Data, and all these technologies apply a core infrastructure of the API to work.

As a final note, you can keep following inequalities in mind:

- ❑ ASP.NET != ASP.NET WebForms
- ❑ ASP.NET > ASP.NET WebForms
- ❑ ASP.NET > ASP.NET MVC
- ❑ ASP.NET > ASP.NET Dynamic Data

In this book, we make a clear distinction of the use of these words in all our chapters, so keep this classification in mind.

The Implementation of the MVC Pattern in ASP.NET MVC

Before wrapping up in this chapter, let's go over the implementation of the *Model-View-Controller* (MVC) pattern in ASP.NET MVC and how this software development pattern is adapted to be implemented in Microsoft Web server development technology.

First of all, there is an important point to note about the implementation of the MVC pattern in ASP.NET MVC. You usually implement this pattern in the order of M, C, and V, not in the order of M, V, and C. In other words, you usually implement your model, then your controller, and finally your view. We'll use the same order throughout much of this book and it's the case for many of the sample code and projects written with ASP.NET MVC available on the Web.

The reason to have this implementation is that the structure of ASP.NET MVC needs this order to route requests from a client to a controller and then connect the model data to the views that render the user interface, so it makes perfect sense to have this be the order of implementation.

In Chapter 1 you learned about the MVC pattern in good detail and saw its advantages for developers and the way it splits the project code into three components: model, view, and controller. This section introduces you to the implementation of the MVC pattern in ASP.NET MVC, how these three elements are implemented in this technology, and how some additional concepts come into play to ameliorate your development experience.

The Model in ASP.NET MVC

The model is where you implement your data interaction code and main business logic. The model component in ASP.NET MVC can be implemented in several ways. Which approach you should use varies from project to project based on your requirements and the data storage system that you want to use.

This is the only part of ASP.NET MVC where Microsoft hasn't implemented anything by default for your code. Actually, only a folder called Models is generated by Visual Studio for you and the rest is left to you.

However, in ASP.NET MVC you can use a wide range of data storage tools and systems such as databases, XML files, and text files. Likewise, you have many options to use with each of these storage systems. For example, you can use data objects, LINQ to SQL, ADO.NET Entity Framework, or many Object/Relational Mappers to use various databases such as SQL Server, Access, or Oracle.

Generally, the model is just an implementation of data storage with business logic. You read more about model implementation with a practical approach in Chapter 4.

The Controller in ASP.NET MVC

The controller component is where you receive requests from the client and respond accordingly using the controller as a bridge between the model and the view.

In ASP.NET MVC, the controller is implemented as a class derived from the `System.Web.Mvc.Controller` base class. Each controller class can contain a set of methods that are called *action methods*.

An action method is a specific type of method in ASP.NET MVC that responds to user requests and returns some specific objects to views. Inside action methods you write your own code to load appropriate data from the model and pass it to the appropriate views that will render the data for the user. Likewise, you can use action methods to get user input and pass it to the model in order to update data storage.

Listing 2-1 shows a sample controller class that is automatically generated by the ASP.NET MVC project template in Visual Studio.

Listing 2-1: Sample controller

```
using System;
using System.Collections.Generic;
using System.Linq;
using System.Web;
using System.Web.Mvc;

namespace SampleApplication.Controllers
{
    [HandleError]
    public class HomeController : Controller
    {
        public ActionResult Index()
        {
            ViewData["Message"] = "Welcome to ASP.NET MVC!";

            return View();
        }

        public ActionResult About()
        {
            return View();
        }
    }
}
```

Here `HomeController` is a controller that contains two action methods called `Index` and `About`.

The other related concept in ASP.NET MVC that is used in conjunction with controller and action methods is the *action filter*. The action filter is a class or method attribute that acts as an additional feature for these components for extra functionality, configuration, or customization. For example, an action filter can help with caching the output of an action method or all the action methods in a controller.

You read more about the controller, action methods, and action filters in Chapter 5.

The View in ASP.NET MVC

The last main component of MVC pattern is the view. The view is actually the user interface element of an MVC application where you implement your HTML code and other code logic to present data to end users.

In ASP.NET MVC you deal with the concept of the view engine, which is actually an engine that runs and parses view files to render them in browsers. There is a default engine in ASP.NET MVC that works with .aspx, .master, and .ascx files that have similar responsibilities as Web pages, master pages, and user controls in ASP.NET WebForms with some differences.

You can write your user interface code and distribute it using these three file types and organize them in the Views folder in your projects based on the corresponding controller and action method name. Actually you need to put all the views for a controller in a subfolder with the exact same name as your controller name, and create the view corresponding to an action method with the exact same name as the method. So for the controller introduced in Listing 2-1, there must be a subfolder called Home placed in the Views folder that contains two view files called Index.aspx and About.aspx.

As with ASP.NET WebForms, you can use .master files and .ascx files to share a constant layout and/ or user interface element across your application.

Listing 2-2 shows the Index view corresponding to the Index action method shown in Listing 2-1. It works with a master page to show the content of the index page to the end user.

Listing 2-2: Sample view

```
<%@ Page Language="C#" MasterPageFile="~/Views/Shared/Site.Master"
Inherits="System.Web.Mvc.ViewPage" %>

<asp:Content ID="indexTitle" ContentPlaceHolderID="TitleContent" runat="server">
    Home Page
</asp:Content>
<asp:Content ID="indexContent" ContentPlaceHolderID="MainContent" runat="server">
    <h2>
        <%= Html.Encode(ViewData["Message"]) %></h2>
    <p>
        To learn more about ASP.NET MVC visit <a href="http://asp.net/mvc"
title="ASP.NET MVC Website">
            http://asp.net/mvc</a>.
    </p>
</asp:Content>
```

This view should be familiar to you because it's very similar to .aspx files in ASP.NET WebForms and contains some HTML code. The only significant difference in this code is the highlighted code, which is something new in ASP.NET MVC. In this part of the code, a text message is retrieved from the data fields in the view.

The way that master files, views, and user controls are implemented in ASP.NET MVC is discussed in detail in Chapter 6.

Routing in ASP.NET MVC

Although the model, view, and controller are main concepts in the MVC pattern that are implemented in ASP.NET MVC, there is an additional concept called *routing* available in ASP.NET MVC to improve the development experience and help developers when building applications.

Routing is a mechanism that lets you map incoming requests in your application based on their RESTful URI patterns to corresponding resources. These resources are usually controllers and action methods.

In other words, routing helps you to define some URL patterns in your application. When a request is made and matches one of the patterns, that request will be routed to the corresponding controller and action method.

Routing adds significant power to ASP.NET MVC because it enables RESTful access to resources, drops the usage of .aspx page extensions, and makes beautiful URLs. It also yields a better organization of URLs in an application.

Listing 2-3 shows the default routing definition for an ASP.NET MVC application available in the Global.asax file.

Listing 2-3: Sample routing definition

```
public static void RegisterRoutes(RouteCollection routes)
{
    routes.IgnoreRoute("{resource}.axd/{*pathInfo}");

    routes.MapRoute(
        "Default",                                        // Route name
        "{controller}/{action}/{id}",                     // URL with
parameters
        new { controller = "Home", action = "Index", id = "" }  // Parameter
defaults
    );
}
```

The RegisterRoutes method is where you can define your routing mechanism patterns. First, there is a line where some specific patterns are excluded from processing, which is actually for .axd resource files. Then there is a general pattern that maps all the requests in the format of {controller}/{action}/{id} to the controller class, action method, and an optional parameter called id. For example, if a request is made to home/about/1, it will be routed to the About action method in the HomeController with an id parameter set to 1. Of course, if a request is made to home/about, it will be mapped to the same action method without a parameter.

Routing is a very powerful feature in ASP.NET MVC and is one of the areas where ASP.NET MVC works much better than ASP.NET WebForms. You read more about routing in Chapter 7.

Summary

This chapter is the first place in this book where you get your hands on ASP.NET MVC. After a detailed introduction to the MVC pattern in Chapter 1, you got started with the main concepts of ASP.NET MVC and the way that the MVC pattern is implemented in ASP.NET MVC technology. You also contrasted what you already knew about ASP.NET WebForms with what is new in ASP.NET MVC.

The chapter started with an overview of ASP.NET history and how ASP.NET was expanded to new derivations such as ASP.NET MVC.

The second section of the chapter contrasted ASP.NET WebForms with ASP.NET MVC by outlining the weaknesses and problems with ASP.NET WebForms and how ASP.NET MVC has been able to address them.

The next section was about the programming model in ASP.NET WebForms and ASP.NET MVC, and how ASP.NET MVC has improved the programming model.

Next we discussed the clear distinction between ASP.NET, ASP.NET WebForms, and ASP.NET MVC as three concepts in the architecture of ASP.NET technology.

Finally, you went through the implementation of MVC pattern concepts in ASP.NET MVC and talked about additional concepts that act as helpers in ASP.NET MVC.

The upcoming chapters of the book discuss ASP.NET MVC concepts and how to implement your Web applications using the power of this new technology. Of course, all the concepts introduced in this chapter are elaborated on further in these chapters to get you started.

Exercise

Try to think about the possible ways that you can convert an ASP.NET WebForms application to an ASP.NET MVC application and split its components so they work in the MVC pattern. List your theoretical results. Later in this book, we go over this topic in detail, and you can compare your findings with our content.

Getting Started with ASP.NET MVC

After reading the first two chapters of the book, you should now have a good understanding of the general principles behind the Model-View-Controller (MVC) pattern and how ASP.NET MVC differs from traditional ASP.NET, particularly regarding the use of WebForms. You are now ready to get started with ASP.NET MVC.

ASP.NET MVC consists of a set of concepts and corresponding techniques that help you implement an application. It is not possible to cover all these aspects in one chapter, but this chapter gives you some grounding in and simple examples of the fundamentals of ASP.NET MVC to prepare you for the rest of the book. It's important to read this chapter carefully and to understand its points very well because you deal with these concepts frequently throughout the book. In the next few chapters, you use some of the basic concepts in examples that are discussed later, and you need to have the background from this chapter to understand them.

You start with installing ASP.NET MVC on a machine and creating a new ASP.NET MVC application and then examining the structure of an ASP.NET MVC project. You also take a look at test projects and their key role in ASP.NET MVC development. Right after this, you step into more details about the general structure of the main elements of a solution (such as the controller, view, and model) to give you a good perspective about these basic elements. There is also a discussion that covers Web configuration files in ASP.NET MVC. In the rest of the chapter, you examine an example of ASP.NET MVC and the process of development.

Don't worry about anything that you do not understand in depth in this chapter. The purpose of this chapter is to give you a general perspective and get you started with some concepts, and many of these main concepts are explored further in dedicated chapters throughout this book.

Some basic concepts that you need to learn from this chapter include how to install ASP.NET MVC on your machine, creating an ASP.NET MVC project, and understanding the structure of ASP.NET MVC projects.

Installing ASP.NET MVC

Obviously, the first stage in ASP.NET MVC development is creating a local installation of this technology on your development machine. ASP.NET MVC comes as a standalone package that installs on your machine and adds some features to Visual Studio.

Since its infancy, ASP.NET MVC has been available as a shared and open source project on a CodePlex workspace, and regular preview releases were dropped to the community during its development and will continue to be released in the future. You can navigate to `http://codeplex.com/aspnet` to get the most recent source code and installer of the ASP.NET MVC. After downloading the installer package, you can run it to install the software on your machine. Before installation, you need to have .NET Framework 3.5 (maybe with Service Pack 1) and Visual Studio 2008 installed on your machine. Of course, the latter requirement is in case you want to develop an ASP.NET MVC application and the .NET Framework is enough for the ASP.NET MVC runtime.

> *If you don't follow the community news, you may wonder why ASP.NET MVC is an open source project despite the traditional Microsoft approach of not releasing the source code. In 2007 Microsoft implemented a new strategy to release the source code of the .NET Framework and its different portions to allow developers to learn some development techniques from the code and be able to debug their code more easily and quickly. This strategy continued to develop, and Microsoft released the source code of some new Web development technologies on a workspace on CodePlex (the Microsoft open source community that hosts thousands of open source projects). Therefore, Microsoft has put the source code of ASP.NET WebForms, ASP.NET MVC, ASP.NET AJAX, and ASP.NET Dynamic Data on this workspace, and it is available for everyone. ASP.NET MVC was a shared source project but after the final release, it became an open source project under the Microsoft Public License (Ms-PL). This allows much space for community contributions and adoption of the code. For example, this allows a Mono developer to port it into the framework for Linux.*

The ASP.NET MVC installer is a straightforward installer with a few steps:

1. On the Welcome screen, click Next.

2. The next step of the wizard requires you to agree to the End User License Agreement (EULA) of the ASP.NET MVC. You must accept the terms, after which you can print out the agreement and click Next.

3. In the next step, click the Install button. This begins your installation process automatically and installs the necessary files at the appropriate paths for you.

4. The last page notifies you that the installation of the ASP.NET MVC on your machine was successful. Click Finish.

This installation copies some Visual Studio project templates to the appropriate paths to let you create and work with the ASP.NET MVC projects more easily and quickly. It also registers ASP.NET MVC assemblies in the GAC (Global Assembly Cache).

In Chapter 13, you read more about how ASP.NET MVC consists of a few assemblies that bring additional functionality to ASP.NET and can be deployed as independent assemblies with your projects or be referenced from the GAC, so you may see these assemblies in some of your ASP.NET MVC projects.

Creating an ASP.NET MVC Project

After installing the ASP.NET MVC on your development machine, you're able to create ASP.NET MVC projects and start developing Web applications based on the MVC pattern.

The ASP.NET MVC installer installs a project template for ASP.NET MVC projects. This template is available in Visual Studio in the New Project dialog box. It is under the Web category in the Project types pane on the left side of the dialog box. You can choose this item and set a project name for your project just as you would for any other Visual Studio project (see Figure 3-1).

> *Because ASP.NET MVC is built on top of .NET Framework 3.5, you need to choose .NET Framework 3.5 as your target framework version in the New Project dialog. Otherwise, you can't see the ASP.NET MVC project template.*

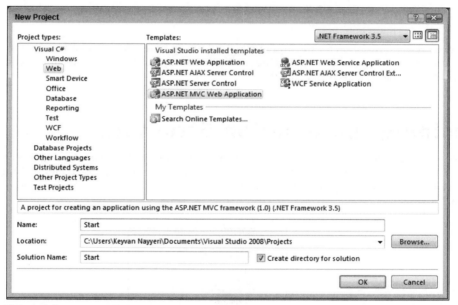

Figure 3-1

After confirming your settings and clicking OK, a new dialog shows up in the middle of your screen asking you whether you want to create a corresponding test project for your ASP.NET MVC application (see Figure 3-2).

Here, you can choose to create a new unit test project by giving a project name and choosing a test framework, or you can skip this step and not create a unit test project. Of course, the MVC pattern is tied to having a unit test project, and having a test project is an integral part of MVC development. Later in the chapter, you uncover more details about test projects in the ASP.NET MVC and Visual Studio 2008.

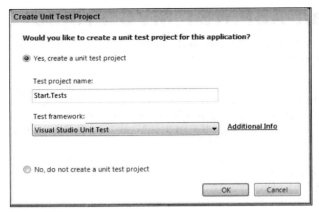

Figure 3-2

After you select your option for the unit test project, Visual Studio starts creating one or two projects in a solution for you (the second project being the unit test project, of course). The next section analyzes the structure of these projects in general.

Examining the Solution Structure

As you read in the previous section, Visual Studio creates a new solution containing one or two projects for you, and this depends on your choice of whether to have a unit test project. Figure 3-3 displays the default solution and the project template that is generated after choosing the Visual Studio Unit Test option.

Figure 3-3

Take a closer look at this project structure. The first project is an ASP.NET MVC project that consists of some files and folders (that have their own subfolders and files). The file types are already familiar to ASP.NET developers. They are some configuration files, programming classes, .aspx files, .master files, and a single Global.asax file.

There is a difference in the organization of project files in ASP.NET MVC in comparison with ASP.NET WebForms projects. Obviously, ASP.NET MVC has a better organization because all the files are placed in separate folders associated with their role in the project. In ASP.NET MVC, controller files are regular classes, and some views are stored as .aspx and .master files. The structure and implementation of models varies from project to project, so there isn't any default implementation for the sample Web site in an ASP.NET MVC project.

Next, you take a closer look at the main ASP.NET MVC-focused elements in this project template. For now you are not going to look at the theoretical concepts; you just focus on the aspects that are related to the storage structure of elements in the project template.

The Controller

The controller is a special type of class that derives from the Controller base class directly or indirectly. These files are pretty straightforward in the ASP.NET MVC project template. These class files are stored as regular .cs files in Visual Studio (or .vb for Visual Basic language). You read about controllers and their development process in detail in Chapter 5.

As an example, Listing 3-1 shows the source code of HomeController, a default controller class generated by Visual Studio.

Listing 3-1: HomeController

```
using System;
using System.Collections.Generic;
using System.Linq;
using System.Web;
using System.Web.Mvc;

namespace Start.Controllers
{
    [HandleError]
    public class HomeController : Controller
    {
        public ActionResult Index()
        {
            ViewData["Message"] = "Welcome to ASP.NET MVC!";

            return View();
        }

        public ActionResult About()
        {
            return View();
        }
    }
}
```

The View

The other common element in the MVC pattern is view. In the ASP.NET MVC project template, views are stored as `.aspx` and `.master` files, but there is no relationship between these `.aspx` and `.master` files with corresponding file types in ASP.NET WebForms. These file extensions are preserved for views, which may cause confusion.

An `.aspx` view represents a view page that is derived from the generic `ViewPage` base class and a `.master` view represents a view master page that is derived from the `ViewMasterPage` class. The only commonality between these files and their corresponding file types in ASP.NET WebForms is their role in presenting and sharing a constant user interface in an application.

Unlike with ASP.NET WebForms where you had three files for a page, in ASP.NET MVC, view and master page files consist of only a single file, which gives a better organization to project files.

Figure 3-4 exhibits the previously mentioned structure of file storage for view pages and master pages in the ASP.NET MVC.

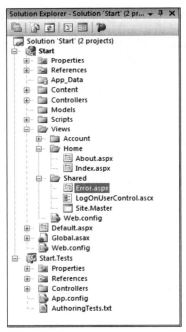

Figure 3-4

The Model

Because the model is dependent on your data storage system, which can vary from project to project, there isn't one specific implementation strategy for model files in your application. You may choose to use LINQ to SQL or LINQ to XML to manipulate data in your database or XML files, or you may choose to use regular database calls to accomplish this. In either case (or any other possible case), there is a different implementation for your model.

However, regardless of your storage provider, it's strongly recommended to encapsulate your main model implementation in programming classes that are included in the Models folder in your project.

The ASP.NET MVC Application Class

There is also a single Global.asax file included in your ASP.NET MVC applications that has a more important role than the same file in an ASP.NET WebForms application because it's responsible for managing URL routing (you learn more about URL routing in Chapter 7). This file routes URLs, maps routes, and registers routes in your application, so it connects user requests to your controller classes. However, it isn't necessary to get into the internal workings of this class here.

This class, which is derived from the HttpApplication base class, is placed in the root folder of your ASP.NET MVC application and has default generated code like that in Listing 3-2.

Listing 3-2: MvcApplication

```
using System;
using System.Collections.Generic;
using System.Linq;
using System.Web;
using System.Web.Mvc;
using System.Web.Routing;

namespace Start
{
    // Note: For instructions on enabling IIS6 or IIS7 classic mode,
    // visit http://go.microsoft.com/?LinkId=9394801

    public class MvcApplication : System.Web.HttpApplication
    {
        public static void RegisterRoutes(RouteCollection routes)
        {
            routes.IgnoreRoute("{resource}.axd/{*pathInfo}");

            routes.MapRoute(
                "Default",
                // Route name
                "{controller}/{action}/{id}",
                // URL with parameters
                new { controller = "Home", action = "Index", id = "" }
                // Parameter defaults
            );

        }

        protected void Application_Start()
        {
            RegisterRoutes(RouteTable.Routes);
        }
    }
}
```

Later in this chapter, you learn how to add your own routes to this file, so your application can handle manifold URL patterns by different controllers.

The Web Configuration File

Configuration files are an inherent part of any .NET application, and ASP.NET MVC comes with a web .config file that keeps the configuration data for the application. The structure of this file should already be familiar to a .NET developer because it has the same schema as other configuration files in the .NET Framework. Moreover, this file is very similar to web.config files for ASP.NET WebForm applications. There are only a few additions and changes to them, and these are outlined in this section. You probably already have a background in the structure of the web.config file for ASP.NET WebForms applications. If this is not the case, try to spend a short time learning about this file (you can find some helpful discussion of this at http://msdn.microsoft.com/en-us/library/kzalyk3a(VS.71).aspx), and then read the rest of this chapter, which just covers the changes and additions to this configuration file in the ASP.NET MVC.

❑   New assemblies have been added to the <assemblies /> element, and some of the older elements have been replaced.

❑   New namespaces have been added to the <namespace /> element and some of older elements have been replaced.

❑   New HTTP Handlers and HTTP Modules have been added within the <httpHandlers /> and <httpModules /> elements under the <system.web /> and <system.webServer /> elements. These new handlers and modules are mainly responsible for some internal workings of the ASP.NET MVC as well as URL routing.

By default, ASP.NET MVC applications are configured to work with ASP.NET membership and role providers in a SQL Express database instance located in the App_Data folder, but you can alter this configuration to not use these providers at all or to use your own data storage or provider system.

The Content Files

The last group of files generated by Visual Studio in the ASP.NET MVC project consists of a Content folder. This folder is responsible for holding some content and static files such as CSS and image files.

The Script Files

There is also a Scripts folder in the default ASP.NET MVC project template that holds JavaScript resources for AJAX features in ASP.NET MVC and jQuery.

Test Projects

All commercial editions of Visual Studio 2008 include unit testing features. (If you are working with Visual Studio 2005, some of the higher-end versions also include unit testing as well.) It's now common for developers to use Visual Studio unit-testing features, known as MsTest.

Though the Microsoft brand is very popular among many developers, others prefer to use open source alternatives such as MbUnit (http://mbunit.com) or NUnit (http://nunit.org), which are two well-known testing frameworks that are older than MsTest.

As you saw earlier in this chapter, when you are creating a new ASP.NET MVC project, Visual Studio asks you about your interest in creating a corresponding test project to test your applications (as was shown in Figure 3-2). If you have installed more testing frameworks on your machine, you can see them in the drop-down list of testing frameworks, and you can choose from them to build your unit test projects using these alternatives.

Figure 3-5 shows the same dialog when you have installed MbUnit on your machine as a secondary test framework, and Figure 3-6 provides a sample of the generated MbUnit test project.

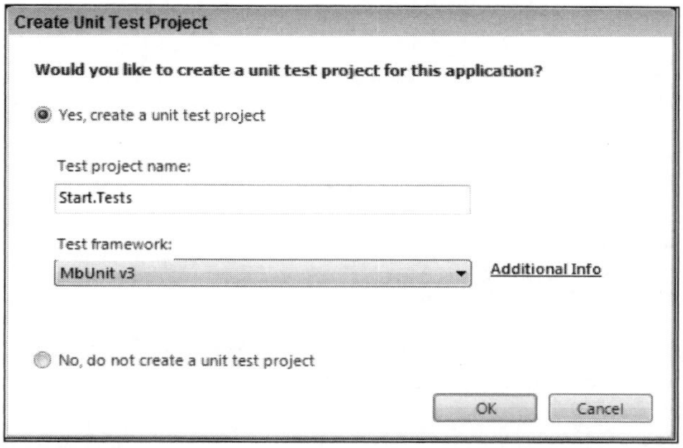

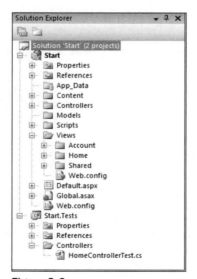

Figure 3-5

Figure 3-6

Talking about unit testing concepts and working with testing frameworks is beyond the scope of this chapter or even this book. However, we can give a general introduction to what you need to get started with ASP.NET MVC. Chapters 8 and 9 give more details and information about unit-testing concepts and testing frameworks and their applications in ASP.NET MVC.

The generated test project contains a single unit test class for the HomeController class that is named HomeControllerTest to show you how to deal with unit testing. While you're working on ASP.NET MVC projects, you can add more test classes to unit test your controllers. Listing 3-3 shows the source code of this test class, which tests two controller actions. You need to follow the same pattern in order to test the returned values from action methods in controllers with what you expect to get from them. This is the main part of unit testing an MVC application. Note the highlighted code lines in this class.

Listing 3-3: HomeControllerTest

```
using System;
using System.Collections.Generic;
using System.Linq;
using System.Text;
using System.Web.Mvc;
using Microsoft.VisualStudio.TestTools.UnitTesting;
using Start;
using Start.Controllers;

namespace Start.Tests.Controllers
{
    [TestClass]
    public class HomeControllerTest
    {
        [TestMethod]
        public void Index()
        {
            // Arrange
            HomeController controller = new HomeController();

            // Act
            ViewResult result = controller.Index() as ViewResult;

            // Assert
            ViewDataDictionary viewData = result.ViewData;
            Assert.AreEqual("Welcome to ASP.NET MVC!", viewData["Message"]);
        }


        [TestMethod]
        public void About()
        {
            // Arrange
            HomeController controller = new HomeController();

            // Act
            ViewResult result = controller.About() as ViewResult;

            // Assert
            Assert.IsNotNull(result);
        }
    }
}
```

An ASP.NET MVC Example

This section develops a simple example with ASP.NET MVC by customizing the existing default application generated by Visual Studio (dropping some parts and adding new parts). The full source code of this application is available as a part of the download package for this chapter, and you can simply grab it from www.wrox.com. However, you are encouraged to work along with the example. Doing so will more solidly ground you in the basics of working with ASP.NET MVC before you move on to the other chapters.

Throughout this book we develop our applications in the order of Model, Controller, View, Routing. This may be a little confusing for some readers who might initially be inclined to think about the MVC pattern in the order of Model, View, and Controller. There is no technical limitation that prevents us from following different orders, but based on our experience, our order (Model, Controller, View, and Routing) is one of the better practices specifically for ASP.NET MVC and helps you have a better development experience.

Try It Out   Creating Your First ASP.NET MVC Application

This application tries to retrieve a list of people from a SQL Express database using LINQ to SQL and then displays them in the output to end users. Moreover, it displays the information for individual people in unique URLs when the user navigates to them. For example, when the user navigates to http://site.com/person/1 she can see the information for the person whose ID is 1.

The Database

The first step in building the application is designing a database for it. This database, which is a SQL Express database, has a pretty simple structure with a single table (named Persons) that includes three columns that keep an ID, name, and creation date of persons (see Figure 3-7).

Here, we should clarify something about the usage of the word "persons," which is incorrect as a plural of "person" in the English language. LINQ to SQL generates the singular form of a table name for the entity name in code, so it drops the "s" from the end of plural words to get the singular form. "Persons" is used as a replacement for "people" for this specific context to handle the situation. In real-world scenarios, unless you are constrained by needing to match such names to terms used in existing business terminology, you can choose to use words where the plural form is created by simply adding an "s" to the singular form.

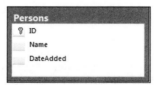

Figure 3-7

The Model

Obviously, you need a data model to communicate with the database and manipulate data. You have various options to choose from based on your requirements in a project, but this sample application uses LINQ to SQL to retrieve data from the database.

Therefore, you need to add a new LINQ to SQL project item to the `Models` folder and assign a `Persons` name. Then you drag the `Persons` table and drop it into the LINQ to SQL designer from the Server Explorer, which results in something like Figure 3-8.

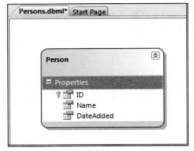

Figure 3-8

In the next section, this data context is applied to fetch and pass data from the database to views through the controller.

The Controller

The next step is to create a controller that acts like a bridge between the model (data) and the view (user interface). Create a new controller called `PersonController` that has two action methods called `Index` and `IndividualPerson`. The first method handles requests for the index of persons and the second method handles requests for individual persons.

The source code for this controller is presented in Listing 3-4.

Listing 3-4: PersonsController

```
using System.Linq;
using System.Web.Mvc;
using Start.Models;

namespace Start.Controllers
{
    [HandleError]
    public class PersonController : Controller
    {
        public ActionResult Index()
        {
            ViewData["Message"] = "Persons List";

            PersonsDataContext dataContext = new PersonsDataContext();
            ViewData["Persons"] = dataContext.Persons.ToList();

            return View();
        }

        public ActionResult IndividualPerson(int id)
        {
            PersonsDataContext dataContext = new PersonsDataContext();
```

```
                Person person = dataContext.Persons.Where
                    (p => p.ID == id).Single();
                ViewData["PersonName"] = person.Name;
                ViewData["Person"] = person;

                return View();
            }
        }
    }
```

Let's examine this class briefly. As you see, this controller class is derived from the `Controller` class located in the `System.Web.Mvc` namespace. Moreover, it contains two methods that return `ActionResult` objects as their results. Such methods are called action methods and are responsible for handling requests to a particular URL.

Each action method is responsible for retrieving data based on user input from the data model. The method passes them to a particular view appropriate for the request and then returns this view to the runtime engine. When working with controllers, you have access to the `ViewData` object from the base class that is of the `ViewDataDictionary` type and that keeps a list of items and their corresponding objects. There is also a `View` object in the base class of the `ViewResult` type that will be configured with this `ViewData` object behind the scenes, and you need to return it at the end.

The first action method, named `Index`, doesn't have any parameters. It sets two items in the `ViewData` objects. The first one is a literal title text and the second one is a list of persons retrieved from the LINQ to SQL data context.

The second action method, `IndividualPerson`, has a dynamic id parameter that it gets from the request URL. Like the first action method, it sets two items in `DataView` object. The first item is the name of the person retrieved from the model to be shown in the page title, and the second is a `Person` object whose data should be displayed.

The Views

The next stage in the development of this sample application is building appropriate views to display data that is passed from controllers to end users. You need to create a master page and two views: the site master, the `Index` view, and the `IndividualPerson` view.

First you create the site master. To start, you create a view master page to share the constant part of the user interface across all pages. For this purpose, you just customize the existing `Site.Master` file generated by Visual Studio and simplify it for the application. Listing 3-5 presents the source code of the new file.

Listing 3-5: Site.Master

```
<%@ Master Language="C#" Inherits="System.Web.Mvc.ViewMasterPage" %>

<!DOCTYPE html PUBLIC "-//W3C//DTD XHTML 1.0 Strict//EN"
 "http://www.w3.org/TR/xhtml1/DTD/xhtml1-strict.dtd">
<html xmlns="http://www.w3.org/1999/xhtml">
<head runat="server">
    <title>
        <asp:ContentPlaceHolder ID="TitleContent" runat="server" />
    </title>
```

Continued

Listing 3-5: Site.Master *(continued)*

```
        <link href="../../Content/Site.css" rel="stylesheet" type="text/css" />
    </head>
    <body>
        <div class="page">
            <div id="header">
                <div id="title">
                    <h1>
                        Getting Started</h1>
                </div>
                <div id="menucontainer">
                    <ul id="menu">
                        <li>
                            <%= Html.ActionLink("Home", "Index", "Home")%></li>
                    </ul>
                </div>
            </div>
            <div id="main">
                <asp:ContentPlaceHolder ID="MainContent" runat="server" />
                <div id="footer">
                    Wrox Beginning ASP.NET MVC
                </div>
            </div>
        </div>
    </body>
</html>
```

For the rest of the work, you need two views that display the index data and the individual person's data. The naming of these views should follow a specific pattern based on the parameters that were passed to the routes in the preceding step. Therefore, you create two view pages called `Index` and `IndividualPerson` located in `Person` subfolder in `Views` folder.

The `Index` view (see Listing 3-6) retrieves the list of persons from the `ViewData` object and displays them to the visitor.

Listing 3-6: Index view

```
<%@ Page Language="C#" MasterPageFile="~/Views/Shared/Site.Master"
Inherits="System.Web.Mvc.ViewPage" %>

<asp:Content ID="indexTitle" ContentPlaceHolderID="TitleContent" runat="server">
    Persons List
</asp:Content>
<asp:Content ID="indexContent" ContentPlaceHolderID="MainContent" runat="server">
    <h2>
        <%= Html.Encode(ViewData["Message"]) %></h2>
    <p>
        <%
            IList<Start.Models.Person> persons = ViewData["Persons"]
                as IList<Start.Models.Person>;
```

```
            if (persons != null)
            {
    %>
    <ul>
        <% foreach (Start.Models.Person person in persons)
            { %>
        <li><a href="/person/<%= Html.Encode(person.ID) %>">
            <%= Html.Encode(person.Name) %></a></li>
        <% } %>
    </ul>
    <% } %>
    </p>
</asp:Content>
```

As you might notice, this view consists of programming and HTML code that are combined together to accomplish a single goal. The main job is done in the highlighted code, which gets a list of `Person` objects from `ViewData` and then iterates through all items in the list and adds them to a bulleted list with appropriate HTML code.

This type of programming (a combination of programming code and HTML markup) may be new to you, but this is something that you frequently use when working with ASP.NET MVC. You can compare this with the model that you may have seen in classic ASP development where markup and programming code were in the same file, but here the programming code is not doing all the work. It's only responsible for rendering the output from the model data.

The second view of the sample application is the `IndividualPerson` view, which displays the information for an individual person based on the identifier that is passed via the URL.

The source code of this view (see Listing 3-7) is not very different from the source code for the `Index` view, except that it works based on a single instance of the `Person` object retrieved from the `ViewData` rather than a list of `Person` objects.

Listing 3-7: IndividualPerson view

```
<%@ Page Title="" Language="C#" MasterPageFile="~/Views/Shared/Site.Master"
Inherits="System.Web.Mvc.ViewPage" %>

<asp:Content ID="Content1" ContentPlaceHolderID="TitleContent" runat="server">
    <%= Html.Encode(ViewData["PersonName"]) %>
</asp:Content>
<asp:Content ID="Content2" ContentPlaceHolderID="MainContent" runat="server">
    <h2>
        <%= Html.Encode(ViewData["PersonName"]) %></h2>
    <p>
        <%
        Start.Models.Person person = ViewData["Person"]
            as Start.Models.Person;
        if (person != null)
        {
    %>
        <p>
```

Continued

Listing 3-7: IndividualPerson view *(continued)*

```
            Name:
            <%= Html.Encode(person.Name) %>
        </p>
        <p>
            Date Added:
            <%= Html.Encode(person.DateAdded) %>
        </p>
        <% } %>
    </p>
</asp:Content>
```

Routing

So far, you have retrieved the data from the database in the data model and then written a controller to get this data and pass it to views. However, before running the application, you need to connect the URLs to their corresponding action methods in the controller.

The different ways to do this are discussed in Chapter 7. For now, you just customize the URL routing in ASP.NET application class named `Global.asax`.

There is a `RegisterRoutes` static method in this class that gets a `RouteCollection` parameter and is the appropriate place to define your routes and add them to this collection.

For this example, you create two routes: one for the index page and another for the individual person page. Listing 3-8 shows the source code for the ASP.NET MVC application class.

Listing 3-8: MvcApplication

```
using System.Web.Mvc;
using System.Web.Routing;

namespace Start
{
    public class MvcApplication : System.Web.HttpApplication
    {
        public static void RegisterRoutes(RouteCollection routes)
        {
            routes.IgnoreRoute("{resource}.axd/{*pathInfo}");

            // Index
            routes.MapRoute(
                "Default",
                "",
                new { controller = "Person", action = "Index" }
                );

            // Individual Person
            routes.MapRoute(
                "IndividualPerson",
                "person/{id}",
                new { controller = "Person", action = "IndividualPerson" }
                );
```

```
        }

        protected void Application_Start()
        {
            RegisterRoutes(RouteTable.Routes);
        }
    }
}
```

Here, the emphasis is on the highlighted code where you define and add the routes. The first part is where you exclude .axd resources from the routing mechanism. The second part is where you define and add the route for the index page. As you see, you pass a name, a URL pattern, and a list of default object data for the route. This list of object data contains the name of the controller and action method that should handle requests to the specified URL pattern. Note that here the controller name doesn't have the "controller" suffix in its name, and ASP.NET MVC automatically detects the controller class.

Likewise, you define the route for the individual person page, but this time you define a dynamic URL pattern based on person IDs.

How It Works: Testing the Application

All that is left is to test the application (not to be confused with unit testing), the easiest step! You can navigate to the root Default.aspx of the project to see the index page (see Figure 3-9).

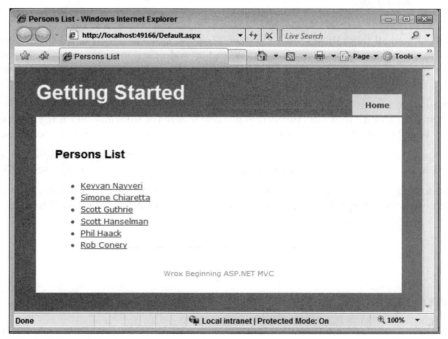

Figure 3-9

By clicking individual person names, you'll be redirected to the individual person's page to see his information (see Figure 3-10). Don't forget to check the URL in the address bar.

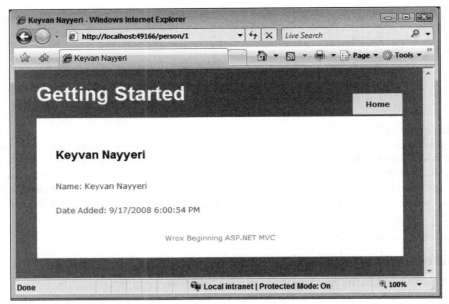

Figure 3-10

Let's look at how all these things work together. First you make a request to the index page, which matches to the pattern for `PersonController` and its `Index` action methods, so the request is routed to `Index` in `PersonController` and it loads the list of all persons and passes them to the `Index` view where you render them.

When you click an individual person's name, the request URL matches the `IndividualPerson` action method pattern and it's routed to this action method where the information for the individual person is retrieved based on his ID and then passed to the `IndividualPerson` view to be rendered.

As you see, this workflow is pretty simple and of course, the simplest type of request workflow in ASP.NET MVC. Throughout the book you discover more real-world examples in ASP.NET MVC.

The unit-testing part of this project is omitted for this chapter because it requires some extra discussion about unit-testing concepts that are explored later in the book and aren't relevant to the focus of this chapter.

Summary

In this chapter, you started getting your feet wet with ASP.NET MVC development with a quick overview of some common topics. The chapter began with a short guide on how to install ASP.NET MVC on your development machine, followed by the process of creating a new ASP.NET MVC project in Visual Studio. Then you examined the structure of ASP.NET MVC projects and took a closer look at main groups of elements. At this point, there was a short discussion about test projects in Visual Studio, alternative options from the community, and the structure of a unit test project in the ASP.NET MVC. The last part of the chapter focused on an example with the main emphasis on showcasing common concepts that you may need in the rest of the book.

Exercises

This chapter concludes with exercises to help you to understand some basic differences between ASP.NET WebForms and ASP.NET MVC and to learn about ASP.NET development with Visual Studio.

1.   Try to rewrite the ASP.NET MVC example that you examined in the chapter with ASP.NET WebForms applications and list the differences that you notice.

2.   Modify the example in this chapter to change the routing pattern for individual person pages to be "person/individual/{id}".

The Model

Throughout the first few chapters of this book you became familiar with basic Model-View-Controller (MVC) principles, how working with ASP.NET MVC differs from working with ASP.NET WebForms, and the general workings of ASP.NET MVC. Here in Chapter 4 your in-depth examination of the ASP.NET MVC begins with a discussion of the first element in the Model-View-Controller pattern: the model.

Any implementation of software in the MVC pattern consists of three main components, and the first element is the model. The model is the component responsible for encapsulating the data layer manipulations of your application in a simple API that can be used in the controller component easily and quickly. Moreover, it's responsible for including your business logic for what's going to happen with your data. This not only helps to reduce the coupling between your components but also improves the readability of your code significantly.

There is no one specific way to build your models, especially in ASP.NET MVC where a wide range of options exist for building your data storage infrastructure. You have various options for implementing your model component, including traditional data interactions with relational databases, different Object Relational (O/R) Mappers, and programming components for working with other data storage types such as XML or even text files. This gives you the flexibility to work in a variety of ways, and you can choose whatever way is most comfortable for you and fits the needs of your organization or project. Due to the variety of storage methods and the level of detail that would be required to cover each one, it is beyond the scope of this chapter to offer a complete guide to developing one. Some titles dedicated to teaching different data storage systems are listed in Appendix A.

ASP.NET MVC is a part of the new wave of development technologies introduced by Microsoft in the past couple of years focused on speeding up the development process. In addition to ASP.NET MVC and prior to it, Microsoft released LINQ technology (and different providers such as LINQ to SQL and LINQ to XML) as a part of .NET Framework 3.5 and ADO.NET Entity Framework as a part of .NET Framework 3.5 Service Pack 1. Both these technologies are built as adjuncts to traditional built-in mechanisms for working with data storage systems, and they make working with storage systems easier and faster. Moreover, they bring modern data interaction methods to the .NET world.

After the advent of the ASP.NET MVC, Microsoft, its employees, its partners, and many community members who authored content about this novel technology, preferred using LINQ (and its derivations such as LINQ to SQL or LINQ to XML) to develop their applications, and this seems to be a common method of facilitating data interaction in ASP.NET MVC applications. Besides, Microsoft has released a more professional implementation of such a technology named ADO.NET Entity Framework that is supposed to go further than LINQ to SQL and become a main option for data interactions in the .NET Framework 4.0.

Therefore, this chapter focuses on newer technologies, especially LINQ, and gives you a short introduction with a few examples to enhance your knowledge in this field with a pragmatic approach. Specifically, here we use LINQ to SQL and the ADO.NET Entity Framework to present two main sample applications and get you started with the model development.

Finally, note that you should adapt this development method to your data storage system in order to build your own model.

What Microsoft Provides for the "M" in MVC

As a powerful technology, you might expect ASP.NET MVC to implement all of the components of the MVC pattern and provide all the tools and means necessary for developing Web applications with this pattern.

Although ASP.NET MVC does a great job of providing very powerful mechanisms to develop controllers, action methods, action filters, views, routes, and many other components, and also has provided a high level of extensibility and customizability for them, Microsoft hasn't implemented anything for the model component.

The model component in ASP.NET MVC is limited to a folder in the default project template generated for you called Models, and the rest is left to you to implement. Moreover, Microsoft hasn't provided an official way for building model components in ASP.NET MVC.

Therefore the "M" in MVC (and the model in ASP.NET MVC) is an unclear part of the ASP.NET MVC learning process. This can be an advantage or a disadvantage, based on your point of view. On one hand it empowers developers to choose whatever method they want for creating their models, and on the other hand, it doesn't provide a best practice or method for developing your models. Another disadvantage is the lack of tools to ameliorate model development in ASP.NET MVC. Of course, most of Microsoft data technologies that you would use for the model (ADO.NET data objects, LINQ to SQL, LINQ to XML, or ADO.NET Entity Framework) are easy to use, but there might be some space for providing better tooling and development experience in the specific field of ASP.NET MVC development.

Because no model is provided in ASP.NET MVC's Models folder, you need to create your own model. Fortunately, you have a lot of options for doing this, as you see in the following sections.

An Overview of the Model

As introduced in Chapter 1, the model is the part of the application that is responsible for retrieving data from the database, converting it to objects, and applying domain-specific elaboration to them. In a simple but not necessarily complete comparison, the model can be compared to the data layer of your application in commonplace n-tier architectures, which most likely you have used in developing your applications, but with a major addition, which is the implementation of business logic in this component. The model is mainly responsible for acting like a bridge between data storage, low-level data interaction components, and controllers. In fact, the model is where you conceal all your data code and encapsulate it in a manner that allows you to achieve independence between your programming components.

As described in the introduction to this chapter, there isn't a specific method for building the model component because a wide range of data storage systems are available, and a model implementation varies by application because of the differences in data requirements. Therefore, no distinct set of methods exists for building the model component.

Based on your requirements, skills, and preferences, you may choose a specific data storage type or a combination of multiple data storage types for building the data infrastructure of your application. At the moment, there is a wide range of data storage technologies such as relational databases (SQL Server, Access, Oracle, and MySql), XML files, and other, less common types such as text files. Moreover, many components, libraries, and technologies have been built to simplify the process of working with one of these data storage systems or a combination of them. Some options are built into the .NET Framework, and some have been released by third-party software vendors as commercial products or by open source teams as nonprofit community projects.

As long as numerous data storage types and data interaction technologies exist, it's clear that we don't have to have a single definitive method for building our models. We are free to use whichever technologies we choose. The next section looks at some of the options.

Different Options for Building the Model

The .NET Framework comes with a rich set of data APIs that are mainly grouped into ADO.NET technologies out-of-the-box. The four technologies that are common choices when working with the ASP.NET MVC are:

❑ **LINQ to SQL** — This is a new technology in .NET Framework 3.5 that brings O/R (Object Relational) Mapper features to the .NET Framework. It's easier to use than other options (such as database objects), and you can build your data infrastructure in a short time, so LINQ to SQL is likely to become a good alternative for traditional data interaction methods.

❑ **Database Objects** — The most common and frequently used way of working with various database types (SQL Server, Access, Oracle, or MySql) is with traditional data interaction APIs that are built specifically for a specific type of database; they all provide similar methods and properties and the same programming model. However, data objects are likely to lose their role in data interaction with new technologies like ASP.NET MVC and they're being replaced by new alternatives such as LINQ to SQL and the ADO.NET Entity Framework.

❑ **ADO.NET Entity Framework** — Like LINQ to SQL, this is a new technology that is released as a part of .NET Framework 3.5 Service Pack 1; it also targets the goal of mapping data objects to programming classes, but it has a more professional structure and level of customizability and control. In the context of ASP.NET MVC, this is better than LINQ to SQL because it allows you to have more control on the definition of your entity classes to apply your necessary changes.

❑ **XML** — Some built-in APIs are available for working with XML files and performing common tasks, such as selecting, editing, deleting, and inserting data, that allow you to use XML files as your storage systems. Older APIs for XML manipulation are a part of `System.Xml` namespace, whereas `System.Xml.Linq` introduces new LINQ to XML APIs to accomplish the same goals based on LINQ expressions in .NET Framework 3.5. Generally, XML is used for small applications and configuration purposes.

This chapter shows examples for each of these four technologies to give you a good background for working with them. We try to focus on some of the options more than others because they're likely to be of more interest to developers.

The chapter provides ASP.NET MVC applications but doesn't go over the details of some components like views or routing, which are not our focus here. These components are discussed in the chapters that follow, but for now we only use their default code, which is introduced in Chapter 3.

LINQ to SQL

One of the options for working with data in the .NET Framework is LINQ, which is commonly used by developers when working with the ASP.NET MVC.

LINQ, which stands for *Language Integrated Query*, is a new technology added to .NET Framework 3.5 that enables native data-querying capabilities in the .NET development languages. Besides this, several technologies provide functionality to work a wide range of different data sources, and in fact act like a mapper in which you map database tables or XML elements to programming classes, thus making working with these classes much easier than working with database objects or XML elements. These technologies work in conjunction with LINQ to provide an easy and readable way of working with data and programming classes.

Various providers in this family are available today. The vast majority of commonly used providers are a built-in part of the .NET Framework, and companies and open source teams have built other providers as well.

Here is a short list of built-in providers:

❑ **LINQ to XML** — LINQ to XML or XLINQ, which is used later in an example in this chapter, maps XML elements to programming objects and allows you to query among them using LINQ operators.

- ❑ **LINQ to SQL** — LINQ to SQL, also known as DLINQ, maps SQL Server database objects to programming classes and then helps you in manipulating data through the use of LINQ operations rather than direct database operations. Besides, Entity Framework, which is discussed later in this chapter, is a more professional implementation of functionality in LINQ to SQL, and it has more features. Entity Framework, which is discussed later in this chapter, is a more professional implementation of functionality in LINQ to SQL, and it has more features.

- ❑ **LINQ to Objects** — This provider of LINQ provides the fundamental operations for other providers and enables in-memory operations with LINQ, which can be applied to various data types, especially enumerator types (such as lists and other collection types).

- ❑ **LINQ to DataSets** — Because LINQ to SQL works only with SQL Server, Microsoft also provides LINQ to DataSets, which works with `DataSet` objects in the .NET Framework and can be used with any other data source type through ADO.NET objects.

In addition, there are some other providers including LINQ to ADO.NET Data Services, LINQ to Entities (ADO.NET Entity Framework), and LINQ to NHibernate. Some helpful providers such as LINQ to Flickr are built for specific purposes like working with Flickr Web 2.0 APIs.

Now that you have this background, the following Try It Out is a simple example of these providers, specifically LINQ to SQL, which is the main provider for LINQ.

Try It Out   Using LINQ to SQL

In this example, you create a new SQL Server database with a single table that holds data for some Pink Floyd albums and their release year. Through a step-by-step guide, you see how to use LINQ to map this table to programming objects and use them in an ASP.NET MVC application to display the list of albums and information for a specific album. Here a list of Pink Floyd albums will be displayed in the home page with a link to an individual album page where visitors can find more details about the album.

1. You start by building your standard SQL Server database. (A standard SQL Server database will work fine for this scenario.) This database needs to include an `Albums` table with the properties `ID`, `Name`, and `ReleaseYear`.

2. The next step is to build the data model. To do so you add a new LINQ to SQL Classes project item to the `Models` folder and name it `PinkFloyd`. While the LINQ to SQL designer is open (Visual Studio automatically opens the designer when you add the project item), choose the `Albums` table from Server Explorer and drag and drop it into the designer surface (see Figure 4-1).

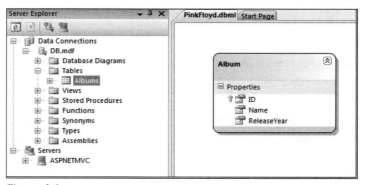

Figure 4-1

3. Now you add a new class to the `Models` folder and name it `AlbumsDataContext`. The class, shown in Listing 4-1, has two static functions that return a list of all albums and the information for a single album, respectively.

Listing 4-1: AlbumsDataContext

```
using System.Collections.Generic;
using System.Linq;

namespace LinqToSql.Models
{
    public class AlbumsDataContext
    {
        public static IEnumerable<Album> GetAlbums()
        {
            PinkFloydDataContext dataContext = new PinkFloydDataContext();
            return dataContext.Albums.ToList<Album>();
        }

        public static Album GetAlbum(int id)
        {
            PinkFloydDataContext dataContext = new PinkFloydDataContext();
            return dataContext.Albums.Where
                (album => album.ID == id).Single();
        }
    }
}
```

In the main part of this code (the highlighted piece) are two methods that use LINQ to SQL data context to retrieve the appropriate data and return it to the caller, and both use simple LINQ operations to accomplish this. The rest of the story is concealed from your eyes because .NET manages the process of mapping the `Albums` table from the database to the `Albums` object available in the `PinkFloydDataContext` class.

4. Next, you build an `AlbumController` class with two action methods that can be written in a few lines of code and don't need any explanation (see Listing 4-2). (Controllers are discussed in detail in Chapter 5.)

Listing 4-2: AlbumController

```
using System.Web.Mvc;
using LinqToSql.Models;

namespace LinqToSql.Controllers
{
    public class AlbumController : Controller
    {
        public ActionResult Index()
        {
            ViewData["Albums"] = AlbumsDataContext.GetAlbums();

            return View();
```

```
        }

        public ActionResult Album(int id)
        {
            Album album = AlbumsDataContext.GetAlbum(id);

            ViewData["Title"] = album.Name;
            ViewData["Album"] = album;

            return View();
        }
    }
}
```

This example skips the steps to set up routing and build master pages and views (which are available in the source code package for this chapter on the Wrox site) and moves directly to the test stage. Running this example, you get the outputs shown in Figures 4-2 and 4-3.

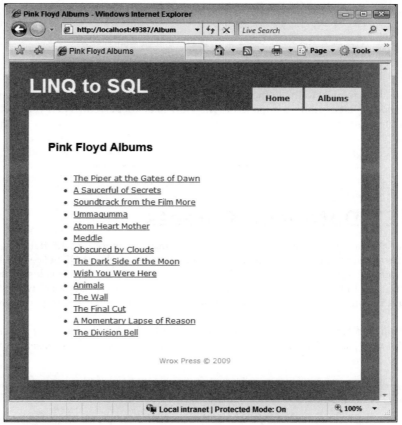

Figure 4-2

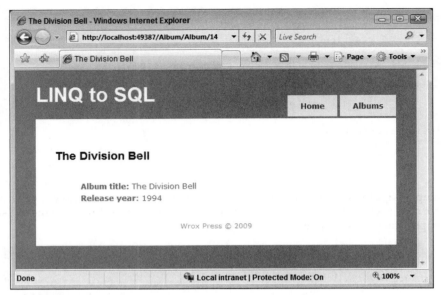

Figure 4-3

When you make a request to the home page, that request is routed to the Index action method of the controller, and the list of albums is loaded to the view to be displayed. When you click a link of an album, it routes your request to the Album action method and loads the data for that album into the view again.

ADO.NET Database Objects

An oldie but goodie, and the most commonly used method for working with data, uses built-in database objects that are designed to work with various database types such as SQL Server, OLE databases, and Oracle. Of course, as stated earlier in this chapter, the usage of these objects is losing its popularity to newer techniques. In the next Try It Out you build another example that works with SQL Server as its database and uses text commands rather than stored procedures to keep things simple.

Using built-in database objects is not covered here because it is a broad subject, and you need to learn about them as a part of acquiring knowledge of ADO.NET. This knowledge is considered an important prerequisite for reading this book.

Try It Out   Using SQL Server

The example in this section uses a SQL Server database that contains a table that stores information about some historical and natural places in Iran that are frequently visited by tourists. This table stores the name of the place, the city where it is located, and a link to the Wikipedia page about the place.

1.   Obviously, the first step is creating a database with the appropriate table. The example uses a SQL Express database. A single Places table holds data for the historical places.

2. After creating the database, you build a data model by defining a new class called `Place` in the `Models` folder (see Listing 4-3).

Listing 4-3: Place

```
using System;

namespace DBObjects.Models
{
    public class Place
    {
        public int ID { get; set; }

        public string Name { get; set; }

        public string City { get; set; }

        public Uri Url { get; set; }
    }
}
```

3. Now, you need to create a new class that acts like a data context. (Call it `PlacesDataContext`.) It has a single static function, named `GetPlaces`, which uses built-in database objects to retrieve data for historical places and returns a list of `Place` objects (see Listing 4-4).

Listing 4-4: PlacesDataContext

```
using System;
using System.Collections.Generic;
using System.Configuration;
using System.Data.SqlClient;

namespace DBObjects.Models
{
    public class PlacesDataContext
    {
        public static IEnumerable<Place> GetPlaces()
        {
            List<Place> places = new List<Place>();

            string connectionString =
                ConfigurationManager.ConnectionStrings["DB"].ConnectionString;

            using (SqlConnection connection = new SqlConnection(connectionString))
            {
                string commandText = "SELECT ID, [Name], City, Url FROM Places";

                using (SqlCommand command = new SqlCommand
                    (commandText, connection))
                {
```

Continued

53

Listing 4-4: PlacesDataContext *(continued)*

```
                    connection.Open();

                    SqlDataReader reader = command.ExecuteReader();
                    while (reader.Read())
                    {
                        Place place = new Place();

                        place.ID = (int)reader["ID"];
                        place.Name = (string)reader["Name"];
                        place.City = (string)reader["City"];
                        place.Url = new Uri((string)reader["Url"]);

                        places.Add(place);
                    }

                    connection.Close();
                }
            }

            return places;
        }
    }
}
```

In this simple class, especially in the highlighted code, `SqlConnection`, `SqlCommand`, and `SqlDataReader` are the three built-in database classes for connecting to the SQL Server database and retrieving a list of places.

If at this point you have difficulty understanding the code in Listing 4-4, we would strongly recommend that you read a good general programming book about C# or more specifically about ADO.NET programming. Appendix A lists some great books in this field.

4. Building the data model is the main step that we're focusing on, but you also need to create a new controller. Listing 4-5 shows the `PlacesController`, which responds to incoming requests via the `Index` action method.

Listing 4-5: PlacesController

```
using System.Web.Mvc;
using DBObjects.Models;

namespace DBObjects.Controllers
{
    public class PlacesController : Controller
    {
        public ActionResult Index()
        {
            ViewData["Places"] = PlacesDataContext.GetPlaces();

            return View();
        }
    }
}
```

As you may have noticed, this action method calls `PlacesDatacontext.GetPlaces` to get and pass the list of historical places to the view.

The controller is covered in detail in Chapter 5.

This example skips the steps to create the views and customize the routing mechanism (which are fully available in this chapter's download package on `wrox.com` and are introduced in Chapter 3). The last step, testing the application, produces output like that shown in Figure 4-4. When you run the application and make a request, it's routed to the controller and its single action method. This method loads data and passes it to the view where it is rendered to the end users.

Figure 4-4

ADO.NET Entity Framework

ADO.NET Entity Framework is the newest technology that we're covering in this chapter by examining an example. ADO.NET Entity Framework targets mapping data objects to programming classes and was introduced as a part of the .NET Framework 3.5 Service Pack 1.

As a prerequisite for this book, especially this chapter, you need to have the .NET Framework 3.5 Service Pack 1 installed on your machine; otherwise, you can't see the items that are used in the example.

ADO.NET Entity Framework provides functionality similar to that offered by LINQ to SQL but is more advanced and gives you more options for customization and using extensions. Moreover, it works on top of LINQ operations, so after building your data model with this framework, you can simply use LINQ operations to deal with data.

This chapter provides a very simple example to help you get started with this technology. Note that this example doesn't reflect the actual power and full features of the Entity Framework that make it something different from LINQ to SQL, but it's still worth exploring here because of the wide use of the Entity Framework and the probability that you will use it in your future .NET projects.

Try It Out   Using ADO.NET Entity Framework

In this example, you build an ASP.NET MVC application that lists some ASP.NET MVC community leaders with links to their Twitter accounts. Twitter is an excellent resource for staying up-to-date with the ASP.NET MVC stream.

1. First, you build the database. This database has a single table called TwitterAccounts with three columns, including ID, Name, and TwitterPage, which are self-explanatory.

2. Next, you add a new ADO.NET Entity Data Model project item to the Models folder and name it TwitterAccounts (see Figure 4-5).

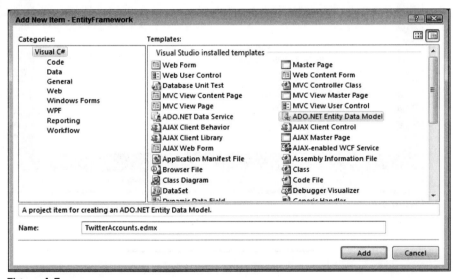

Figure 4-5

3. In the next step the Entity Data Model Wizard appears and asks you whether you want to use an existing database to generate your model or build a clean model (see Figure 4-6). Choose the first option (Generate from database), and click Next.

Figure 4-6

4. In the second step of this wizard, you choose your data connection from existing connections or add a new one, and then decide whether you want to add the connection string to `Web.config`. Enter the information as shown in Figure 4-7.

Figure 4-7

5. In the next step, you select the tables, views, and stored procedures that you'd like to include in your model. Choose the single table, and set an appropriate root namespace name for the model, as shown in Figure 4-8.

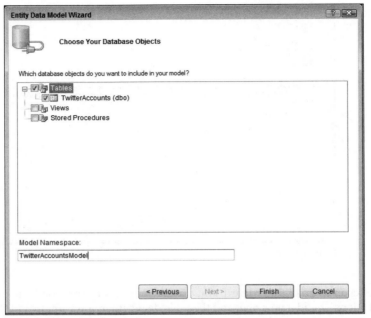

Figure 4-8

6. After this, Visual Studio generates a schematic view of your model in ADO.NET Entity Framework designer (see Figure 4-9), and you can apply necessary changes in your model in a classic form.

Figure 4-9

7. At this point, most of the work to build the data model is completed. You just need to add a new class called `TwitterAccountsDataContext` to your `Models` folder and a short piece of code to select information in its static `GetAccounts` function (see Listing 4-6).

Listing 4-6: TwitterAccountsDataContext

```
using System.Collections.Generic;

namespace EntityFramework.Models
{
    public class TwitterAccountsDataContext
    {
        public static IEnumerable<TwitterAccounts> GetAccounts()
        {
            DBEntities entities = new DBEntities();
            return entities.TwitterAccounts;
        }
    }
}
```

Note the highlighted code that creates an instance of the `DBEntities` class, which acts like LINQ to SQL data context classes. .NET does the job for you behind the scenes, and you can simply use this class to get access to your data and manipulate it.

8. In the next step, you create your controller class called `TwitterContoller`. The source code of this class is shown in Listing 4-7.

Listing 4-7: TwitterController

```
using System.Web.Mvc;
using EntityFramework.Models;

namespace EntityFramework.Controllers
{
    public class TwitterController : Controller
    {
        public ActionResult Index()
        {
            ViewData["Accounts"] = TwitterAccountsDataContext.GetAccounts();

            return View();
        }
    }
}
```

After customizing the routing mechanism and building the master page and views (available in the source code package for this chapter on the Wrox site), you can run your application to get the output presented in Figure 4-10.

Figure 4-10

The workflow of the events to produce this output is simple. A request is made to the site and routed to the action method where data is loaded from the model and passed to the view. There data objects are processed and displayed in the correct format.

XML

XML files are suitable for small applications and configuration purposes. They are also good for storage when you don't want to work with very complicated relationships between your data and you're not dealing with a lot of data rows.

In the .NET Framework, two groups of classes are available for working with XML files: traditional XML classes (which have been a part of this framework since the early days) and new LINQ to XML classes, which are introduced in .NET Framework 3.5 to enable LINQ expressions on XML data.

LINQ to XML is a part of .NET that assists developers, when working with XML data, to select, update, delete, and insert data. This technology enables the same human-readable syntax for XML manipulations and, more importantly, allows you to map XML data to programming objects.

Let's dive right in and look at an example of how you can use XML files with LINQ to XML technology.

Try It Out   Using XML Files and LINQ to XML

This Try It Out has an XML file containing a list of .NET community members and leaders along with their blog URLs. The goal is to display this list in a page with links to their blogs. You apply LINQ to XML classes to retrieve the URLs in the model and pass them to controllers. Obviously, the main step is building the data model.

1.   Listing 4-8 represents an XML file that holds the data, a list of well-known ASP.NET community leaders and members that is worth checking by any developer.

Listing 4-8: XML file of ASP.NET community leaders with their blog URLs

```
<?xml version="1.0" encoding="utf-8" ?>
<Leaders>
  <Leader name="Scott Guthrie">
    http://Weblogs.asp.net/scottgu
  </Leader>
  <Leader name="Scott Hanselman">
    http://hanselman.com/blog
  </Leader>
  <Leader name="Phil Haack">
    http://haacked.com
  </Leader>
  <Leader name="Rob Conery">
    http://blog.wekeroad.com
  </Leader>
  <Leader name="Keyvan Nayyeri">
    http://nayyeri.net
  </Leader>
  <Leader name="Simone Chiaretta">
    http://codeclimber.net.nz
  </Leader>
</Leaders>
```

As you see, there is a root `<Leaders />` element with multiple `<Leader />` elements as its children, and each `<Leader />` subelement has a `name` attribute as well as a value that refers to the blog URL.

2.   Now suppose that you have a `Leader` class (located in the `Models` folder in the solution) representing a community leader with two properties as shown in Listing 4-9.

Listing 4-9: The Leader class

```csharp
using System;

namespace LinqToXml.Models
{
    public class Leader
    {
        public string Name { get; set; }

        public Uri BlogUrl { get; set; }
    }
}
```

61

3. Having these requirements, you create a new class in the `Models` folder called `LeadersDataContext`, which is mainly responsible for data manipulation operations and encapsulating the data operations.

We chose the name `LeadersDataContext` just to be consistent with the names that Visual Studio generates for LINQ to SQL data contexts. You aren't required to use the same naming convention, but we recommend that you adhere to your own conventions to improve the organization of your project files and make it more readable.

Listing 4-10 shows the source code for `LeadersDataContext`, which has a single method that retrieves `Leader` objects and returns a list of the results.

Listing 4-10: LeadersDataContext

```
using System;
using System.Collections.Generic;
using System.IO;
using System.Linq;
using System.Web;
using System.Xml.Linq;

namespace LinqToXml.Models
{
    public class LeadersDataContext
    {
        public static IEnumerable<Leader> GetLeaders()
        {
            string filePath = HttpContext.Current.Server.MapPath
                ("~/App_Data/Leaders.xml");

            XElement xmlData = XElement.Parse(File.ReadAllText(filePath));

            var leaders = from leader in xmlData.Elements()
                    select new Leader
                    {
                        Name = leader.Attribute("name").Value,
                        BlogUrl = new Uri(leader.Value)
                    };

            return leaders;
        }
    }
}
```

4. Obviously, you need a controller component for your application. Next you create the `LeadersController` in Listing 4-11.

Listing 4-11: LeadersController

```
using System.Web.Mvc;
using LinqToXml.Models;

namespace LinqToXml.Controllers
{
    public class LeadersController : Controller
    {
        public ActionResult Index()
        {
            ViewData["LeadersList"] = LeadersDataContext.GetLeaders();

            return View();
        }
    }
}
```

As you can see, the action method can get its data from the data model by calling a single method, and this is an important point in the MVC development.

To save paper, we omitted the rest of the process, including the creation of views and master page, and leave it to you to download the sample package for this chapter from wrox.com and get your hands on the code. It mostly has the default implementation generated by the Visual Studio project template that we discussed in Chapter 3. Figure 4-11 shows you the output of this example.

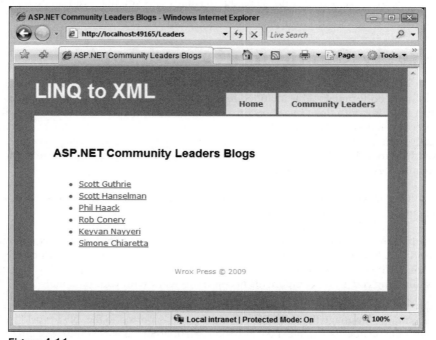

Figure 4-11

Important Considerations about Creating Data Models

Reading this chapter, you need to understand two important points about building a data model in general.

The first point is about storing your data model classes and related content in an organized manner in the `Models` folder. As you saw in the examples, we stored all our model classes and data contexts in this folder. For the sake of consistency, it is very important to store your classes in this folder. This is the one part of ASP.NET MVC where Microsoft has left a footprint for model development for developers to follow.

The second and more important point is about keeping your model classes and data contexts separate and independent from your controllers and other components. It's critical to have a complete encapsulation for data models and keep all your components (including the model) in an isolated mode, so you can change everything in your data model without applying changes in controllers or views.

We used data context classes to conceal the data manipulation portion of the code from controllers, and all our controllers have a single call to the data model to retrieve only their required data, so if we change anything behind the scenes (even our data storage system), we shouldn't change anything in other components.

It's also recommended that you apply some data operations such as sorting and grouping in your data model and hide them from your controllers, but in some cases you may want to do that somewhere else.

Third-Party Components and Tools

Software developers are always looking for new methods to speed up their development and make it easier. Although built-in data APIs included in the .NET Framework are really easy to use and you can accomplish anything with them in a short time, software developers have tried to make this development process even easier and faster. The result is a varied set of tools, components, and technologies that are basically built on top of these built-in APIs but hide them behind the scenes. However, new technologies like LINQ to SQL and ADO.NET Entity Framework may challenge the usage of these tools to some extent because they target the same areas.

Here are some well-known tools and projects that many professional developers use in their day-to-day development:

❑ **SubSonic** — This open source project that started as a community project was mainly managed and developed by Rob Conery and some active community members prior to the birth of the ASP.NET MVC. SubSonic assists you in building your data model quickly by generating all programming codes and components necessary to work with your data tables.

❑ **NHibernate** — Hibernate is a famous and popular open source O/R Mapper for the Java programming language that is built by Red Hat, and is ported to the .NET world by this company with the NHibernate name. Like SubSonic, NHibernate assists you in speeding up your development by auto-generating your data access layer code.

❏ **LightSpeed** — As a young, powerful, and commercial (with limited free edition) O/R Mapper tool built by Mindscape, LightSpeed provides a set of modern features for developers such as a better visual designer, LINQ support, and design for testability features (which may be a very good advantage for ASP.NET MVC scenarios).

❏ **LLBLGen** — Another commercial O/R Mapper with many modern features that, like other tools, can speed up the generation of the data access layer for you.

It's left to you to decide whether you need to use such a code-generator tool, and which code generator is suitable for your needs.

Summary

This chapter was all about the first component in the MVC pattern: the model. As you read in the introduction, how you build a model is dependent on your knowledge of the data storage system that you want to use.

The chapter started by looking at some common data storage systems and technologies available for .NET developers to use in their applications. It outlined the most common methods for building ASP.NET MVC models.

The rest of the chapter provided sample implementations of the built-in data technologies in the .NET Framework, including LINQ to SQL, built-in database objects, ADO.NET Entity Framework, and LINQ to XML.

The last sections of the chapter discussed a couple of the more important points in building ASP.NET MVC models and introduced third-party tools and generators.

Exercise

Regarding the model component in an MVC application, you need to practice with your preferred data storage system or the one that you commonly use. However, we have provided an exercise that will enhance your knowledge of the important sections of this chapter.

1. Apply the example for built-in database objects (Iranian historical places) in a LINQ to SQL example. Try to create a new application that uses two tables with a relationship and retrieves and displays their data using LINQ to SQL. You can create a new table that holds the province name of the historical place and relates each place to its province.

The Controller

The controller is the last letter of MVC, but if the naming followed the real correlation between the components of the pattern, it would have been placed in the middle. The controller is the orchestrator of the operations and is the component that stands between the model and view and passes data between the two.

The previous chapter covered the model part of the pattern. In this chapter, you learn in detail about the controller.

Specifically, you learn:

❑   The responsibilities of the controller

❑   How to create the controller

❑   How to read inputs and pass data to the view

❑   How to access the core ASP.NET objects, like `Response`, `Cache`, and similar objects

What the Controller Does

You already had a quick overview of how the controller fits into the MVC pattern in Chapter 1. In this section, you learn in detail what its responsibilities are.

The controller is the main component of an MVC application, and its role is even more important here in the ASP.NET MVC framework, which adopts the Passive View pattern. One common misconception is that the main role of the controller is to keep the model and the view separated, but its main role is to mediate between the end user and the application: The fact that it also connects the model with the view is just a side effect. In fact, not including the routing mechanism, the controller is the first component of the application that receives the input from the users.

The tasks that the controller has to perform are capturing and validating the user input, delegating all the complex operations (business logic rules and data access) to the model, and when the results come back, deciding which view to render and handing the data to the selected view.

Before you dive into the technical aspects of how to write a controller with the ASP.NET MVC framework, I want to stress one important concept: Because the controller is the first thing being hit by a request, the temptation is to stuff it with lots of code and forget about the model. This is something you must avoid at all costs, or you risk making it just another `Page_Load` method. One thing that you must remember when developing an MVC application is that the controller must be as thin as possible, and all the complex business logic, data access, and data manipulation must be handled inside the model. Coming from the Ruby on Rails world, this concept is synthesized with the following tenet:

> **MVC applications must have a fat model and skinny controller (and a dumb view).**

Enough with theoretical concepts. From the next paragraph on you learn how to create a controller using the ASP.NET MVC framework.

Creating a Controller

In ASP.NET MVC, a controller is just a class that implements the `IController` interface and whose name ends with `Controller` (if the name of your controller is `Image`, the name of the class must be `ImageController`). But you don't really have to implement the interface from scratch: To make things easier for developers, the framework provides the base controller class `System.Web.Mvc.Controller`, which implements the `IController` interface and also provides other useful methods to help with the development of controllers.

The only purpose of the controller class is to act as a container of *actions*, which is where the requests are handled. An action is just a public method that can have any number of parameters, from zero to many, and typically returns an object of type `System.Web.Mvc.ActionResult`. Usually it sets the data that needs to be passed to the view in the `ViewData` object and calls the `View` method to render the view.

Other than the few rules just outlined, you are free to organize the controller class and the action methods any way you prefer.

Just a quick note before starting with the code samples: In Chapter 3, when you learned how to create an ASP.NET MVC Web site, you saw that the default routing rule is `{controller}/{action}/{id}` and that with this rule the ASP.NET MVC framework does the processing of the request with the controller and action that are specified as part of the URL. You also had a brief overview of how a view works. Because the controller is just a brick in the whole application, the examples in this chapter take that basic knowledge for granted. Further details on routing and views come in the following chapters.

Try It Out   Write Your First Controller

In this example, you create an ASP.NET MVC basic Web site, with a controller that is a bit more complex than the one that comes out of the project template.

1.   Create a new ASP.NET MVC Web site, using the Visual Studio template (as you read about in Chapter 3).

2. Navigate to the Controllers folder in Solution Explorer, open the `HomeController` class in the code editor, remove the `About` method (created by the project template), and add the following method:

```
public ActionResult About(int id)
{
    ViewData["ID"] = String.Format("Requested id = {0}",id);

    return View();
}
```

3. Now go in the `Views/Home` folder, open the `About.aspx` file, and add the following line of code somewhere in the body of the page:

```
<h1><%= Html.Encode(ViewData["ID"]) %></h1>
```

4. Press F5 or select the menu command Debug ⟿ Start Debugging, acknowledge any dialog that might appear, wait for the browser to open, type the following URL in the address bar, and press Enter:

```
http://localhost:<portnumber>/Home/About/12
```

5. You get the results shown in Figure 5-1 in the browser.

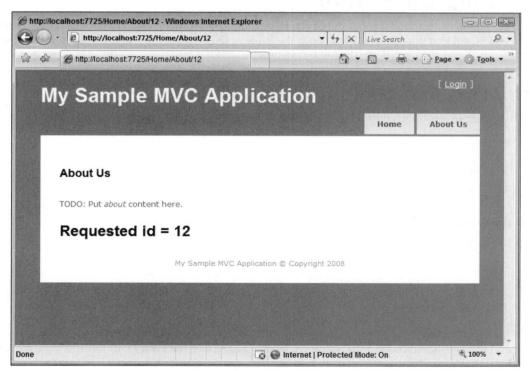

Figure 5-1

How It Works

You have just written an action that is a bit more complex than the one automatically created by the project template.

You requested the URL /Home/About/12. This instructs the framework to instantiate the HomeController class and call the About method, supplying 12 as the value of the id parameter.

The value is then concatenated into a string, and it's stored inside the ViewData object. Finally, the View method is called, and the default view for this action is called.

Notice that the value coming from ViewData is rendered through the Encode method. This method prevents scripting attacks to the site. You read more about this in the next chapter, but it's important to start keeping a focus on security aspects right from the beginning.

You now have an overview of all the steps required to write a controller. In the next section, you learn in detail about all the aspects of the controller.

Defining an Action

In the previous section you learned that just by adding a public method to a controller class you create an action and that the name of the action is the name of the method. Most of the time this is true, but some attributes can modify the default behavior.

Attributes That Control Action Definition

Three built-in attributes control how an action is defined inside a controller class:

- ❏ NonAction
- ❏ ActionName
- ❏ AcceptVerbs

The NonAction Attribute

A public method marked with this attribute will not be treated as an action.

```
[NonAction]
public void ThisIsNotAnAction()
{
    //do something
}
```

If the browser should request the action ThisIsNotAnAction, the server will return a Page Not Found error (HTTP error 404).

The ActionName Attribute

The default name for an action is the name of the method that implements it, but it can be changed by marking the method with the `ActionName` attribute.

Why would you want to change the name of the action? If you want an action named `View`, you cannot just create a method named `View`, because one of the methods of the controller base class is already named `View` (which is the one that renders the view to the browser). But with this attribute you can create a method with an arbitrary name and set the action name to `View`.

```
[ActionName("View")]
public ActionResult NotTheSameView()
{
    ViewData["Message"] = "Welcome from the method NotTheSameView";

    return View();
}
```

The AcceptVerbs Attribute

This attribute sets the HTTP verbs that the action can respond to. For example, to create a form that edits a product's details, you need to write two different methods: one that writes the form with its values, and one that stores the form's values to the repository. To do this you have three options:

- ❏ Write two separate actions, one named `WriteForm` and another named `ProcessForm`. This is not a good solution, because it gives two names to the same feature and exposes the internals to the users.

- ❏ Write just one action named `Update` that contains two branches. This is a bit better than the previous option but is still not quite right. It makes the controller too "fat" and puts two completely different functionalities inside the same method.

- ❏ Use the `AcceptVerbs` attribute and write two methods with the same action name that respond to different verbs.

The most commonly used HTTP verbs are GET and POST. (The other verbs are PUT and DELETE.) The first is used when clicking a link or typing the URL in the address bar, and the second is used when an HTML form is submitted. Here is an example of how the `AcceptVerbs` attribute is used:

```
[AcceptVerbs("GET")]
public ActionResult Update()
{
    //ShowUpdateForm

    return View();
}
```

```
[AcceptVerbs("POST")]
public ActionResult Update(FormCollection form)
{
    //ProcessUpdateForm

    return View();
}
```

The attribute accepts an array of strings. If you want to have the same method handle two or more verbs, all you need to do is to supply all the verbs as parameters.

```
[AcceptVerbs("GET","POST")]
```

If you don't like strings, it's also possible to specify the verbs accepted, using the overload that takes in the values of an enum. You can specify that an action can only be called via POST with this line of code:

```
[AcceptVerbs(HttpVerbs.Post)]
```

If the actions can be called with two or more verbs, you can use the binary or operator:

```
[AcceptVerbs(HttpVerbs.Post | HttpVerbs.Get)]
```

Building Your Own Attribute

If you want finer control of how an action is selected, you can build your own attribute that derives from the `ActionMethodSelectorAttribute` base class. You see how to do it in Chapter 16, the one about the extensibility points of the framework.

Now that you know how to create a controller and how to define an action, it's time to learn how to get data from the request and how to pass data to the view.

Passing Data to the View

The ultimate goal of an action is to collect data and then return it to the user. Most of the time this is done by a view that receives the data retrieved by the action. You have three different ways to do this:

❑   Using the `ViewData` object

❑   Using a strongly typed Presentation Model object

❑   Using the `TempData` object

ViewData

The first and probably more approachable way of passing data to the view is to use the `ViewData` object, which is just a simple dictionary that stores a collection of name-value pairs. You can store any type of value you want, from a simple message string to a complex hierarchical model object.

```
ViewData["Title"] = "About Page";
ViewData["LoggedUser"] = new User("Simone Chiaretta");
ViewData["CurrentDate"] = DateTime.Now;
```

In the code, you set a string, a custom model object, and a `DateTime` into the `ViewData` object.

To display these values in a view, unless you want their bare string representation (which in some situations can be enough), you have to cast them to the appropriate type and render them.

Try It Out   **Using the ViewData Object**

In this example, you write a simple application that displays a text message with details about a user and the current date and time.

1.   Create a new ASP.NET MVC Web site, and inside the Models folder add a class named User. Replace the contents added by Visual Studio with the code in Listing 5-1.

Listing 5-1: Sample User model class

```
namespace Passing_Data.Models
{
    public class User
    {
        public string Username { get; set; }
        public string Email { get; set; }
        public Address HomeAddress { get; set; }
    }

    public class Address
    {
        public string Country { get; set; }
        public string City { get; set; }
        public string Street { get; set; }
    }
}
```

2.   Open the Controllers\HomeController.cs file and replace the definition of the method About with the code in Listing 5-2:

Listing 5-2: About action

```
public ActionResult About()
{
    User loggedUser = new User
                        {
                            Username = "MVCDeveloper",
                            Email = "mvcdev@wrox.com",
                            HomeAddress = new Address
                                            {
                                                Country = "Italy",
                                                City = "Milano",
                                                Street = "Viale Monza"
                                            }
                        };

    ViewData["Title"] = "Modified About Page";
    ViewData["Message"] = "This page uses loosely typed ViewData";
    ViewData["LoggedUser"] = loggedUser;
    ViewData["CurrentDate"] = DateTime.Now;

    return View();
}
```

3. Finally, open `Views\Home\About.aspx` and add to the new page the code shown in Listing 5-3.

Listing 5-3: About ViewPage

```
<%@ Page Language="C#" MasterPageFile="~/Views/Shared/Site.Master"
AutoEventWireup="true" Inherits="System.Web.Mvc.ViewPage" %>
<%@ Import Namespace="Passing_Data.Models"%>

<asp:Content ID="aboutTitle" ContentPlaceHolderID="TitleContent" runat="server">
About Us
</asp:Content>

<asp:Content ID="aboutContent" ContentPlaceHolderID="MainContent" runat="server">
    <h2><%= Html.Encode(ViewData["Message"]) %></h2>
    <p>
    Today is <%= ((DateTime)ViewData["CurrentDate"]).ToLongDateString()%>
    and the current user is <b><%=((User)ViewData["LoggedUser"]).Username %></b>
    and he comes from <%=((User)ViewData["LoggedUser"]).HomeAddress.City %>
    (<%=((User)ViewData["LoggedUser"]).HomeAddress.Country %>)
    </p>
</asp:Content>
```

4. Start the Web site and browse to the URL `http://localhost:<portnumber>/Home/About`. You see a page that shows the current date formatted in long format, the username, the city, and the country of the user currently logged in.

How It Works

In the action you added four objects to the `ViewData` dictionary: two strings, one `DateTime`, and the custom `User` class that you created as the model in step 1 (in that sample the instance of the user was created using the new C#3.0 object initializer syntax).

Then, in the view, the objects are retrieved from the `ViewData` object. But this approach has a small problem: All the objects are stored in the dictionary as `object`, so they must be cast to the correct type before using them:

```
<%=((User)ViewData["LoggedUser"]).HomeAddress.City %>
```

Another problem of this approach is that all the objects are retrieved through their name, so, unless the action is documented very well, it's easy to forget which values are available or to mistype a name and discover the error only at runtime.

There is another approach that solves this problem: the strongly typed model object.

A Strongly Typed Model Object

Instead of storing the data you want to pass to the view in the `ViewData` dictionary, you can create a custom transfer object and pass it to the view with one of the various overloads of the `View` method:

```
ViewResult View(object model)
```

To enable the use of this object in a strongly typed manner instead of inheriting from the base class `ViewPage`, the view class must inherit from its generic counterpart `ViewPage<TModel>`, where `TModel` is the type of the custom transfer object.

On the view side no more casting is needed. You can access the transfer object from the `Model` property of `ViewPage`.

```
<%=Model.LoggedUser.HomeAddress.City %>
```

This approach solves the problems of the loosely typed one:

❏ No more casting is necessary to access the properties and methods of the object passed to the view.

❏ You have a compile-time check of the correctness of the application.

❏ You have the support of IntelliSense, which lists all the available objects contained in the custom transfer object, as shown in Figure 5-2.

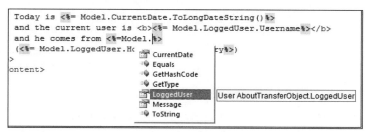

Figure 5-2

Try It Out   Using the Strongly Typed Model Object

In this example, you create a slightly modified version of the previous example, this time using the strongly typed object instead of the loosely typed `ViewData` dictionary.

1. Start by creating a new MVC Web application, and add the same `User` class that you added previously to the `Models` folder. (The code is listed in Listing 5-2.)

2. Add another class to the `Models` folder, `AboutTransferObject`, and write the code shown in Listing 5-4.

Listing 5-4: Custom Model transfer object

```
using System;

namespace Passing_Data.Models
{
    public class AboutTransferObject
    {
        public DateTime CurrentDate { get; set; }
```

Continued

Listing 5-4: Custom Model transfer object *(continued)*

```
            public User LoggedUser { get; set; }
            public string Message { get; set; }
        }
    }
```

3. Open the `Controllers\HomeController.cs` file, and replace the definition of the `About` method with the code in Listing 5-5.

Listing 5-5: About Action with strongly typed data

```
public ActionResult About()
{
    User loggedUser = new User()
                        {
                            Username = "MVCDeveloper",
                            Email = "mvcdev@wrox.com",
                            HomeAddress = new Address()
                                            {
                                                Country = "Italy",
                                                City = "Milano",
                                                Street = "Viale Monza"
                                            }
                        };

    ViewData["Title"] = "Modified Strongly-typed About Page";
    AboutTransferObject ato = new AboutTransferObject
                        {
                            CurrentDate = DateTime.Now,
                            LoggedUser = loggedUser,
                            Message = "This page uses strongly typed object"
                        };

    return View(ato);
}
```

4. Finally, open the markup for the `About` view, and add the code in Listing 5-6.

Listing 5-6: Strongly typed About ViewPage

```
<%@ Page Language="C#" MasterPageFile="~/Views/Shared/Site.Master"
AutoEventWireup="true" Inherits="System.Web.Mvc.ViewPage<AboutTranferObject>" %>
<%@ Import Namespace="Passing_Data.Models"%>

<asp:Content ID="aboutTitle" ContentPlaceHolderID="TitleContent" runat="server">
    Modified Strongly-typed About Page
</asp:Content>

<asp:Content ID="aboutContent" ContentPlaceHolderID="MainContent" runat="server">
    <h2><%= Html.Encode(Model.Message) %></h2>
    <p>
```

```
        Today is <%=Model.CurrentDate.ToLongDateString()%>
        and the current user is <b><%=Model.LoggedUser.Username%></b>
        and he comes from <%=Model.LoggedUser.HomeAddress.City%>
        (<%=Model.LoggedUser.HomeAddress.Country%>)
    </p>
</asp:Content>
```

5.   Start the Web site, browse to the `About` view, and you'll see exactly the same page as you saw in the previous Try It Out section.

How It Works

Unlike the previous example, now you had to write one more class, `AboutTransferObject`, to store all the information that you want to pass to the view. Notice that in the action you populated both `ViewData` and the model object: One doesn't preclude the usage of the other, and you can use both at the same time.

You may wonder which of the two approaches you should use. As with everything in the IT world, both have advantages and disadvantages. In this specific case, the advantages of one approach are also the disadvantages of the other. I recommend using the strongly typed approach for chunks of data that are recurrent in many views of the application or if the data is an entity that already exists in your Presentation Model. For everything else — error messages, general messages, and unimportant objects that are specific to a single view — use the `ViewData` loosely typed dictionary.

TempData

The life of `ViewData` and the strongly typed object are limited to the current request, so their values are not accessible after the view is returned to the browser. If you want the data to be available also outside the page, you can use the good old `Session` object or the new `TempData` object. It's a loosely typed dictionary, just like `ViewData`, but its contents live until the next request.

```
TempData["Message"] = "Redirected from About";
```

This is useful when you are building a wizard-like interface and each page sends some data to the next one. It is also useful if you are redirecting to another page, for example a page with the error details, and want to display some data you collected in the previous page.

Retrieving Data from the Request

Now that you know all about passing data from the controller to a view, in this section you learn how to collect data from the request.

You have two ways of retrieving data: The first involves the usage of the action parameters, both for simple types (integer, strings, numeric, and so on) and, with the help of a ModelBinder, for complex types (your own model objects). The second involves using the ModelBinder directly inside the action method.

Action Parameters

The first approach to retrieve data from the request is to have the data passed to the action as method parameters. In the following sections you learn the different ways in which data can be passed as a parameter for action methods.

Passing Simple Types to the Action

The easiest scenario is when you want to supply parameters that come with the URL itself or from POST operations that contain just a few parameters. In this case what you are doing is passing into the action methods only data that can be represented through simple types, like integer or string.

The Value Retrieved from the URL

You learn about routing in detail in Chapter 7, but, as you already saw with the default routing rule, the URL of a request is matched to the route rule and each of the folders of the URL is assigned to a token. Briefly, if the default rule is {controller}/{action}/{id} and the URL requested is http://localhost/Home/Edit/12, Home becomes the value of the controller token; Edit becomes the value of the action token; and finally, 12 becomes the value of the id token. The first two tokens (controller and action) are used by the framework to identify the action to execute, but all the other tokens are then passed to the action as parameters. Furthermore, if the URL has a query string, its query variables are passed as parameters as well.

You have an action named Post that accepts a few parameters:

```
public ActionResult Post(int year, int month, int day, string title, int commentId)
```

and you have the following route rule: {controller}/{action}/{year}/{month}/{day}/{title}.

When you browse to the URL http://localhost/Blog/Post/2008/09/11/My-Birthday?commentId=4577, the Post method is called with the following parameters:

Parameter	Value
year	2008
month	09
day	11
title	My-Birthday
commentId	4577

The first four parameters have been retrieved from the URL path and mapped to the tokens defined in the route rule, whereas the last one was retrieved from the query string variable with the same name.

The same approach can also be used with data coming from the post of an HTML form.

The Value Retrieved from Post Data

In addition to retrieving the values for the parameters from the URL or from the query string, the ASP .NET MVC framework can also get the values from an HTML form submitted using POST.

To make this work, you just have to name the HTML input controls as the name of the parameters.

Try It Out   **Method Parameters from Form Post**

1. As always, start by creating a new ASP.NET MVC Web site.

2. Create a controller class named BlogController, and add two methods to it:

```
using System;
using System.Web.Mvc;

namespace PassingDataToAction.Controllers
{
    public class BlogController: Controller
    {
        public ActionResult Create()
        {
            return View();
        }

        public ActionResult Save(string postTitle, string postText)
        {
            ViewData["Message"] = String.Format("Title: {0}<br/>Text: {1}",
                                                postTitle, postText);
            return View();
        }
    }
}
```

3. Add a new folder under Views, and name it **Blog**.

4. Inside that new folder add one Content View Page named Create.aspx:

```
<%@ Page Title="" Language="C#" MasterPageFile="~/Views/Shared/Site.Master"
Inherits="System.Web.Mvc.ViewPage" %>

<asp:Content ID="Content1" ContentPlaceHolderID="TitleContent" runat="server">
    Create
</asp:Content>

<asp:Content ID="Content2" ContentPlaceHolderID="MainContent" runat="server">
<form action="/Blog/Save" method="post">
    Title: <input type="text" id="postTitle" name="postTitle" /><br />
    Text: <input type="text" id="postText" name="postText" /><br />
    <input type="submit" />
</form>
</asp:Content>
```

5. And another Content View Page named `Save.aspx`:

```
<%@ Page Title="" Language="C#" MasterPageFile="~/Views/Shared/Site.Master"
Inherits="System.Web.Mvc.ViewPage" %>

<asp:Content ID="Content1" ContentPlaceHolderID="TitleContent" runat="server">
    Save
</asp:Content>

<asp:Content ID="Content2" ContentPlaceHolderID="MainContent" runat="server">
 <h2><%= ViewData["Message"] %></h2>
</asp:Content>
```

6. Now start the Web site, browse to `/Blog/Create`, type some text in the two textboxes, click the Submit button, and see on the next page the text you typed in.

How It Works

In this example, the action has been implemented exactly the same as in the previous example. It just accepts two parameters. But instead of being collected from the URL parts or from the query strings, this time the values of the parameters are retrieved from the form submitted by the browser.

Binding Complex Objects Using the Model Binder

The previous way to retrieve data from the request showed how binding works with simple types like integer, string, numeric, and so on. But if you want to pass a complex object, like the `User` object shown in Listing 5-1, things are slightly different.

The default binding mechanism of ASP.NET MVC tries to map the values of HTML controls to the parameter based on their naming. If the action method accepts a parameter whose name is `user` and of type `User`, the default binder looks for HTML controls named `user.propertyName`. It also navigates through the nested objects to try and bind the entire hierarchy of objects. This is easier to show with an example. The following code is the action method:

```
public ActionResult Save(User user)
{
    //do something
}
```

For the framework to automatically fill the properties of the user parameter, the HTML controls should be named as in the code that follows:

```
UserName: <input type="text" id="username" name="user.Username" />
Email: <input type="text" id="email" name="user.Email" />
City: <input type="text" id="city" name="user.HomeAddress.City" />
Street: <input type="text" id="street" name="user.HomeAddress.Street" />
```

If it doesn't find any HTML control named `parameterName.propertyName`, the default binder falls back on looking for controls named with only the name of the property. So, the following code sample leads to the same result as the previous one. Notice that now the controls are just named with the property name without the name of the parameter (`propertyName`).

```
UserName: <input type="text" id="username" name="Username" />
Email: <input type="text" id="email" name="Email" />
City: <input type="text" id="city" name="HomeAddress.City" />
Street: <input type="text" id="street" name="HomeAddress.Street" />
```

The default model binder allows you to further control how the binding is done by annotating the action parameter with the `Bind` attribute. This attribute contains three properties you can set to specify how the binding should work:

❑   Prefix

❑   Include

❑   Exclude

Prefix

The `Prefix` property allows you to change the prefix that is added to the model's property name when searching for a matching HTML control. By default, it's the name of the parameter passed to the action method, but you can change it to whatever you prefer, for example to `userToSave`:

```
public ActionResult Save([Bind(Prefix = "userToSave")]User user)
```

With the action defined as in the preceding line, you need to define the HTML controls with just the properties' names:

```
UserName: <input type="text" id="username" name="userToSave.Username" />
Email: <input type="text" id="email" name="userToSave.Email" />
City: <input type="text" id="city" name="userToSave.HomeAddress.City" />
Street: <input type="text" id="street" name="userToSave.HomeAddress.Street" />
```

Include

The `Include` property allows you to specify which properties of the model object you want to be automatically bound to the action parameter. It can be used as a "whitelist" of all the properties you want to be bound. By default, all the properties of the model object are taken into account, even the ones that are not set via the HTML controls. Imagine that the `User` object also had a password property that you don't want to be changed via the `Save` action. If a hacker understands that all the properties are populated with the naming convention you saw a few lines ago, he could sniff the transmission and tamper with it, adding a value for a fake HTML control named `user.Password` so that he can set the password of the user. That's why it's important to explicitly set the model's properties you want to be bound via the `Include` property:

```
public ActionResult Save([Bind(Include = "Username, Email")]User user)
```

Exclude

The `Exclude` property is the opposite of `Include`. It allows you to specify which model object's properties you don't want to be bound. In the preceding example, it would have been easier to just say "exclude the password property" than "include all the others."

```
public ActionResult Save([Bind(Exclude = "Password")]User user)
```

Besides annotating the action parameter, you can also apply the same attribute directly to the object model definition:

```
[Bind (Exclude = "City")]
public class Address
{
    //Class
}
```

This is useful if you want to specify the binding options for all the instances of an object model (and not only for a single action method) or for classes that are only used as properties (and the binding cannot be modified with a parameter attribute, because it applies only to the outer object).

Binding Data Inside the Action

Parameter model binding is great when you want to instantiate new objects and pass them as methods of the action, but in other scenarios you want to create the object inside the action and update it with the values that are coming from the request. For example, you retrieve a user from the DB and then you want to update only the e-mail with the values submitted with the form. To do this, you have to use the `UpdateModel` or the `TryUpdateModel` methods.

Their usage is pretty simple:

```
User user = new User();
UpdateModel(user);
```

First, you create the instance of the object you want to update, and then you call the `UpdateModel` method, passing it the object you want to update and the properties of the object you want to update.

To specify the binding options, you can either add attributes to the type that is being bound, or you can use one of the several overloads of the `UpdateModel` method. These include specifying the prefix (unlike the other approach, here the default is no prefix, and if you want it to be the name of the property, you have to specify it in the call), and the whitelist and the blacklist of properties.

```
UpdateModel (user, "user" , new[] {"username", "email"});
```

But there is also a more idiomatic and strongly typed way of defining the properties that need to be bound. You can define an interface with the allowed properties and then have a real model object implement it. (See Listing 5-7.)

Listing 5-7: User object with forbidden property

```
public interface IUserBindable
{
    string Username { get; set; }
    string Email { get; set; }
}

public class User : IUserBindable
{
    public string Username { get; set; }
    public string Email { get; set; }
    public string Password { get; set; }
}
```

Then you call the `UpdateModel` method, using the generic version and specifying the bindable interface as the type:

```
UpdateModel<IUserBindable>(user);
```

The difference between `UpdateModel` and `TryUpdateModel` is that, whereas the first raises an exception, the second returns a Boolean indicating whether or not some binding error occurred.

> One cool bonus feature you get with model binding is `ModelState`. This is a dictionary that contains all the properties that have been bound, with their name and original value. If the framework cannot correctly bind a property of an object, either via the parameter binding or via the `UpdateModel` method, it will add an error message to the item related to the property that is failing. This way the controller can take actions based on what kind of error happened. You read more about `ModelState` and how it is used to validate the user input in Chapter 14.

Types of Action Results

The last thing an action must do is return the result to the end user. But a result is not only an HTML view page; it can be anything from a small part of a HTML page, to a JSON result, file, or just a string of text. And it can even be just a redirect to another URL or another action.

In the ASP.NET MVC framework, actions are all represented as classes inheriting from the base class `ActionResult`. In this section, you learn about all the different kinds of action results that are available in the framework.

ViewResult

The first and probably most important action result is the `ViewResult`. When returned by an action, it instructs the framework to render a view, optionally supplying a custom model object.

There is a helper method that simplifies the process of creating an instance of this action result with all its optional properties. It is the method you already saw in all the previous examples: The `View` method is available in eight different overloads that are used with permutations of the three main parameters:

❑ `viewname` — The name of the view that needs to be rendered

❑ `model` — The custom model object that you want to pass to the view

❑ `mastername` — The name of the master page that will include the specified view

The following table contains the list of all the available overloads and their purpose:

Method Signature	Description
`View()`	Renders the view that has the same name as the action being executed
`View(object model)`	Renders the view that has the same name as the action being executed and supplies the custom model object
`View(string viewname)`	Renders the view of the name specified
`View(IView view)`	Renders the view specified
`View(string viewname, object model)`	Renders the view of the specified name and supplies the custom model object
`View(string viewname, string mastername)`	Renders the view of the specified name with the specified master page
`View(IView view, object model)`	Renders the specified view and supplies the custom model object
`View(string viewname, string mastername, object model)`	Renders the view of the specified name with the specified master page and supplies the custom model object

For example, the following code instructs the framework to render a view named List, inside a master page named AdminMaster, and supplies a custom model object:

```
return View("List","AdminMaster",listOfCustomers);
```

Most of the time, you will probably find yourself using this action result and this helper method at the end of your actions.

PartialViewResult

A user of your Web application clicks a button on a page, and your application has to do some server-side processing and update a portion of the page. You have two options: You do a full postback that reloads the entire page, or you use a bit of JavaScript and change only the contents you really need to change, avoiding the full postback, emulating the partial rendering that was introduced with ASP.NET AJAX.

In this scenario, you cannot render a complete view, but only the HTML needed for the portion of the page you want to update: In that case the action must return the `PartialViewResult`.

As with the `ViewResult`, this job is made easier by a helper method that takes care of the creation of the instance of the class; its name is `PartialView`, but it has fewer parameters, because there is no need for a master page for a partial view and no need for an already instantiated view. You can create the partial view by setting the view name, supplying the model object, or both.

```
return PartialView("LoginStatus",currentUser);
```

There is also the overload that takes no parameters and renders the view with the same name as the action, and that partial view will only have access to the `ViewData` dictionary.

RedirectResult

An action usually displays a view but can also redirect the user to another URL or action; this is done by returning an object of type `RedirectResult` or `RedirectToRouteResult`.

This return type is useful when you want to apply the *POST/Redirect/GET* (PRG) pattern. An HTML form is submitted and the action is processed, but instead of directly returning a confirmation message or any other contents, the flow is redirected to another page that is responsible for returning the results to the user.

This pattern makes it unlikely to post the same data twice and removes the confirmation dialog that appears when you click the Reload button on a page that has been requested using the POST HTTP verb.

If you want to redirect the user to a specific URL, you can use the `Redirect` method, which redirects the browser to the specified URL.

```
return Redirect("/Blog/Create");
```

Try It Out   **Implementing the PRG Pattern**

In this example, you write a small application that makes use of the `Redirect` method and the `TempData` object to implement the POST/Redirect/GET pattern.

1. As always, start by creating a new ASP.NET MVC Web application.

2. Inside the `Controllers` folder, create a new controller named `BlogController`, and copy the code in Listing 5-8.

Listing 5-8: Blog controller that implements the PRG pattern

```
using System.Web.Mvc;

namespace PRGPattern.Controllers
{
    public class BlogController : Controller
    {
        public ActionResult Edit()
        {
```

Continued

Listing 5-8: Blog controller that implements the PRG pattern *(continued)*

```
            if (TempData["title"] != null)
                ViewData["Title"] = TempData["title"];
            else
                ViewData["Title"] = "[Type Title]";
            if (TempData["text"] != null)
                ViewData["Text"] = TempData["text"];
            else
                ViewData["Text"] = "[Type Text]";
            return View();
        }

        public ActionResult Save(string title, string text)
        {
            TempData["Message"] = "Post Updated!";
            TempData["title"] = title;
            TempData["text"] = text;
            return Redirect("/Blog/Edit");
        }
    }
}
```

3. Create a new folder under `Views` and call it **Blog**.

4. Create a new view content page named **Edit**, and type in the code in Listing 5-9.

Listing 5-9: Edit page

```
<%@ Page Title="" Language="C#" MasterPageFile="~/Views/Shared/Site.Master" "
Inherits="System.Web.Mvc.ViewPage" %>

<asp:Content ID="Content1" ContentPlaceHolderID="TitleContent" runat="server">
    Edit
</asp:Content>

<asp:Content ID="Content2" ContentPlaceHolderID="MainContent" runat="server">
<b><%= TempData["Message"] %></b>
<p>
<form action="/Blog/Save" method="post">
Title:<br />
<input type=text name="title" id="posttitle" value="<%= ViewData["Title"] %>"/><br />
Text:<br />
<textarea name="text" id="posttext"><%= ViewData["Text"] %></textarea><br />
<input type="submit" value="Post" />
</form>
</p>
</asp:Content>
```

5. Now start the Web site, browse to `/Blog/Edit`, type some text in the two textboxes, click the Post button, and on the next page you will see the text you typed in.

6. Click the Reload button to see that the form is not submitted again, but instead that the empty form is displayed.

How It Works

In this example, you put into practice some of the concepts you read about in this chapter:

❑ ViewData, which has been used to contain the data that needs to be rendered in the view

❑ TempData, used to maintain the data during the redirect operation

❑ Action parameters used to pass the values from the HTML form to the action

❑ RedirectResult, used to send the redirect to the Edit action

❑ The POST/Redirect/GET pattern, which is how all the workflow of the example has been organized

The flow of this application is the typical one of the PRG pattern. First, the page with the form is requested. Once the user submits the form, the Save method is called. This is where in a real application the form is processed, saving the object to the database and so on. In this example, the values are stored in the TempData collection together with a message. Then the user is redirected to the Edit form again, directly specifying the URL of the action.

The Edit form checks whether there is something in the TempData data and renders the view, with the data saved if the page is the result of a post, or with the default data if it's the first time the page is accessed or if the user clicks the Reload button.

The POST/Redirect/GET pattern is typically used in these kinds of situations — where the operation performed when the user clicks the Submit button changes the state of the application; for example, when you add an entity to the database or update its details.

RedirectToRouteResult

The Redirect method is great if you want to redirect to some outside URL or to a carved-in-stone internal URL. But if the URL in the application changes, you risk having to change all the occurrences of the URL string. This scenario happens more frequently than you might think. To help with this scenario, the framework includes RedirectToRouteResult, which redirects the user to a specific route.

You can use two helper methods to return this type of ActionResult:

❑ RedirectToAction — Computes a route based on the action you want to redirect to.

❑ RedirectToRoute — Directly selects the route to redirect to.

Two of the parameters that these methods accept are related to the routing engine that you see in Chapter 7:

❑ RouteValueDictionary is a dictionary with the route tokens that are used to match the route rule and invoke the action specified.

❑ routeName is the optional friendly name that you give to a route when you register it in the application startup code.

RedirectToAction

The first helper method is useful when you want to redirect to a URL based on the controller action it represents. The following table lists the available overloads:

Method Signature	Description
`RedirectToAction(string actionName)`	Redirects to the action specified in the same controller
`RedirectToAction(string actionName, object values)`	Redirects to the action specified in the same controller, and with the action parameter supplied inside an anonymous type
`RedirectToAction(string actionName, string controllerName)`	Redirects to the action in the controller specified
`RedirectToAction(string actionName, RouteValueDictionary values)`	Redirects to the action specified in the same controller, and with the action parameter supplied inside a `RouteValueDictionary`
`RedirectToAction(string actionName, string controllerName, object values)`	Redirects to the action in the controller specified, and with the action parameter supplied inside an anonymous type
`RedirectToAction(string actionName, string controllerName, RouteValueDictionary values)`	Redirects to the action in the controller specified, and with the action parameter supplied inside a `RouteValueDictionary`

The following example redirects to the action `About` in the controller `Home` and supplies two parameters, `id` and `name`, specified as an anonymous type:

```
return RedirectToAction("About", "Home", new {
                             id = 12,
                             name = "Wrox"
                       });
```

RedirectToRoute

This second helper method is useful when you don't want to work with action names but prefer working directly with the routes. Because it mainly deals with route names and `RouteValueDictionary`, I tend to consider it a less abstracted version of the `RedirectToAction` method. In fact, whereas with `RedirectToAction` you supply the action name, the controller name, and other parameters as separate entities, with this method you pass in the fully populated `RouteValueDictionary` that contains all the tokens needed.

If you want to redirect to the action `About` in the `Home` controller, first you have to populate the `dictionary` object and then pass it to the method:

```
public ActionResult RedirectToRouteSample()
{
    RouteValueDictionary dictionary = new RouteValueDictionary();
    dictionary["action"] = "About";
```

```
dictionary["controller"] = "Home";
dictionary["id"] = 12;
dictionary["name"] = "Wrox";

return RedirectToRoute(dictionary);
}
```

This method also has other overloads, some of which accept an anonymous type that includes all the tokens as in the example illustrating the `RedirectToAction` method. These are discussed in the following table:

Method Signature	Description
`RedirectToRoute(object values)`	Redirects to the route that results from evaluating all the tokens supplied as an anonymous type
`RedirectToRoute(string routeName)`	Redirects to the route with the specified friendly name
`RedirectToRoute (RouteValueDictionary values)`	Redirects to the route that results from evaluating the `RouteValueDictionary`
`RedirectToRoute(string routeName, object values)`	Redirects to the route with the specified friendly name with the additional tokens supplied inside an anonymous type
`RedirectToRoute(string routeName, RouteValueDictionary values)`	Redirects to the route with the specified friendly name with the additional tokens supplied inside a `RouteValueDictionary`

JsonResult

If you want do real AJAX development, the partial view is not enough; you want to be able to send back to the browser an object graph formatted in a way that is easy to manipulate with a client-side JavaScript function. The format that is used the most is called *JavaScript Object Notation*, or *JSON*. The nice thing about this format is that it can be parsed very easily just by executing it as if it was a set of JavaScript statements.

AJAX and JSON are discussed further in Chapter 12.

The following is the JSON representation of the `User` class defined in Listing 5-2:

```
{
    "username": "MVCDeveloper",
    "Email": "mvcdev@wrox.com",
    "HomeAddress": {
        "Country" = "Italy",
        "City" = "Milano",
        "Street" = "Viale Monza"
    }
}
```

To return to the user a message formatted in JSON, you can use the helper method named Json. It takes as parameters the object to be formatted, the content type (the default value, if the parameter is not supplied, is application/json), and the content encoding.

```
public ActionResult JsonSample()
{
    Models.User loggedUser = new User()
    {
        Username = "MVCDeveloper",
        Email = "mvcdev@wrox.com",
        HomeAddress = new Address()
        {
            Country = "Italy",
            City = "Milano",
            Street = "Viale Monza"
        }
    };

    return Json(loggedUser);
}
```

If you compare this with Listing 5-3, which renders a view, you will notice that they are pretty similar; in fact, the only difference is that this one calls the Json method, whereas the other calls the View method.

JavaScriptResult

If instead of sending a JSON-formatted object graph you just want to send a few lines of JavaScript to be executed on the browser, your action can return JavaScriptResult, which is created through the helper method JavaScript. This method has just one parameter: the string with the JavaScript code.

```
return JavaScript("alert(\"Hello MVC\"");
```

This action result is used if you want to generate script that will be referenced inside views using the <script> tag.

ContentResult

If you want to have complete control over the response that is sent back to the user, you don't like how JSON is formatted, or your JavaScript function expects custom formatting, you can return an action result of type ContentResult. To do so, you can use the helper method Content.

The following example shows you how to return a custom format for a JavaScript function that expects the message to be pipe separated. You call the Content method, supplying the string to be rendered and the content-type:

```
return Content("Italy|Simone|Iran|Keyvan","text/plain");
```

The Content method has three overloads that allow you to specify just the string, the string and the content-type, or also the content encoding.

FileContentResult

This action result instructs the framework to send a generic binary stream to the user.

There is a helper method for this action result as well. Its first parameter, which specifies the content to be returned, can be any of three different objects:

- ❑ An array of bytes
- ❑ A `Stream` object
- ❑ Simply the name of the file

```
return File(Path.GetFullPath("Content/WroxPicture.gif"),
        "image/gif","picture.gif");
```

The other two parameters are the content type of the file and the name with which the user will see the file.

EmptyResult

`EmptyResult` is pretty simple. It says that the framework doesn't have to do anything. This is useful when you want to handle the rendering by yourself; for example, if you want to return an image or a PDF document generated on the fly.

Like the previous result type, there is no helper method to return an `EmptyResult`. You have to create an instance of the class and return it.

```
return new EmptyResult();
```

To return an empty result, you can also just return null and the framework will automatically translate it to an `EmptyResult`.

Using the Core ASP.NET Objects

From inside a controller, you can access all the usual objects that were available in the traditional WebForm programming: `Response`, `Request`, `Session`, `Server`, and so on.

The `Controller` base class exposes all these objects, so trying to get the `Request` object is just a matter of accessing the `Request` property on the `Controller` class.

For example, to get the current URL inside an action, the only thing you have to do is:

```
String url = Request.Url.ToString();
```

The same easy approach is possible for most of the objects of more frequent use such as:

- ❑ `Request`
- ❑ `Response`
- ❑ `Server`

❑   Session

❑   User

To access the other objects typical of WebForm development, such as the `Application` object or the `Cache` collection, you have to use the `HttpContext` property, which contains everything.

For example, you could store the current time in the cache with this line of code:

```
HttpContext.Cache.Insert("time",DateTime.Now);
```

and read it with this other line of code:

```
HttpContext.Cache["time"]
```

Summary

The controller is the coordinator of an application based on the Model-View-Controller pattern and its main tasks are getting the input from the user and from the request and, after having delegated the operations to the model, sending the response back to the user.

In this chapter you learned:

❑   That a controller is a collection of actions

❑   How to pass data from an action to the view in both a loosely and a strongly typed manner

❑   How to read data from the request and assemble it in a model object, using the Model Binder

❑   That to render a result to the user, the action must return an instance of type `ActionResult`

❑   The different kinds of results that can be sent back to the user

❑   How to use the POST/Redirect/GET pattern and how to implement it using the `RedirectResult` and the `TempData` collection

In the next chapter, you learn about the part of the application that interacts with the user: the view. But before you move on to the next concept, please spend some time reviewing the chapter and working through the following exercises to test your knowledge of the controller part of the MVC pattern.

Exercises

1.   Create a controller that contains an action named `Content` and that has a string parameter.

2.   Modify the action just created to have it pass to the view a custom model object for an image (title, URL, description, creation date), and make a view to show that content.

3.   Implement an action (named `Edit`) that renders an HTML form to submit the above-mentioned image object.

4.   Add an action that processes the submission and redirects to the `Content` action, displaying the image just submitted.

The View

The view is the part of a Model-View-Controller application that interacts with the end-users and that lays out the data retrieved by the controller on an HTML page. Even though its purpose is just writing some HTML code, if done wrong, a view can turn the application into a maintenance nightmare.

In this chapter you learn:

❏ How to create a view

❏ What the responsibilities of the view are

❏ How to write HTML forms

❏ How to extend a view

The Responsibilities of the View

In the previous chapter you probably noticed that the MVC mantra about having a skinny controller and a fat model also includes an adjective for the view: *dumb*. This means that the view must not have business logic, but should only take the data it receives from the controller and insert it into the page's HTML. The only logic allowed inside the view is some conditional formatting or hiding/showing areas of the page based on certain conditions, but that should be all.

You already read this guideline in the previous chapter. We're stressing it here because it is a very important concept, which if not applied can make the use of MVC useless. But enough with theoretical concepts: The rest of the chapter is all about how to create a view and write HTML in it.

The Anatomy of a View

You already created some views in the examples in previous chapters, so you might already have guessed what the rules for creating a view might be. Now it's time to lay them down in detail.

Before diving deeply into the view, there is a part of the framework you have to know about: the *view engine*. The view engine is the part of the framework that takes care of finding and rendering a view: As with everything inside the ASP.NET MVC framework, the default view engine can be replaced with a custom one.

> *This chapter is based on the WebForm view engine, which adopts the same concepts of the traditional ASP.NET WebForm paradigm. Some of the concepts might not apply to other view engines. You learn about other view engines in Chapter 16.*

A view is an `.aspx` file that, instead of inheriting from the usual `System.Web.UI.Page` base class of all the ASP.NET pages, inherits from the `System.Web.Mvc.ViewPage` class. Additionally it doesn't have the code-behind as you are used to. For that reason the base class is declared directly in the markup page inside the `Page` directive:

```
<%@ Page Inherits="System.Web.Mvc.ViewPage" %>
```

The only other rule is that a view must be created in a subfolder of the `Views` folder that matches the name of the controller from which the view will be rendered or, if the view needs to be shared among many controllers, inside the subfolder named `Shared`.

Figure 6-1 shows the default Web site as created by the ASP.NET MVC Web application project template. There is a main folder named `Views`, and under it there is a folder for each controller (you may notice the `Home` folder for the views related to the `HomeController` and the `Account` folder, for the views related to the `AccountController`). In addition, there is also a folder named `Shared`, which contains all the views used in more than one controller.

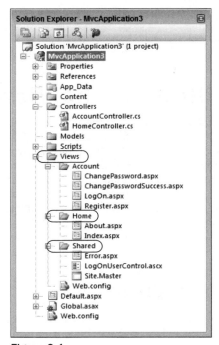

Figure 6-1

When the controller requests a view with the default parameterless method overload, the framework looks for an .aspx page with the same name as the current action, inside a folder with the same name as the controller. If it doesn't find it, it looks in the Shared folder.

For example, if the View method is called inside the About action of the Home controller, the paths probed are:

❑   \Views\Home\About.aspx

❑   \Views\Shared\About.aspx

If neither path exists, an exception is thrown (not a 404 error, which is returned when an action doesn't exist).

Creating a View with Visual Studio

The Visual Studio project template comes to the rescue when you have to create a new view.

Instead of manually creating a new ASP.NET page, deleting the code-behind and changing its base class, you can use the page templates provided with the project template. Right-click the folder where you want to create the new view, and click Add ➪ New Item. The dialog box shown in Figure 6-2 will appear.

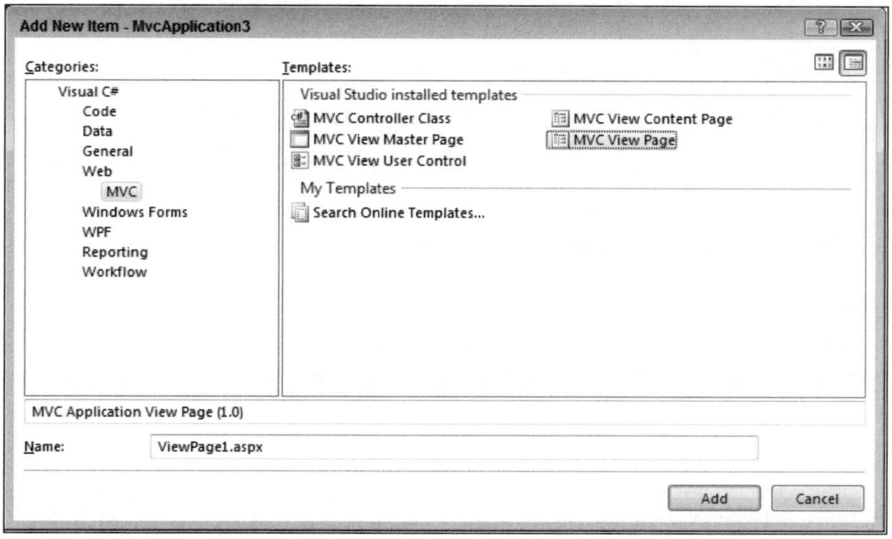

Figure 6-2

You have the following options:

❑   **MVC View Page** — This option automatically creates an ASP.NET page that inherits from the ViewPage.

❑ **MVC View Content Page** — This option is the counterpart of a WebForm content page, a page that will be put inside a master page.

❑ **MVC User Control** — This creates a user control that can be used inside other views or rendered directly as a result of the `PartialViewResult` object returned by the action.

❑ **MVC View Master Page** — This is the MVC version of the usual master page of ASP.NET.

❑ **MVC Controller Class** — This creates a new controller class. Because it's not related to views, this option isn't discussed in this chapter.

As you already learned in the previous chapter, views can be loosely typed or strongly typed. In the next sections, you learn how to do this.

Loosely Typed Views

By default, all views are loosely typed when you create them, which means that the data they receive from controllers is available only inside the `ViewData` dictionary object.

```
ViewData["Message"];
```

The following table contains the base classes for all the types of loosely typed views you can create with the WebForm view engine.

View Type	Base Class
View Page	System.Web.Mvc.ViewPage
View Content Page	System.Web.Mvc.ViewPage
View User Control	System.Web.Mvc.ViewUserControl
View Master Page	System.Web.Mvc.ViewMasterPage

The following sections show you how to use each of these loosely typed views.

View Page

Similar to what a WebForm page is, a view page contains all the HTML code need by a Web page: headers, layout, and contents. As mentioned at the beginning of the chapter, the only difference is the base class it inherits from.

In this chapter you won't see samples of view pages but only of view content and master pages. This is because it is good practice to separate the layout of a page from its contents, and also because the only difference between view pages and view content pages is that view pages include all the markup, whereas view content pages contain only the content specific to the page. But from the ASP.NET MVC standpoint, they work exactly the same way.

View Master Pages and View Content Pages

Master pages and content pages work exactly the same way as they work in the traditional WebForm development. The master page defines the layout of the page and contains placeholders for the actual contents; the content page contains only the portion that changes in every page. Listing 6-1 shows the code for the `Wrox.master` master page.

Listing 6-1: View master page

```
<%@ Master Language="C#" Inherits="System.Web.Mvc.ViewMasterPage" %>

<!DOCTYPE html PUBLIC "-//W3C//DTD XHTML 1.0 Transitional//EN"
    "http://www.w3.org/TR/xhtml1/DTD/xhtml1-transitional.dtd">

<html xmlns="http://www.w3.org/1999/xhtml" >
<head runat="server">
    <title><asp:ContentPlaceHolder ID="TitleContent" runat="server" /></title>
</head>
<body>
    <div>
        <asp:ContentPlaceHolder ID="MainContent" runat="server">

        </asp:ContentPlaceHolder>
    </div>
</body>
</html>
```

The preceding code is for a view master page. As you might notice, the only difference between this and the master page used in traditional WebForms is the base class. Listing 6-2 contains the code for the content page.

Listing 6-2: View content page

```
<%@ Page Title="" Language="C#" MasterPageFile="~/Views/Shared/Wrox.Master"
Inherits="System.Web.Mvc.ViewPage" %>

<asp:Content ID="title" ContentPlaceHolderID="TitleContent" runat="server">
    WroxContent
</asp:Content>

<asp:Content ID="main" ContentPlaceHolderID="MainContent" runat="server">
    <h2><%= Html.Encode(ViewData["Message"]) %></h2>
    <p>
        This is the contents page for the Wrox MasterPage
    </p>
</asp:Content>
```

One thing that is interesting to notice is that in the controller, through one of the many overloads of the `View` method, you can ask the rendering engine to render a content view inside a master page that is different from the one specified in the `MasterPageFile` attribute of the content page.

For example, if you want to render the `WroxContent` view inside the `Site.master` master page (the one created by default by the project template) instead of `Wrox.master`, you have to call the `View` method with the following syntax:

```
return View("WroxContent", "Site");
```

97

View User Controls

User controls are, as in traditional WebForm development, a convenient way to encapsulate a portion of the UI of a view.

As with the view page and the master page, the only differences from the WebForm user control are the base class it extends and the fact that there is no code-behind. To define a view user control, you have to define it like this:

```
<%@ Control Language="C#" Inherits="System.Web.Mvc.ViewUserControl" %>
```

The nice thing about the user control is that it has access to the `ViewData` dictionary without anything needing to be done by the developer who writes the page.

You learn more about user controls and the other ways to componentize your views in Chapter 10, which is all about components.

Strongly Typed Views

The project template creates all the views as loosely typed, but if you want to access the custom model object in a strongly typed manner, you have to change the base class from the normal to the generic one.

The following table shows the base classes that need to be used to obtain a strongly type view:

View Type	Base Class
View Page	System.Web.Mvc.ViewPage<TModel>
View Content Page	System.Web.Mvc.ViewPage<TModel>
View User Control	System.Web.Mvc.ViewUserControl<TModel>
View Master Page	System.Web.Mvc.ViewMasterPage<TModel>

Apart from the base class, all the rest is the same as the loosely typed ones. In the next Try It Out, you experiment with all the concepts that you have learned about views.

Try It Out   Strongly Typed View Master Page

1. After creating a new ASP.NET MVC Web application Web site, go to the `Models` folder and add the following sample custom model object:

```
using System;

namespace SimpleView.Models
{
    public class User
    {
        public string Name { get; set; }
        public DateTime Time { get; set; }
    }
}
```

2. Add to the `HomeController.cs` file the action that handles the request and creates the data:

```
public ActionResult UserLogged()
{
    ViewData["Message"] = "Welcome to ASP.NET MVC!";

    User user = new Models.User
                    {
                        Name = "Simone",
                        Time = DateTime.Now
                    };

    return View(user);
}
```

3. Create a new view master page inside the `Views\Shared` folder and name it `Wrox.master`. Also remember to specify the correct base class it inherits from, the one with the type it accepts as model:

```
<%@ Import Namespace="SimpleView.Models"%>
<%@ Master Language="C#" Inherits="System.Web.Mvc.ViewMasterPage<User>" %>

<!DOCTYPE html PUBLIC "-//W3C//DTD XHTML 1.0 Transitional//EN"
    "http://www.w3.org/TR/xhtml1/DTD/xhtml1-transitional.dtd">

<html xmlns="http://www.w3.org/1999/xhtml" >
<head runat="server">
    <title><asp:ContentPlaceHolder ID="TitleContent" runat="server" /></title>
</head>
<body>
    <p>Now it's <%= Model.Time %> and
    the current user is <%= Html.Encode(Model.Name) %></p>
    <div>
        <asp:ContentPlaceHolder ID="MainContent" runat="server">

        </asp:ContentPlaceHolder>
    </div>
</body>
</html>
```

4. Finally, create a new view content page in the `Views\Home` folder and name it `UserLogged.aspx`:

```
<%@ Page Title="" Language="C#" MasterPageFile="~/Views/Shared/Wrox.Master"
Inherits="System.Web.Mvc.ViewPage" %>

<asp:Content ID="Content1" ContentPlaceHolderID="TitleContent" runat="server">
    User Logged
</asp:Content>

<asp:Content ID="Content2" ContentPlaceHolderID="MainContent" runat="server">
    <h2><%= Html.Encode(ViewData["Message"]) %></h2>
    <p>
        This is the contents page for the Wrox MasterPage
    </p>
</asp:Content>
```

99

5. Compile the application, run it, and browse to `http://localhost:<portnumber>/Home/UserLogged`. You will see the current time and user displayed in the master page portion of the page.

How It Works

In this example, you created a custom model object, and in the action, you both populated the `ViewData` dictionary and passed the custom object to the `View` method.

Then, because the master page has been declared as strongly typed, you were able to access the properties of the model object directly without the need to cast to the correct type. Notice that the object passed to the view with the `View` method is available to both the view content page and to the master page. This is an important thing to remember: The `ViewData` dictionary and the custom model object created in the control and passed to the view will be available to all the views that will be used during the rendering phase, be they view content pages, master pages, and even view user controls.

Until now, you have been learning how to create a view, but now it's time to write some HTML. In the remaining sections of this chapter, you learn how.

Writing HTML the ASP.NET MVC Way

As you might have already noticed, one other big difference between the WebForm approach and the ASP.NET MVC approach is that the concept of server controls doesn't exist in the latter. One of the philosophical design decisions of the framework was to give the developer the maximum control over the HTML rendered to the user. But every decision has its drawbacks: There are no `<asp:Link />` or `<asp:Button />` controls that build the HTML code to display a link or a button for you.

But don't worry, you don't have to write all the HTML by yourself. All the most commonly used HTML elements, links, HTML forms, textboxes, and all the other form fields can be created using the helper methods available in the `Html` object.

For example, to create a link to another action, you could use the `Html` helper method named `ActionLink`:

```
<%= Html.ActionLink("Go to the About page","About","Home") %>
```

Next you learn about the available helper methods and how to use them.

One note before starting with the list of all the helper methods: The ASP.NET MVC framework also comes with an external add-on library called MvcFutures that you can download from CodePlex. It includes experimental features that might be included in future versions of the framework but that do not meet the quality standards of an officially supported release. Anyway, we consider some of these future features very useful, so in the next sections you will also find some of them. When that happens, you will find a note to avoid any possible confusion.

Link-Building Helpers

The first group of helpers contains methods that help you to create links to other actions and routes.

The ActionLink Method

The `ActionLink` method builds the HTML code for a link and automatically generates the URL to go to a specific action.

This method has several different overloads that work with strings, and two that work with lambda expressions. The last ones are part of MvcFutures, but they are nice add-ons that help to catch any potential mistyping and to enable IntelliSense support during the coding of the page.

String-Based Overloads

The parameters that can be passed to the method are:

❑ `linkText` — The text that will be linked.

❑ `actionName` — The name of the action you want the link to go to.

❑ `controllerName` — The name of the controller where you want the link to go to. This one is optional, and if it is missing the current controller will be used.

❑ `routeValues` — An optional list of parameters that must be passed to the action. It can be provided both as an anonymous type and as an instance of a `RouteValueDictionary` (just like it was for the `RedirectToAction` method in the controller).

❑ `htmlAttributes` — A list of HTML attributes that will be injected inside the anchor tag for the link. This parameter is optional and can be defined both as an anonymous type and as `IDictionary<string, object>`.

❑ `protocol, hostname, fragment` — These three optional parameters can be used to fine-tune the link, changing the protocol, for example, to `https`, changing the hostname, or asking to scroll the page until a certain position is reached.

The easiest overload takes only the first two parameters:

```
<%= Html.ActionLink("Go to the About page", "About") %>
```

The preceding code creates a link to the `About` action of the current controller (which happens to be `Home`):

```
<a href="/Home/About">Go to the About page</a>
```

On the opposite side is the overload that takes all the parameters specified previously:

```
<%= Html.ActionLink("Go to the About page",
                    "About",
                    "Home",
                    "http",
                    "localhost:7448",
                    "footer",
                    new
```

```
                {
                    id=11,
                    name="Simone"
                },
                new
                {
                    style="border:1px solid black",
                    onclick="alert(\"Hello MVC\")",
                    target="_blank"
                })
    %>
```

This code creates a link to the About action, passing a few parameters (id = 11 and name = Simone) and setting the style and the target and adding an onclick event that opens a JavaScript alert box before opening the link in another window. The code that is generated is the following:

```
<a href="http://localhost:7448/Home/About/11?name=Simone#footer"
    onclick="alert(&quot;Hello MVC&quot;)"
    style="border:1px solid black"
    target="_blank">Go to the About page</a>
```

Also notice that the quotation marks have been automatically HTML escaped and rendered as the HTML entity ".

The other overloads are just convenient shortcuts that supply the default values for the parameters that are not specified.

Lambda Expression–Based Overloads

The other two overloads, which are available inside the MvcFutures bonus pack, adopt a different approach: Instead of specifying the action name, the controller name, and the parameters as string and anonymous types, they use a lambda expression to specify the action that must be linked to.

This approach has advantages and disadvantages: You gain the compile-time check of the correctness of the action and controller names, and you can use IntelliSense to write the link without the need to remember by heart the exact name of the action. But, as a downside, it works only if the actions have the same name of the methods that implement them. These overloads will not work if the action name has been specified using the ActionName attribute.

```
<%= Html.ActionLink<HomeController>( c => c.About(),"Link to about") %>
```

Figure 6-3 demonstrates that the action name can be selected by using IntelliSense.

If the method required some parameter, you would have known it directly from looking at IntelliSense.

If you are not used to lambda expressions, the way this method's overload is called can seem a little bit cryptic, but once you start using it you will never go back to the other string-based overloads (unless, of course, you want to link to an action whose name is different from the name of the method that implements it).

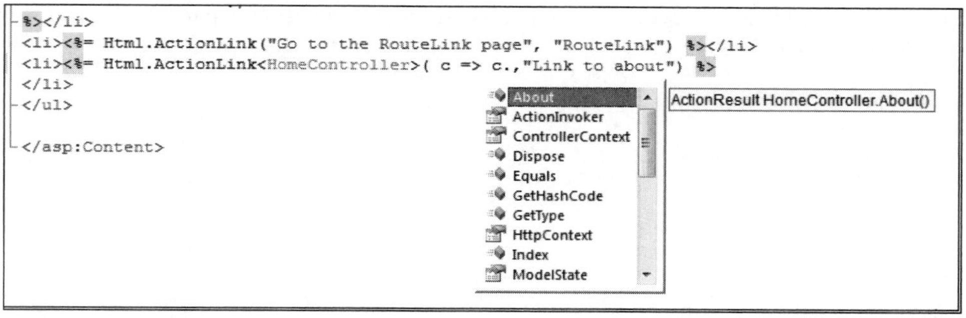

```
%></li>
<li><%= Html.ActionLink("Go to the RouteLink page", "RouteLink") %></li>
<li><%= Html.ActionLink<HomeController>( c => c.,"Link to about") %>
</li>
</ul>

</asp:Content>
```

```
About
    ActionInvoker
    ControllerContext
    Dispose
    Equals
    GetHashCode
    GetType
    HttpContext
    Index
    ModelState
```

```
ActionResult HomeController.About()
```

Figure 6-3

One way to memorize the usage of this method is to visualize it as follows: The lambda expression is just the plain method call (in the example it is c.About()), and the generic type of the method is the controller where the method is defined.

The second lambda expression–based overload only adds the htmlAttributes parameter to specify other attributes such as the style or event handlers.

To use the features available inside the MvcFutures pack, you need to add the highlighted line inside the <system.web><pages><namespaces> *section of the* web.config *file:*

```
<pages>
    <controls>
    ....
    </controls>
    <namespaces>
        <add namespace="System.Web.Mvc"/>
        <add namespace="Microsoft.Web.Mvc"/>
        <add namespace="System.Web.Mvc.Ajax"/>
        <add namespace="System.Web.Mvc.Html"/>
        <add namespace="System.Web.Routing"/>
        <add namespace="System.Linq"/>
        <add namespace="System.Collections.Generic"/>
    </namespaces>
</pages>
```

The RouteLink Method

If you prefer to work with routes instead of action and controller names, there is another method you can use: RouteLink.

The parameters are the same as the previous ActionLink method, but in this one the routeValues parameter must include the values for the action and the controller names. There is one more parameter: routeName. This is the friendly name with which the route has been registered at the application's startup.

To create a link for the `About` action on the `Home` controller and pass two parameters, you should use the following lines of code:

```
<%= Html.RouteLink("Link to About",
        new {
            action ="About",
            controller ="Home",
            id=12,
            name ="Simone"
        },null) %>
```

This code creates the following HTML code:

```
<a href="/Home/About/12?name=Simone">Link to About</a>
```

The other overloads available also allow you to specify the list of additional HTML attributes and the route name, and to change the protocol, hostname, or page fragment.

Routing is discussed further in Chapter 7.

Form Helpers

In this section, you learn about the methods that help you create HTML forms and populate them with data coming from the controller.

The first and most important one is the `BeginForm` helper. Its job is similar to the one of the `ActionLink` method: It helps create the URL for the POST operation, given the action and the controller that will handle the request.

The first and easiest version of this method is parameterless. It creates an HTML form that sends the data to the URL of the current request (including a possible query string) using the POST method.

The syntax for creating a form uses the `using` statement to help visualize the beginning and the end of the form:

```
<% using(Html.BeginForm()) { %>
<!-- Form Content  -->
<% } %>
```

Given that the current URL is `FormHelpers/FormSample?name=Simone` this code is transformed into the following HTML:

```
<form action="http://localhost:7448/FormHelpers/FormSample?name=Simone"
        method="post">
<!-- Form Content  -->
</form>
```

You can notice two things:

❑   The `action` attribute of the form contains exactly the same URL that was called to request the current page, and it also includes the query string.

❑   The closing brace after the form content area is rendered as the closing tag of the HTML form.

If you want to fine-tune the code for the form or send the data to another action or controller, other, richer, overloads exist for this method, some that work with strings and others that work with lambda expressions.

The syntax for the string-based overload with the most parameters is:

```
<% using (Html.BeginForm("Home", "About", FormMethod.Post,
        new { onclick="alert('Hello Mvc')" }
        ))
    { %>
<!-- Form Content   -->
<% } %>
```

The first two parameters are the name of the controller and the name of the action. Then you can optionally specify the method to use for the submit operation (Post or Get), and as a last parameter, you can pass an anonymous type with the list of all the HTML attributes for the `form` tag.

Then, as for the `ActionLink` method, you have the lambda expression–based overloads that are part of the MvcFutures library.

The syntax is:

```
<% using(Html.BeginForm<HomeController>(c => c.About(), FormMethod.Post,
        new { onclick = "alert('Hello Mvc')" }))
    { %>
<!-- Form Content   -->
<% } %>
```

Now that you know how to create the containing tag for the HTML form element, in the next section you learn how to fill it with contents and with the usual form fields.

If you don't like the `using` approach, you can call the `EndForm` method to explicitly close the form without the need to remember to close a curly bracket.

```
<% Html.BeginForm();  %>
<!-- Form Content   -->
<% Html.EndForm();  %>
```

Both approaches do the exact same thing. You are free to use the one you feel most comfortable with.

Form Field Helpers

The helpers for all the types of input fields have in common one parameter: `htmlAttributes`. You already saw it in the previous helpers, and it is possible to specify it as an optional parameter for all the field form helper methods. So, even if you are not going to see it repeated in all the methods that follow, remember that it is available.

Following are the various types of form field helpers that come with ASP.NET MVC.

The TextBox Helper

The first type of input field is the textbox. This helper method comes in two flavors: The first accepts only the name of the field, and the second accepts the name of the field and the value that will appear in the field when the page loads.

Imagine that you have the following action method:

```
public ActionResult TextBoxSample()
{
    ViewData["booktitle"] = "Beginning ASP.NET MVC";
    return View();
}
```

Suppose that you want to edit the title of the book inside a textbox. You could use the second overload and call the helper method, supplying both the name and the value.

```
<%= Html.TextBox("booktitle", ViewData["booktitle"])%>
```

Usually, also to make the processing of the submit operation easier, you name the form field with the same name as the property it represents, especially when the action provides a custom Presentation Model object to the view. That's why the first overload exists; it automatically looks for any data that has the name specified, inside either the `ViewData` or a property of the custom object.

For example, the following action method sends a custom book object to the view:

```
public ActionResult TextBoxSample()
{
    ViewData["booktitle"] = "Beginning ASP.NET MVC";
    var data = new TransferObject
        {
            Book = new Book
            {
                Title = "Beginning ASP.NET MVC",
                Publisher = "Wrox"
            }
        };
    return View(data);
}
```

You can use the name-only overload to automatically retrieve the properties from the model object. This way the form is ready to be submitted and automatically bound back to the same object, using the default model binder you saw in Chapter 5 in the section about binding complex objects.

```
<%= Html.TextBox("book.title")%><br />
<%= Html.TextBox("book.publisher")%>
```

Try It Out   Creating the Book Details Editing Form

In this Try It Out, you put in practice all the concepts you learned about form and textbox helpers as well as the model binder you learned in Chapter 5.

1. As, usual start by creating a new ASP.NET MVC Web application, and then add a new model object to the `Models` folder in a file named `Books.cs`, as shown in Listing 6-3.

Listing 6-3: Book Presentation Model object

```
using System;

namespace BookEditing.Models
{
    public class Book
    {
        public String Title { get; set; }
        public int Id { get; set; }
        public String Summary { get; set; }
        public String Publisher { get; set; }
    }

    public class EditBookViewData
    {
        public Book Book { get; set; }
    }
}
```

2. Next, create a new controller class file, named `BookController.cs`, and add the code in Listing 6-4.

Listing 6-4: Book controller and edit actions

```
using System;
using System.Web;
using System.Web.Mvc;
using BookEditing.Models;
using Microsoft.Web.Mvc;

namespace BookEditing.Controllers
{
    public class BookController : Controller
    {
        [AcceptVerbs("GET")]
        public ActionResult Edit()
```

Continued

Listing 6-4:Book controller and edit actions *(continued)*

```
        {
            Book book = new Book ();
            if (TempData["EditedBook"] != null)
            {
                book = (Book)TempData["EditedBook"];
            }
            return View(book);
        }

        [AcceptVerbs("POST")]
        public ActionResult Edit(
                    Book book)
        {
            TempData["EditedBook"] = book;
            return RedirectToAction("Edit");
        }
    }
}
```

3.   Add a new folder under Views named **Book**, then add a new view named Edit.aspx, and enter the code in Listing 6-5.

Listing 6-5: Edit view

```
<%@ Page Title="" Language="C#" MasterPageFile="~/Views/Shared/Site.Master"
    Inherits="System.Web.Mvc.ViewPage" %>

<asp:Content ID="Content1" ContentPlaceHolderID="TitleContent" runat="server">
    Edit Book
</asp:Content>

<asp:Content ID="main" ContentPlaceHolderID="MainContent"
        runat="server">
<h2>Edit Book</h2>
<p>
<% using (Html.BeginForm())
    { %>
    Title: <%= Html.TextBox("title") %><br />
    Publisher: <%= Html.TextBox("publisher") %><br />
    Summary: <%= Html.TextBox("summary") %><br />
    <input type="submit" value="Save" />
<% } %>
</p>
</asp:Content>
```

4.   Now, build the Web application, run it, point your browser to http://localhost:<portnumber>/Book/Edit, type in some text, and click Save. You will see the same text you entered displayed in the form.

How It Works

This example shows how to write a complete Web application that shows an editing form and processes the submit operation, using the POST/Redirect/GET (PRG) pattern.

The controller contains two actions with the same name, but, thanks to the different verbs accepted, one will only be called to respond to the form submission and the other will only process the plain GET. The action that handles the POST, after having received the Book object, saves it in the TempData collection (in a real-world scenario, it would have been saved to a database) and then redirects the operation flow to the other action that displays the saved object back to the user.

One last important thing to note is the default model binder, which populates the parameter with the data that arrives from the form submission, as long as the parameter's properties adopt the same naming convention that is used by the TextBox helper method: Form elements must be named with the name of the properties of the parameter passed to the action's method (in our example, the parameter book contains the properties *title*, *publisher*, and *summary*).

The TextArea Helper

If you want to display more than just one line of text, you have to use a textarea. The name of this HTML helper method is TextArea. It works exactly the same way as the TextBox helper method. If you specify just the name of the field, it will look inside the ViewData or the custom object to look for a property with the same name.

In addition to the name and optional default value, the TextArea method also accepts the number of rows and columns of the area.

Imagine the action is also sending the summary of the book in a property named Summary, and you want to give the user a big area to edit it. The method call will be:

```
<%= Html.TextArea("summary",null,7,80,null)%>
```

This will result in the following HTML code being rendered:

```
<textarea cols="80" id=" summary"
    name=" summary"
    rows="7">Lorem ipsum...</textarea>
```

The Password Helper

The Password helper method works the same way as the TextBox, but instead of rendering a normal input box of type text, it will render one of type password. This means that any character typed inside the field will be masked with an asterisk by the browser.

```
<%= Html.Password("password")%>
```

The Hidden Helper

Hidden fields are useful if you want to store some data in the HTML page so that it is passed back again when the form is submitted (and you will find yourself doing it a lot now that you don't have the ViewState anymore). Even though it serves a different purpose than the normal textbox and password textbox, the Hidden helper method works just like the previous methods:

```
<%= Html.Hidden("pageNum")%>
```

Remember that even if a hidden field is not displayed inside the browser, its value can be read just by looking at the source code of the page. So do not write sensitive data like passwords or authorization code. Also don't make the assumption that the value that is submitted with the form is the same that you wrote on the page. Anyone with a basic knowledge of how the HTTP protocol works can change the value of the field before it's submitted. So, always encrypt sensitive data you write inside hidden fields, or, better yet, use them only for unimportant values.

The CheckBox Helper

Another important HTML control is the checkbox. It is rendered using the CheckBox helper method. Unlike the previous controls, the valid value for a checkbox can only be a Boolean: true if you want the checkbox to be checked; false if you want it to be unchecked.

Everything else is the same, so pass just the control name to automatically probe the ViewData for data with the same name, or if the control name is different from the name of the property that contains its data, pass both the name and the value.

```
public ActionResult CheckBoxSample()
{
    ViewData["Visible"] = true;
    return View();
}
```

With that ViewData, you can render a checkbox on a view, using the following syntax:

```
This should be unchecked: <%= Html.CheckBox("Published",false) %>
This should be checked: <%= Html.CheckBox("Visible")%>
```

The first line specifies both the name of the control and whether it must be checked. The second line uses automatic binding to find the checked state of the checkbox. When submitted, the value of the checkbox will be true or false, depending on the checked state of the control. In the preceding example, the value of the Published parameter will be false, whereas Visible will be true.

Before moving to the next helper, it's worth noticing that the HTML includes a hidden field to make the retrieval of the values easier, especially retrieving the checked state of unchecked controls. (The HTML specification says that an unchecked checkbox should not be submitted inside the POST operation.)

The RadioButton Helper

The RadioButton method helps with rendering an HTML radio button. Unlike the checkbox, whose value is always true or false, the value of a radio button can be any string. For this reason, the signature of the method is a bit different and contains both the value and the checked Boolean flag.

110

As with the `CheckBox` helper method, you can either use the automatic binding or you can explicitly specify whether a radio button must be checked.

When relying on the automatic binding, the `ViewData` must contain the value of the radio button that has to be rendered as checked.

```
public ActionResult RadioButtonSample()
{
    ViewData["Gender"] = "male";
    return View();
}
```

With the `ViewData` populated as in the preceding lines of code, you can render two radio buttons by just specifying the name of the control and its value.

```
Male <%= Html.RadioButton("Gender","male") %><br />
Female <%= Html.RadioButton("Gender","female")%>
```

The result on the page will be the same as if you explicitly specified which button to check.

```
Male <%= Html.RadioButton("Gender","male",true) %><br />
Female <%= Html.RadioButton("Gender","female",false)%>
```

When submitted, in both cases, the value of the field `Gender` will be `"male"`.

The DropDownList Helper

Until now you learned how to use controls that take only one value. But there is another kind of control, which is probably the most used after the textbox: the HTML select control, also known to ASP.NET developers as `DropDownList`.

Its peculiarity is that, in order to render it on the page, you need two separate elements:

❑   The list of items that will go into the drop-down list

❑   The item that will be selected by default when the page loads

The automatic binding feature of all the helpers binds only one element per control, so, in order to have the `DropDownList` working, there is one more step you need to take: In the action, you have to create a collection with the items you want to display in the drop-down menu.

Depending on your personal preferences, you can use two different approaches to creating a drop-down list, but they both make use of a custom Presentation Model object called `SelectListItem`.

The `SelectListItem` class represents a single option of the drop-down list, and has the following properties:

❑   `Text` — The string that will be displayed as text of the option

❑   `Value` — The string that will be used as value of the option

❑   `Selected` — A Boolean indicating whether this option is selected

Inside the action you have to create and populate a list of SelectListItem and then pass it to the view either inside the ViewData or inside a strongly typed object.

Autobinding the Item List

The first approach is setting everything inside the list of SelectListItem in the action method:

```
public ActionResult DropDownListWithIEnumerableSample()
{
    var list = new List<SelectListItem>();
    list.Add(new SelectListItem
    {
        Text = "Professional ASP.NET MVC",
        Value = "1"
    });
    list.Add(new SelectListItem
    {
        Text = "Beginning ASP.NET MVC",
        Value = "2",
        Selected = true
    });
    list.Add(new SelectListItem
    {
        Text = "Professional ASP.NET 3.5",
        Value = "3"
    });
    list.Add(new SelectListItem
    {
        Text = "Professional Visual Studio Extensibility",
        Value = "4"
    });
    ViewData["Books"] = list;
    return View();
}
```

Once you have set up the list of SelectListItem, creating the DropDownList in the view is pretty easy: Call the helper method specifying just the name of the control so that it matches the name of the ViewData item containing the list of all the options. You can also specify the *label* of the drop-down, which is the first element that will appear in the list.

```
<%= Html.DropDownList("Books","Select the book...") %>
```

Figure 6-4 shows how the drop-down list created this way is rendered inside the browser.

Autobinding the Selected Item and Specifying the Item List

If you don't like the previous all-in-one approach, you can store the list of options and the selected values in two separate items inside the ViewData. Alternatively, you may want the name of the selected HTML control to match the name of the selected value field and not the collection of all options. To accomplish this, you can use another approach.

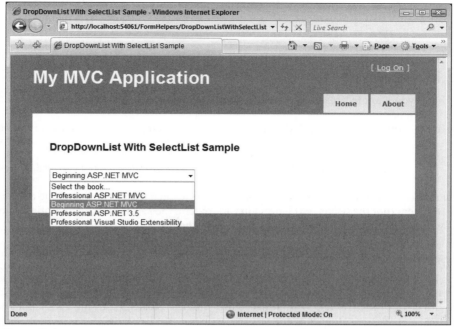

Figure 6-4

You still have to create the list with all the options, but this time without specifying the `Selected` parameter for any of the `SelectListItem` of the list.

```
public ActionResult DropDownListWithIEnumerableSample()
{
    var list = new List<SelectListItem>();
    list.Add(new SelectListItem
    {
        Text = "Professional ASP.NET MVC",
        Value = "1"
    });
    list.Add(new SelectListItem
    {
        Text = "Beginning ASP.NET MVC",
        Value = "2"
    });
    list.Add(new SelectListItem
    {
        Text = "Professional ASP.NET 3.5",
        Value = "3"
    });
    list.Add(new SelectListItem
    {
        Text = "Professional Visual Studio Extensibility",
```

```
            Value = "4"
    });
    ViewData["BooksList"] = list;
    ViewData["SelectedBook"] = 3;
    return View();
}
```

Notice that if you want to preselect an option, you also have to store its Value in the ViewData.

Finally, in the view, you have to call the helper method, but using a different syntax than before:

```
<%= Html.DropDownList("SelectedBook",
        (IEnumerable<SelectListItem>)ViewData["BookList"],"Select the book...")%>
```

The first parameter is the name of the control, which now must match the key of the object that contains the selected item (not the list as in the previous approach), the second is a list of options, now specified explicitly, and the third is the label added before any other option.

Using the SelectList Class to Help Create the Options

Creating a list of SelectListItem is fine if you are doing it manually to display a few options, but if you receive the list of options from your business logic, iterating over it just to fill the new list can be tedious and error prone. To help with this scenario, the ASP.NET MVC framework comes with a helper class, named SelectList, that converts any list of objects to a list of SelectListItem, automatically filling its properties.

The SelectList class encapsulates all the elements needed to create a drop-down list in one place:

❑   Items — The list of the options inside the drop-down list

❑   SelectedValue — The option that will be selected by default

❑   DataTextField — The name of the item's property that will be used as text of the option

❑   DataValueField — The name of the property used as the value of the option

Using this class, the example of the preceding section would have been created as follows:

```
public ActionResult DropDownListWithSelectListSample ()
{
    var list = new List<Book>();
    list.Add(new Book {
        Id = 1,
        Title = "Professional ASP.NET MVC"
    });
    list.Add(new Book {
        Id = 2,
        Title = "Beginning ASP.NET MVC"
    });
    list.Add(new Book {
        Id = 3,
        Title = "Professional ASP.NET 3.5"
    });
```

```
list.Add(new Book {
    Id = 4,
    Title = "Professional Visual Studio Extensibility"
});
ViewData["Books"] = new SelectList(list, "Id", "Title", 2);
return View();
}
```

The preceding code sample creates a collection containing four `Book` objects (but imagine that this list has been returned by your business logic or by your data access layer), and it creates a `SelectList` and stores it inside the `ViewData` collection. Notice how the `SelectList` is created:

```
new SelectList(list, "Id", "Title", 2)
```

The first parameter is the list of items (here it is a `List`, but it can be any `IEnumerable` object), the second one is the name of the data value field, and the third one is the name of the text value field. The last parameter is the selected value. In the example its value is 2, because that's the value of the property specified as `dataValueField` for the item that you want to be selected by default.

The ListBox Helper

The HTML select control can also allow the user to select multiple options at the same time. This flavor of select can be obtained using the `ListBox` helper, which is the same as the `DropDownList`, with just one difference: You can set the `Select` property to `true` for more than one `SelectListItem`.

As for the `DropDownList`, for the `ListBox` there is a class that helps with the creation of the list of `SelectListItem`. It is called `MultiSelectList` and has a `SelectedValues` property that holds the values of all the options that must appear as preselected (as opposed to the `SelectedValue` of the `SelectList`, which holds only one value).

That's the way to create a `MultiSelectList`, specifying the list of selected values:

```
new MultiSelectList(list, "Id", "Title", new []{1,2});
```

On the view side, the syntax for creating a select control with multiple selections is:

```
<%= Html.ListBox("Books")%>
```

Notice that in this method the label parameter is not available.

By default the listbox will grow in height in order to display all the options available. This might be fine with 4 or 5 options, but not if you have 20 of them. If you want to reduce the number of rows displayed, you have to add the HTML attribute `size` and set it to the number of rows.

```
<%= Html.ListBox("Books", null, new { size=3 })%>
```

Before moving to the validation helpers, in the next Try It Out you write a `ListBox` using the other approach, the one where you autobind the selected values and specify the list of options, using the `MultiSelectList` helper class.

ListBox

1. As usual, everything starts by creating a new ASP.NET MVC Web application.

2. Then go inside the `Models` folder, create a new class file named **Book.cs**, and type in the following code:

```
using System;

namespace ListBoxSample.Models
{
    public class Book
    {
        public String Title { get; set; }
        public int Id { get; set; }
        public String Summary { get; set; }
        public String Publisher { get; set; }
    }
}
```

3. Open the `HomeController.cs` file, and change the `Index` method like Listing 6-6.

Listing 6-6: Action method that populates the MultiSelectList

```
public ActionResult Index()
{
    ViewData["Message"] = "ListBox Samples";
    var list = new List<Book>();
    list.Add(new Book
    {
        Id = 1,
        Title = "Professional ASP.NET MVC"
    });
    list.Add(new Book
    {
        Id = 2,
        Title = "Beginning ASP.NET MVC"
    });
    list.Add(new Book
    {
        Id = 3,
        Title = "Professional ASP.NET 3.5"
    });
    list.Add(new Book
    {
        Id = 4,
        Title = "Professional Visual Studio Extensibility"
    });
    list.Add(new Book
    {
        Id = 5,
        Title = "Professional ASP.NET Ajax"
    });
```

```
    });

    ViewData["Books"] = new MultiSelectList(list, "Id", "Title");
    ViewData["SelectedBooks"] = new[] { 1, 2, 5 };
    return View();
}
```

4. Open the view inside \Views\Home\Index.aspx, and add the code shown in Listing 6-7.

Listing 6-7: View with ListBox

```
<%@ Page Language="C#" MasterPageFile="~/Views/Shared/Site.Master"
Inherits=" System.Web.Mvc.ViewPage" %>

<asp:Content ID="indexTitle" ContentPlaceHolderID="TitleContent" runat="server">
    Home Page
</asp:Content>

<asp:Content ID="indexContent" ContentPlaceHolderID="MainContent"
    runat="server">
    <h2><%= Html.Encode(ViewData["Message"]) %></h2>
    <% using (Html.BeginForm())
        { %>
        Select the books you own:<br />
        <%= Html.ListBox("SelectedBooks",
            (IEnumerable<SelectListItem>)ViewData["Books"], new { size = 3 })%>
            <br />
        <input type="submit" value="Save" />
    <% } %>
</asp:Content>
```

5. Now run the application, and you will get a page with a listbox like the one in Figure 6-5.

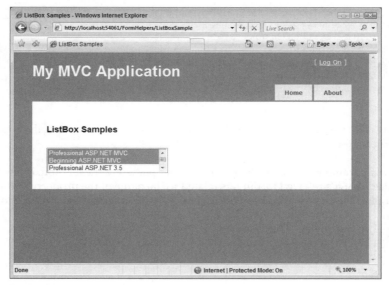

Figure 6-5

How It Works

In this example, you created a view that displays a listbox with only three lines. To do this, you used the overload that autobinds the list of selected items and makes you explicitly specify the list of options.

```
<%= Html.ListBox("SelectedBooks",
    (IEnumerable<SelectListItem>)ViewData["Books"], new { size = 3 })%>
```

Notice that the element that contains the selected items was created as an array of anonymous objects and the list of `htmlAttributes` is an anonymous type.

```
ViewData["SelectedBooks"] = new[] { 1, 2, 5 };
```

ASP.NET MVC makes an extensive use of and encourages developers to take advantage of all the new features of the C# 3.0 compiler.

Validation Helpers

The last group of helpers contains the methods that help display error messages to the users. Form field validation is a vast topic, and it is covered in detail in Chapter 14. However, because some helper methods are involved in the validation process, they are included here for the sake of completeness.

There are two helpers: one that shows a message next to the field that contains the value that caused the error to happen and the other that shows a summary of all error messages.

The ValidationMessage Helper

This helper renders an error message related to a single property or `ViewData` object. There are mainly two overloads: one that renders the error message provided by the action for the specific model property and one that overrides it in the view.

```
<% using (Html.BeginForm()) { %>
Title: <%= Html.TextBox("BookTitle") %>
<%= Html.ValidationMessage("BookTitle")%> <br />
Summary: <%= Html.ValidationMessage("Summary","*")%><br />
<%= Html.TextArea("Summary") %> <br />
<input type="submit" />
<% } %>
```

The preceding code uses both the overloads, and the resulting form, when both properties are missing, is shown in Figure 6-6.

The `modelName` parameter, which is the first parameter passed to the method, is not related to the name of the form field that it's referred to, but it is related to the name of the property of the Presentation Model object that is bound to it. To keep things easier to understand, it's better not to differentiate the two names.

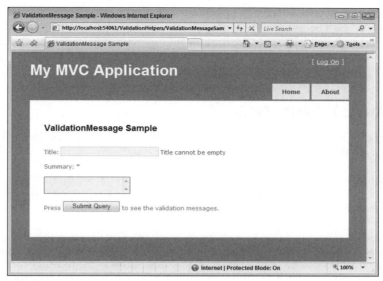

Figure 6-6

The ValidationSummary Helper

The other validation helper is ValidationSummary. On the page it renders a bulleted list with all the validation errors that happened in the action.

```
<%= Html.ValidationSummary() %>
```

This short line of code, when applied to the previous example, will be rendered as shown in Figure 6-7.

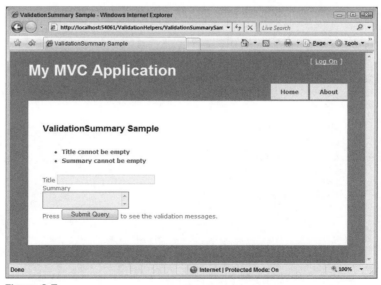

Figure 6-7

In this figure and in the one before, you might notice that the textboxes are styled with a red border and background. That's because the `TextBox` and `TextArea` helpers are adding an error-specific CSS class (`input-validation-error`) to the controls that are named as the properties with errors, and the default style is red.

What about the rest?

All of this is good, but where are all the nice controls that make adding complete grids, menus, and even login screens without having to write a line of HTML so easy?

They all disappeared, because they hid too much of the code rendered on the page. Furthermore, the view should only be an HTML rendering and most of the operations should be possible using only the basic C# statements.

There is an anecdote about this that shows the approach used by the team that developed the framework: There was a meeting with someone from the marketing department, and after the demo of the framework he said: "We need a helper that does the same thing as the repeater control." Phil Haack, program manager of the ASP.NET MVC team said: "We already have one: It's called a foreach loop."

Imagine that you want to write a list of books in an HTML table, with alternating row colors. You don't need any fancy Web control to do that, just the plain old `foreach` and `if` statements:

```
<%@ Page Title="" Language="C#" MasterPageFile="~/Views/Shared/Site.Master"
    Inherits="System.Web.Mvc.ViewPage<IList<Book>>" %>
<%@ Import Namespace="HTMLHelpers.Models"%>

<asp:Content ID="Content1" ContentPlaceHolderID="TitleContent" runat="server">
    Book List without helpers
</asp:Content>

<asp:Content ID="Main" ContentPlaceHolderID="MainContent"
    runat="server">
<h2>Book List without helpers</h2>
<table>
<tr>
    <td>Id</td>
    <td>Title</td>
    <td> </td>
</tr>
<%
    int rowIndex = 0;
    foreach (var book in Model)
    {%>
    <% if (rowIndex++ % 2 == 0) { %>
    <tr style="background-color:Yellow">
    <% } else {%>
    <tr>
    <% } %>
        <td><%=book.Id %></td>
        <td><%=book.Title %></td>
        <td><%=Html.ActionLink("Details","Details",
                new { id=book.Id}) %></td>
```

```
    </tr>
<% } %>
</table>
</asp:Content>
```

This code snippet is rendered as shown in Figure 6-8.

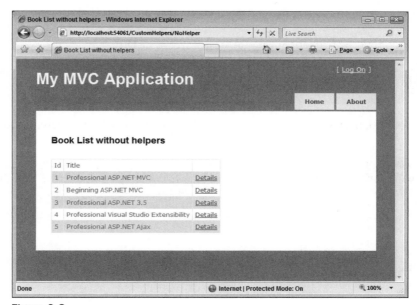

Figure 6-8

This was a pretty simple example, but as you might have noticed, even in this case, there is too much mixing of HTML tags and C# code. If this code becomes more complex, maybe with more conditional styling or other links and buttons, the risk is that this might become so-called "tag soup." You see how to solve this problem in the next section, where you learn about how to write your helper methods.

Writing Your Own Helper Methods

One rule of thumb to follow to avoid transforming an MVC view into an ASP Classic-like page is that, if the code is more than just a property and if it includes some conditional operations, you should write your own helper method.

One way to create a helper method is to write a protected method in the code-behind of the view. Yes, you read code-behind. Even if the default way of writing views is to make them without code-behind, you can still add it to address special scenarios like this one.

For example, you could replace the portion of code that renders the link to the details page adding the code-behind file with the following method:

```
using System.Collections.Generic;
```

121

```csharp
using System.Web.Mvc.Html;
using System.Web.Mvc;
using HTMLHelpers.Models;

namespace HTMLHelpers.Views.CustomHelpers
{
    public partial class CustomHelper : ViewPage<IList<Book>>
    {
        protected string WriteDetailsLink(Book book)
        {
            return Html.ActionLink("Details", "Details",
                new { id = book.Id });
        }
    }
}
```

Using this method, the view becomes easier to read (remember to add the references to the code-behind):

```aspx
<%@ Page Title="" Language="C#" MasterPageFile="~/Views/Shared/Site.Master"
    AutoEventWireup="true" CodeBehind="CustomHelper.aspx.cs"
    Inherits="HTMLHelpers.Views.CustomHelpers.CustomHelper" %>

<asp:Content ID="Content1" ContentPlaceHolderID="TitleContent" runat="server">
    Book List with custom helper
</asp:Content>

<asp:Content ID="Content1" ContentPlaceHolderID="MainContent"
        runat="server">
<h2>Book List with custom helper</h2>
<table>
<tr>
    <td>Id</td>
    <td>Title</td>
    <td> </td>
</tr>
<%
    int rowIndex = 0;
    foreach (var book in ViewData.Model)
    {%>
    <% if (rowIndex++ % 2 == 0) { %>
    <tr style="background-color:Yellow">
    <% } else {%>
    <tr>
    <% } %>
        <td><%=book.Id %></td>
        <td><%=book.Title %></td>
        <td><%=WriteDetailsLink(book)%></td>
    </tr>
<% } %>
</table>
</asp:Content>
```

This approach is fine if the helpers are used only in a specific view. However, if you want to write a wider-scope helper, for example one that formats in yellow every other row in a table, you have to write it as an *extension* method of the same Html object that is used by the core helpers.

Extension methods are a new feature introduced with C# 3.0 that allow the developer to add a method to an existing type without the need to subclass or modify it. They are easy to implement: Just declare them as static methods on a static type and add the type you want to extend as the first parameter with the modifier this.

For example, to create an extension method for the Html property of each view, you have to use the following syntax:

```
public static string AlternateRowColor(this HtmlHelper helper, … )
```

Using this approach, now you can write a general-purpose extension method that writes the background-style CSS attribute based on the row count.

To help organize the extension methods, a good practice is to put all the ones that refer to a certain area in the same class. That class must be a static class.

```
using System.Web.Mvc;

namespace HTMLHelpers.Helpers
{
    public static class TableHelpers
    {
        public static string AlternateRowColor(this HtmlHelper helper,
            int row, string color )
        {
            if (row % 2 == 0)
                return "background-color:" + color ;
            else
                return "";
        }
    }
}
```

Using this method, the view now becomes:

```
<%@ Page Title="" Language="C#" MasterPageFile="~/Views/Shared/Site.Master"
    AutoEventWireup="true" CodeBehind="CustomHelper.aspx.cs"
    Inherits="HTMLHelpers.Views.CustomHelpers.CustomHelper" %>
<%@ Import Namespace="HTMLHelpers.Helpers" %>

<asp:Content ID="Content1" ContentPlaceHolderID="TitleContent" runat="server">
    Book List with custom helper
</asp:Content>


<asp:Content ID="Content1" ContentPlaceHolderID="MainContent" runat="server">
<h2>Book List with custom helper</h2>
<table>
```

123

```
<tr>
    <td>Id</td>
    <td>Title</td>
    <td> </td>
</tr>
<% int rowIndex = 0;
    foreach (var book in Model)
    {%>
    <tr style="<%=Html.AlternateRowColor(rowIndex++, "Yellow") %>">
        <td><%=book.Id %></td>
        <td><%=book.Title %></td>
        <td><%=WriteDetailsLink(book)%></td>
    </tr>
<% } %>
</table>
</asp:Content>
```

If you compare it to the first one you wrote, you will notice that this is much more readable, and also more powerful. For example, you could easily expand it to change colors every 10 rows or display a red background if a book was out of order (in that case, you would need to pass the instance of the book to the method) without touching the code of the view.

Writing custom helpers is as important as writing skinny controllers. This way the HTML code stays clean and will not scare HTML designers who have to make your pages look prettier. Also, because the code for the conditional formatting is in an external method, it can be tested to ensure that your application is behaving correctly.

A Shortcut for Creating Views

Before wrapping up the chapter, it's worth mentioning that Visual Studio provides an even tighter integration with the ASP.NET MVC framework, and it has a nice shortcut for creating a view: the Add View dialog, as shown in Figure 6-9.

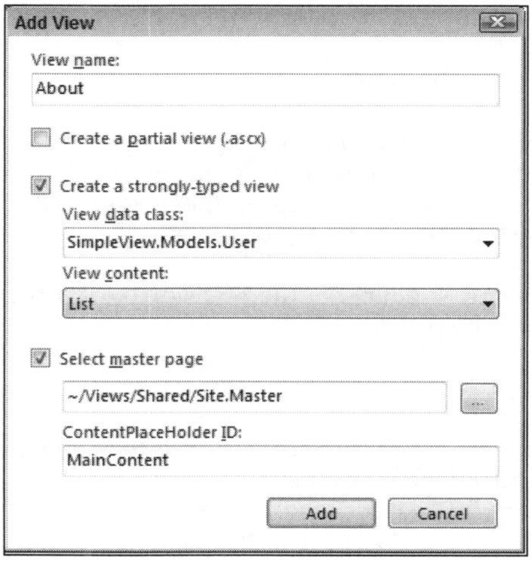

Figure 6-9

In this dialog you can choose the name of the view, whether it is contained inside a master page, whether it's a strongly typed view, and the type of the model object (letting you choose from any type defined inside the project).

It also lets you choose what the contents of the view you want to create are. This is because Visual Studio will create for you a page that contains all the HTML controls needed.

For example, if you want to create a page to edit the User object that you saw in the first Try It Out example of this chapter (which had Name and Time of the last login) all you have to do is select (as shown in Figure 6-10) the User class as "View data class" and Edit as "View content."

Figure 6-10

After clicking the Add button, Visual Studio will generate for you a page to edit the User object, with all the textboxes and the validation messages required.

```
<%@ Page Title="" Language="C#" MasterPageFile="~/Views/Shared/Site.Master"
Inherits="System.Web.Mvc.ViewPage<SimpleView.Models.User>" %>

<asp:Content ID="Content1" ContentPlaceHolderID="TitleContent" runat="server">
    EditUser
</asp:Content>

<asp:Content ID="Content2" ContentPlaceHolderID="MainContent" runat="server">

    <h2>EditUser</h2>

    <%= Html.ValidationSummary(
    "Edit was unsuccessful. Please correct the errors and try again.") %>

    <% using (Html.BeginForm()) {%>

        <fieldset>
            <legend>Fields</legend>
            <p>
```

125

```
        <label for="Name">Name:</label>
        <%= Html.TextBox("Name", Model.Name) %>
        <%= Html.ValidationMessage("Name", "*") %>
    </p>
    <p>
        <label for="Time">Time:</label>
        <%= Html.TextBox("Time", String.Format("{0:g}", Model.Time)) %>
        <%= Html.ValidationMessage("Time", "*") %>
    </p>
    <p>
        <input type="submit" value="Save" />
    </p>
</fieldset>

<% } %>

<div>
    <%=Html.ActionLink("Back to List", "Index") %>
</div>

</asp:Content>
```

This dialog can be accessed either by right-clicking a view folder and selecting Add ⇨ View or by right-clicking anywhere inside a controller's action, as in Figure 6-11.

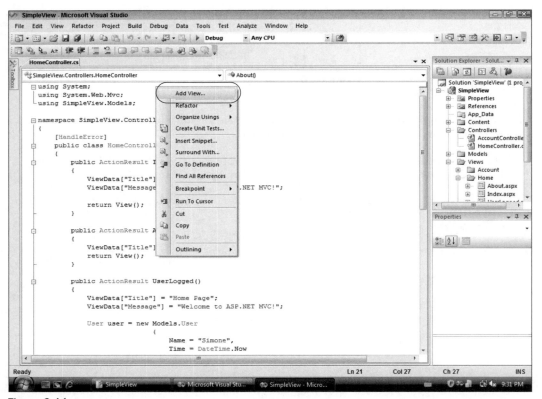

Figure 6-11

Using this shortcut, the name of the view will automatically match the name of the action in which you clicked.

Summary

Views are the front end of your application. They are not pure .NET but a mix of many languages (HTML, CSS, JavaScript, and C#). They must be developed with the same care as and by applying the same concepts used for the controller and the model: separation of concerns, a single responsibility per class/method, and good design for testability.

In this chapter, you learned:

- ❑ How views are organized inside a solution
- ❑ How to create a view using the Visual Studio project template
- ❑ About loosely and strongly typed views and master pages
- ❑ Why using helpers is important
- ❑ What the MvcFutures pack is
- ❑ How the link helper works
- ❑ How to use the various overloads of the form helper
- ❑ How to write all the standard HTML form controls
- ❑ How the autobinding of controls works
- ❑ How to add drop-down lists and listboxes to a view
- ❑ What the basics of form validation are
- ❑ How to write your own helpers
- ❑ How Visual Studio helps with creating views

In the next chapter, you learn how the routing engine works and how to customize the URLs of an ASP .NET MVC Web application.

But before moving on to the next chapter, please take a moment to try the following exercises. They cover all the aspects of writing forms using the WebForm view engine.

Exercises

1. Take exercise 4 in Chapter 5, and change the view to use helper methods.

2. Add a property named License to the Image class. This will store the license with which the image is provided. Also, add a method for a fictitious ImageRepository class that returns the list of available licenses.

3.   Add a drop-down list that allows the user to select the license for a given image.

4.   Display the selected `License` in the content view.

5.   Write a custom helper method to remove all the occurrences of `if` from the content view.

Routing

Now that you have completed your journey exploring the three parts of an MVC application, it's time for you to learn about the places where a request meets the application: the routing engine.

In this chapter, you learn:

- ❑ What routing is
- ❑ How to define routing rules
- ❑ How to debug routes

Life before Routing

In a typical WebForm-based Web application, the user types a URL in the address bar of his browser, and then the request is sent to the server. The server takes the URL, looks at the file system for a file that is located in the folder and with the name specified in the URL, executes the code-behind that is mapped to the file, and finally sends the response back to the user. To display the listing of all the books in the category ASP.NET, you would type `http://example.com/catalog/booklisting.aspx?id=345`. But this URL is not a very good one. For the user it's not obvious that 345 is the ID of the category of books on ASP.NET.

Speaking of search engine optimization (SEO), because all categories are retrieved using the same path (catalog/booklisting.aspx), search engines might not do a very good job of indexing the bookstore catalog. A URL like `http://example.com/catalog/ASPNET` would have been both more SEO-friendly and easier to remember and understand for the end user, who could just change the last part to `ASPNETMVC` to get all the books on ASP.NET MVC.

Over the years, many solutions have been implemented to make WebForm URLs more user- and SEO-friendly, the most notable of which is called URL rewriting. With URL rewriting, the user types in a user-friendly URL, like the preceding one, and a component of the server transforms all the folders into query string parameters passed to the dynamic page.

For example, the URL of a typical blog is `http://example.com/archive/2009/09/28/`. The URL rewriting component changes it to `/posts.aspx?year=2009&month=09&day=28` so that the standard WebForm engine can handle the request.

But this approach has its problems as well: What happens if the user types a non-numeric character instead of the month number? Or what if you want to handle the request in different ways based on the URL? With URL rewriting, you have to implement all this validation in the WebForm.

Another reason why the traditional approach of binding the URL to the physical file is not the solution anymore is that with MVC applications the first component hit by the request is the controller, not the view, and controllers don't have physical paths.

The routing engine has been designed to solve all these issues, introducing a solution that supports SEO-friendly URLs that map directly to controllers. It proved to be such a great solution that, even though it was initially designed specifically for the MVC framework, during development it was made more general-purpose and made available for other technologies as well. It was released to the world inside ASP.NET 3.5 SP1, which shipped a few months before ASP.NET MVC.

Key Concepts

You have already encountered the default ASP.NET MVC route in previous chapters. In the following sections, you read more about the concepts behind routing and how it works.

Routing encompasses three key concepts: routes, route handlers, and the global route table.

❑ **Routes** — A route is a class that contains a URL pattern and other constraints that will be evaluated against the requests to determine the route.

❑ **Route handlers** — A route handler is a class that handles a specific request.

❑ **Global route table** — The global route table lists all the routes registered in the application. It is typically initialized with the user's routes when the application is first started.

To better understand the concepts of routes and route handlers, have a look at how the routing engine works. When a request reaches the application, the routing engine loops through all the registered routes, finds the first one that matches the URL requested, and then uses the route handler specified for the route to handle the request. This way, you can have different routes handled in different ways. In an ASP.NET MVC application, the route handler must always be `System.Web.Mvc.MvcRouteHandler`. If you use the routing engine in a WebForm application, you have to implement your own route handlers, but doing so means that you are not going to use ASP.NET MVC anymore. If you are interested in this topic, you can read more about it in Chapter 16, the chapter about extending ASP.NET MVC. Within the context of this chapter, the only key concept you have to remember is the route.

The Anatomy of a Route

The `Route` object contains all the information needed to determine whether a URL matches a certain route and how to handle the request. This class has five properties:

❑ `Url`

❑ `Defaults`

❑ `Constraints`

❑   DataTokens

❑   RouteHandler

Because all the "complexity" of the routing engine lies inside these properties, you learn more about them in the following sections, starting with the most important one: the Url.

The URL Property

The first, and most important, property to set for a route is its URL pattern. In the traditional way of thinking, a URL represents a physical path on the server. It consists of a folder structure, which is a sequence of names delimited by the / character, followed by an optional file name. In the URL pattern of a route, a "folder" is called a *segment*. Segments can be either literal constants or, if enclosed between curly braces ({ and }), placeholders for the URL parameter. The pattern applies only to the part of the URL after the application name.

An example will help demonstrate this concept better: In the URL `http://example.com/blog/archive/2009/10/06`, where the application name is `blog`, the pattern applies only to `archive/2009/10/06`. This URL will be matched by a pattern with four segments, for example by `archive/{year}/{month}/{day}`.

After a URL is matched to a route, the routing engine retrieves the values from the request and assigns them to the corresponding URL parameters. In the preceding sample, it will result in the year being `2009`, the month being `10`, and the day being `06`. Later, all the URL parameters will be handed to the route handler inside a property named `RouteData`.

The `Url` and the `RouteHandler` are the only two mandatory parameters that have to be specified during the construction of a new `Route` object.

```
Route blogArchiveRoute = new Route(
    "archive/{year}/{month}/{day}",
    new MvcRouteHandler()
    );
```

The `MvcRouteHandler` is the handler that must be used in order to handle the request in the ASP .NET MVC way. You see later in this chapter that the ASP.NET MVC framework provides an extension method that helps with the creation of routes.

A special URL parameter is the catch-all parameter. If you want to catch any number of segments, including separators, the name of the parameter must start with an asterisk (*). For example, the `archive/{*date}` pattern will match anything, from `archive/2009` to `archive/2009/10/09/23/41/25/This-is-a-post-written-almost-at-midnight`. In the second situation, the value of the date parameter would be `2009/10/09/23/41/25/This-is-a-post-written-almost-at-midnight` and then you'd have to parse it yourself in the action method.

The Defaults Property

It can happen that a URL contains fewer segments than the number of URL parameters in the matched pattern. For example, the URL `http://example.com/blog/archive/2009/10` doesn't specify a value for the `day` parameter. In this situation, you need to specify a default value for the missing parameter. You do this through the `Defaults` property.

The `Defaults` property is a `RouteValueDictionary` object that contains an entry for each of the parameters you want to supply a default value for. Additionally, you can specify other URL parameters that are not retrieved from the URL but that you want to supply to the route handler or the action method. For example, in an ASP.NET MVC application, there must always be two URL parameters named `controller` and `action`. If you don't collect them, as in the case of the blog archive example, you have to specify them manually in the `Defaults` property.

The `RouteValueDictionary` class is a collection of key/value pairs like a normal dictionary, but with some methods specific for the routing engine to work and to make the creation of the instance easier. You can create a `RouteValueDictionary` in two ways: with an anonymous type or with a collection initializer.

Using the anonymous type, each property will be treated as the name of the key:

```
blogArchiveRoute.Defaults = new RouteValueDictionary(
                              new
                              {
                                year = 2009,
                                month = 0,
                                day = 0
                              });
```

Using the collection initializer, you pass to the constructor a collection of key/value pairs:

```
blogArchiveRoute.Defaults = new RouteValueDictionary
                              {
                                {"year",2009},
                                {"month",0},
                                {"day", 0}
                              };
```

Both of the syntaxes produce the same result: They instruct the route engine that when some parameters are not found in the URL, the value of the `day` parameter should be 0, the value for the `month` should be 0, and if all the parameters are missing (this happens if the URL is `http://example.com/blog/archive`), the `year` is 2009.

The Constraints Property

The `Constraints` property contains a dictionary of validation rules for the URL parameters. Again it is a `RouteValueDictionary`, where the key is the name of the parameter and the value is the validation rule.

The `Constraints` property has two types of validation rules:

❑ Regular expressions
❑ `IRouteConstraint`

Regular Expression Constraints

The first and easiest way to define a constraint is to specify it with a regular expression. Regular expressions are a vast topic, so you won't read everything about regular expressions here. Instead, you see only the basics and then a few samples of usage.

A regular expression is a special text string that represents a pattern. You can think of a regular expression as a much more powerful version of a wildcard. When you search for a text file in your file system, you write `*.txt`; with a regular expression, you can make the search more precise. For example, you can say that you want all the files that start with an `a`, that contain a number from two to four digits in length, that can or cannot contain the string `"view"`, and finally that end with the `.txt` extension. This pattern is matched by many file names:

❑ a45view.txt

❑ a3456.txt

❑ a22.txt

The regular expression for this kind of search is `a\d{2,4}(view)?\.txt`.

This short string helps introduce most of the important elements of regular expressions:

❑ `a` — *Constant literal*: The exact character must be found.

❑ `\d` — *Character class*: Any character that is part of the class. In the preceding sample `\d` means any digit. (Another class is `\w` for any word character.)

❑ `{2,4}` — *Quantifier*: The preceding element (in the sample it is "any digit") must be present at least two times and no more than four times.

❑ `(view)` — *Grouping*: The exact string

❑ `?` — *Quantifier*: The preceding element (in this case, the string "view") can be present zero or one times. (The other quantifiers are +, which stands for one or more times, and *, which stands for zero or more times.)

❑ `\.` — *Escape character*: The dot is a special character (it means any single character), so, in order to include a dot, it must be escaped with the backslash character (\).

❑ `txt` — *Constant literal*: The exact sequence of characters

The other important concepts that were not part of the sample regular expression are:

❑ `[ ]` — *Character groups*: Matches one of the characters included between the brackets; for example `[abc]` matches a, b, or c. The list of characters can also be specified as a range: `[a-z]` means any character between a and z.

❑ `[^ ]` — *Negation*: Matches any character not included in the brackets; `[^aeiouy]` means any nonvowel.

❑ `|` — *Option*: Matches either the element before or the element after the pipe character; `(view|master)` matches either the string `view` or the string `master`.

Going back to routing, if you want to specify that the year, month, and day must be in the right format (only numeric values allowed), you should write the following lines:

```
blogArchiveRoute.Constraints = new RouteValueDictionary(
                new
                {
                    year = @"\d{2}|\d{4}",
                    month = @"\d{1,2}",
                    day = @"\d{1,2}"
                });
```

The first rule says that the year can only be two or four digits (not three digits, because you don't expect posts being written at the time of Charles the Great). The other two lines say that the month and day can be specified with either one or two digits.

Just to keep the ball rolling, look at some more regular-expression–based constraints:

❑   A valid language locale (it-it) must be two characters, a dash (-), and then another two characters: `[a-z]{2}-[a-z]{2}`.

❑   A zip code must be five digits: `\d{5}`.

❑   If you want to provide a print-specific or mobile version of a view, you might want to add a URL parameter for that. But this can only accept the string `print` or the string `mobile`: `print|mobile`.

If you already know about regular expressions, two things make their usage in ASP.NET MVC different from the general usage in most languages:

❑   Regular expressions normally are case sensitive by default; however, the ones used in ASP.NET MVC are configured to be always case insensitive.

❑   A general-purpose regular expression can match any part of the string, be it at the beginning, at the end, or in the middle. This is not possible with ASP.NET MVC. For example, when not using ASP.NET MVC, with the regular expression `\d{1,2}` you would get a match for the string `abc03rt`, because it contains a valid month in the middle. So, for the purpose of routing, a regular expression must match the whole string, not just part of it.

The IRouteConstraint Constraint

If a simple syntax validation is not enough and you need a more complex logic to validate the input, you can write your own route constraint by writing a class that implements the `IRouteConstraint` interface.

This interface specifies only one method, called `Match`, whose signature is:

```
bool Match(
    HttpContextBase httpContext,
    Route route,
    string parameterName,
    RouteValueDictionary values,
    RouteDirection routeDirection
)
```

The regular-expression–based constraint of the blog archive URL in the previous section is not really optimal for complex validation. It checks whether the day is a two-digit number, but it accepts 45 as a valid day, and it also accepts February 30th as valid date.

First, you have to write the RouteConstraint class, as shown in Listing 7-1.

Listing 7-1: DateIsValidConstraint

```
public class DateIsValidConstraint: IRouteConstraint
{
    public bool Match(HttpContextBase httpContext, Route route,
        string parameterName, RouteValueDictionary values,
        RouteDirection routeDirection)
    {
        try
        {
            DateTime date = new DateTime(
                Convert.ToInt32(values["year"]),
                Convert.ToInt32(values["month"]),
                Convert.ToInt32(values["day"])
                );
            return true;
        }
        catch
        {
            return false;
        }
    }
}
```

This tries to create a DateTime object using the year, month, and date URL parameters. If the three parameters make a valid date, the return value of the Match method will be true. Otherwise, if the constructor of the DateTime object throws an exception, this means that the date is not valid, so the return value must be false. Notice that the code doesn't check the correctness of the single parameters, because their syntax is already checked by the regular expression constraints that verify they are numeric values.

Next, you need to change the Constraints property with the new value:

```
blogArchiveRoute.Constraints = new RouteValueDictionary(
                new
                {
                    year = @"\d{4}",
                    month = @"\d{1,2}",
                    day = @"\{1,2}",
                    date = new DateIsValidConstraint()
                });
```

Notice that the custom constraint is applied to a fictitious URL parameter (date). That's done for two reasons: The first is that in order to create the date, the three values must be numbers, and because the framework already provides a way to check this, checking it inside the validation function would be a pointless duplication. The second reason is that the constraint is not about one specific parameter but about all of them, so it is not a good idea to connect the constraint to only one of them.

This way of setting constraints, in an external method made on purpose for the job, is another proof of two of the main pillars used in the design of the framework: single responsibility and separation of concerns. If the validation of the date was done inside the action, this would have performed both the validation and the post archive retrieval, thus breaking the two rules.

Constraints are processed after the default values are applied to missing parameters, so, if you want a URL parameter to be optional and also to adhere to certain limits, remember to put in a default value that satisfies the constraints as well.

The DataTokens Property

This property is a collection of other additional custom values that are passed to the route handler but that don't take part in the route-matching process. This property is more useful when using custom route handlers with traditional WebForm development than it is with ASP.NET MVC, but with enough imagination, you can also find a way to use the `DataTokens` property with ASP.NET MVC.

With ASP.NET MVC the values of URL parameters are used for the parameters of the controller's actions, but `DataTokens` is not. The only way you have to access the values contained in the `DataTokens` property inside an action is through the `RouteData` property of the controller.

For example, suppose that you have a news site, and based on the URL you have to access one database or another. This can be accomplished in different ways; for example, by treating the discriminating URL passed as the URL parameter, passing it to the action method, and using it to switch from one database to another (as shown in Listings 7-2 and 7-3).

Listing 7-2: Route definition with URL parameter

```
Route blogArchiveRoute = new Route(
        "archiveParam/{database}/{year}/{month}/{day}",
        new MvcRouteHandler()
        );
blogArchiveRoute.Defaults = new RouteValueDictionary(
                new
                {
                    controller = "Home",
                    action = "IndexParam"
                });
blogArchiveRoute.Constraints = new RouteValueDictionary(
                new
                {
                    database = "sport|technology",
                    year = @"\d{2}|\d{4}",
                    month = @"\d{1,2}",
                    day = @"\d{1,2}"
                });
routes.Add(blogArchiveRoute);
```

Listing 7-3: Action method that uses URL parameters

```
public ActionResult IndexParam(string database, int year, int month, int day)
{
    string connString = string.Empty;
    switch (database)
    {
        case "sport":
            connString = "sportConnString";
            break;
        case "technology":
            connString = "techConnString";
            break;
    }
    ViewData["Message"] = String.Format("Connecting to database {0}",
            connString);
    return View("Index");
}
```

Another solution would be to define two different routes (as shown in Listing 7-4) and send them to the same action (shown in Listing 7-5), but pass a different data token.

Listing 7-4: Route definition using DataTokens

```
Route blogSportArchiveRoute = new Route(
    "archiveDT/sport/{year}/{month}/{day}",
    new MvcRouteHandler()
    );

blogSportArchiveRoute.Defaults = new RouteValueDictionary(
                new
                {
                    controller = "Home",
                    action = "IndexDT"
                });

blogSportArchiveRoute.Constraints = new RouteValueDictionary(
                new
                {
                    year = @"\d{2}|\d{4}",
                    month = @"\d{1,2}",
                    day = @"\d{1,2}"
                });

blogSportArchiveRoute.DataTokens = new RouteValueDictionary(
                new
                {
                    database = "sportConnString"
                });
```

Continued

137

Listing 7-4: Route definition using DataTokens *(continued)*

```
routes.Add(blogSportArchiveRoute);

Route blogTechnologyArchiveRoute = new Route(
    "archiveDT/technology/{year}/{month}/{day}",
    new MvcRouteHandler()
    );

blogTechnologyArchiveRoute.Defaults = new RouteValueDictionary(
                    new
                    {
                        controller = "Home",
                        action = "IndexDT"
                    });

blogTechnologyArchiveRoute.Constraints = new RouteValueDictionary(
                    new
                    {
                        year = @"\d{2}|\d{4}",
                        month = @"\d{1,2}",
                        day = @"\d{1,2}"
                    });

blogTechnologyArchiveRoute.DataTokens = new RouteValueDictionary(
                    new
                    {
                        database = "techConnString"
                    });

routes.Add(blogTechnologyArchiveRoute);
```

Listing 7-5: Action method that uses DataTokens

```
public ActionResult IndexDT(int year, int month, int day)
{
    ViewData["Message"] = String.Format("Connecting to database {0}",
        RouteData.DataTokens["database"]);
    return View("Index");
}
```

As you see, you get the same result from the different approaches. The first approach is better from the testability standpoint, because the database to use is passed as a parameter to the action, but then you have to deal with that new parameter inside the method. Furthermore, if you need to change the database or want to add a new connection string, you have to change the method implementation. With the data token approach, you only need to add a new route or change the value of the connection string name passed as a data token.

Another reason why DataTokens is important in ASP.NET MVC is that you can use it to call controllers that are inside namespaces different from the default one (*applicationname.Controllers*) or even in a different assembly.

To do this, you have to register a route specifying the namespace inside the `DataTokens` property:

```
Route externalBlogRoute = new Route(
    "blog/{controller}/{action}/{id}",
    new MvcRouteHandler()
    );
externalBlogRoute.Defaults = new RouteValueDictionary(
    new
        {
            controller = "Home",
            action = "Index",
            id = ""
        });
externalBlogRoute.DataTokens = new RouteValueDictionary(
    new
        {
            namespaces = new[] { "ExternalClassLibrary" }
        });
routes.Add(externalBlogRoute);
```

In this example, when a URL matches the blog route, the framework will look for the controller in the namespaces provided inside the `DataTokens` property. If no controller is found in the namespace specified, the usual search pattern will be used. Notice that the namespace value is not a single string but an array of strings.

The RouteHandler Property

This contains an instance of the class that will handle the request in case the route is matched. As you already read, in an ASP.NET MVC application this is always `MvcRouteHandler`. If you don't want the default MVC handler to process a route, you have to write a new route handler by implementing the `IRouteHandler` interface and its only method, `GetHttpHandler`. But, as already noted earlier in the "Key Concepts" section of this chapter, this will result in not using ASP.NET MVC anymore. You read about how you could do this in Chapter 16.

How to Register Routes

Now that you know everything about routes, it's time to learn how to inform the routing engine about them. In the previous examples, you saw that every route was added to a collection named `routes`. This variable holds an instance of the `RouteCollection`, which contains all the routes defined for the application. A best practice, which is also suggested by the default project template, is to place all the routes inside a helper method and to not directly add them to the static `RouteTable` of the application. Doing this not only helps in separating the elements, but also makes testing easier.

The routes must be added before any request is processed, so the only possible location is inside the `Application_Start` event in the `Global.asax` file.

```
public class MvcApplication : System.Web.HttpApplication
{
    public static void RegisterRoutes(RouteCollection routes)
    {
```

```
            Route blogRoute = new Route(
                "blog/{controller}/{action}/{id}",
                new MvcRouteHandler()
                );
            routes.Add(blogRoute);
        }

        protected void Application_Start()
        {
            RegisterRoutes(RouteTable.Routes);
        }
    }
```

The highlighted line is the call to the helper method that contains all the route definitions.

When you add a route to the collection, you can also specify a name for it. Inside controllers or when you want to create a link to a specific route, you can refer to it through its friendly name. To do this, there is another overload of the Add method:

```
    routes.Add("BlogRoute",blogRoute);
```

You can add as many routes as you like. When a request hits the application, the routing engine loops through all the registered routes, checks whether the request URL matches the URL pattern, and then verifies that the URL parameters that are retrieved are valid based on the constraints specified.

The routing engine stops looping through the routes as soon as it finds the first match. For this reason, the order in which the routes are registered is very important. You have to register the routes from the most specific to the most generic.

For example, imagine you want the URL blog/post/3 to be handled by a controller named CMSController and by the action Show. With the default rule, such a URL would be handled by BlogController.Post, so you have to write a specific routing rule that maps it to the desired controller and action. To achieve this result, you have to register the routes in the following order:

```
Route showBlogRoute = new Route(
    "blog/post/{id}",
    new MvcRouteHandler()
    );
showBlogRoute.Defaults = new RouteValueDictionary(
    new
        {
            controller = "CMS",
            action = "Show",
            id = ""
        });

Route blogRoute = new Route(
    "blog/{action}/{id}",
    new MvcRouteHandler()
    );
blogRoute.Defaults = new RouteValueDictionary(
    new
        {
            controller = "CMS",
```

```
                    action = "Index",
                    id = ""
               });

    Route defaultRoute = new Route(
        "{controller}/{action}/{id}",
        new MvcRouteHandler()
        );
    defaultRoute.Defaults = new RouteValueDictionary(
        new
            {
                controller = "Home",
                action = "Index",
                id = ""
            });

    routes.Add("ShowBlog",showBlogRoute);
    routes.Add("Blog",blogRoute);
    routes.Add("Default",defaultRoute)
```

When the /blog/post/3 URL hits the application, the routing engine starts evaluating the list of routes; because the URL matches the first parametric route, it stops evaluating the routes. If you had registered the routes in the opposite order, the URL would have matched the default route and so the Post method in the BlogController would have been called, which was not what you wanted.

Before moving to the next topic, you should know about two other features of the RouteCollection:

❑   StopRoutingHandler

❑   RouteExistingFiles

The first one is a special handler that stops the routing engine from handling the route and lets the default handler do its job. This is typically used for resource files (.axd) or Web services (.asmx).

```
    routes.Add(
        new Route("{resource}.axd/{*pathInfo}",
            new StopRoutingHandler())
            );
```

The second property belongs to the RouteCollection object. If set to true it instructs the routing engine to also handle the requests to existing files; otherwise, the request will be handled directly by the existing ASP.NET page. If not set, the value of the property is false. But remember that setting it to true means that the routing engine will try to handle requests for images, style sheets, and static JavaScript files, so be prepared for this overhead.

Easier Route Management with ASP.NET MVC

Specifying routes can be a long task, especially with ASP.NET MVC, where you don't want to repeat the same RouteHandler for every route. For that reason, the ASP.NET MVC framework provides a helper method to ease the process.

As with all helpers, it's implemented as an extension method for the `RouteCollection` and provides three benefits over the standard API:

❏ You don't have to specify the same route handler for all the routes.

❏ You can specify the default values and the constraints directly as an anonymous type. (There is no need to create the `RouteValueDictionary` object.)

❏ You have an easy way to specify the namespaces.

To specify the route for the blog archive, together with its default values and constraints, the code is as follows:

```
routes.MapRoute(
    "BlogArchive",
    "archive/{year}/{month}/{day}",
    new {
        controller = "Home",
        action = "Index",
        year = "2009",
        month = "00",
        day = "00" },
    new {
        year = @"\d{4}",
        month = @"\d{2}",
        day = @"\d{2}"},
    new[] { "ExternalClassLibrary" }
);
```

Notice that now all the properties and the namespace for the controller are specified without the overhead of creating a `RouteValueDictionary` object to hold them.

The other method that comes with the MVC framework is `IgnoreRoute`. It's a handy helper that registers a `StopRoutingHandler` for the pattern specified.

```
routes.IgnoreRoute("{resource}.axd/{*pathInfo}");
```

This line of code achieves the same result as the one in the previous page, just with less code to write and with an easier-to-understand method name.

Debugging Routes

Now you know almost everything there is to know about routing. As you saw, there are only a few major concepts, and building simple routing rules is pretty easy. The problems come when there are many routes, especially when some routes must be treated in a way that is different from the generic case and you are struggling with route precedence.

To help troubleshoot routing issues and also to help you better understand how routing works, Phil Haack, ASP.NET MVC program manager at Microsoft, wrote a handy RouteDebugger. You can download it from Phil's blog (http://haacked.com/archive/2009/03/13/url-routing-debugger .aspx) or in the code that accompanies this book (www.wrox.com).

To enable the route debugger, you have to add a reference to the RouteDebug assembly and then register the route handler inside the Application_Start event, like this:

```
protected void Application_Start()
{
    RouteTable.Routes.RouteExistingFiles = true;
    RegisterRoutes(RouteTable.Routes);
    RouteDebug.RouteDebugger.RewriteRoutesForTesting(RouteTable.Routes);
}
```

This registers the RouteDebugger (which is a route handler) for all the routes defined. Then, just request any URL to have it show you all the information on the routes.

For example, Figure 7-1 shows an MVC application with all the routes you saw in the previous examples, with route debugging enabled.

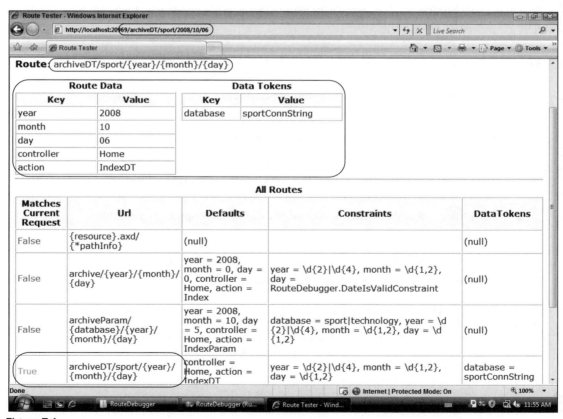

Figure 7-1

143

All the relevant areas of the report page are surrounded by circles:

❑   In the address bar is the URL that was requested by the user: `archiveDT/sport/2009/10/06`.

❑   The pattern that matches the URL requested

❑   The list of all the routes with all the properties of the route (Defaults, Constraints, DataTokens). The first column says whether the route matches the URL. There might be more than one route that matches an incoming URL, but, because they are processed from top to bottom, only the first one is the real match.

❑   The values of all URL parameters and data tokens related to the matched route

Another way to verify that routes are working correctly is to unit test them, but that's a topic you learn about in Chapter 9, which is about testing ASP.NET MVC applications.

Summary

Search engine optimization is an important feature that is made possible by the routing engine provided with the ASP.NET MVC framework.

In this chapter, you learned about how routing works and that it can even be used outside ASP.NET MVC applications. You learned:

❑   What the benefits provided by the routing engine are

❑   How a route is defined

❑   How to supply default values or metadata for a route

❑   How to use regular expressions to write constraints for URL parameters

❑   How to write constraints that are based on custom logic, implementing the `IRouteConstraints` interface

❑   How to call controllers that are defined in external namespaces or assemblies

❑   How to register routes and how to set exceptions that must not be considered

❑   How to use the MVC helpers to register routes in an easier way

❑   How to debug routes using the `RouteDebugger`

This is the last chapter that covers the basics of the ASP.NET MVC framework. From here on, you learn about advanced topics such as unit testing, working with the AJAX and JavaScript frameworks, extending the framework, and putting an application into production. But before you move on to the next chapter, which discusses unit testing, take some time to test the knowledge you have acquired in this chapter with the following exercises.

Exercises

1. Using as a starting point the DateIsValidConstraint method implemented in Listing 7-1, write a custom constraint that accepts only dates that occur in the past.

2. To expand your knowledge of regular expressions, find a tutorial (for example, http://www .regular-expressions.info/) and write a regular expression that matches valid project names (only alphanumeric characters or underscores are allowed in the name) with a time-stamp and version number (valid names are aspnetmvc-20081007-1.0.34.567 and aspnet_ mvc-20081007-1.0.34.567).

3. Use the Debug Route Helper to play with routes and get a better feeling for how route priority works.

Unit Testing Concepts

One of the main differences between the ASP.NET MVC framework and the classic WebForm paradigm is that the first has been designed and implemented with testability in mind. Adopting the MVC pattern is a big step toward testability, but it's not enough; the MVC framework includes a lot of other features and requires API design decisions to make sure that it will support any kind of unit testing.

In Chapter 9 you learn how to test a Web application developed with the ASP.NET MVC framework and what all these test-facilitating features are. To help you fully understand them, this chapter covers the basic concepts of unit testing.

In this chapter you learn:

- ❑ What unit testing is and why it is important
- ❑ How to write tests
- ❑ What patterns enable unit testing in complex applications

What Is Unit Testing?

Unit testing is a vast topic and probably even a whole book would not be enough to cover all the aspects of this important practice. In this section, you learn the basic concepts and why you should start testing your applications right now.

Unit testing is a practice used in software development to verify that individual units of code are working the way they were originally supposed to. What a unit is depends on the kind of programming language you are using, but in object-oriented programming, the smallest testable unit is a method.

The main reason why you might want to use a unit test to validate that a single piece of your source code is working properly is that you can automate its execution. This way, you can have a full suite of test cases that prove the correctness of your application every time you build it. With this safety net in place, you can add new features or *refactor* (change the internal behavior of a method without changing the external interface) parts of the code without the fear of breaking something elsewhere in the application.

> **A test must isolate and prove the correctness of a single part of the application.**

If a test doesn't isolate a single unit of your application, it might fail for reasons that don't depend on the portion of code you want to test. It might fail because another part of the application it depends on is not behaving the way it is intended to, or, even worse, because an external service, be it a remote Web service or even your database server, is experiencing some issues.

The Benefits of Unit Testing

Now that you understand rule number one of unit testing (because it's the most important concept of unit testing, you will find it repeated in different ways throughout this chapter), this section shows you the benefits of doing unit testing.

I already said that one of the main advantages of unit testing is that, with a full suite of tests that covers all your code, you can modify your application without worrying, because if your changes break something, the automated testing process will notify you immediately.

Other benefits you get with unit testing are that tests can act both as specification and documentation of your API. They can be viewed as a specification because a test case says how a piece of software should behave, and they are the best kind of specification because they can be automatically verified. You learn how to write a unit test later, but take a look at the following test sample taken from the test suite of a mathematical library:

```
[TestMethod]
public void AddTest()
{
    int result = MathLib.Add(2, 2);
    Assert.AreEqual(4, result);
}
```

The highlighted line states that the mathematical library must have a method named Add and that, when called with two parameters whose values are 2 and 2, it should return 4.

The same test also acts as documentation because it tells you that to sum two numbers you just have to call the static method Add of the class MathLib.

All these benefits gain an even higher value within today's IT projects, which are usually designed and prototyped by a team of developers, actually implemented by another team, sometimes even an offshore team, and finally maintained in house by a team inside the company that commissioned it. The executable specifications are a great help to the team that is going to implement the application, and the maintenance team can start working on someone else's code quickly and with more confidence because the tests document how the code works and act as a safety net that prevents new features and bug fixes from breaking other parts of the application.

Before you start writing your unit tests later in this chapter, you first learn how a unit test is structured.

The Structure of a Unit Test

Before starting Visual Studio and writing your first test, you need to learn a few concepts about how a test is structured and how it is executed by the *test runner*, the application that runs all the tests.

Many frameworks exist for writing unit tests in C# and .NET: NUnit, MbUnit, and MSTest, to name a few. Even if each of them has its own peculiarities, they all work in the same way, so for the purposes of this chapter, you learn how to use the framework that comes with Visual Studio 2008, which is called MSTest.

The testing tools are available with Visual Studio 2008 starting from the Professional edition upward. The Express and the Standard editions don't have MSTest. If you have one of these two editions, you can use one of the other open source frameworks; the API and the tooling experience change, but the concepts remain the same.

The Four Phases of a Test

All testing frameworks that derive from the original work of Kent Beck (collectively known as *xUnit*) are based on a four-phase test:

1. **Setup phase** — The preconditions (also known as the *test fixture*) for the test are set.

2. **Exercise phase** — The test code interacts with the *system under test* (the thing you are testing, also known as *SUT*).

3. **Result Verification phase** — The results of the methods invoked on the SUT are compared with the expected results.

4. **Teardown phase** — The test fixture you set up in the first phase of the test is destroyed in order to bring the external situation back to the condition that it was in before the test.

In order to be run automatically by test runners or inside build procedures, the tests are organized into a TestSuite, Testcase classes, and test methods. Relating these terms to the practical implementation in .NET, a *TestSuite* is the .NET assembly that is compiled by Visual Studio, a *Testcase class* is a .NET class inside the assembly, and the *test method* is a method inside the class.

Fixtures

A *fixture* is the set of preconditions that needs to be restored before each test, and it's set up during the Setup phase of the test. Because all the test methods inside a Testcase class usually share the same fixture, most of the xUnit frameworks have a way to define a method to set up the same fixture for all the tests. Some also have a method to create a *SuiteFixture*, which is created before the first test runs and is torn down after the last test.

MSTest has a way to specify the `FixtureSetup` and `FixtureTearDown` methods, but it doesn't have a method to set up and tear down the SuiteFixture. Instead it brings a new feature to the table, the *ClassFixture*, which contains the code to set up the preconditions before the first test in a Testcase class runs.

The Order of Execution

Taking into account all the phases of testing and all the various fixture setup and teardown methods, the order of execution of a Testcase class with two methods is the following:

1. `ClassFixture` setup from Testcase Class 1
2. `FixtureSetup` from Testcase Class 1
3. `TestMethod1` in Testcase Class 1
4. `FixtureTearDown` from Testcase Class 1
5. `FixtureSetup` from Testcase Class 1
6. `TestMethod2` in Testcase Class 1
7. `FixtureTearDown` from Testcase Class 1
8. `ClassFixture` teardown for Testcase Class 1

Attributes That Control Testing

If the tests are specified as normal .NET classes and methods, how does the test runner know which classes inside an assembly are Testcase classes and which are only helper classes? And which are test methods and which are only private helpers?

MSTest, like most of the xUnit-like .NET testing frameworks, uses attributes. The following table lists the attributes used in MSTest and what they are used for:

Attribute Name	Description
TestClass	Marks a class as Testcase class
ClassInitialize	Marks a method as ClassFixture setup
ClassCleanup	Marks a method as ClassFixture teardown
TestMethod	Marks a test as a test method
TestInitialize	Marks a method as fixture setup
TestCleanup	Marks a method as fixture teardown

Result Verification

Each test method, after having exercised the SUT, has to verify that the test was successful. There are two main types of result verification: *simple success tests* and *expected exception tests*.

Assertions

The simple success test, as you might guess by the name, verifies that the results returned by the SUT are the ones the test was expecting. This is done with `assertions`.

Assertions are static helper methods whose only goal is to validate the actual result against the expected result and display a message if the assertion fails.

Figure 8-1 shows the start syntax for calling an assertion method:

1. First is the name of the helper class. In Figure 8-1 `Assert` is the name used by MSTest.

2. Then comes the name of the assertion method, which usually is the name of the comparison the method performs.

3. The first parameter is always the value you want to compare the actual result with.

4. The second parameter is the value returned by the SUT.

5. Then, usually as last parameter, there is the message you want the test runner to display in its GUI or in the log files if the assertion fails.

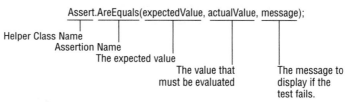

Figure 8-1

MSTest has 11 different assertion methods that you can use in your tests, as described in the following table:

Method Name	Description
`AreEqual`	Asserts that two objects are equal
`AreNotEqual`	Asserts that two objects are not equal
`AreSame`	Asserts that two specified variables contain the reference to the same reference type value
`AreNotSame`	Asserts that two specified variables do not contain the reference to the same reference type value
`IsTrue`	Asserts the condition supplied as the parameter is true
`IsFalse`	Asserts the condition supplied as the parameter is false
`IsNull`	Asserts the parameter supplied is null
`IsNotNull`	Asserts the parameter supplied is not null
`IsInstanceOfType`	Asserts the parameter supplied is an instance of the specified type
`IsNotInstanceOfType`	Asserts the parameter supplied is not an instance of the specified type
`Fail`	Makes the assertion fail unconditionally

Expected Exceptions

Simple assertions work fine when you want to test that your method is returning the correct results, but it's important to test for unexpected outcomes as well, such as when exceptions are thrown.

You could wrap your test in a `try-catch` block and assert that an exception was thrown and that it was of the expected type, but this is repetitive and requires too much effort for you to implement.

MSTest provides an easy way to verify that the test threw an exception: the `ExpectedException` attribute.

The following code snippet shows you how to test that a division by zero raises a `DivideByZeroException`:

```
[TestMethod]
[ExpectedException(typeof(DivideByZeroException))]
public void DivideByZeroIsThrownWithZeroDivisor()
{
    MathLib.Divide(12, 0);
}
```

You just have to supply information to the constructor of the attribute about the type of the exception you want the code inside the test to throw. If an exception of the given type is not thrown, the test fails; otherwise it passes.

Code Coverage

Another important concept you have to learn before writing your tests is *code coverage*.

Code coverage is the percentage of application code that your tests are exercising. If the method contains two lines of code and both are executed during the exercise phase of the test, the code coverage on that specific method is 100%. If, for example, it contains an `if` statement and only one branch is exercised, the code coverage will be 50% (supposing that the two branches have the same number of instructions).

Code coverage is an important indicator of how well-tested an application is. If you have 100 tests and all of them are passing, but the code coverage is only10%, it means that you are testing only one tenth of your application, and 90% is still untested.

Writing Tests with Visual Studio

Now that you have learned how a unit test must be structured and how MSTest implements the unit-testing guidelines, it's time to open Visual Studio and see how to use it to write a test project.

All the screenshots and the samples that you find later in this section are based on the simple mathematical library shown in Listing 8-1.

Listing 8-1: A simple mathematical library

```
using System;

namespace CalculatorLib
{
    public class MathLib
    {
        //Adds two numbers
        public int Add(int addend1, int addend2)
        {
            return addend1 + addend2;
        }

        //Subtract two numbers
        public int Subtract(int minuend, int subtrahend)
        {
            return minuend  - subtrahend;
        }

        //Should multiply two numbers
        //This method is wrong on purpose
        public int Multiply(int multiplicand, int multiplier)
        {
            return multiplicand + multiplier;
        }

        //Divide two numbers
        public float Divide (float dividend, float divisor)
        {
            if (divisor==0)
                throw new DivideByZeroException();
            return dividend/divisor;
        }
    }
}
```

This sample library just implements the four basic arithmetic operations (sum, subtraction, multiplication, and division). Notice that the `Multiply` method is wrong (it sums instead of multiplying). This will be used later to show a failing test.

The Visual Studio Testing User Interface

Visual Studio 2008, from the Professional version upward, includes a test runner for MSTest. In this section, you learn how Visual Studio facilitates the management of unit tests.

The Test Project Template

The first thing you encounter when you want to create a unit test in Visual Studio is the Test Project template, shown in Figure 8-2. (To get there, open Visual Studio and select File ➪ New Project.) This template helps you set up a project specifically made for testing, by adding all the additional files needed by Visual Studio to manage the testing process.

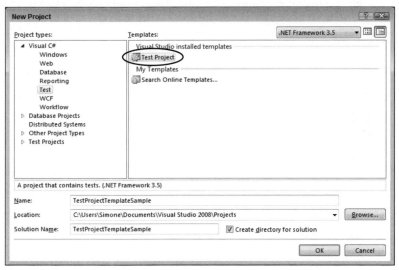

Figure 8-2

Visual Studio comes with more than just unit testing, so, when the test project is first added (look at Figure 8-3), it includes a template for the Word document for manual testing (ManualTest1.mht) and a text file (AuthoringTests.txt) that explains all the different kinds of tests that are available with Visual Studio 2008. It includes a sample unit test class as well.

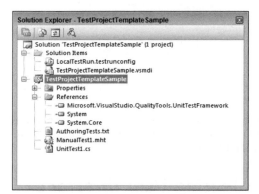

Figure 8-3

It also adds two files to the Solution Items folder of the testing solution:

❑   LocalTestRun.testrunconfig is the configuration file for the test run. It includes settings for timeouts, scripts to run before or after the run, whether to run the tests locally or on a remote test machine, whether to enable code coverage, and others.

❑   TestProjectTemplateSample.vsmdi is the Test List, which allows you to enable or disable some tests and organize them in lists.

The Test Tools Toolbar

The next thing you encounter after having created a test project is the Test Tools toolbar shown in Figure 8-4. If it's not automatically displayed, you have to add it manually: Go to View ➪ Toolbars and select Test Tools from the drop-down list.

Figure 8-4

The toolbar consists of four main areas:

❑   The first button opens the Add New Test dialog.

❑   The next four buttons allow you to run or debug the tests in the *current context* or in the entire solution. The term "current context" can be a bit confusing; it's related to the current position of the mouse caret. If the caret is inside a test method, only that test will be executed; if the caret is inside a test class but outside a method, the test runner will run all the methods of the current class.

❑   The next five buttons open various management windows: Test View, Test List, Test Results, Code Coverage, and Test Runs.

❑   The last three buttons are enabled only when you are looking at a file with code coverage enabled. They allow you to enable coverage coloring and jump to the next and previous uncovered statements.

The Add New Test Dialog

The Add New Test dialog, which is opened by clicking the first button of the Test Tools toolbar, allows you to create, with the help of a user-friendly dialog, all the types of tests that are available inside Visual Studio.

If you select Unit Test Wizard from among the many options available, you will get the dialog shown in Figure 8-5.

If your solution contains a class library project, the wizard lists all the classes and methods available and allows you to select the methods you want to create a test for. Then it automatically creates the skeleton for the test for each of the methods you selected.

The code in Listing 8-2 is the code generated for testing the Add method of the sample math library.

Listing 8-2: Test skeleton for Add method

```
/// <summary>
///A test for Add
///</summary>
```

Continued

Listing 8-2: Test skeleton for Add method *(continued)*

```
[TestMethod()]
public void AddTest()
{
    MathLib target = new MathLib(); // TODO: Initialize to an appropriate value
    int addend1 = 0; // TODO: Initialize to an appropriate value
    int addend2 = 0; // TODO: Initialize to an appropriate value
    int expected = 0; // TODO: Initialize to an appropriate value
    int actual;
    actual = target.Add(addend1, addend2);
    Assert.AreEqual(expected, actual);
    Assert.Inconclusive("Verify the correctness of this test method.");
}
```

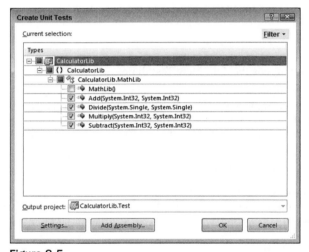

Figure 8-5

As you can see, the test is declared inconclusive and will never succeed until you remove the line with `Assert.Inconclusive` and set up and exercise the method correctly.

Test Management Windows

These windows, opened by clicking the toolbar buttons Test View, Test List, and Test Results, show all the tests in the solution, allowing you to group them in lists for easier management, especially when they are used together with a build process. Probably the most useful window is the Test Results window. Figure 8-6 shows the Test Results view with three possible outcomes of a test: Passed, Failed, and Inconclusive.

Code Coverage

Code coverage is disabled by default, so in order to see the percentage of code covered, and, more importantly, which lines of code were not covered, it must be enabled. Double-click the test run configuration file (`LocalTestRun.testrunconfig`), go to the Code Coverage page, as shown in Figure 8-7, and check the assemblies for which you want the coverage enabled.

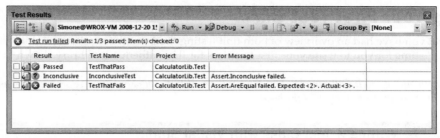

Figure 8-6

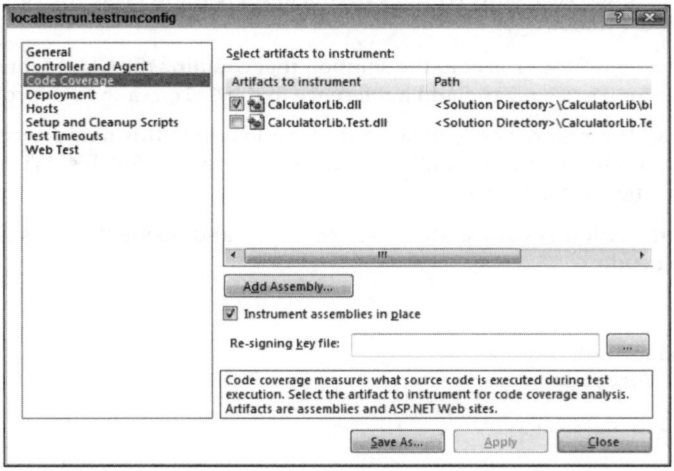

Figure 8-7

Now with code coverage enabled, you can run the tests and see which lines were covered and which were not in the code editor. Figure 8-8 shows the code coverage on the `Divide` method of the sample math library after the test `DivideByZeroIsThrownWithZeroDivisor` ran. Highlighted in pink are the statements that were not covered by the test, and the lines that were covered are in azure.

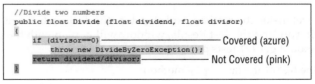

Figure 8-8

Unlike MSTest, which is available from the Professional edition of Visual Studio upward, the code coverage feature is available only in the Team edition. And it's not enabled in the 64-bit version of Visual Studio.

If you don't have a version that supports code coverage, you could achieve the same result using a third-party commercial application, such as NCover (http://www.ncover.com), which also provides a free "community edition," and running your test through its test runner.

Writing Your First Test Class

Now that you have had an overview of both unit testing theory and how testing is done inside Visual Studio, it's time for you to write your first test class for the mathematical library shown in Listing 8-1.

As with all the Try It Out samples, you can get the code from the www.wrox.com *Web site, as explained in the introduction of the book.*

Try It Out   Writing a Test Class with Visual Studio

1. Create a new Class Library project and name it `CalculatorLib`.

2. Add a new Class file, name it `MathLib.cs`, and copy and paste the code from the math library of Listing 8-1 into it.

3. Now add a new Test Project to the solution that contains the Class Library project, name it `CalculatorLib.Test`, and add a reference to the `CalculatorLib` project.

4. Remove all the automatically generated files and add to this new project a Unit Test file using the button on the Test Tools toolbar. Instead of using the Unit Test Wizard, just use Unit Test. Name the file `MathLibTest.cs`.

5. Remove the automatically added `TestMethod1`, and inside the class definition enter the following code:

```
private MathLib _lib;

[TestInitialize]
public void SetupLib()
{
    _lib = new MathLib();
}
```

6. Add the test for the `Add` method of the library:

```
[TestMethod]
public void CanAddNumbers()
{
    int result = _lib.Add(2, 2);
    Assert.AreEqual(4, result);
}
```

7. Place the caret inside the method, and click the Run Tests in Current Context toolbar button. The test will run, and the Test Results window will pop up with the results of the current test run. (You should get 1/1 tests passed.)

8. Now add the test of the `Multiply` method:

```
[TestMethod]
public void CanMultiplyNumbers()
{
    int result = _lib.Multiply(3, 2);
    Assert.AreEqual(6, result);
}
```

9. This time place the cursor outside the method you just added so that it is in the class definition, and click the same button as before. Now both tests will be executed, and the one for the `Multiply` method will fail. Your results will show that 1/2 tests passed.

10. Now go back to the `MathLib.cs` file, and change the `Multiply` method so that it passes the test:

```
//Multiplies two numbers
public int Multiply(int multiplicand, int multiplier)
{
    return multiplicand * multiplier;
}
```

11. Run the tests again. Now the results show that 2/2 tests passed.

12. Now, finish testing the whole library by adding the tests for the other methods. Once added, the test class looks like Listing 8-3.

Listing 8-3: Complete test class for the sample math library

```
using System;
using CalculatorLib;
using Microsoft.VisualStudio.TestTools.UnitTesting;

namespace CalculatorLib.Test
{

    [TestClass]
    public class MathLibTest
    {
        private MathLib _lib;

        [TestInitialize]
        public void SetupLib()
        {
            _lib = new MathLib();
        }

        [TestMethod]
        public void CanSubractNumbers()
        {
            int result = _lib.Subtract(6, 2);
            Assert.AreEqual(4, result);
        }

        [TestMethod]
        public void CanAddNumbers()
        {
            int result = _lib.Add(2, 2);
            Assert.AreEqual(4, result);
        }

        [TestMethod]
        public void CanMultiplyNumbers()
        {
            int result = _lib.Multiply(3, 2);
```

Continued

159

Listing 8-3: Complete test class for the sample math library *(continued)*

```
        Assert.AreEqual(6, result);
    }

    [TestMethod]
    public void CanDivideNumbers()
    {
        float result = _lib.Divide(12, 4);
        Assert.AreEqual(3, result);
    }

    [TestMethod]
    [ExpectedException(typeof(DivideByZeroException))]
    public void DivideByZeroIsThrownWithZeroDivisor()
    {
        _lib.Divide(12, 0);
    }
}
}
```

How It Works

In the example, you put into practice all the concepts you learned in the first half of this chapter. First, you created the test class, and then you added a method marked with the `TestInitialize` attribute. This method is executed before each test method of the class. The method creates an instance of the mathematical library that will be used by the test. In the example the initialization is very simple, but there might be cases where it can be pretty complex, and having the code in only one place makes the maintenance of the test easier.

Next, you added the first test, written inside a method marked with the `TestMethod` attribute, and ran it inside the Visual Studio test runner. You also saw a test fail and fixed the code that was causing the problem: The `Multiply` method was adding the numbers instead of multiplying them.

Finally, you added the tests for all the methods of the library. Furthermore, you added two different tests for the `Divide` method, one to test the expected result and another test to verify that an exception is thrown if you try to divide by zero. In order to do so, you marked the test method with the attribute `ExpectedException` and supplied the type of the exception that should be thrown as a parameter.

One thing you might have noticed is the naming of the test project, class, and methods:

❏ The test project and the namespace of the assembly built by the project are named as the project it is testing followed by `.Test`. Therefore, `CalculatorLib` becomes `CalculatorLib.Test`.

❏ The test class is usually named like the class it is testing followed by `Test`. Thus, `MathLib` becomes `MathLibTest`.

❏ The naming of the methods is less automatic. The name should be a sentence that tells what the test is doing. Just by reading `DivideByZeroIsThrownWithZeroDivisor` you should understand that you expect a DivideByZero exception to be thrown when the divisor is zero.

It's not a strict rule, and people using different testing libraries may have different naming conventions, but if you follow it consistently, it helps you manage the test projects better and helps you immediately understand what a test is testing.

Now that you know how to write tests for isolated classes, in the next section you learn how to test classes that depend on other components.

Testing Classes That Depend on External Components

Earlier in this chapter you learned that a test must isolate a single part of an application. With the MathLib of the previous example that was easy; all the methods were already isolated. But in real life most of the classes depend on other components, like the model part of the MVC or even external Web services. If you test a method that uses these *depended-on components* (that's the globally accepted name for these external components, sometimes also shortened as DOC), you are verifying not only that the method works but also that its DOCs work. Your test can fail because of a DOC, which is something you'd want to avoid.

The solution to this problem is the *test double*. It's like the "stunt double" in the movie industry (which is actually where the name comes from). It replaces the real actor, in this case the real DOC, just for the purpose of the test. If it replaces the model, it might return prebaked responses instead of really hitting the database. In this specific scenario, it also helps you avoid the pain of setting up a testing database. You will always have the data needed for the test from the test double.

In the following sections, the math library is expanded to include a method that computes the circumference of a circle, given its radius. The formula for this is:

$$C = 2\pi \times r$$

where C is the circumference, r is the radius, and π is Archimedes' constant, usually approximated to 3.14. For the purposes of the samples, this constant will be retrieved using a remote Web service. (The exact value of pi is not known, so we rely on an external source to get the best possible approximation.)

The code for the method that computes the circumference is:

```
PiWebService _ws;
public MathLib()
{
    _ws = new PiWebService();
}

//Compute the circumference of a circle
public float ComputeCircumference(float radius)
{
    float pi = _ws.GetPi();
    return 2 * pi * radius;
}
```

The instance of the Web service wrapper is created directly inside the constructor of the library. This is good for encapsulation, because the caller doesn't have to know that the library uses a Web service in its internals, but if you want to write a test for this method it will be impossible to isolate the verification of the formula from the retrieval of the value of pi. Figure 8-9 shows the relationship between the math library and the external Web service that is used to retrieve the value of pi.

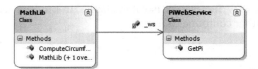

Figure 8-9

In the next section, you learn how to change the library in order to make it testable with a test double.

Patterns That Make Testing Easier

Two patterns can help working with test doubles and external components:

❑ **Dependency Injection** — A way to design classes so that their dependencies can be specified by the caller

❑ **Inversion of Control** — Complements the Dependency Injection pattern by adding an external component (called the container) that takes care of specifying the DOC

The following sections go deeper into these concepts.

Dependency Injection

The first pattern that allows easier testing in the presence of depended-on components is called *Dependency Injection*, often shortened to *DI*.

Instead of having the dependency created inside the constructor as in the previous example, the DOC is created by the caller and then supplied to the library. This is made possible by modifying the constructor to allow the client to pass in the Web service to use.

```
public MathLib(PiWebService ws)
{
    _ws = ws;
}
```

This constructor accepts only an instance of the real Web service, so it is ineffective for enabling the usage of a test double. The optimal way to implement the DI pattern is to create an interface with all the methods that the Web service supplies (in the sample, only the GetPi method) and to use it inside the method that uses the DOC. This way the caller can use the real Web service for the production code, and use the test double, which also implements the same interface, for the test.

The diagram in Figure 8-10 shows this scenario:

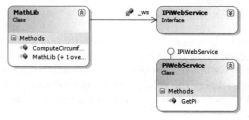

Figure 8-10

Using the interface, the math library becomes as shown in Listing 8-4.

Listing 8-4: Math library with Dependency Injection

```
namespace CalculatorLib
{
    public interface IPiWebService
    {
        float GetPi();
    }

    public class MathLib
    {

        IPiWebService _ws;

        public MathLib(IPiWebService ws)
        {
            _ws = ws;
        }

        //Compute the circumference of a circle
        public float ComputeCircumference(float radius)
        {
            float pi = _ws.GetPi();
            return 2 * pi * radius;
        }
    }
}
```

Using this new version is a bit more complicated than using the one with the internally created Web service. Instead of just instantiating the library and then calling `ComputeCircumference`, now the caller has to set up the instance of the external component as well.

```
PiWebService ws = new PiWebService();
MathLib lib = new MathLib(ws);
float circ = lib.ComputeCircumference(3);
```

As you just saw now it's up to the developer to create the dependencies. This poses two problems:

- ❑ You lose the encapsulation principle of the object-oriented design. The user must know how the component works inside.

- ❑ You have a lot more code to write. Imagine the math library also has two other DOCs: a logger and an external scientific calculator. The logger itself depends on a data access object that it uses to store logs to the database. That makes four external components that you have to correctly instantiate in the right order.

To complement Dependency Injection for bringing back the encapsulation of components, another pattern evolved: It's called *Inversion of Control*.

Inversion of Control Containers

Inversion of Control Containers (IoCCs) are lightweight containers that manage on your behalf the instantiation of all the components on which the main class depends.

More than 10 different IoCCs are available for .NET, all with different ways to be configured and different side features, but all provide the same utility. They automatically resolve all the dependencies of a component so that the developer can focus just on using it, instead of having to know how to set it up.

The next example shows how to call `ComputeCircumference` using Ninject (version 2.0), one of the IoCCs for .NET that I like the most:

```
MathLib lib = container.Get<MathLib>();
float circ = lib.ComputeCircumference(3);
```

As you see, all you have to do is "ask" the container to get an instance of `MathLib`. It will automatically resolve all the dependencies, instantiate the components in the right order and, finally, hand you the instance ready to be used.

But how does the container know how to resolve all the dependencies? There are different techniques for configuring a container. They can be configured with XML configuration files, marking the class definitions with attributes, or through code. Different IoCCs use different techniques, and sometimes a combination of them.

In the next section, you learn how to configure Ninject to automatically resolve the dependencies. If you want to learn more about Ninject, I recommend you go to the official Web site (`http://ninject.org/`), download the version 2.0 (in beta at the time of writing), and browse through the documentation and samples.

Configuring Ninject

Unlike other IoCCs that use XML files to configure the dependencies of a given component, in Ninject the type mappings are configured with a few lines of code collected into groups called *modules*. That's because in large applications with many components, XML files can grow large and become difficult to manage and read.

Each module defines the mapping of a single portion of the application, and they can be organized in whatever way you prefer. Writing a module is easy. Just extend the base class `Module` and override the `Load` method. (See Listing 8-5.)

Listing 8-5: Module to configure the dependencies of the math library

```
using Ninject.Modules;

namespace CalculatorLib
{
    public class PiWebServiceModule: NinjectModule
    {
        public override void Load()
        {
```

```
                        Bind<MathLib>().ToSelf();
                        Bind<IPiWebService>().To<PiWebService>();
                }
        }
}
```

The highlighted lines of code tell the container that, when you ask for an object of type MathLib, it should instantiate the class itself, but when you request an object whose type is IPiWebService, it should return an instance of the concrete class PiWebService.

Another step is required to have Ninject understand how to correctly instantiate a component with its dependencies. You have to tell it how to inject the dependencies. You do this through the [Inject] attribute on the constructor:

```
[Inject]
public MathLib(IPiWebService ws)
{
    _ws = ws;
}
```

Getting an Instance of a Component with Ninject

Now that you have configured the container, the only thing missing is setting it up and using it to get a ready-to-use instance of the component you need:

```
IKernel container = new StandardKernel(new PiWebServiceModule());
MathLib lib = container.Get<MathLib>();
float circ = lib.ComputeCircumference(3);
```

First, you load the container Kernel supplying the modules that will help resolve the dependencies, and then you ask it to Get an object of type MathLib.

Using a Test Double

An IoCC is great and helps a lot in your production code, but it must not be used inside your tests. Otherwise, your test will depend on that external library and will not be independent. Furthermore, in test code you are not using real components, but instead are using fake components made for each specific test, so having to manage all these configurations can be a nightmare and a waste of time.

In this section, you learn how to use a test double for testing components with references to other components. As you have already learned, a test double is used in test code to replace the real depended-on component in order to remove the dependency on an external component or service. But not all test doubles are born equal. There are four different types of test doubles: *dummy*, *stub*, *fake*, and *mock*. Even though they might sound like the same thing to you, some subtle differences exist:

❑   A *dummy* is an object that is only passed around (like a placeholder in method's calls) or that is used when no results are expected back from the call. For example, a dummy logging component receives the calls to the log method but does nothing and doesn't verify anything.

❑   A *stub* provides canned responses to the calls made during the test and only to the ones strictly needed by the test. For example, a Web service stub always returns the same fixed result to any request.

❑ Next comes the *fake* object, which is an actual working implementation of the same component but is usually implemented quickly and in a manner not suitable for production; for example, a data access layer that acts as an in-memory database instead of talking to a real one.

❑ The *mock* object is completely different from the other test doubles. Besides acting as the component it is replacing, the mock object also verifies that the expected methods are called and raises an exception, thus making the test fail, if the expectations are not met.

You learn more about mock objects in the next section, but before moving on, the following Try It Out gives you an example of a test developed using a stub.

Try It Out   **Testing with a Stub Object**

In this Try It Out example, you test the math library shown in Listing 8-4.

1. As in the previous Try It Out, create a class library for the math library (named CalculatorLib) and copy the code of Listing 8-4 into a file named MathLib.cs.

2. Next, create a testing project called CalculatorLib.Test and a new test class named MathLibTestWithStub.cs, and delete the automatically created TestMethod1.

3. Add a reference to the CalculatorLib, and then add the following using statement at the top of the file:

```
using CalculatorLib;
```

4. Inside the same file, add the class for the Web service stub:

```
internal class StubPiWebService: IPiWebService
{
    public float GetPi()
    {
        return 3.1416f;
    }
}
```

5. Add the following method for the fixture setup in MathLibTestWithStub:

```
private MathLib _lib;
[TestInitialize]
public void SetupLib()
{
    StubPiWebService ws = new StubPiWebService();
    _lib = new MathLib(ws);
}
```

6. And finally add the test method:

```
[TestMethod]
public void CircumferenceIsComputedCorrectly()
{
    float result = _lib.ComputeCircumference(3f);
    Assert.AreEqual(18.8496f,result);
}
```

7. Now run the test and see it pass.

How It Works

In this example, you tested a method that uses an external component. First you created a stub object, `StubPiWebService`, that mimics the behavior of the real Web service wrapper and always returns a low-precision approximation of pi.

Next, in the test initialization method, you set up an instance of the stub object and passed it to the constructor of the math library. Finally, you added the test, which bases its outcome on the value of pi provided by the stub implementation.

Mock Objects

As you learned in the previous section, a mock object is a test double that also verifies it has been used correctly by the SUT. Why is a simple stub not enough? Because, if you look at the previous example, the test didn't verify that the Web service was really called to retrieve the value of pi. The test would have passed even if the value of pi was stored directly inside the method. This practice is also called *interaction-based testing* or *behavior verification*.

Furthermore, mock objects are not classes written specifically for the test, but they are usually libraries that can be configured to mimic any component and to perform any kind of verification. Therefore, their setup is a bit more complicated than the previously mentioned stubs.

The life of a mock object can be divided into five phases:

1. **Setup** — First, the mocking framework is initialized and the mock object is created.

2. **Record** — Next, the mock object is configured, setting the expectations and the return results of method calls.

3. **Installation** — The mock is then injected into the SUT.

4. **Replay** — The SUT is exercised, which in turn calls the mock object (sometimes also called Playback).

5. **Verification** — The assertions are verified, and the interactions with the mock object are verified.

The example that follows uses one of the most famous and probably most used mocking frameworks for .NET: Rhino Mocks. Specifically, it refers to version 3.5. You can download this library from its official Web site at `http://ayende.com/projects/rhino-mocks.aspx`

Try It Out   Testing with Rhino Mocks

To try this example, just add a new test class named `MathLibTestWithMock.cs` to the testing project from the previous example and clear all the contents and write the code shown in Listing 8-6.

To make the class compile, you also have to get the Rhino Mocks library and add a reference to it.

Listing 8-6: Test class that uses Rhino Mocks

```
using Microsoft.VisualStudio.TestTools.UnitTesting;
using Rhino.Mocks;

namespace CalculatorLib.Test
{
    [TestClass]
    public class MathLibTestWithMock
    {
        private MathLib _lib;
        private MockRepository mocks;

        [TestInitialize]
        public void SetupLib()
        {
            mocks = new MockRepository();

            IPiWebService mockedWS = mocks.DynamicMock<IPiWebService>();

            Expect.Call(mockedWS.GetPi()).Return(3.1416f);
            _lib = new MathLib(mockedWS);
            mocks.ReplayAll();
        }

        [TestMethod]
        public void CircumferenceIsComputedCorrectly()
        {
            float result = _lib.ComputeCircumference(3f);
            Assert.AreEqual(18.8496f, result);
            mocks.VerifyAll();
        }
    }
}
```

If you run the test, you will see that it succeeds. If you want to see it fail, you have to change the compute method to work without calling the external Web service.

Open the MathLib class, and change the ComputeCircumference method:

```
public float ComputeCircumference(float radius)
{
    float pi = 3.1416f;
    return 2 * pi * radius;
}
```

If you run the test again, it will fail with this error message: "Rhino.Mocks.Exceptions .ExpectationViolationException: IPiWebService.GetPi(); Expected #1, Actual #0.."

How It Works

In the test initialization method, first the code initializes the mocking framework (MockRepository) and then it asks it to generate a mock object that mimics the behavior of the IPiWebService:

```
IPiWebService mockedWS = mocks.DynamicMock<IPiWebService>();
```

Then the expectation is set:

```
Expect.Call(mockedWS.GetPi()).Return(3.1416f);
```

The preceding code means: "Expect a call to the method `GetPi` on the mock object, and when that happens return the specified value as result."

Finally, the mock object is injected into the math library, and finally it is set in replay mode, which means that from now on it will mimic the interface, following the expectations that have been set before.

```
mocks.ReplayAll();
```

The test then proceeds as usual, but at the end of the method, after the normal assertions, the mocking framework verifies that all the expectations have been satisfied:

```
mocks.VerifyAll();
```

You also saw an error message when you changed the code of the math library to make the test fail on purpose. The message you got was: *Rhino.Mocks.Exceptions.ExpectationViolationException: IPiWebService .GetPi(); Expected #1, Actual #0.*. It means that the mocking framework expected that the method `GetPi` would be called once (#1), but it was instead called zero times (#0).

Something to keep in mind about the `VerifyAll` method is that it verifies all the expectations that have been set. So, if you don't want to verify that the methods have been really called, you don't have to use it.

Rhino Mocks is a very wide topic, so a detailed coverage of its features is outside the scope of this book. However, you learn a bit more about this in the next chapter, where you use it to test an application developed with ASP.NET MVC.

What you just learned is the so-called "Record/Replay/Verify" approach for mocking. With version 3.5, Rhino Mocks added a new approach called "Arrange/Act/Assert" (AAA), which makes the setup of mocks objects more similar to standard unit testing: Instead of setting the expectations before using the object and verifying them later, with the AAA approach, you write assertions after having exercised the system under test, just like you do with standard unit testing.

To give you the feeling of how this approach works, the following code is an example of the test written in Listing 8-6:

```
[TestMethod]
public void CircumferenceIsComputedCorrectly()
{
    var webservice = MockRepository.GenerateMock<IPiWebService>();
    webservice.Stub(x => x.GetPi()).Return(3.1416f);

    var _lib = new MathLib(webservice);

    float result = _lib.ComputeCircumference(3f);

    Assert.AreEqual(18.8496f, result);
    webservice.AssertWasCalled(x => x.GetPi());
}
```

This new syntax is becoming more and more popular because it's more concise and better expresses the intents. Other mocking frameworks are adopting it, but in order to get the most out if it, it requires a good knowledge of the new features of C#3 such as lambda expressions and object initializers.

Throughout the book all the samples use the Record/Reply/Verify approach, but, because it's only a change of syntax, it is easy, if you prefer to use the AAA approach, to adapt them.

Summary

Unit testing is a practice that helps you develop high-quality applications, and this alone should be enough reason to start using ASP.NET MVC, which was developed to be easily testable.

In this chapter, you learned:

❑ What unit testing is and what benefits it brings

❑ What user interface elements Visual Studio has that allow you to write unit tests

❑ How a test is structured

❑ What an SUT, a fixture, and an assertion is

❑ How to use MSTest to write a unit test

❑ How Dependency Injection helps you in writing tests for components that depend on other components

❑ How Inversion of Control Containers help you in managing DI in large applications

❑ How to use Ninject

❑ What a test double is

❑ What a mock object is

❑ How to use Rhino Mocks

In the next chapter, you put all that knowledge to practice and you learn how to test an application developed with the ASP.NET MVC framework. However, before proceeding, try the following exercises to test your understanding of the unit-testing concepts covered in this chapter.

Exercises

1. The math library is extended by adding a method that computes the percentage. The method is implemented as follows:

```
public float Percent(float part, float total)
{
    if (total == 0)
        throw new DivideByZeroException();
    if (part > total)
```

```
        return -1;
    return (part/total)*100;
}
```

It's a particular implementation of Percent. It throws an exception if the total is zero, and it returns –1 if you want to compute a percent that will be greater than 100%.

Implement a test to verify the correctness of the method and that it has 100% coverage.

2. Expand the math library you built in the Try It Out section named "Testing with a Stub Object" to include CalculateMass, which computes the mass of a solid given its weight. The formula for it is $m = W/g$, where g is the acceleration of gravity. The acceleration of gravity depends on the current position on the Earth, so to calculate the mass of on object, you have to get the current acceleration of gravity from a Web service, supplying you current location. The signature of the Web service is:

```
public float GetGravity(string location);
```

Implement the method so that it uses the external Web service and in a way that will make testing possible.

3. Implement a test for the CalculateMass method, using the stub object approach.

4. Implement the same test as exercise 3, but use a mock object.

Testing ASP.NET MVC Applications

The ASP.NET MVC framework has been developed to be testable out-of-the-box. After having learned in the previous chapter what unit testing is and how to test applications, in this chapter you apply these concepts together with the ASP.NET MVC–specific features made to facilitate testing.

In the chapter, you learn:

❑ How to create a new testing project for an ASP.NET MVC application

❑ How to test controllers' actions and routes

❑ How the ASP.NET MVC framework facilitates testing

❑ How to test an end-to-end application

❑ A bit of TDD approach

Creating a Test Project for ASP.NET MVC

Every ASP.NET MVC application should have a companion test project, so the project template for this process is super. When you create an ASP.NET MVC Web application, as soon as you click the OK button, another dialog pops up (see Figure 9-1), asking you whether you want to create a unit test project for the application. In this dialog, you can choose the name of the test project; by default, it's named like the MVC project name dot Tests (for example `mvcapplication.Tests`) and the testing framework you want to use to create the tests with. With the installation, there is only the Visual Studio Unit Test template, which uses MSTest, but you can add other testing frameworks if you like. (In Figure 9-1 MbUnit v3 is shown.)

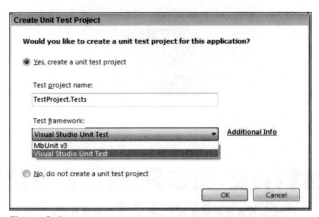

Figure 9-1

If you choose Yes, a new project will be created, with a tiny test class that tests the controller created by the project template: `HomeControllerTest`.

In the previous chapter, you read about mock objects and Dependency Injection, but to test the actions of a controller you often don't need to bring these concepts to the table. The ASP.NET MVC team did a very good job of removing many of the needless dependencies on the environment so that you can test actions just by instantiating the controller and calling the method. This is true for most of the common scenarios.

In the next section, you read about these easily testable common scenarios and later you see how the environment is abstracted so that you can also test the scenarios that interact directly with the HTTP runtime.

Testing without Mocking

As you might remember from Chapter 8, a test is performed in four phases: Setup, Exercise, Verification, and Teardown. In that chapter you also read that mocking frameworks are starting to adopt a new syntax called Arrange, Act, Assert (AAA).

Given the rising popularity of the AAA syntax for mocking frameworks, and to make the symmetry even stronger, the Visual Studio project template creates a sample testing class and refers to the phases of unit testing using the AAA naming. (The Teardown phase is not included because this phase is usually in the `TearDown` method of the unit test class.)

Unlike mocking frameworks, in the context of test phases, the AAA naming doesn't bring in a different way of writing tests, but just different names for the various phases of unit tests. The AAA naming for test phases equates to the "traditional" test phases in the following way:

❑   Arrange = Setup

❑   Act = Exercise

❑   Assert = Verify

Because it's just a name shift, and because the Visual Studio project template is using it, throughout the rest of this chapter, the new AAA naming is used.

Following is the test method as created by the Visual Studio project template:

```
[TestMethod]
public void Index()
{
    // Arrange
    HomeController controller = new HomeController();

    // Act
    ViewResult result = controller.Index() as ViewResult;

    // Assert
    // Here goes the verify phase
}
```

When testing an action, the first two phases are pretty simple: the setup (Arrange) is just the instantiation of the controller, and the exercise (Act) phase is just calling the action you want to test. The teardown phase, most of the time, is implicitly performed by the garbage collector, so the only phase that needs your attention is the verification (or Assert) one, where the test looks inside the result of the action to prove the correctness of the method.

The Assert phase is different, depending on what you want to test. You will learn about the different ways to do testing later in the chapter. You can split the outcomes of the controller actions into two main groups:

❑   The actions that render a view or other outputs

❑   The actions that send the request flow to another action, via a redirect

These two types of actions need different approaches.

Testing Actions That Render Something

The first, and probably most used, type of action sends some kind of output to the browser. This can be a view, a partial view, a direct text response, a JSON response, or other custom response types.

So, the first thing you have to verify is that the type returned by the action is the one you are expecting. Call the action method, which usually returns an object that inherits from ActionResult, and cast it to the specific type of result you are expecting, using the as statement.

The as statement behaves differently from the usual cast operation. If the cast cannot be completed, instead of raising an InvalidCastException it assigns a null value to the variable.

```
// Act
ActionResult actionResult = controller.Index();
// Assert
ViewResult result = actionResult as ViewResult;
Assert.IsNotNull(result,"The result is not a view result");
```

After you determine that the action is returning the correct kind of result, you have to verify the correctness of the data being passed to the view.

`ViewData` is a property of the result object, so verifying its content is pretty easy:

```
ViewDataDictionary viewData = result.ViewData;
Assert.AreEqual("Home Page", viewData["Title"]);
```

If the view data also contains a custom Presentation Model supplied to the view in a strongly typed manner, you can access it through the `Model` property.

```
MyCustomObject myObject = viewData.Model as MyCustomObject;
Assert.IsNotNull(myObject, "The custom object has not been passed");
Assert.AreEqual("Simone", myObject.Username);
```

This approach is similar to the one used to test the type of the response. First, you cast the model object to the expected type, then verify that it's not null, and finally, check the value of the properties that need to be tested. This is pretty much all you have to do to verify that the data retrieved and manipulated inside the actions is the data you expected.

In case your action has logic that chooses the view to render based on certain conditions, you also have to test that the view that is going to be rendered is the correct one. To facilitate this scenario, the `ViewResult` and the `PartialViewResult` objects contain properties that you can access to check for these conditions:

❑   `ViewName` — The exact name of the view that is going to be rendered

❑   `MasterName` — The name of the master page

With this in place, if you want to test that the view that is going to be rendered is the view named "Index," you just need to write:

```
Assert.AreEqual("Index",result.ViewName);
```

The process is the same if you want to test the master page name (only if it has been set explicitly in the action method):

```
Assert.AreEqual("AdminMaster",result.MasterName);
```

In the following Try It Out, you test an ASP.NET MVC application that renders views.

Try It Out   Testing an Action That Renders a View

In this Try It Out, you write an application that renders different views based on the time of the day. The example contains only the code of the controller and the tests. This is to show that you can start your application even before having created a view.

1.   Create a new ASP.NET MVC Web application and create a testing project, selecting the "Yes, create a unit test project" option when asked.

2. Create a new file in the `Model` folder, name it **Time.cs**, and add the following code:

```
namespace TestingRenderView.Models
{
    public class Time
    {
        public int Hour { get; set; }
    }
}
```

3. Open the `Controllers\HomeController.cs` file, and add the following method:

```
public ActionResult DayPart(int hour)
{
    Time time = new Time {Hour = hour};
    if (hour <= 6 || hour >= 20)
        return View("NightTimeView", time);
    if (hour > 6 && hour < 20)
        return View("DayTimeView", time);
    return View("Index");
}
```

4. Now focus your attention on the other project, the testing one. Open the `HomeControllerTest.cs` file and write a new test method:

```
[TestMethod]
public void DayTimeView_Is_Rendered_At_Midday()
{

}
```

5. Inside this method start writing the setup of the test:

```
HomeController controller = new HomeController();
```

6. Then exercise the system under test:

```
ActionResult actionResult = controller.DayPart(12);
```

7. Finally, add the code to verify all the conditions. After adding the code the method will be:

```
[TestMethod]
public void DayTimeView_Is_Rendered_At_Midday()
{
    // Arrange
    HomeController controller = new HomeController();

    // Act
    ActionResult actionResult = controller.DayPart(12);

    // Assert
    ViewResult result = actionResult as ViewResult;
    Assert.IsNotNull(result,"Not a RenderView Result");
    Assert.AreEqual("DayTimeView", result.ViewName);
```

```
        ViewDataDictionary viewData = result.ViewData;
        Time model = viewData.Model as Time;
        Assert.IsNotNull(model,"Model is not the correct type");
        Assert.AreEqual(12, model.Hour);
    }
```

8. Then add another test method, one that verifies the other possible outcome of the action:

```
[TestMethod]
public void NightTimeView_Is_Rendered_At_Midnight()
{
    // Arrange
    HomeController controller = new HomeController();

    // Act
    ActionResult actionResult = controller.DayPart(0);

    // Assert
    ViewResult result = actionResult as ViewResult;
    Assert.IsNotNull(result, "Not a RenderView Result");
    Assert.AreEqual("NightTimeView", result.ViewName);
    ViewDataDictionary viewData = result.ViewData;
    Time model = viewData.Model as Time;
    Assert.IsNotNull(model, "Model is not the correct type");
    Assert.AreEqual(0, model.Hour);
}
```

9. Now run the tests (use the command menu Test ➪ Run ➪ All Tests in Solution) and see them "green."

How It Works

In the first part of the example, a normal action has been created. Based on the hour supplied as parameter (in a real production environment this would have been passed as part of the URL and mapped through the routing engine), it renders a different view and passes it a custom model object (the Time object). To make sure that all the possible outcomes are tested, you need to write two tests: one with a parameter in the day range and the other in the night range. The first is called DayTimeView_Is_ Rendered_At_Midday and the second one is NightTimeView_Is_Rendered_At_Midnight. They are the same method but have different parameters and expected values, so the explanation of the code will be based only on the day time parameter.

At step 4 the test method is created, annotating the method with the TestMethod attribute, as required by the MSTest framework. Then an instance of the controller is created, and finally the SUT is exercised by calling the action method DayPart with the parameter 12 (midday).

But all the complexity lies in what you add during step 7: all the assertions.

The action result is first cast to the expected result type (ViewResult), and you verify that the returned object is really as expected:

```
ViewResult result = actionResult as ViewResult;
Assert.IsNotNull(result,"Not a RenderView Result");
```

Then the name of the view is verified:

```
Assert.AreEqual("DayTimeView", result.ViewName);
```

And, finally, the test verifies that a custom model object of the correct type was returned and that the Hour is really set to the one passed as the parameter of the action method (in this example, 12):

```
ViewDataDictionary viewData = result.ViewData;
Time model = viewData.Model as Time;
Assert.IsNotNull(model,"Model is not the correct type");
Assert.AreEqual(12, model.Hour);
```

The other test method is the same, just with 0 passed as the value of the parameter of the action and, obviously, with a different expected ViewName (NightTimeView).

It was not implemented in this example, but usually it's a good idea to test the boundary conditions, to make sure that the inclusion of the limit has been implemented correctly. In the example, the night goes from 8PM to 6AM, limits included, so you have also written two tests named something like NightTimeView_Is_Still_Rendered_At_6AM and NightTimeView_Is_Already_Rendered_At_8PM. The first passed 6 as the value of the action and the second passed 20.

These boundary tests are included in the code samples that come with the book, together with a full implementation of the Web application, with the two different views and the routing rules.

Testing Actions That Redirect to Another Action

The other group of actions contains the ones that, instead of rendering something, redirect the flow of the application to another action or URL.

The test flow is the same as the previous one, although the details are slightly different: The type of the action result must be either RedirectResult or RedirectToRouteResult.

```
RedirectResult result = actionResult as RedirectResult;
Assert.IsNotNull(result, "The result is not a redirect");
```

Then, you have to verify that the processing is being redirected to the right URL.

If the result is a RedirectResult, this is pretty easy: Just check for the Url property.

```
Assert.AreEqual("/Home/NotLogged", result.Url);
```

If the action is returning a RedirectToRouteResult, things are a bit more complex. In this case you can check either the RouteName or the RouteValues collection, which is an instance of the usual RouteValueDictionary class. For example, if you want to verify that the flow is redirected to the action named "Login", this is the code to write:

```
Assert.AreEqual("Login",result.RouteValues["action"]);
```

Once you have verified that the request will be redirected to the correct action, the other element that needs to be tested is the `TempData` collection. This collection is not part of the result but is a property of the controller.

```
Assert.AreEqual("Simone", controller.TempData["Name"]);
```

Now that you know about testing controller actions, in the next Try It Out, which builds on the previous one, you put everything together inside the same application.

Try It Out   **Testing for Both Render and Redirect**

In the previous Try It Out, the code didn't handle very well the case when the user specifies a value that is not a valid hour of the day, for example 44. In this example, you enhance the code of the application so that it redirects the user to a specific view if the value of the hour is not valid.

1. Building on the previous Try It Out, in the `Controllers\HomeControllers.cs` file replace the `DayPart` action with the following one:

```
public ActionResult DayPart(int hour)
{
    if(hour <0 || hour > 24)
    {
        TempData["Hour"] = hour;
        return RedirectToAction("NotValid");
    }
    Time time = new Time { Hour = hour };
    if (hour <= 6 || hour >= 20)
        return View("NightTimeView", time);
    return View("DayTimeView", time);
}
```

2. Then, add to the same controller the action that handles the error situation:

```
public ActionResult NotValid()
{
    ViewData["UserSuppliedTime"] = TempData["Hour"];
    return View("NotAValidHour");
}
```

3. Finally, add to the `HomeControllerTest` class the test method for the new "not valid" scenario:

```
[TestMethod]
public void Not_Valid_Hours_Are_Redirected_To_NotValid_Action()
{
    // Arrange
    HomeController controller = new HomeController();

    // Act
    ActionResult actionResult = controller.DayPart(44);

    // Assert
    RedirectToRouteResult result = actionResult as RedirectToRouteResult;
    Assert.IsNotNull(result, "Not a RedirectToRouteResult Result");
    Assert.AreEqual("NotValid", result.RouteValues["Action"]);
    Assert.AreEqual(44, controller.TempData["Hour"]);
}
```

4. The complete test class should now look like Listing 9-1:

Listing 9-1: The complete test class

```
using System.Web.Mvc;
using Microsoft.VisualStudio.TestTools.UnitTesting;
using RenderAndRedirect.Controllers;
using RenderAndRedirect.Models;

namespace RenderAndRedirect.Tests.Controllers
{
    /// <summary>
    /// Summary description for HomeControllerTest
    /// </summary>
    [TestClass]
    public class HomeControllerTest
    {
        [TestMethod]
        public void DayTimeView_Is_Rendered_At_Midday()
        {
            // Arrange
            HomeController controller = new HomeController();

            // Act
            ActionResult actionResult = controller.DayPart(12);

            // Assert
            ViewResult result = actionResult as ViewResult;
            Assert.IsNotNull(result, "Not a RenderView Result");

            Assert.AreEqual("DayTimeView", result.ViewName);
            ViewDataDictionary viewData = result.ViewData;
            Time model = viewData.Model as Time;
            Assert.IsNotNull(model, "Model is not the correct type");
            Assert.AreEqual(12, model.Hour);
        }

        [TestMethod]
        public void NightTimeView_Is_Rendered_At_Midnight()
        {
            // Arrange
            HomeController controller = new HomeController();

            // Act
            ActionResult actionResult = controller.DayPart(0);

            // Assert
            ViewResult result = actionResult as ViewResult;
            Assert.IsNotNull(result, "Not a RenderView Result");
            ViewDataDictionary viewData = result.ViewData;
            Assert.AreEqual("NightTimeView", result.ViewName);
            Time model = viewData.Model as Time;
            Assert.IsNotNull(model, "Model is not the correct type");
            Assert.AreEqual(0, model.Hour);
```

Continued

181

Listing 9-1: The complete test class *(continued)*

```
        }

        [TestMethod]
        public void Not_Valid_Hours_Are_Redirected_To_NotValid_Action()
        {
            // Arrange
            HomeController controller = new HomeController();

            // Act
            ActionResult actionResult = controller.DayPart(44);

            // Assert
            RedirectToRouteResult result = actionResult
                    as RedirectToRouteResult;
            Assert.IsNotNull(result, "Not a RedirectToRouteResult Result");
            Assert.AreEqual("NotValid", result.RouteValues["Action"]);
            Assert.AreEqual(44, controller.TempData["Hour"]);
        }
    }
}
```

5. Now run the tests, including the one you created in the previous Try It Out to confirm that they all pass.

How It Works

In the previous Try It Out, the action didn't handle invalid hours very well. In this new version of the action, the code first checks whether the hour supplied is positive and less than 24. If it's not, the code redirects the user to another action, called NotValid, and passes the original value to it. This is done using the TempData collection.

Notice that the implementation of the part of the day has been changed a bit, but the tests you put in place will tell you whether you broke something, so you can do your refactoring free from worry.

The action that handles the error condition just takes the original value from the TempData collection and stores it inside the ViewData collection and then renders the view with the error message.

The new test method, called Not_Valid_Hours_Are_Redirected_To_NotValid_Action, calls the action to test with an invalid parameter (44 in this example) and then verifies that everything is as expected.

As before, first the type of the action result is tested for correctness:

```
RedirectToRouteResult result = actionResult as RedirectToRouteResult;
Assert.IsNotNull(result, "Not a RedirectToRouteResult Result");
```

Then the code proves the correctness of the action to which the flow will be redirected:

```
Assert.AreEqual("NotValid", result.RouteValues["Action"]);
```

And, finally, the value inside the TempData is tested:

```
Assert.AreEqual(44, controller.TempData["Hour"]);
```

> Most of the parameters inside the action results, such as the `ViewName` or the name of the controller inside the `RouteValueDictionary`, are available to use inside a test method only if they are explicitly set by the developer. If you call the `View()` method without parameters, the `ViewName` will be empty. So remember this when testing actions that rely on the default values for the view name: Either test it to see if it is empty or explicitly set the name of the view.

System.Web.Abstractions

In the previous section, you tested the controllers' actions as if they were a general-purpose library that doesn't have anything to do with the Web and HTTP. A big round of applause to the ASP.NET MVC team for coming up with such an easy-to-test framework.

But these are Web applications, and unfortunately at some time you might have to interact with the HTTP runtime to get, for example, a value from the browser's cookies or you might need to interact with `Session` object. Even in these scenarios, however, you'd want to go on testing the actions without setting up the Web server environment. That's what the assembly `System.Web.Abstractions` is for. All the methods in the ASP.NET framework that interact with the HTTP runtime are actually interacting with a wrapper that, in the end, calls the real `System.Web` assembly so that you don't need the Web server runtime to test these interactions. When writing tests, you can replace the implementation of the wrapper with a stub/mock object made on purpose for your test.

This namespace, like the routing one, was developed with ASP.NET MVC in mind, but it was later considered of wider interest and was shipped as part of the SP1 of .NET 3.5 at the end of August 2008.

In the next section, you learn how to mock the objects of the HTTP runtime in order to test HTTP-specific interactions, such as cookies.

Testing with Mocking

In the previous chapter, you learned about mock objects and Rhino Mocks. In this section you use Rhino Mocks to test the interaction of actions with the `http` objects.

Imagine that you want to read the value of a cookie. To do this, you have to access the `HttpRequest` object and read the `Cookies` property. The code for this action is:

```
public ActionResult About()
{
    string lastLogin = Request.Cookies["LastLogin"].Value;
    ViewData["LastLogin"] = lastLogin;

    return View();
}
```

Now, you want to test that the action actually reads the data from the browser cookie and then passes it over to the view.

In ASP.NET MVC, all the references to the HTTP runtime are made through the abstraction layer provided by the `System.Web.Abstractions` assembly. This allows you to inject your own implementation or a mock object instead of using the real implementation.

The `Request` object is stored inside the `HttpContext` property of the `ControllerContext` object, which, in a production environment, is created by the framework when it handles the request. But during unit testing there is no framework that sets everything up for you, so you have to do it yourself.

As you might have guessed, setting up all the dependencies is not easy. You first need to mock the context, then mock the request, set the expected result, and finally create the cookie you expect to find in the user's browser when the application runs in production.

To keep things neat, it's usually better to encapsulate the mock's setup inside a method marked with the `TestInitialize` attribute that will run before each test method:

```
private MockRepository mocks;
private HttpContextBase mockHttpContext;

[TestInitialize]
public void SetupHttpContext()
{
    mocks = new MockRepository();
    //Mock setup
    mockHttpContext = mocks.DynamicMock<HttpContextBase>();
    HttpRequestBase mockHttpRequest = mocks.DynamicMock<HttpRequestBase>();
    SetupResult.For(mockHttpContext.Request).Return(mockHttpRequest);

    HttpCookieCollection cookies = new HttpCookieCollection();
    cookies.Add(new HttpCookie("LastLogin","Yesterday"));

    Expect.Call(mockHttpRequest.Cookies).Return(cookies);

    mocks.ReplayAll();
}
```

The first line of the method creates an instance of the mock repository, as you already saw in the previous chapter. Next, using the `DynamicMock` method, a mock object of both the context and the request is created. The context mock object is then instructed to return the mocked request object when the `Request` property is called:

```
SetupResult.For(mockHttpContext.Request).Return(mockHttpRequest);
```

And finally, the cookie with the test case value is created and the expectation is set on the request object:

```
Expect.Call(mockHttpRequest.Cookies).Return(cookies);
```

Notice the difference between the two instructions: The first one — the one that uses the `SetupResult` `.For` syntax — tells the only mocked object that whenever someone calls the `Request` property, it must return the given object. The second one that uses `Expect.Call` does a bit more. It still sets the return value, but it also instructs the mock framework to verify that this method is actually called during the execution of the test.

Now that all the mock objects are ready, the `ReplyAll` method ends the record phase and puts the mock objects in replay mode.

This test method is not much different from the ones that run without mocking. The controller is instantiated, the action is executed, and the results are verified.

```
[TestMethod]
public void About()
{
    // Arrange
    HomeController controller = new HomeController();
    controller.ControllerContext = new ControllerContext(
        mockHttpContext,
        new RouteData(),
        controller);

    // Act
    ActionResult actionResult = controller.About();

    // Assert
    ViewResult result = actionResult as ViewResult;
    Assert.IsNotNull(result, "Not a RenderView Result");
    ViewDataDictionary viewData = result.ViewData;
    Assert.AreEqual("Yesterday", viewData["LastLogin"]);
    mocks.VerifyAll();
}
```

The only differences are the lines highlighted in grey.

The first one is the highlighted section that does the same thing that the framework does when it handles the request in a live application: It injects the `ControllerContext` in the controller. However in this case the context is not the real `HttpContext` but the mocked version created in the test initialization method.

The other highlighted line instructs the mock repository to verify all the expectations. If the action method cheated and didn't retrieve the `LastLogin` value from the cookies, this would have made the test fail. To experiment with this behavior, run the test now, and see everything pass. Then change the action method, replacing the line that reads the cookie with one that sets a static value, like this:

```
public ActionResult About()
{
    string lastLogin = "Yesterday";
    ViewData["LastLogin"] = lastLogin;
    return View();
}
```

Now run the test again. It will fail because the cookie's properties have never been accessed.

The same approach can be used to test actions that access the ASP.NET `Cache` object, the `Session` object, or any of the objects that are inside the current HTTP execution context.

Testing Routes

Now that you have tested all the components of an ASP.NET MVC Web application, there is one last component that you might want to test: the routes. In Chapter 7 you saw that there is a route handler that helps you debug routing rules, but it's always better to be able to automate the testing.

The routing engine relies on `HttpContext` and `HttpRequest` to get the URL of the current request, so, in order to test routes, you still need to mock these two objects. You do this the same way as before:

```
MockRepository mocks = new MockRepository();
//Mock setup
HttpContextBase mockHttpContext = mocks.DynamicMock<HttpContextBase>();
HttpRequestBase mockHttpRequest = mocks.DynamicMock<HttpRequestBase>();
SetupResult.For(mockHttpContext.Request).Return(mockHttpRequest);
```

Once the mock HTTP stack is set up, you need to supply the URL that you want to test:

```
SetupResult.For(mockHttpRequest.AppRelativeCurrentExecutionFilePath)
    .Return("~/archive/2008/10/15");
```

You do this by setting the result for the property of the `HttpRequest` that contains the URL relative to the application root path.

The exercise phase consists of calling the helper method that registers the routes in the `global.asax.cs` file. It then acts as part of the routing engine and calls the framework methods that search the collection with all the registered routes and retrieves the one that matches the URL supplied: the `GetRouteData` method.

```
RouteCollection routes = new RouteCollection();
MvcApplication.RegisterRoutes(routes);
RouteData routeData = routes.GetRouteData(mockHttpContext);
```

And, finally, the test needs to verify that the segments have been evaluated correctly and the route data has been populated with the right values:

```
RouteData routeData = routes.GetRouteData(mockHttpContext);
Assert.IsNotNull(routeData, "Should have found the route");

Assert.AreEqual("Blog", routeData.Values["Controller"]
    , "Expected a different controller");

Assert.AreEqual("Index", routeData.Values["action"]
```

```
        , "Expected a different action");

    Assert.AreEqual("2008", routeData.Values["year"]
        , "Expected a different year parameter");

    Assert.AreEqual("10", routeData.Values["month"]
        , "Expected a different month parameter");

    Assert.AreEqual("15", routeData.Values["day"]
        , "Expected a different day parameter");
```

Putting It All Together

Now that you know everything about testing specific elements of an ASP.NET MVC application, it's time to test a real-world application. You learn how to do this by making the application used as an example in Chapter 4 testable.

Analyzing a Legacy Application

The code sample you will focus on is the application that retrieves a list of Pink Floyd albums. It used a repository developed with LINQ to SQL. But this is a *legacy* application, which, among the other things, means "not developed to be testable." The controller directly depends on the repository. The complete code of the controller is shown in Listing 4-2, but the parts relevant to show this approach are included here:

```
public class AlbumController : Controller
{
    public ActionResult Index()
    {
        ViewData["Title"] = "List of Pink Floyd Albums";
        ViewData["Albums"] = AlbumsDataContext.GetAlbums();

        return View();
    }

    public ActionResult Individual(int id)
    {
        var album = AlbumsDataContext.GetAlbum(id);

        ViewData["Title"] = album.Name;
        ViewData["Album"] = album;

        return View();
    }
}
```

The lines where all the problems lay are highlighted in grey. The data access layer is using a "hard" reference that makes it impossible to test the controller in isolation.

The other problem is that the methods used to access the repository are static methods. So, even if the controller didn't use the reference to the implementation of the data access layer, it would have been impossible to abstract out this method, because static methods cannot be part of interfaces.

```
namespace LinqSample.Models
{
    public class AlbumsDataContext
    {
        public static List<Album> GetAlbums()
        {
            ...
        }

        public static Album GetAlbum(int id)
        {
            ...
        }
    }
}
```

Last, but not least, the `Album` class was generated by the LINQ designer and is part of the `LinqDataContext`, so it might not be available to the application if the test code doesn't have a reference to the assembly that contains the data access layer.

To verify that the controller is behaving correctly in isolation from the data access layer, you need to refactor the code in order to make it testable.

Refactoring to Testable

Dependency Injection is the key for this refactoring process, which will be based on the following steps:

1. Define the `Album` model class.
2. Define the `IAlbumContext` interface.
3. Have the concrete `AlbumDataContext` implement it.
4. Change the `AlbumController` to use the DI pattern.

Step 1 — The Model Object

This step is quite easy: Just copy the same class autogenerated by the LINQ designer, as shown in Listing 9-2.

Listing 9-2: Album object

```
namespace TestingDAL.Models
{
    public class Album
    {
        public int ID { get; set; }
        public string Name { get;  set; }
        public string ReleaseYear { get; set; }
    }
}
```

Step 2 — The Data Access Layer Interface

To make it possible to swap the implementation of the data access layer without changing and recompiling the application, the methods needed by the application to work must be extracted to an interface that will later be used as the only way controllers and other clients refer to the data access layer (DAL). (See Listing 9-3.)

Listing 9-3: IAlbumDataContext interface

```
using System.Collections.Generic;

namespace TestingDAL.Models
{
    public interface IAlbumDataContext
    {
        List<Album> GetAlbums();
        Album GetAlbum(int id);
    }
}
```

Step 3 — The Concrete DAL Implements the Interface

Because this example is only about testing, you could have skipped this step, but if you want to completely refactor the application, you also need to have the original data access layer implement the new IAlbumDataContext interface. (See Listing 9-4.)

Listing 9-4: The concrete AlbumDataContext

```
using System.Collections.Generic;

namespace TestingDAL.Models
{
    public class AlbumDataContext: IAlbumDataContext
    {
        public List<Album> GetAlbums()
        {
            ...
        }

        public Album GetAlbum(int id)
        {
            ...
        }
    }
}
```

If you compare this with the old version, you will notice that the only difference besides the implementation of the interface is that the methods are now instance methods and not static ones.

Step 4 — Writing the Controller Using the DI Pattern

The biggest changes need to be applied to the implementation of the controller. As you already know from the previous chapter, the central concept of Dependency Injection is that the methods must not create their own private instance of the depended-on component (in this example of the `AlbumDataContext`), but they must use the instance that has been passed to the controller when it was instantiated. To do that, there must be a private field inside the controller to hold the instance of the DOC:

```
private readonly IAlbumDataContext _albumDataContext;
```

Furthermore, a constructor of the controller must allow the caller to supply the instance of the data access layer that needs to be used:

```
public AlbumController(IAlbumDataContext albumDataContext)
{
    _albumDataContext = albumDataContext;
}
```

In a live production environment, the default controller factory of the ASP.NET Framework instantiates the controller by using its parameterless constructor, so you need to add another constructor that creates an instance of the LINQ-to-SQL–based data access layer:

```
public AlbumController()
{
    _albumDataContext= new AlbumDataContext();
}
```

This constructor creates a compile-type dependency to a specific concrete implementation of the data context class, so it makes the implementation of the DI pattern a bit dirty. In Chapter 16 you see that this can be avoided by replacing the default controller factory with one factory that uses an Inversion of Control Container to instantiate the controllers supplying the right dependencies.

And finally, the methods that use the data context to retrieve the albums must be changed to use the private field and not the static method as before:

```
_albumDataContext.GetAlbums();
```

The new version of the `AlbumController`, after all the changes, is shown in Listing 9-5.

Listing 9-5: AlbumContoller

```
using System.Web.Mvc;
using TestingDAL.Models;

namespace TestingDAL.Controllers
{
    [HandleError]
    public class AlbumController : Controller
    {
        private IAlbumDataContext _albumDataContext;

        public AlbumController()
```

```
        {
            _albumDataContext= new AlbumDataContext();
        }

        public AlbumController(IAlbumDataContext albumDataContext)
        {
            _albumDataContext = albumDataContext;
        }

        public ActionResult Index()
        {
            ViewData["Title"] = "List of Pink Floyd Albums";
            ViewData["Albums"] = _albumDataContext.GetAlbums();

            return View();
        }

        public ActionResult Individual(int id)
        {
            var album = _albumDataContext.GetAlbum(id);

            ViewData["Title"] = album.Name;
            ViewData["Album"] = album;

            return View();
        }

    }
}
```

This implementation takes only a few more lines of code but is much more testable than before. It is also more maintainable and extensible, as you see in the next sections.

Testing the Application

Now that the application has been refactored, it's possible to test the controllers in isolation, without the overhead of hitting the database for every test. The key concept of these tests is that the data context will be automatically created at runtime by the mocking framework.

In the previous chapter, you learned that mock objects have two modes: the record mode and the replay mode. In all the previous examples, you made the switch calling the method mocks.ReplayAll() when you finished recording all the expectations, and calling the method mocks.VerifyAll() when you finished exercising the SUT and verifying all the expectations. But Rhino Mocks also has another syntax to mark the beginning and the end of the two modes. This syntax uses the using statement to group all the instructions that belong to each mode.

The record mode is defined like this:

```
using(mocks.Record())
{
    //All the expectations are set here
}
```

And the replay mode (sometimes also referred to as the playback mode as a consequence of the name of the method) is:

```
using (mocks.Playback())
{
    //The exercise phase and the asserts are inside this block
}
```

In my opinion this is an easier syntax because it clearly separates the two modes and will not lead to unexpected results if you forget to call one of the two methods.

In the next Try It Out, you finally write the test for the AlbumController.

Try It Out   Testing a Controller

This example builds on the refactored code for the application that lists music albums. So, before you begin with the steps, create a new ASP.NET MVC project, click Yes when asked if you want to create a test project, and copy all the code of the previous listings in the newly created project (Album and IAlbumDataContext in the Model folder and AlbumController in the Controllers folder). Then follow these steps:

1.   Create a new test file in the test project, and call it **AlbumControllerTest.cs**.

2.   Erase all the content of the class, leaving only the class declaration.

3.   Inside the class add the two following fields:

```
private MockRepository mocks;
private IAlbumDataContext mockContext;
```

4.   Add a new method, marked with the TestInitialize attribute:

```
[TestInitialize]
public void SetupMocks()
{
    mocks = new MockRepository();
    mockContext = mocks.DynamicMock<IAlbumDataContext>();
}
```

5.   The first test will prove the correctness of the Index method of the controller:

```
[TestMethod]
public void Index_Returns_10_Albums()
{
}
```

6.   Inside this method add the code for the setup phase of the test:

```
// Arrange
List<Album> albumList = new List<Album>();
for (int i = 0; i < 10; i++)
{
    albumList.Add(new Album());
}
using(mocks.Record())
{
    Expect.Call(mockContext.GetAlbums()).Return(albumList);
```

```
    }

    AlbumController controller = new AlbumController(mockContext);
```

7. Then enter the playback mode:

```
using (mocks.Playback())
{
}
```

8. Inside the playback mode block, exercise the `Index` method and verify that it returns the expected results:

```
// Act
ActionResult result = controller.Index();

// Assert
ViewResult viewResult = result as ViewResult;
Assert.IsNotNull(viewResult, "Not a view result");

IList<Album> list = viewResult.ViewData["Albums"] as IList<Album>;
Assert.AreEqual(10, list.Count);
Assert.AreEqual(String.Empty, viewResult.ViewName);
```

9. Then add the test method that verifies the `Individual` action:

```
[TestMethod]
public void Can_Get_Specific_Album()
{
    // Arrange
    Album specificAlbum = new Album()
                                {
                                    ID = 34,
                                    Name = "The Division Bell",
                                    ReleaseYear = "1994"
                                };
    using (mocks.Record())
    {
        Expect.Call(mockContext.GetAlbum(0)).IgnoreArguments()
            .Return(specificAlbum);
    }

    AlbumController controller = new AlbumController(mockContext);

    using (mocks.Playback())
    {
        // Act
        ActionResult result = controller.Individual(0);

        // Assert
        ViewResult viewResult = result as ViewResult;
        Assert.IsNotNull(viewResult, "Not a view result");

        Assert.AreEqual("The Division Bell", viewResult.ViewData["Title"]);

        Album album = viewResult.ViewData["Album"] as Album;
        Assert.IsNotNull(album, "No Album provided");
        Assert.AreEqual("1994", album.ReleaseYear);
```

193

```
                Assert.AreEqual("The Division Bell", album.Name);
                Assert.AreEqual(34, album.ID);

                Assert.AreEqual(String.Empty, viewResult.ViewName);
            }
        }
```

10. The complete test class will look like Listing 9-6.

Listing 9-6: AlbumControllerTest

```
using System;
using System.Collections.Generic;
using System.Web.Mvc;
using Microsoft.VisualStudio.TestTools.UnitTesting;
using Rhino.Mocks;
using TestingDAL.Controllers;
using TestingDAL.Models;

namespace TestingDAL.Tests.Controllers
{
    /// <summary>
    /// Summary description for AlbumControllerTest
    /// </summary>
    [TestClass]
    public class AlbumControllerTest
    {

        private MockRepository mocks;
        private IAlbumDataContext mockContext;

        [TestInitialize]
        public void SetupMocks()
        {
            mocks = new MockRepository();
            mockContext = mocks.DynamicMock<IAlbumDataContext>();
        }


        [TestMethod]
        public void Index_Returns_10_Albums()
        {
            // Arrange
            List<Album> albumList = new List<Album>();
            for (int i = 0; i < 10; i++)
            {
                albumList.Add(new Album());
            }
            using(mocks.Record())
            {
                Expect.Call(mockContext.GetAlbums()).Return(albumList);
            }

            AlbumController controller = new AlbumController(mockContext);

            using (mocks.Playback())
```

```
        {
            // Act
            ActionResult result = controller.Index();

            // Assert
            ViewResult viewResult = result as ViewResult;
            Assert.IsNotNull(viewResult, "Not a view result");

            IList<Album> list = viewResult.ViewData["Albums"]
                as IList<Album>;
            Assert.AreEqual(10, list.Count);
            Assert.AreEqual(String.Empty,viewResult.ViewName);
        }
    }


    [TestMethod]
    public void Can_Get_Specific_Album()
    {
        // Arrange
        Album specificAlbum = new Album()
                                {
                                    ID = 34,
                                    Name = "The Division Bell",
                                    ReleaseYear = "1994"
                                };
        using (mocks.Record())
        {
            Expect.Call(mockContext.GetAlbum(0)).IgnoreArguments()
                .Return(specificAlbum);
        }

        AlbumController controller = new AlbumController(mockContext);

        using (mocks.Playback())
        {
            // Act
            ActionResult result = controller.Individual(0);

            // Assert
            ViewResult viewResult = result as ViewResult;
            Assert.IsNotNull(viewResult, "Not a view result");

            Assert.AreEqual("The Division Bell",
                viewResult.ViewData["Title"]);

            Album album = viewResult.ViewData["Album"] as Album;
            Assert.IsNotNull(album, "No Album provided");
            Assert.AreEqual("1994", album.ReleaseYear);
            Assert.AreEqual("The Division Bell", album.Name);
            Assert.AreEqual(34, album.ID);

            Assert.AreEqual(String.Empty, viewResult.ViewName);
        }
    }
}
```

11. Now run the tests and see them pass, as shown in Figure 9-2.

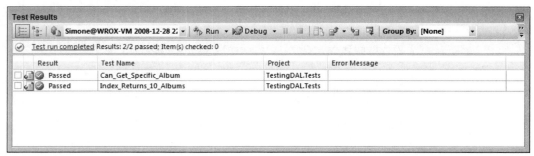

Figure 9-2

How It Works

This test uses the mocking library Rhino Mocks, as did the other tests in the chapter, so let's focus only on the new elements that are coming out in this specific sample.

At step 4, in the test initialization method, the mock object of the data context is created, asking the mocking framework to use the `IAlbumDataContext` interface:

```
mockContext = mocks.DynamicMock<IAlbumDataContext>();
```

The test you are writing wants to prove that when the database returns 10 albums, the controller populates the `ViewData` collection with a list containing 10 `Album` objects, and the view rendered is the default one (the one whose name is automatically retrieved by the name of the action). So first a list of 10 empty objects is created and then the mock object is instructed to return it as the return value for the call to the `GetAlbums` method.

```
List<Album> albumList = new List<Album>();
for (int i = 0; i < 10; i++)
{
    albumList.Add(new Album());
}
using(mocks.Record())
{
    Expect.Call(mockContext.GetAlbums()).Return(albumList);
}
```

Notice that the expectation is set inside the using code block that delimits the record mode of the mock repository. The most important line of the test method is the one that creates an instance of the controller, using the constructor that accepts the data context to use as a parameter:

```
AlbumController controller = new AlbumController(mockContext);
```

After this, the mock repository goes in playback mode, exercises the action method, and verifies the expectations. There's not much to be said about this part, because it's the same as in the other examples in this chapter. The only line worth noticing is the one that verifies the name of the view rendered:

```
Assert.AreEqual(String.Empty, viewResult.ViewName);
```

The `ViewName` is empty when the controller doesn't request any specific view to be rendered and relies on the `ActionName` at runtime to get the name of the view.

The other test method wants to prove that when the `Individual` action is called, the album titled "*The Division Bell*," released during 1994 is rendered on the screen. The expectation for this action is set in a slightly different way than the other test: Instead of specifying a specific ID as the parameter for the action, the `IgnoreArguments` method is used. This instructs the mock framework not to care about the value of the parameter, as long as the method is called.

```
Expect.Call(mockContext.GetAlbum(0)).IgnoreArguments()
    .Return(specificAlbum);
```

The rest of the test method is the same as the other one, so there is no point in repeating the same things again.

This approach to testing can be applied to almost all the actions that depend on a data access layer or any external component. The next step in the journey through testing is Test Driven Development (TDD), which you learn about in the next section.

Developing with a TDD Approach

Thanks to the design for testability in the ASP.NET MVC framework, another methodology that can be used is Test Driven Development, or, as it's usually called, TDD.

This methodology adopts an iterative approach that consists of a few phases:

1. First, the developer adds a new test that covers a new desired feature or improvement that has yet to be implemented.

2. Then the test suite is run. This ensures that the test is well designed. If the test passes, it means that the test was not written correctly, because the new feature hasn't been implemented yet.

3. The production code to implement this feature or improvement is written to make the test pass.

4. The code is then refactored to remove duplications and clean it up.

5. Tests are re-run to verify that the refactoring didn't break anything.

This process is also referred to as the TDD Mantra: "*Red, Green, Refactor*," from the colors of the icons that show the result of a test run.

This approach has some benefits over the classic "testing after coding" approach:

❑ It ensures that the developer understands the requirements before writing the code.

❑ The resulting code is inherently designed with testability in mind. It has a clear separation of concerns, low coupling (which means that modules of the application depend on interfaces and not on their implementation), and adheres to the single responsibility principle.

❏ Only the code that makes the test pass is implemented, so there is no needless complexity.

❏ It always provides 100 percent code coverage.

❏ The tests, if written using terms coming from the business/domain, also act as additional documentation of how the code works.

A lot has been written on TDD, and if you are interested in this topic, I really encourage you to read a book about Test Driven Development. In the remaining pages of this chapter, you get a feel for how to write an application using TDD.

Requirements

The first step is writing the requirements. They will be formalized in a series of tests, and then the code will be written to pass the tests and implement the application.

The requirements that you are going to implement are:

❏ If it's Christmas, the view rendered will be the StoreClosed one.

❏ When it's not Christmas, the Index view will be rendered.

Testing for Christmas Day

The first test verifies that on the day of Christmas the store is closed:

```
[TestMethod]
public void HomePage_Renders_StoreClosed_View_When_Its_Xmas()
{
    MockRepository mocks = new MockRepository();
    IDateProvider provider =
        mocks.DynamicMock<IDateProvider>();
    using (mocks.Record())
    {
        DateTime xmas = new DateTime(2008,12,25);
        SetupResult.For(provider.GetDate()).Return(xmas);
    }
    HomeController controller = new HomeController(provider);

    using (mocks.Playback())
    {

        ViewResult result = controller.Index() as ViewResult;

        Assert.IsNotNull(result, "A view has not been rendered");
        Assert.AreEqual("StoreClosed", result.ViewName);
    }
}
```

The Test Fails

You don't want to wait for Christmas to test your application. It's better to use an external provider that returns the current date: `IDateProvider`. The real production implementation will return the current date (`DateTime.Now()`), but the mock one will always return the day of Christmas.

```
namespace TDDSample.Models
{
    public interface IDateProvider
    {
        DateTime GetDate();
    }
}
```

If you now run the test, the application will not compile, because, obviously, the `HomeController` has not been implemented yet. So, because you first want the test to fail, you "fake" the `HomeController` and implement a nonworking implementation of it:

```
namespace TDDSample.Controllers
{
    public class HomeController : Controller
    {
        public ActionResult Index()
        {
            throw new NotImplementedException();
        }
    }
}
```

The Test Passes

Now that the test fails, you can write the controller action to make the test pass, which will be just:

```
namespace TDDSample.Controllers
{
    public class HomeController : Controller
    {
        public ActionResult Index()
        {
            return View("StoreClosed");
        }
    }
}
```

The test verifies that the `StoreClosed` view is rendered when it's Christmas, but nothing has been discussed yet about what to do when it's not. Therefore, to keep the code as simple as possible, it always returns `StoreClosed`.

Testing for Any Other Day

Now the second requirement leads to the following test:

```
[TestMethod]
public void HomePage_Renders_Index_View_When_Its_Not_Xmas()
```

```
    {
        MockRepository mocks = new MockRepository();
        IDateProvider provider =
            mocks.DynamicMock<IDateProvider>();
        using (mocks.Record())
        {
            DateTime xmas = new DateTime(2008, 3, 20);
            SetupResult.For(provider.GetDate()).Return(xmas);
        }
        HomeController controller = new HomeController(provider);

        using (mocks.Playback())
        {
            // Execute
            ViewResult result = controller.Index() as ViewResult;

            Assert.IsNotNull(result, "A view has not been rendered");
            Assert.AreEqual("Index", result.ViewName);
        }
    }
}
```

You repeat all the processes, run the test, and watch it fail. (The controller will still return the StoreClosed view.) (See Figure 9-3.)

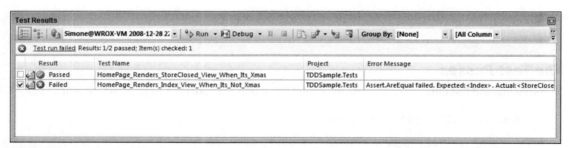

Figure 9-3

Now it's time to really implement the check for the day of Christmas:

```
namespace TDDSample.Controllers
{
    public class HomeController : Controller
    {
        private IDateProvider _provider;
        public HomeController(IDateProvider provider)
        {
            _provider = provider;
        }

        public ActionResult Index()
```

```
        {
            DateTime current = _provider.GetDate();
            if(current.Day==25 && current.Month==12)
                return View("StoreClosed");
            return View("Index");
        }
    }
}
```

Now you run all the tests and they all pass.

Testing for New Year's Day

Let's do it one more time. You want to test that on New Year's Day there is yet another view. You write the test:

```
[TestMethod]
public void HomePage_Renders_HappyNewYear_View_When_Its_NewYear()
{
    MockRepository mocks = new MockRepository();
    IDateProvider provider =
        mocks.DynamicMock<IDateProvider>();
    using (mocks.Record())
    {
        DateTime day = new DateTime(2008, 1, 1);
        SetupResult.For(provider.GetDate()).Return(day);
    }
    HomeController controller = new HomeController(provider);

    using (mocks.Playback())
    {
        // Execute
        ViewResult result = controller.Index() as ViewResult;

        Assert.IsNotNull(result, "A view has not been rendered");
        Assert.AreEqual("HappyNewYear", result.ViewName);
    }
}
```

Again, the test fails and you implement the new code that also takes New Year's Day into account:

```
public ActionResult Index()
{
    DateTime current = _provider.GetDate();
    if(current.Day==25 && current.Month==12)
        return View("StoreClosed");
    if (current.Day == 1 && current.Month == 1)
        return View("HappyNewYear");
    return View("Index");
}
```

It's Refactoring Time

Now all three tests pass, but the logic in the controller is not very sound, so you decide to remove the `if` statements in order to reduce the complexity of the method (there are currently three exit paths) and increase the readability of the method. It's refactoring time. (See Listing 9-7.)

Listing 9-7: Home Controller after the refactoring

```
using System;
using System.Collections.Specialized;
using System.Globalization;
using System.Web.Mvc;
using TDDSample.Models;

namespace TDDSample.Controllers
{
    public class HomeController : Controller
    {
        private IDateProvider _provider;
        private StringDictionary _holidayViews;

        public HomeController(IDateProvider provider)
        {
            _provider = provider;
            _holidayViews = new StringDictionary();
            _holidayViews.Add("25-12", "StoreClosed");
            _holidayViews.Add("01-01", "HappyNewYear");
        }

        public ActionResult Index()
        {
            return View(GetViewByDate(_provider.GetDate()));
        }

        private string GetViewByDate(DateTime date)
        {
            return _holidayViews [date.ToString("dd-MM",
                CultureInfo.InvariantCulture)] ?? "Index";
        }
    }
}
```

After the refactoring, all the three tests keep on passing, as shown in Figure 9-4.

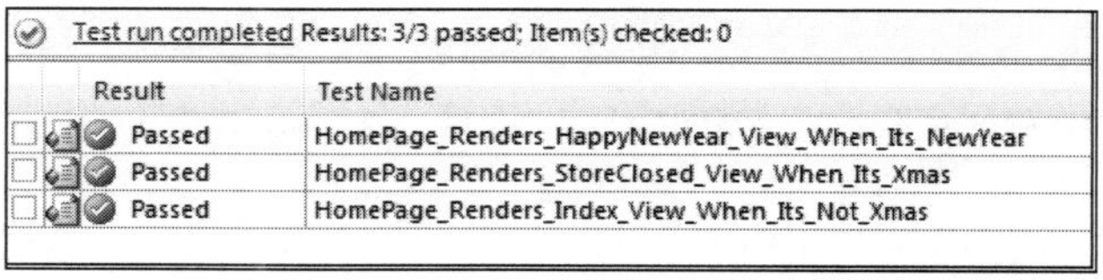

	Result	Test Name
	Passed	HomePage_Renders_HappyNewYear_View_When_Its_NewYear
	Passed	HomePage_Renders_StoreClosed_View_When_Its_Xmas
	Passed	HomePage_Renders_Index_View_When_Its_Not_Xmas

Test run completed Results: 3/3 passed; Item(s) checked: 0

Figure 9-4

The `Index` action changed from six lines of code to just one and from three exit paths to just one. Furthermore, now the code is more readable, and it is easier to add a new view for a new holiday. In a real application, you would probably have extracted the dictionary of views to an external repository that the application reads the list of holidays from. This way the controller would only act as the controller and not behave as the model.

Summary

Even if you decide not to adopt a Test Driven Development approach, testing your applications is something you should do to ensure they are easily maintainable, are well designed, and meet high-quality standards. Because testing WebForm applications was not very easy, Microsoft fully embraced these new development methodologies and designed the ASP.NET MVC framework to be test-friendly and allow the developer to easily test an application.

In this chapter, you learned:

- ❑ How to create a test project for an ASP.NET MVC application
- ❑ How to test actions
- ❑ How to verify `ActionResults`
- ❑ How to verify that an action renders the correct view or redirects to the correct action
- ❑ What the `System.Web.Abstractions` assembly is
- ❑ How to mock the `HttpContext` in order to test interaction with the `Http` runtime
- ❑ How to test routes
- ❑ How to spot when an application is not testable
- ❑ How to refactor code so that it is more testable
- ❑ How to mock a data access layer used inside a controller's actions
- ❑ Another way of switching between record and playback mode in mock objects
- ❑ How to design an application using the TDD methodology

In the following chapters, you learn about more advanced features of the ASP.NET MVC framework, starting from building a view that makes use of components. But before moving on to the next topic, take the time to test your knowledge of what you just learned in this chapter.

Exercises

For these exercises, you have the following controller action:

```
public ActionResult Index(string pageTitle, string language)
{
    ViewData["Message"] = pageTitle +" "+language.toUpperInvariant();
    if (!language.Equals("it") && !language.Equals("en"))
```

```
    {
        TempData["Language"] = language;
        return RedirectToAction("NotSupported");
    }

    return View("Index");
}
```

And the `global.asax.cs` file contains the following route registration:

```
routes.MapRoute(
    "Language",
    "{language}/{pageTitle}",
    new { language = "en",
        controller = "Home",
        action = "Index",
        pageTitle = "Home" }
);
```

1. Test that the URL /it sends the URL to the Index action in the Home controller with the title. set to "Home Page."

2. Test that the Index view is rendered when the languages it or en are supplied.

3. Add a test that verifies that the test rendered on the page is in the format "*<pagetitle>* *<LANG>*" and that if the parameters are BookList and en, the text rendered is BookList EN.

4. Verify that when someone requests a page in French the flow is redirected to the NotSupported action.

5. Expand the last test to verify also that the TempData contains the original language supplied.

Components

With ASP.NET MVC, you gain a cleaner way to separate the responsibilities of a Web application and an easier testing experience. Because it's a complete break with the traditional WebForm model, however, it lacks some of WebForms' basic features.

The feature of WebForms you are going to miss the most is server controls. How are you going to achieve the same results using ASP.NET MVC? Can it still be achieved?

In this chapter you see how to encapsulate some portions of your application in components that can be reused in many of your views.

You learn:

- ❑ How to use the server controls
- ❑ How to exploit the partial views
- ❑ How to include behaviors in your components

Before talking about how to achieve this result with ASP.NET MVC, it's important to see why using the server controls available from WebForms is not the best solution anymore.

Why Are There No Server Controls?

The traditional use of server controls won't work with ASP.NET MVC for a couple of reasons.

Reason number one: For a server control to handle its own interactions, the post operation needs to always go back to the same page where the controller has been declared. This was done by using the infamous postback concept that is not used in ASP.NET MVC.

Reason number two: The control has to manipulate things only inside its boundaries and everything that is outside must be sent back to the user as it was before. Again, this was achieved by storing all the contents of a page inside the viewstate of the page. This abstraction is also not used in ASP.NET MVC.

These two concepts have not been reintroduced in ASP.NET MVC because they hid too much of what was going on with the HTTP interaction and with the rendering of HTML. But it's indisputable that the possibility of having components that encapsulate part of UI is invaluable.

In the rest of this chapter, you learn about some possible approaches to solving this problem, starting with reusing the "old" server controls.

Server Controls

You and your company might have already invested a lot in ASP.NET, so moving to ASP.NET MVC might seem like you have to learn everything again from scratch, but that's not true.

If you are approaching ASP.NET Web application development for the first time using the MVC frame-work, this section can still provide a lot of insight regarding the differences in functionality between ASP.NET and ASP.NET MVC, even if you don't have to transfer your Web development efforts from ASP.NET WebForms to ASP.NET MVC.

First, as you have already read in the early chapters of the book, ASP.NET MVC is an alternative approach to WebForms, not a replacement. If you feel like you don't need all that separation of concerns, testability, and increased control over your page, you don't have to make the switch, and you can go on using server controls. That said, if you want to move to ASP.NET MVC, remember that it's still ASP.NET. The only things that change are the logic of how you build your application and how interactions are handled, but the foundations are still the same ones you used with C# (or VB.NET if you prefer). You also use the same core class library and the same ASP.NET features such as providers, the cache, and master pages. You read more on how to use the "old" ASP.NET features inside ASP.NET MVC in Chapter 14.

Even some server controls keep on working as before, or, kind of. Most of the server controls rely on viewstate and postback to accomplish their duties. So, as a general rule of thumb, controls will stop working as soon as they start leveraging one of these two features. This means that, for the most part, only the rendering part of controls will work.

A few other problems are related to the use of server controls built for WebForms. One is that most of them need to be included inside a `<form runat="server">` tag. This means that the hidden tag containing the viewstate will be included even if it will be not be used at all. Just adding the aforementioned form tag means that the page will contain the following HTML:

```
<form name="aspnetForm" method="post" action=""
    id="aspnetForm">
<div>
<input type="hidden" name="__VIEWSTATE"
    id="__VIEWSTATE"
    value=" /wEPDwULLTE0NjI0ODU4NThkZB9hwbPJMe89wezYKPCBZ6v4zVBQ" />
</div>
...
</form>
```

Another change is that the ID of the control will be autogenerated by the framework, and with the usual hierarchical naming convention that you are used to seeing. For example, if you add an asp:Label tag, the code will be as follows:

```
<span id="ctl00_MainContent_lbl">That's a label</span>
```

The last change is that most of the controls render HTML in a suboptimal way (with nested tables, CSS properties, and JavaScript specified directly inside the tags).

These behaviors are going against what the ASP.NET MVC is trying to accomplish, which is giving back to the developer full control over the HTML markup that is rendered.

If you still want to use WebForm server controls, because you need to reuse some of your developed work or because you need to quickly prototype something, in the next pages you see how to do it.

We don't recommend using server controls, for the three reasons you just read. You see other more MVC-friendly ways later in this chapter, and that you already saw in Chapter 6.

A Simple Form Control

One of the controls you might want to use is the `RadioButtonList`. It renders a list of radio buttons and allows you to add options in a declarative way, as shown in Figure 10-1.

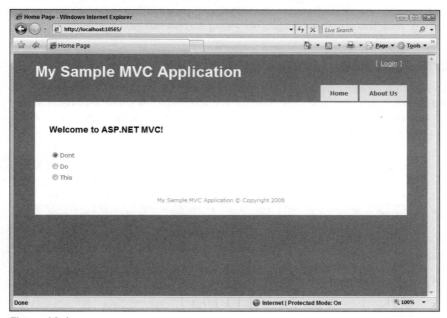

Figure 10-1

The code for this control looks like this:

```
<asp:RadioButtonList runat="server" ID="list">
    <asp:ListItem Value="0" Text="Dont" Selected="True"></asp:ListItem>
    <asp:ListItem Value="1" Text="Do"></asp:ListItem>
    <asp:ListItem Value="2" Text="This"></asp:ListItem>
</asp:RadioButtonList>
```

In order to work, it needs to be enclosed inside a `<form runat="server">` tag. But be aware that the HTML code is rendered as shown in Figure 10-2.

```
            <form name="aspnetForm" method="post" action="" id="aspnetForm">
<div>
<input type="hidden" name="__VIEWSTATE" id="__VIEWSTATE" value="/wEPDwUKMTMyMjkzMTA3MWRkBMwA3D6IsCcrERISErVrapKp+88=" />
</div>

    <h2>Welcome to ASP.NET MVC!</h2>
    <p>

        <table id="ct100_MainContent_list" border="0">
        <tr>
            <td><input id="ct100_MainContent_list_0" type="radio" name="ct100$MainContent$list" value="0" checked="checke
        </tr><tr>
            <td><input id="ct100_MainContent_list_1" type="radio" name="ct100$MainContent$list" value="1" /><label for="c
        </tr><tr>
            <td><input id="ct100_MainContent_list_2" type="radio" name="ct100$MainContent$list" value="2" /><label for="c
        </tr>
</table>


    </p>
<div>
        <input type="hidden" name="__EVENTVALIDATION" id="__EVENTVALIDATION" value="/wEWBQKgvr/NCgK60fepCgKl0fepCgKk0fepCgKqv
</div></form>
```

Figure 10-2

The `form` tag is rendered with an empty `action` attribute (because this is the index page, and the post-back goes to the same page). You could use some JavaScript to change the `action` attribute later, but this is really not recommended. One of the HTML helpers available in the MVCFutures library reaches the same goal, with less obtrusive HTML rendering and overall baggage.

Components with Rendering Only

You saw that using a server control to render a form field is not good. Let's try using something that has been thought from the beginning to only do the rendering. For example, let's consider the `TreeView` control. It renders a tree of elements and adds the JavaScript needed to expand and collapse nodes that contain subnodes. An example of this is shown in Figure 10-3.

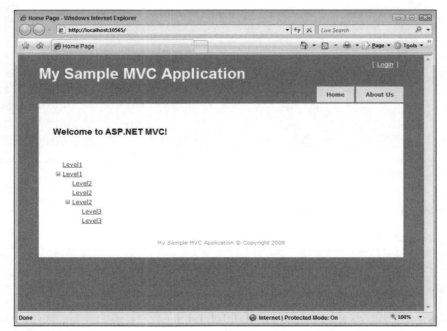

Figure 10-3

The output is fine, and it works pretty well, and if you care to specify the URLs for all the nodes, it doesn't even rely on the postbacks. The only problem left is the ugly (to say the least) HTML rendered, as shown in Figure 10-4.

Figure 10-4

Adding to the bad HTML of the `RadioButtonList`, this not only has nested tables and hard-coded styles; it also downloads images inside resource files and has all that JavaScript added at the bottom of the page.

This works, and if you don't care about all that complex HTML, this is one of the few server controls that can be still be used. But, as you read later, you have better ways to handle the collapsible/expandable tree.

Controls with Databinding

The last, and probably most frequently used (and abused), category of server controls includes `DropDownList`, `ListView`, `Repeater`, and the one-control-fits-all `GridView`. Basically, these are all the ones that render a list of data, allowing some kind of interactivity, such as sorting, paging, and editing in place.

Such controls are very useful, because they allow you to add an editable, sortable, and paging-enabled table of data with just a few lines of code:

```
<form runat="server">
<asp:GridView runat="server" ID="list"
    AllowSorting="true"
    AllowPaging="true" PageSize="3">
</asp:GridView>
</form>
```

Then you add to the `OnLoad` event these lines and do the binding of the `ViewData` model to the grid:

```
protected override void OnLoad(EventArgs e)
{
    list.DataSource = ViewData.Model;
    list.DataBind();
}
```

This control looks into the object bound to it, retrieves the column names and the values, and displays a good looking table, as shown in Figure 10-5, with links on top of each column for sorting and links at the bottom to move to the second page of data.

But (and there is always a "but" when it comes to server controls in the context of ASP.NET MVC) making the table look nice is the only thing this control does. Because the postback doesn't work, you cannot re-sort the columns or move to the next page. And to create this control, you also went against one of the conventions of the framework, which is to never put code in the code-behind (and to enforce that rule, the code-behind is not even added by Visual Studio when creating new views). That's too bad, because this time what the HTML code rendered was not as bad as in the previous examples.

But don't fear. The one-control-to-rule-them-all editable/sortable grid also can be achieved with ASP .NET MVC. You see how to do it later in this chapter.

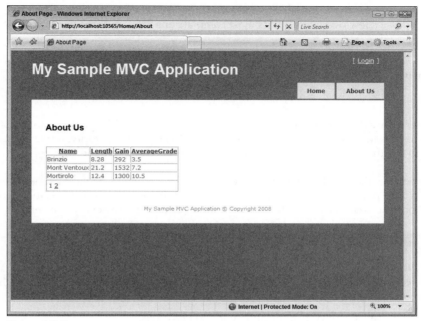

Figure 10-5

So, what are the recommended ways to componentize an ASP.NET MVC application? You have four different possible ways to do it:

❑ Using partial views

❑ Writing a custom `HtmlHelper`

❑ Rendering the result of an action

❑ Writing client-side components written in JavaScript

Let's start with partial views.

Using Partial Views

In previous chapters, you read about elements related to partial views: we introduced the `PartialViewResult` in Chapter 5 and MVC User Control in Chapter 6.

What is a partial view? Actually it is the MVC User Control we mentioned before: a small and reusable piece of the view. Its purpose is to render a portion of the view, getting the data either from the `ViewData` of the parent or by using a model object specifically passed into it. Technically speaking it's just a view, with a page fragment, whose extension, when using the default WebForm view engine, is `.ascx`.

A partial view can be easily inserted inside a view using the HTML helper method `RenderPartial`. This method has a few overloads but its most complete one takes in three parameters:

❑ `partialViewName` — The name of the partial view, without the extension

❑ `model` — The model object passed to the partial view

❑ `viewData` — The `ViewData` dictionary you want to pass into the partial view

If you specify only the view name, the `ViewData` of the parent will be passed into the partial view. If you want to pass in a model object, the `ViewData` dictionary will be empty. If you want to have both, you have to use the most complete overload and pass everything into the view.

This method uses the usual view engine to look for the partial view: So first it looks inside the same folder where the parent view is, and then in the `Shared` folder. This also means that partial views can be shared only between views rendered by the same controller or by every controller.

Try It Out   Reusing a Partial View

In this Try It Out, you apply the few concepts about partial rendering you just learned. You build a small application that renders a list of climbs in the index page, and the details of one climb plus the list of all the climbs in the details page. You do this using a partial view.

1. First, create a new Web application with no test project.

2. Then add in the `Models` folder the three classes shown in Listings 10-1, 10-2, and 10-3.

Listing 10-1: Climb.cs

```
namespace PartialRendering.Models
{
    public class Climb
    {
        public string Name { get; set; }
        public DifficutlyLevel Difficutly { get; set; }
        public double Length { get; set; }
        public double Gain { get; set; }
        public double AverageGrade { get; set; }
    }

    public enum DifficutlyLevel
    {
        Easy,
        Medium,
        Hard,
        Strenuous,
        ArmstrongLevel
    }
}
```

Listing 10-2: ClimbList.cs

```
using System.Collections.Generic;

namespace PartialRendering.Models
{
    public class ClimbList : List<Climb>
    {
        public ClimbList()
        {
        }

        public ClimbList(IEnumerable<Climb> collection) : base(collection)
        {
        }
    }
}
```

Listing 10-3: ClimbRepository.cs

```
using System.Linq;

namespace PartialRendering.Models
{
    public class ClimbRepository
    {
        private ClimbList _climbs;
        public ClimbRepository()
        {
            _climbs = new ClimbList();

            _climbs.Add(new Climb()
                        {
                            Name = "Passo dello Stelvio",
                            Length = 24.3,
                            AverageGrade = 7.4,
                            Gain = 1808,
                            Difficutly = DifficutlyLevel.Hard
                        }
                );

            _climbs.Add(new Climb()
                        {
                            Name = "Mont Ventoux",
                            Length = 21.2,
                            AverageGrade = 7.2,
                            Gain = 1532,
                            Difficutly = DifficutlyLevel.Medium
                        }
                );

            _climbs.Add(new Climb()
                        {
```

Continued

213

Listing 10-3: ClimbRepository.cs *(continued)*

```
                                    Name = "Mortirolo",
                                    Length = 12.4,
                                    AverageGrade = 10.5,
                                    Gain = 1300,
                                    Difficutly = DifficutlyLevel.Strenuous
                        }
                );

            _climbs.Add(new Climb()
                        {
                            Name = "Mount Washington",
                            Length = 12.4,
                            AverageGrade = 11.5,
                            Gain = 1420,
                            Difficutly = DifficutlyLevel.ArmstrongLevel
                        }
                );

            _climbs.Add(new Climb()
                        {
                            Name = "Brinzio",
                            Length = 8.28,
                            AverageGrade = 3.5,
                            Gain = 292,
                            Difficutly = DifficutlyLevel.Easy
                        }
                );
        }

        public ClimbList GetTopClimbs()
        {
            var query = from c in _climbs
                        orderby r.Name
                        select c;
            return new ClimbList(query);
        }

        public Climb GetClimb(string name)
        {
            var climb = from c in _climbs
                        where c.Name == name
                        select c;
            return climb.First();
        }
    }
}
```

3. Add a partial view (MVC User Control) in the Views\Home folder, name it **_allclimbs.ascx**, and populate it with the code in Listing 10-4.

Listing 10-4: _allclimbs partial view

```
<%@ Import Namespace="PartialRendering.Models"%>
<%@ Control Language="C#"
Inherits="System.Web.Mvc.ViewUserControl<ClimbList>" %>

<div style="border: 1px solid red">
<ul>
<% foreach (var climb in Model)
    { %>
        <li><%= Html.ActionLink(climb.Name,"Climb",
                    new { name = climb.Name }) %></li>
    <% } %>
    </ul>
</div>
```

4. Clear the Index method inside the Controllers\HomeController.cs file, and replace it with this:

```
public ActionResult Index()
{
    ViewData["Message"] = "Welcome to the climb archive on ASP.NET MVC!";

    var _repository = new ClimbRepository();
    var climbs = _repository.GetTopClimbs();

    ViewData["Climbs"] = climbs;

    return View();
}
```

5. Always, inside the same class, add the Climb method:

```
public ActionResult Climb(string name)
{
    var _repository = new ClimbRepository();

    Climb climb = _repository.GetClimb(name);

    var climbs = _repository.GetTopClimbs();
    ViewData["Climbs"] = climbs;
    return View(climb);
}
```

6. Add the call to the partial view inside the Views\Home\Index.aspx view (replacing the default content with this):

```
<asp:Content ID="indexContent" ContentPlaceHolderID="MainContent"
    runat="server">
    <h2><%= Html.Encode(ViewData["Message"]) %></h2>
    <div>
    <% Html.RenderPartial("_allclimbs", ViewData["Climbs"]); %>
    </div>
</asp:Content>
```

7. Then create a new view, named **Climb.aspx**, with the code in Listing 10-5.

Listing 10-5: Climb.aspx

```
<%@ Page Title="" Language="C#" MasterPageFile="~/Views/Shared/Site.Master"
Inherits="System.Web.Mvc.ViewPage<Climb>" %>
<%@ Import Namespace="PartialRendering.Models"%>

<asp:Content ID="Content1" ContentPlaceHolderID="TitleContent" runat="server">
    Climb
</asp:Content>

<asp:Content ID="Content2" ContentPlaceHolderID="MainContent" runat="server">

    <h2><%= Model.Name %></h2>
    <div style="float:left; width:80%">
        Name: <%= Model.Name %><br />
        Length: <%= Model.Length %> Km<br />
        Altitude Gain: <%= Model.Gain %> m<br />
        Average Grade: <%= Model.AverageGrade %>%<br />
    </div>
    <div style="float:right; width:20%">
        <% Html.RenderPartial("_allclimbs", ViewData["Climbs"]); %>
    </div>
    <br class="clear" />
</asp:Content>
```

8. And then, to have the controller work, add any other rule, as a new routing rule, inside the Global.asax file:

```
routes.MapRoute(
    "Climb",
    "Home/Climb/{name}",
    new { controller = "Home", action = "Climb" }
);
```

How It Works

The code for the model part of the application (step 2) declares a model class, its strongly-typed collection, and the repository with two methods: one that gets the list of all climbs and one that retrieves a climb based on the name. For simplicity, it uses in-memory storage instead of a real DB. It is initialized in the constructor of the repository.

The partial view (added in step 3) is named with a leading "_" (underscore) because most of the view engines around use this convention and we think it helps make spotting partial from "full" views easier than merely using the different extensions. Apart from this, the partial view is just like any other strongly-typed view; it loops through the Model object, which is a ClimbList, and renders an unordered list that links to the Climb action passing the name of the climb to display.

The Index action calls the repository, retrieves the list of climbs, and stores it inside the ViewData dictionary. The Climb action looks for a specific climb and sends it as a model to the view, but because the view rendered must also show the list of climbs, this action also has to retrieve the list of climbs.

Finally both the views, `Index.aspx` and `Climb.aspx`, are including the partial view so that they need to repeat the same code that loops through the climbs:

```
<% Html.RenderPartial("_allclimbs", ViewData["Climbs"]); %>
```

Notice that the model object is specified without casting it to its real type because it will be passed to the partial view, which, in this case, is a strongly-typed one.

The last step of the example adds a new rule to the routing table: The default rule has an `id` parameter, but in this context it's better to name it "name."

Figure 10-6 shows the page with the details of a single climb.

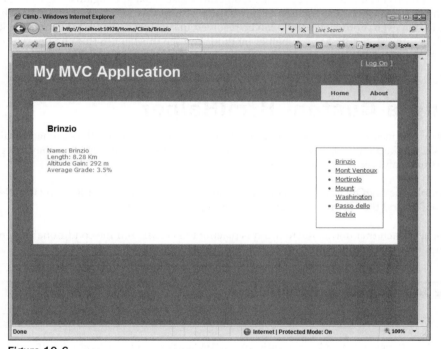

Figure 10-6

You just saw how to use a partial view to encapsulate a piece of HTML that must be rendered in many views. Another example of this is the ubiquitous LogOnUserControl that is added by the default project template. In that case the control is placed inside the `Shared` folder because it is used by all the views. It also differs from the one that renders the list of climbs because it doesn't display anything that comes from the `ViewData`, but it only uses objects that come from the current HTTP context.

```
<%
    if (Request.IsAuthenticated) {
%>
        Welcome <b><%= Html.Encode(Page.User.Identity.Name) %></b>!
```

```
                [ <%= Html.ActionLink("Log Off", "LogOff", "Account") %> ]
    <%
        }
        else {
    %>
                [ <%= Html.ActionLink("Log On", "LogOn", "Account") %> ]
    <%
        }
    %>
```

Before moving to the next possibility, we want you to notice one thing: Both the actions have to retrieve the list of climbs even if their "core" task is something else. That goes against the concept of not repeating portions of code and single responsibility. Things can get worse if this list of climbs must be repeated in even more views. This can be resolved in two ways: the first is by using a kind of sub-controller, with the `RenderAction` helper method. You see this later in this chapter. The other is using `ActionFilters`, which is covered in the next chapter.

Writing a Custom HtmlHelper

In Chapter 6, you saw that custom HTML helpers can be used to reduce the spaghetti coding feel of mixing HTML markup with C# code. If applied to more general-purpose problems, they can provide a way to encapsulate and reuse portions of code.

For example, the LogOnUserControl of the previous example can be rebuilt as an HtmlHelper, because it's so generic and the HTML it renders never changes.

The first approach that may come to mind is placing the HTML and the conditional statements inside the compiled method in a simple method, as in Listing 10-6.

Listing 10-6: LoginControl html helper

```csharp
public static string LoginControl(this HtmlHelper htmlHelper)
{
    HttpContextBase ctx = htmlHelper.ViewContext.HttpContext;
    if (ctx.Request.IsAuthenticated)
    {
        string logoffLink = htmlHelper.ActionLink("Log Off",
            "LogOff", "Account");
        return String.Format("Welcome <b>{0}</b>! [{1}]",
            htmlHelper.Encode(ctx.User.Identity.Name), logoffLink);
    }
    else
    {
        string logonLink = htmlHelper.ActionLink("Log On",
            "LogOn", "Account");
        return String.Format("[{0}]", logonLink);
    }
}
```

But what if you want to change the name of the actions that handle the login and the logout procedure? And what if you want to change the salutation or you don't like the square brackets ("[ ]") that contain the links? The designer cannot change the HTML because it's hard-coded inside the compiled code. How can you reach the same flexibility, while keeping the same level of encapsulation of rendering logic?

A good practice is to allow the caller to specify all the variable parameters in the method call and to provide some overloads for when you don't need all that power.

Try It Out   LoginStatus Helper

In this Try It Out, you implement a helper that encapsulates the creation of the login status text but keeps the same flexibility of the LoginUserControl partial view.

1. Create the usual ASP.NET MVC Web application without a testing project, and create, inside a new folder named Helpers, a class file named LoginExtensions.cs.

2. Next, create the definition of the class:

```
namespace LoginHelper.Helpers
{
    public static class LoginExtensions
    {

    }
}
```

3. Then, inside the class, place the following method:

```
public static string LoginStatus(this HtmlHelper htmlHelper,
    string loginText, string logoutText,
    string loginAction, string logoutAction,
    string loginController, string logoutController,
    string loginFormat, string logoutFormat)
{
    HttpContextBase ctx = htmlHelper.ViewContext.HttpContext;
    if(ctx.Request.IsAuthenticated)
    {
        string logoutLink = htmlHelper.ActionLink(logoutText,
            logoutAction, logoutController);
        return String.Format(logoutFormat,
            htmlHelper.Encode(ctx.User.Identity.Name), logoutLink);
    }
    else
    {
        string loginLink = htmlHelper.ActionLink(loginText,
            loginAction, loginController);
        return String.Format(loginFormat, loginLink);
    }
}
```

4. Then add the following overloads:

```
public static string LoginStatus(this HtmlHelper htmlHelper)
{
    return htmlHelper.LoginStatus("Log On","Log Off");
}

public static string LoginStatus(this HtmlHelper htmlHelper,
    string loginText, string logoutText)
{
    return htmlHelper.LoginStatus(loginText, logoutText,
        "LogOn", "LogOff");
}

public static string LoginStatus(this HtmlHelper htmlHelper,
    string loginText, string logoutText,
    string loginAction, string logoutAction)
{
    return htmlHelper.LoginStatus(loginText, logoutText,
        loginAction, logoutAction,
        "Account");
}

public static string LoginStatus(this HtmlHelper htmlHelper,
    string loginText, string logoutText,
    string loginAction, string logoutAction,
    string controller)
{
    return htmlHelper.LoginStatus(loginText, logoutText,
        loginAction, logoutAction,
        controller, controller);
}

public static string LoginStatus(this HtmlHelper htmlHelper,
    string loginText, string logoutText,
    string loginAction, string logoutAction,
    string loginController, string logoutController)
{
    return htmlHelper.LoginStatus(loginText, logoutText,
        loginAction, logoutAction,
        loginController, logoutController,
        "[{0}]", "Welcome <b>{0}</b>! [{1}]");
}
```

5. Finally, open the Views\Shared\Site.master file and replace the call to
Html.RenderPartial("LoginUserControl") with:

```
<%= Html.LoginStatus()%>
```

How It Works

In step 2 you added the class definition. Because the HTML helper is an extension method, the class that contains it must be a static class. Notice that the name ends with Extensions. This is a good convention to keep, because it helps to identify the class as just a container of the extensions method.

Then in step 3 you added the method that writes the login status. Unlike the one in Listing 10-6, this one renders the HTML taking the text, action names, and controllers from the values supplied as parameters of the method. With such a method, if you wanted to specify all the parameters, you should write:

```
Html.LoginStatus("Log On", "Log Off",
        "LogOn", "LogOff",
        "Account", "Account",
        "[{0}]", "Welcome <b>{0}</b>! [{1}]");
```

But you don't want your view designer to specify all the parameters at all times, because most of them are likely to be the default ones, especially the format. One way to solve this problem, while you wait for the optional parameters that will arrive with the next version of the C# compiler, is to create some method overloads. They start from the one with zero parameters and go up till the most complete one. And each overload calls the next one after supplying default values for the parameters (step 4).

This solution is now more flexible, because you can request the login status with all the default values, or you can specify a custom text for the links or a custom action method, a custom controller, and finally a custom format string to render all the text.

This approach still has a small problem: What if you just want to specify the format of the logout text? With this solution, you cannot, because the format is the last parameter, so you have to specify all the others before it anyway. Another possible approach to solve the problem of the many method parameters is to use a class that contains all the values and rely on the object initializer syntax of C# 3.0.

To do this, you first create the class LoginStatusParameters, which contains all the defaults for the method, and the accessors for each one of the parameters:

```
public class LoginStatusParameters
{
    public LoginStatusParameters()
    {
        LoginText = "Log On";
        LogoutText = "Log Of";
        LoginAction = "LogOn";
        LogoutAction = "LogOff";
        LoginController = LogoutController = "Account";
        LoginFormat = "[{0}]";
        LogoutFormat = "Welcome <b>{0}</b>! [{1}]";
    }

    public string LoginText { get; set; }
    public string LogoutText { get; set; }
    public string LoginAction { get; set; }
    public string LogoutAction { get; set; }
    public string LoginController { get; set; }
    public string LogoutController { get; set; }
    public string LoginFormat { get; set; }
    public string LogoutFormat { get; set; }
}
```

Then you add another overload for the helper method that takes the values out of the class and calls the method's overload that does the real job.

```
public static string LoginStatus(this HtmlHelper htmlHelper,
    LoginStatusParameters parameters)
{
```

```
    return htmlHelper.LoginStatus(
        parameters.LoginText, parameters.LogoutText,
        parameters.LoginAction, parameters.LogoutAction,
        parameters.LoginController, parameters.LogoutController,
        parameters.LoginFormat, parameters.LogoutFormat);
}
```

Now you can just change the format of the logout status by using the object initializer syntax. For example, you can greet the user in Italian:

```
<%= Html.LoginStatus(
    new LoginStatusParameters
        {
            LogoutFormat = "Benvenuto <b>{0}</b>! [{1}]"
        }
) %>
```

These first three options are all you can get using the core ASP.NET MVC framework. Two more options are available from the integration with Microsoft-endorsed external libraries.

Rendering the Result of an Action

The three approaches discussed so far allow you only to encapsulate the UI of the views, but they are not the most straightforward solutions if they rely on specific data. Another possible approach consists of rendering the result of an action directly. This is possible through the use of `RenderAction`, an HTML helper available inside the MVCFutures.

Given an action name (with option parameters), the `RenderAction` method instantiates the controller, calls the action method, and renders its result inside the parent view.

Let's see how the same result obtained with the partial view can be obtained using the `RenderAction` method.

The first step of the process consists of creating the action that retrieves the data that has to be displayed:

```
public ActionResult _AllClimbs()
{
    var _repository = new ClimbRepository();
    var climbs = _repository.GetTopClimbs();
    return PartialView(climbs);
}
```

Then the partial view that renders the result is just the same as the one used at the beginning of the chapter inside the Try It Out example about the partial views.

```
<%@ Import Namespace="RenderAction.Models"%>
<%@ Control Language="C#"
```

```
Inherits="System.Web.Mvc.ViewUserControl<ClimbList>" %>

<div style="border: 1px solid red">
<ul>
<% foreach (var climb in Model)
    { %>
        <li><%= Html.ActionLink(climb.Name,"Climb",
                new { name = climb.Name }) %></li>
    <% } %>
    </ul>
</div>
```

And finally, this partial view is put inside the parent view just by calling the RenderAction method.

```
<asp:Content ID="indexContent" ContentPlaceHolderID="MainContent"
    runat="server">
    <h2><%= Html.Encode(ViewData["Message"]) %></h2>
    <div>
    <% Html.RenderAction("_AllClimbs"); %>
    </div>
</asp:Content>
```

This method can also be called by specifying the controller (by default, the same controller that requested the rendering of the parent view is used) and option parameters. Additionally, the method features the generic-enabled version, which provides compile-time check and IntelliSense support:

```
<% Html.RenderAction<HomeController>(c => c._AllClimbs()); %>
```

Unlike the partial view example, where each action also had to retrieve the data needed by the partial view, with this approach the actions only do what they were meant to do.

Even if this approach allows you not to repeat code, it breaks one of the concepts behind the MVC pattern: the "dumb" view. This can become a problem, because the view knows too much about how the controller is structured and what each action does, so it can become a maintainability issue in the future.

None of the approaches enumerated so far provides a solution for the editable/sortable grid and all the controls that need to handle their own interactions in isolation from the rest of the Web page. This is briefly introduced in the next section.

Writing Client-Side Components with JavaScript

This approach is probably the most powerful one, but it is also the most difficult to achieve. It consists of using JavaScript to call external Web services in order to manipulate data without triggering a reload of the page.

The editable/sortable/paging-enabled grid and the collapsible/expandable treeview can both be achieved by using JavaScript and calls to Web services.

Achieving this result can be compared to creating a custom server control in the traditional WebForm model. For this reason, the process for creating such components is not covered in this book, but it is something that is covered in the more advanced Wrox book about ASP.NET MVC: *Professional ASP.NET MVC 1.0*, by Rob Conery, Phil Haack, Scott Hanselman, and Scott Guthrie by Wrox, 2009.

Nevertheless, in Chapter 12 you read about how to use JavaScript together with ASP.NET MVC for less complicated things.

When to Use Which Option

All these available options make choosing which approach to follow more difficult, so here we try to give you some guidelines that can help you in making the decision:

❑   **Server Controls** — Never use them, unless you want to do a quick prototype.

❑   **Partial Views** — Use them when HTML must be easily modified by a designer or without recompiling the application. It is also a good practice to use the partial view when there are more than just a few lines of HTML and there are not many conditional statements.

❑   **HtmlHelper** — Custom HTML helpers are best suited for situations where there is a lot of conditional rendering and when the HTML doesn't change often (as opposed to partial views, HTML helpers are compiled). Another usage scenario is when the HTML cannot be changed because it contains a hook used by JavaScript libraries. And finally, HTML helpers are probably the only possible solution if you want to encapsulate the component in an external library that can be reused by more than one project.

❑   **RenderAction** — This option is a powerful one, because it directly renders into a page the result of a controller's action. It makes things easier when it comes to components that also contain behaviors, but it can leave a bad taste because it breaks the purity of the MVC pattern. That's one of the reasons why it's not part of the core framework but is part of the MVCFutures library, which means that this method can be included in the core framework, but also that it could be discontinued in the future. And finally, it makes testing a bit more complicated, because it's called directly from the view.

❑   **Javascript and AJAX** — This is probably the most powerful solution. It contains rendering behaviors, and everything is achieved via JavaSript and AJAX calls. The disadvantage is that it must be developed with JavaScript, and not everyone is skilled in that.

Summary

The removal of the postback and the viewstate also means that the server controls of the WebForm approach cannot work anymore. But ASP.NET MVC introduces new ways of encapsulating portions of your Web pages, some of which are even more in line with new trends in Web development.

Even though creating effective components is an advanced topic that is outside the scope of this book, in this chapter you read about the possible approaches that can be used to componentize your application and which scenarios best suit each of the options.

You also learned:

❏ Why it's not possible to use all server controls in all their aspects

❏ What happens if you put a server control in an ASP.NET MVC application

❏ Which server components work and which do not

❏ How to use databinding in ASP.NET MVC

❏ How to use partial views

❏ How you can use custom HTML helpers as a way to encapsulate the UI and reuse it across different projects

❏ How to create an HTML helper with optional parameters

❏ What the `RenderAction` method is and how it allows the encapsulation of UI and logic

❏ Why the `RenderAction` approach breaks the "purity" of the MVC pattern

❏ Why the only way to create a truly interactive and complex component is through the use of JavaScript

❏ What the advantages and disadvantages of each approach are

❏ When to choose which option

In the next chapter you read about another form of encapsulation, this time not about the view, but about logic. This will solve one of the problems of the partial view approach.

Before moving to the next chapter, take a few moments to complete the exercises.

Exercises

1. Play around with various WebForms' server controls and try to find a replacement for each of them.

2. In the partial view section, you saw that all the actions have to retrieve the data needed by the partial view. Even without using the `RenderAction` method or the `ActionFilters` (which are explained in the next chapter), there is a way to reduce the code repetition inside the actions. Try to find a way to do this.

3. Write an HTML helper that renders the list of climbs.

Action Filters

In the previous chapter, you learned how view components and HTML helpers can encapsulate the rendering of the UI, but they cannot be used to encapsulate the process logic. This can be achieved using action filters.

In this chapter, you learn:

- ❑ What you can use action filters for
- ❑ What kinds of filters are available
- ❑ Which core filters are available inside the framework
- ❑ How to write custom filters

What Is an Action Filter?

An action filter is a custom attribute that you can decorate action methods or controllers with. The framework will then execute the logic inside the action filter before or after the execution of the action method.

You probably already have seen a filter being used. It's in the `HomeController` that is added by the project template.

```
[HandleError]
public class HomeController : Controller
```

By being applied directly to the class definition, the filter is automatically applied to all the actions of the controller. This in particular instructs the ASP.NET MVC framework to handle the errors that might happen inside the actions, using the logic that is defined inside the filter.

If you wanted to handle the errors only for a specific action, you would annotate the method directly:

```
[HandleError]
public ActionResult Index()
```

In a typical ASP.NET MVC application, an action is responsible for handling user-initiated requests. The user clicks a button or submits a form, the request is sent and routed through the routing logic to a specific controller, and finally a specific action is executed. But at times you might want to execute some code before the action, for example to verify that the current user is allowed to perform an operation, or to add logging or error handling. One way you could address these scenarios is by writing private methods to encapsulate the logic and call them at the beginning (or at the end) of each action method, but this is repetitive (you have to call the method in each action), error prone, and not really well encapsulated or reusable. That's why action filters exist. They allow you to encapsulate this logic in external components and use it in a nice, clean, declarative way.

Another scenario that can be made easier using filters is the situation in which you have a master page that shows data, for example the name of the user that is logged in or a list of the latest news. For this to happen you have to retrieve the data needed inside the controller and add it to the ViewData collection. However, doing this inside all the actions is not a good separation of concerns. Why should an action that shows the list of comments for a blog post also retrieve the latest posts of the blog? With an action filter you can encapsulate the logic that gets the latest posts and pass it to the master page without touching the code of each single action.

Types of Filters

To implement a filter, all you have to do is create a class that inherits from FilterAttribute or one of its specializations based on the type of filter you want to implement.

Four types of filters exist:

❑   Authorization filters

❑   Exception filters

❑   Action filters

❑   Result filters

Authorization filters are executed before an action, to verify whether the current user is allowed to perform the operation requested. Besides inheriting from FilterAttribute, they also implement the IAuthorizationFilter interface (whose only method is OnAuthorization). You could write your own authorization filter, but for most scenarios you can just use the Authorize filter that is provided by the framework. You read more about how to use this filter in a later section in this chapter.

Exception filters are used to handle exceptions that are not caught inside the action method. Like the previous type, they extend the base filter class and implement the IExceptionFilter (and its only method, OnException). The framework already provides a configurable action, HandleError, that covers almost every error handling scenario. But again, if you don't like how it's done, you can implement your own. You also learn about the HandleError action later in this chapter.

The last, and probably most important, types of filters are the action and result filters. They inherit from the base class ActionFilterAttribute, which allows you to specify methods that will be executed before and after the action method is executed and before and after the result is executed. Unlike the other two types of filters, which mainly exist to support the framework itself, action filters exist to allow you to build your own filters with your custom logic. The framework already comes with one implementation of this kind of action: OutputCache.

> You have probably noticed that the name "action filters" is used both for the filters as a whole and for a specific type of filter. This is a bit confusing, but that's the name Microsoft gave to these components. Once you understand the distinction between the two, the context of a situation generally makes clear whether you are talking about a specific action filter or all action filters collectively.

In the next section, you learn how to use the five core filters that are provided with the framework.

The Core Filters

The framework includes five filters that address some very common scenarios, including error handling, authorization, security, and caching. Let's see each of them in detail.

The HandleError Filter

Usually, when an exception happens during the processing of a Web request, the end-user gets the infamous "Yellow page of death," as shown in Figure 11-1, or, if the developer took the time to enable custom error messages, a static HTML page.

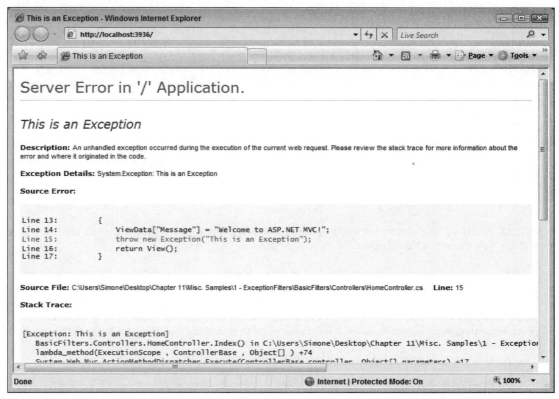

Figure 11-1

With the `HandleError` filter, the framework will render a custom message whenever an uncaught exception happens inside an action as shown in Figure 11-2.

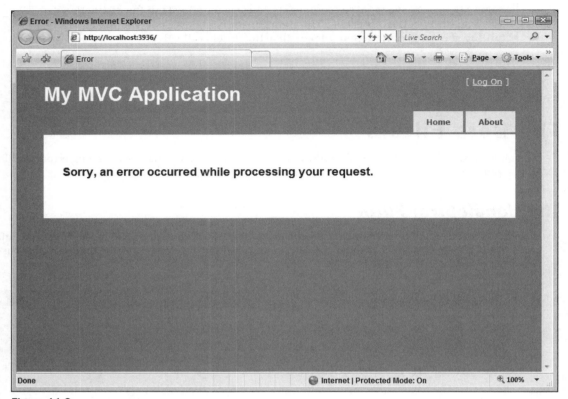

Figure 11-2

To enable this exception handling, you need to perform two steps. First, you have to enable custom errors inside the `Web.config` file:

```
<customErrors mode="On"></customErrors>
```

Second, you need to annotate the action or the controller class with the `HandleError` attribute, as you already saw earlier in this chapter.

By default, the `HandleError` filter will render a view named `Error`. Following the usual pattern for searching the view to render, the view engine will first search inside the folder with the views for the current controller and then search in the `Shared` folder. This allows you to provide different error messages based on the current controller. But this filter allows an even finer tuning of the messages to display: You can specify which view and even master page to render, based on the type of the exception.

```
[HandleError (Order = 1, ExceptionType = typeof(SqlException),
    View = "DatabaseError")]
[HandleError (Order = 2, ExceptionType = typeof(IOException),
    View = "FileSystemError")]
```

```
[HandleError (Order = 3)]
public class ProblematicController : Controller
```

The preceding class definition says that a SqlException will be handled by showing the view name DatabaseError, the IOException using the FileSystemError view, and for all the other exceptions, the default Error view will be fine.

> **For this to work, remember to specify the order in which you want the exceptions evaluated, using the Order property; the one with the lowest number is evaluated first. If you don't specify a value, the default will be –1, and filters with the same order are applied in an undetermined order. These rules are valid also for all the types of filters you see later in the chapter.**

It is good to remember that, unlike the standard custom error, which renders a static HTML page, this filter renders a view, so it can contain a bit of logic. To allow you to customize the error message even more, the ViewData that is passed to the error view is strongly typed and the model is an instance of HandleErrorInfo. This contains all the information regarding where the error comes from: the action name, the controller name, and the original exception.

For debugging, it is useful to have the complete stack trace and history of the exception (in case there is an exception with many inner exceptions). But you don't want to give all these details to the possible malicious user. Listing 11-1 shows the complete stack of exceptions when running on the local machine, or just the friendly message when accessed by a remote browser.

Listing 11-1: Error message view

```
<h2>
    Sorry, an error occurred while processing your request.
</h2>

<% if (ViewContext.HttpContext.Request.IsLocal) { %>
    <h3>
        Action details:
    </h3>
    <div>
    <ul>
    <li><b>Controller name</b>: <%= Model.ControllerName %></li>
    <li><b>Action name</b>: <%= Model.ActionName %></li>
    </ul>
    </div>
    <h3>
        Exception details:
    </h3>
    <div style="overflow: auto;">
        <%
            Stack<Exception> exceptions = new Stack<Exception>();
            for (Exception ex = Model.Exception;
                ex != null;
                ex = ex.InnerException) {
```

Continued

Listing 11-1: Error message view *(continued)*

```
                exceptions.Push(ex);
            }
            foreach (Exception ex in exceptions) {
        %>
                <div>
                    <b><%= Html.Encode(ex.GetType().FullName)%></b>:
                        <%= Html.Encode(ex.Message)%>
                </div>
                <div>
                    <pre style="font-size: medium;">
                        <%= Html.Encode(ex.StackTrace)%></pre>
                </div>
        <%
            }
        %>
        </div>
    <% } %>
```

This code checks whether the request is local (`Request.IsLocal`). Then it loops through all the inner exceptions and renders them on the screen together with the name of the controller and action where the exception originated. (See Figure 11-3.)

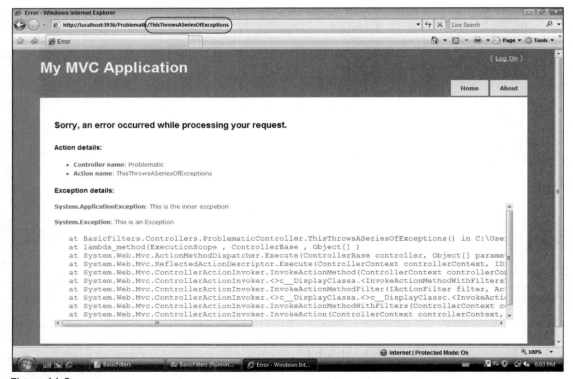

Figure 11-3

232

One last thing that is worth noticing is that, instead of redirecting the user to the error page and changing the URL in the browser's address bar, the URL remains the same with the `HandleError` filter (see the circled area in Figure 11-3). So the end-user can just click the Refresh button on the browser to try to reload the page.

The Authorize Filter

Another very common scenario for which the ASP.NET MVC framework provides a standard solution is authorization. This feature is provided by the `Authorize` filter, which leverages the already existing ASP.NET Membership Provider to verify whether the current user is authenticated and authorized to execute the action. If not, it redirects the user to the login URL, as shown in Figure 11-4, that has been specified in the membership section of the `Web.config` file.

To make the creation of an authentication subsystem for your application easy, the project template creates the login and registration actions for you. It saves the data in the standard ASP.NET membership provider database and does all the error checking and validation, so all you need to do is adapt them to fit your needs and graphic layout.

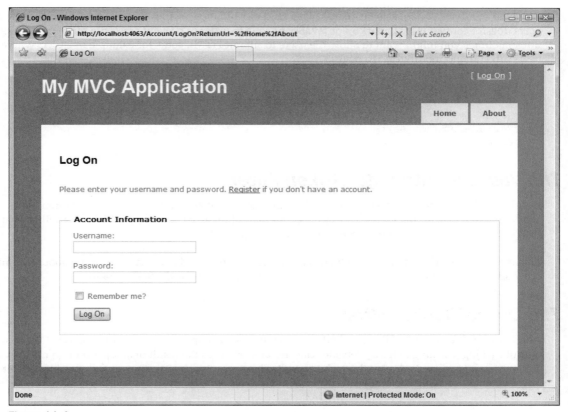

Figure 11-4

Once the underlying authorization system is set up correctly, all you need to do to restrict the access to an action is to annotate it with the `Authorize` attribute:

```
[Authorize]
public ActionResult About() { … }
```

This code means that the `About` action can be executed only if the user has been authenticated. Optionally, you can specify the users or the roles that are authorized to execute the action.

```
[Authorize (Users ="Simone, Keyvan")]
public ActionResult About() { … }
[Authorize (Roles = "Admin")]
public ActionResult About() { … }
```

This topic is covered in much more detail in Chapter 15, which is all about authentication and authorization.

The ValidateInput Filter

ASP.NET validates all requests by default. This kind of validation verifies that all input submitted by the users doesn't contain HTML markup or JavaScript code in order to prevent cross-site scripting attacks. But sometimes you might want to allow the users to submit HTML code, for example in a CMS where users can add and modify HTML pages.

To disable validation for a specific action, all you have to do is decorate that action with the `ValidateInput` attribute and set the only parameter to `false` (true is the default behavior):

```
[ValidateInput(false)]
public ActionResult UpdatePage()
```

The ValidateAntiForgeryToken Filter

Another authorization filter that is part of the framework is the `ValidateAntiForgeryToken` filter. Working together with the `AntiForgeryToken` method of the `HtmlHelper`, it addresses another security problem of Web applications: cross-site request forgery attacks.

This is an advanced security topic, which is not covered in this book. You can read more about this and other advanced topics in *Professional ASP.NET MVC 1.0* (Wrox, ISBN 978-0-470-38461-9).

The OutputCache Filter

Another useful feature of ASP.NET WebForms that has been adapted to work with ASP.NET MVC is output caching. Caching helps a Web site scale, because it stores the result of an operation in memory so that subsequent requests receive the cached result. This saves time and resources; for example, not hitting a database can help the application sustain a higher volume of traffic.

In ASP.NET MVC, you can cache the result of an action by annotating the method with the `OutputCache` attribute:

```
[OutputCache(Duration = 60, VaryByParam = "none")]
public ActionResult Index()
{
    ViewData["Message"] = "Now it's " + DateTime.Now.ToLongTimeString();
    return View();
}
```

The preceding code instructs the ASP.NET runtime to cache the result for 60 seconds, no matter what the parameters of the request are. This means that for one minute the page will show the same time.

Figure 11-5 is just a figure, but if you reload the page, you'll see the same time for one minute. You can try this yourself with the sample code for this chapter.

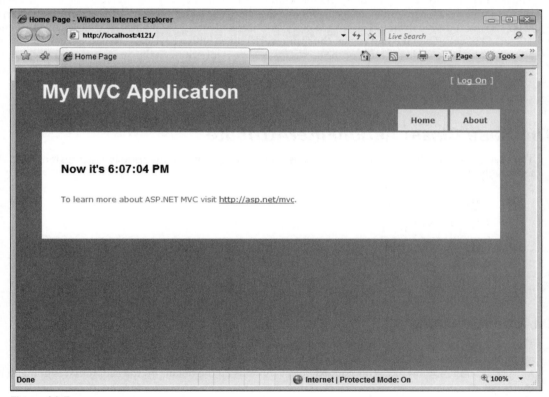

Figure 11-5

As with classic ASP.NET WebForms, you can specify many other parameters, such as `VaryByHeader`, which will create a different version of the result based on the various values of an HTTP header. You can also specify a `SqlDependency` to invalidate the cache when data in a table in the database changes.

To avoid repeating all the attributes over and over in all your actions, you can specify them inside the `Web.config` file in the section about caching profiles and then simply use the profile name in the attributes used to decorate the actions. This saves you time and also makes maintenance easy because it centralizes all the management of the caching configuration.

Because the main topic of this chapter is the action filter, you read more about how to set up caching, using profiles, and `SqlDependency` in Chapter 14, which is about the WebForm features that you can still use in ASP.NET MVC Web applications.

In the next section, you learn how to create a custom action filter.

Building a Custom Action Filter

You learned how to use the action filters that come with the framework, but the real power of the action filter is unleashed when you build a custom one to solve your own problems. This is done by creating a class, having it derive from `FilterAttribute`, and implementing the interfaces `IActionFilter` and `IResultFilter`. To make that easier, the framework comes with a base class that does that for you, so all you really have to do for most of the scenarios is have it inherit from the `ActionFilterAttribute` base class, like this:

```
public class LoggingFilterAttribute: ActionFilterAttribute
```

The Base Class: ActionFilterAttribute

The base class is an abstract class that contains four methods you can override in your custom filter. The four methods are:

❑   `OnActionExecuting`

❑   `OnActionExecuted`

❑   `OnResultExecuting`

❑   `OnResultExecuted`

To make a filter, you have to override at least one of them.

OnActionExecuting

This method will be executed before any action method marked with the filter attribute. All the methods of the base call take a context object as a parameter. In this case, the object is an instance of `ActionExecutingContext`. This context object contains all the details on the action that is going to be executed:

❑   `ActionParameters` — A list of all the parameters that are passed to the action

❑ ActionDescriptor — Contains all the information about the action and controller that are going to be executed, like the action's name, the controller's name, and the type (these last two are inside a property called ControllerDescriptor).

❑ Controller — The instance of the controller that contains the action that is going to be executed

❑ RouteData — All the low-level details on the route that brought the request to the action (all the URL parameters and data tokens)

❑ HttpContext — The current execution context of the HTTP request

There is also another property that allows you to cancel the execution of the action by specifying directly the ActionResult to execute. It is called Result, and you see an example of its usage later in the chapter.

```
public override void OnActionExecuting(ActionExecutingContext filterContext)
{
    // Filter implementation here
}
```

OnActionExecuted

The other action-related method is OnActionExecuted, which the framework calls when the action method has finished. It takes a parameter of type ActionExecutedContext, which contains four parameters in common with the ActionExecutingContext object, ActionDescriptor, Controller, RouteData, and HttpContext, but adds a few more:

❑ Exception — This contains a possible exception that might have been thrown during the execution of the action method.

❑ ExceptionHandled — This is a Boolean that says whether the exception specified in the Exception property has already been handled. (This is relevant only when more than one filter is executed after the same action method.)

❑ Result — This is the action result that has been returned by the action method.

If an exception is provided and your filter handles it, the ExceptionHandled property must be set to true to inform the other filters in the chain of this. This is necessary because the exception will be passed to all the other filters even when it has been handled. This allows, for example, a logging filter to log the exception even after it has been handled.

Another property is Canceled. Its value is true when another filter canceled the execution of the action method by setting the Result property inside the OnActionExecuting method. If the filter relies on the action being executed to perform its logic, it's important to verify that it's false before doing anything.

If your custom filter needs to, it can change the action result returned by the action by changing the Result property.

```
public override void OnActionExecuted(ActionExecutedContext filterContext)
{
    // Filter implementation here
}
```

OnResultExecuting

In addition to the action-related methods there are other methods that surround the execution of the action result. The `OnResultExecuting` method is called by the framework before the `ActionResult` object returned by the action method is invoked. It receives as a parameter an object of type `ResultExecutingContext`, which, besides the standard properties of the other context objects (`Controller`, `HttpContext`, and `RouteData`), contains a reference to the action result that is going to be executed in the property named `Result`. There is also a `Cancel` property that allows the filter to stop the execution of the action result.

```
public override void OnResultExecuting(ResultExecutingContext filterContext)
{
    // Filter implementation here
}
```

OnResultExecuted

The last method is `OnResultExecuted`. It is called after the action result has been executed. It receives as a parameter a `ResultExecutedContext` object, which contains the same properties as `ActionExecutedContext`. The only difference is that you cannot set the `Result` property, because it has already finished executing. But exception handling and the `Canceled` properties act the same way as in the other context.

```
public override void OnResultExecuted(ResultExecutedContext filterContext)
{
    // Filter implementation here
}
```

Try It Out   **Implementing a Logging Filter**

When it comes to action filters and aspect-oriented programming, the *"Hello World!"* example is logging. In this Try It Out, you implement a filter that logs the execution and appends the message at the end of the HTML page.

1. After having created an MVC Web application project, create a folder named `Actions` and add a new class inside it, named `LoggingFilterAttribute.cs`.

2. Make the class inherit from `ActionFilterAttribute`:

```
public class LoggingFilterAttribute: ActionFilterAttribute
```

3. Add a local field to store the logging message throughout the flow of the operations:

```
private string _logMessage = string.Empty;
```

4. Add the `OnActionExecuting` method:

```
public override void OnActionExecuting(ActionExecutingContext filterContext)
{
    string message = String.Format(
        "Executing {0}.{1} with {2} parameters<br>",
        filterContext.ActionDescriptor.ControllerDescriptor.ControllerName,
        filterContext.ActionDescriptor.ActionName,
        filterContext.ActionParameters.Count);

    _logMessage = message;
}
```

5. Add the `OnActionExecuted` method:

```
public override void OnActionExecuted(ActionExecutedContext filterContext)
{
    string message = String.Format(
        "Finished executing action {0}.{1} with result {2}<br>",
        filterContext.ActionDescriptor.ControllerDescriptor.ControllerName,
        filterContext.ActionDescriptor.ActionName,
        filterContext.Result.GetType().Name);

    _logMessage = _logMessage + message;
}
```

6. Add the `OnResultExecuting` method:

```
public override void OnResultExecuting(ResultExecutingContext filterContext)
{
    string message = String.Format(
        "Starting to execute result {0}<br>",
        filterContext.Result.GetType().Name);

    _logMessage = _logMessage + message;
}
```

7. Add the `OnResultExecuted` method:

```
public override void OnResultExecuted(ResultExecutedContext filterContext)
{
    string message = String.Format(
        "Finished executing {0}<br>",
        filterContext.Result.GetType().Name);

    filterContext.HttpContext.Response.Output.WriteLine(
        "<div class=\"trace page\">" + _logMessage + message + "</div>");
}
```

8. Annotate the action with the custom action filter attribute:

```
[LoggingFilter]
public ActionResult Index()
```

9. Add a CSS class to the style sheet `Content\Style.css`:

```
.trace
{
    padding: 30px 30px 15px 30px;
    background-color: #fff;
}
```

10. Run the Web site, browse to `/Home/Index`, and you'll see a logging message at the bottom of the page, as shown in Figure 11-6.

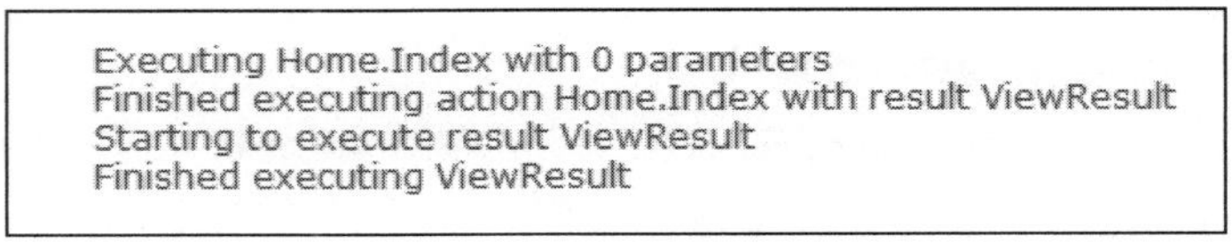

```
Executing Home.Index with 0 parameters
Finished executing action Home.Index with result ViewResult
Starting to execute result ViewResult
Finished executing ViewResult
```

Figure 11-6

How It Works

Congratulations! You have just created an action filter that makes use of all four possible methods, shares data among them, and finally adds text to the response stream. To append the logging message, you needed to share the message between the method's calls, via a private field local to the filter instance, and this is what was done at step 3. This is possible because a filter is instantiated just once per request. All the methods are called on the same instance, and it doesn't have threading synchronization issues, because different requests will not share the same instance.

Then, all four methods read inside the various contexts to collect information on what it is going to be executed or what has already been executed. For example, in the `OnActionExecuting` method you retrieve the action and the controller that are going to be executed by looking into the `ActionDescriptor` property:

```
filterContext.ActionDescriptor.ControllerDescriptor.ControllerName,
filterContext.ActionDescriptor.ActionName,
```

In `OnActionExecuted`, you get the action that has been returned by the action, using the `Result` property:

```
filterContext.Result
```

An interesting thing to point out is what has been done in step 7, inside the `OnResultExecuted` method: The filter appends to the output stream the messages that have been collected during the processing of the request:

```
filterContext.HttpContext.Response.Output.WriteLine(...);
```

The `Output` property is the text writer that writes to the `Http` stream, so by appending a line to it, you are appending some text to the HTML page that will be rendered.

To enable the logging filter, you just needed to decorate the actions with an attribute. Notice that the name of the class is `LoggingFilterAttribute`, but the attribute applied to the method is `LoggingFilter`. That's because the framework design guidelines say that all the classes that implement an attribute must have a name that ends with `Attribute`, so it's not necessary to specify the full name:

```
[LoggingFilter]
public ActionResult Index()
```

Controller-Scoped Filters

Implementing filters as attributes is fine if you want to reuse the logic in many controllers or even in different projects, but if you want to apply a filter to a specific controller, you can do it in a more lightweight fashion by implementing the methods directly inside the controller.

For example, if you want to add to the `ViewData` collection a property named `Title` but don't want to write it inside all the actions of the controller, you could just override the `OnActionExecuted` method, as shown in Listing 11-2.

Listing 11-2: Controller scoped filter

```
namespace ControllerSpecific.Controllers
{
    public class HomeController : Controller
    {
        public ActionResult Index()
        {
            ViewData["Title"] = "Home Page";
            ViewData["Message"] = "Welcome to ASP.NET MVC!";

            return View();
        }

        public ActionResult About()
        {
            ViewData["Title"] = "About Page";

            return View();
        }

        protected override void OnActionExecuted(
            ActionExecutedContext filterContext)
        {
            ViewResult result = filterContext.Result as ViewResult;
            if(result!=null)
            {
                string title = (string)result.ViewData["Title"];
                if (!String.IsNullOrEmpty(title))
                    title = "Home - " + title;
                else
                    title = "Home";
                result.ViewData["Title"] = title;
            }
            base.OnActionExecuted(filterContext);
        }
    }
}
```

If you access any of the actions of this controller, you will see that the title of the page will now always start with Home even if no attribute has been applied to the actions or to the controller class. (See Figure 11-7.)

241

Figure 11-7

The same is valid also for the other three methods of the action filter base class, and even for the methods of the two other types of filters: `OnException` to override the exception handling and `OnAuthorization` for the authorization filter.

The Filter Execution Order

You can specify the order of execution of the filters, which can be applied at the class and method levels. You also know that you can create controller-specific filters without using any attribute. These factors alone make determining the order of execution difficult, but things can get even more complicated. The controller might derive from a base controller, and it can have its own filter attributes as well.

To help you understand the ordering of filter execution, there is the notion of *scope*. A scope is where the action filter has been declared, either at the class level, at the action level, as an override of the methods inside the controller, in the base class, or in the derived class.

The order of execution is the following:

1. First executed are all the filters defined by overriding `OnActionExecuting` and `OnActionExecuted` inside the controller.

2. Then all the attribute-defined filters are ordered, using the value of the `Order` property. If no order is specified, –1 is used as value for the filter. In the same scope, there cannot be more than one filter with the same order.

3. If filters defined in different scopes have the same order, the ones defined at type level will be executed before the ones defined at action level.

It's better to see how the order of execution is applied for real, using a handy action filter that writes a message to the trace log, as shown here in Listing 11-3.

Listing 11-3: Trace filter

```
[AttributeUsage(
    AttributeTargets.Method | AttributeTargets.Class,
    AllowMultiple = true)]
public class TraceFilterAttribute: ActionFilterAttribute
{
    public string Message { get; set; }

    public override void OnActionExecuting(
```

```
        ActionExecutingContext filterContext)
    {
        filterContext.HttpContext.Trace.Write(
            "Trace Filter",
            String.Format("TraceFilter.OnActionExecuting: Order {0}, {1}",
            Order, Message)
            );
    }

    public override void OnActionExecuted(
        ActionExecutedContext filterContext)
    {
        filterContext.HttpContext.Trace.Write(
            "Trace Filter",
            String.Format("TraceFilter.OnActionExecuted: Order {0}, {1}",
            Order, Message)
            );
    }
}
```

To test the order of execution, you need all the possible scenarios:

- ❏ Controller-level defined methods
- ❏ Type-level defined filters
- ❏ Action-level defined filters
- ❏ A controller that derives from a base controller
- ❏ More than one filter per scope

First, shown in Listing 11-4, is the base controller with two filters per scope.

Listing 11-4: Base controller

```
[TraceFilter(Order = 1, Message = "CONTROLLER - MyBaseController")]
[TraceFilter(Order = 2, Message = "CONTROLLER - MyBaseController")]
public class MyBaseController : Controller
{

    [TraceFilter(Order = 2, Message = "ACTION - MyBaseController.Index")]
    [TraceFilter(Order = 1, Message = "ACTION - MyBaseController.Index")]
    public virtual ActionResult Index()
    {
        return View("FilterTracing");
    }
}
```

Then, as in Listing 11-5, you have the derived controller with two filters per scope and the implementation of the OnActionExecuting and OnActionExecuted methods.

Listing 11-5: Derived controller

```
[TraceFilter(Order = 2, Message = "CONTROLLER - MyDerivedController")]
[TraceFilter(Order = 1, Message = "CONTROLLER - MyDerivedController")]
public class MyDerivedController : MyBaseController
{
    [TraceFilter(Order = 1, Message = "ACTION - MyDerivedController.Index")]
    [TraceFilter(Order = 2, Message = "ACTION - MyDerivedController.Index")]
    public override ActionResult Index()
    {
        HttpContext.Trace.Write(
            "Trace Filter",
            String.Format("MyDerivedController.Index ACTION")
            );
        return View("FilterTracing");
    }

    protected override void OnActionExecuting(
        ActionExecutingContext filterContext)
    {
        filterContext.HttpContext.Trace.Write(
            "Trace Filter",
            String.Format(
                "MyDerivedController.OnActionExecuting: VIRTUAL METHOD")
            );
    }

    protected override void OnActionExecuted(
        ActionExecutedContext filterContext)
    {
        filterContext.HttpContext.Trace.Write(
            "Trace Filter",
            String.Format(
                "MyDerivedController.OnActionExecuting: VIRTUAL METHOD")
            );
    }
}
```

To see the results, you have to enable tracing, by setting `Trace="true"` inside the `Page` directive of the view that will be displayed and by adding the following line in the `Web.config`:

```
<trace enabled="true" />
```

When executed, the resulting trace message will be the one shown in Figure 11-8.

As you can see in Figure 11-8, all the action filters with `order = 1` are executed first. Then, among the filters with same order, the ones defined at controller level are executed followed by those at the action level. In the figure, the ones in the derived controller are executed before the ones in the base controller, but because this order is not deterministic in either situation, this order can be different.

Also, notice that the order of execution of OnActionExecuted is symmetric to OnActionExecuting. That way, the most "important" filter can always change the outcome of the action by setting the ActionResult property of the context.

Trace Information		
Category Message	**From First(s)**	**From Last(s)**
Trace Filter MyDerivedController.OnActionExecuting: VIRTUAL METHOD		
Trace Filter TraceFilter.OnActionExecuting: Order 1, CONTROLLER - MyDerivedController	0.00209887010779303	0.002099
Trace Filter TraceFilter.OnActionExecuting: Order 1, CONTROLLER - MyBaseController	0.00247713047328641	0.000378
Trace Filter TraceFilter.OnActionExecuting: Order 1, ACTION - MyDerivedController.Index	0.00601054044578291	0.003533
Trace Filter TraceFilter.OnActionExecuting: Order 1, ACTION - MyBaseController.Index	0.00626392460494281	0.000253
Trace Filter TraceFilter.OnActionExecuting: Order 2, CONTROLLER - MyDerivedController	0.00658267503272206	0.000324
Trace Filter TraceFilter.OnActionExecuting: Order 2, CONTROLLER - MyBaseController	0.00679471832313884	0.000206
Trace Filter TraceFilter.OnActionExecuting: Order 2, ACTION - MyDerivedController.Index	0.00699809612674237	0.000203
Trace Filter TraceFilter.OnActionExecuting: Order 2, ACTION - MyBaseController.Index	0.00720315012103494	0.000205
Trace Filter MyDerivedController.Index ACTION	0.0129248270380733	0.005722
Trace Filter TraceFilter.OnActionExecuted: Order 2, ACTION - MyBaseController.Index	0.0145060335880678	0.001581
Trace Filter TraceFilter.OnActionExecuted: Order 2, ACTION - MyDerivedController.Index	0.0147691955262471	0.000263
Trace Filter TraceFilter.OnActionExecuted: Order 2, CONTROLLER - MyBaseController	0.0149787193623771	0.000210
Trace Filter TraceFilter.OnActionExecuted: Order 2, CONTROLLER - MyDerivedController	0.0151837733566696	0.000205
Trace Filter TraceFilter.OnActionExecuted: Order 1, ACTION - MyBaseController.Index	0.0153977670346371	0.000214
Trace Filter TraceFilter.OnActionExecuted: Order 1, ACTION - MyDerivedController.Index	0.0156014242033555	0.000204
Trace Filter TraceFilter.OnActionExecuted: Order 1, CONTROLLER - MyBaseController	0.0158534115369411	0.000252
Trace Filter TraceFilter.OnActionExecuted: Order 1, CONTROLLER - MyDerivedController	0.0160618179126118	0.000208
Trace Filter MyDerivedController.OnActionExecuted: VIRTUAL METHOD	0.0170468593075377	0.000985

Figure 11-8

Using Action Filters

Now that you know how an action filter is implemented and executed, you might wonder how you can use all that power. In the following section, you see some possible ways you can use action filters.

Canceling the Execution of an Action

One first possible scenario is canceling the execution of an action (for example, if some precondition is not met). Imagine a checkout process where you cannot enter your billing and shipping info if you don't provide the payment details first.

To achieve this, you have to implement the OnActionExecuting method of the filter and set the Result property of the context.

In the next Try It Out, you implement a simplified checkout process to test out this scenario.

Try It Out   Canceling an Action

In this example, you see how to use the Result property to cancel the execution of an action.

1.   Create a new ASP.NET MVC Web application project, and say no to the testing project.

2.   Create a new controller in the file CheckOutController.cs that defines the actions and the workflow, as shown in Listing 11-6.

Listing 11-6: CheckOutController

```
namespace CancelSample.Controllers
{
    public class CheckOutController : Controller
    {
        [RequiredStep(FlowStart = true)]
        public ActionResult Confirm()
        {
            //Collect information on the order
            return View();
        }

        [RequiredStep (PreviousStep = "Confirm")]
        public ActionResult ExecuteOrder()
        {
            //Process the order
            return RedirectToAction("ThankYou");
        }

        [RequiredStep(PreviousStep = "ExecuteOrder")]
        public ActionResult ThankYou()
        {
            return View();
        }
    }
}
```

3. Now define the action filter in the `RequiredStepAttribute.cs` file as shown in Listing 11-7.

Listing 11-7: RequiredStepAttribute

```
namespace CancelSample
{
    public class RequiredStepAttribute: ActionFilterAttribute
    {
        public string PreviousStep { get; set; }
        public bool FlowStart { get; set; }

        public RequiredStepAttribute()
        {
            FlowStart = false;
        }

        public override void OnActionExecuting(
            ActionExecutingContext filterContext)
        {
            if (FlowStart)
                return;
            string previousStep =
                filterContext.Controller.TempData["PreviousStep"] as string;

            if(!String.IsNullOrEmpty(previousStep))
            {
                if (!previousStep.Equals(PreviousStep))
```

```
                            filterContext.Result = new ViewResult()
                                            {
                                                ViewName = "FlowError"
                                            };
            }
            else
            {
                filterContext.Result = new ViewResult()
                                    {
                                        ViewName = "FlowError"
                                    };
            }
        }

        public override void OnActionExecuted(
            ActionExecutedContext filterContext)
        {
            filterContext.Controller.TempData["PreviousStep"] =
                filterContext.ActionDescriptor.ActionName;
        }
    }
}
```

4. Finally, create the three views as content view pages with the usual `Site.Master` master page, as shown in Listing 11-8.

Listing 11-8: The three views

Here is the code for `\Views\CheckOut\Confirm.aspx`:

```
<%@ Page Title="" Language="C#" MasterPageFile="~/Views/Shared/Site.Master"
    Inherits="System.Web.Mvc.ViewPage" %>

<asp:Content ID="Content1" ContentPlaceHolderID="TitleContent" runat="server">
    Confirm
</asp:Content>

<asp:Content ID="Content2" ContentPlaceHolderID="MainContent" runat="server">

    <h2>Confirm</h2>
    <div>
    Are all the information correct?<br />
    <%= Html.ActionLink("OK", "ExecuteOrder")%>
    </div>

</asp:Content>
```

Here is the code for `\Views\CheckOut\ThankYou.aspx`:

```
<%@ Page Title="" Language="C#" MasterPageFile="~/Views/Shared/Site.Master"
 Inherits="System.Web.Mvc.ViewPage" %>

<asp:Content ID="Content1" ContentPlaceHolderID="TitleContent" runat="server">
```

Continued

Listing 11-8: The three views *(continued)*

```
        ThankYou
</asp:Content>

<asp:Content ID="Content2" ContentPlaceHolderID="MainContent" runat="server">
    <h2>Thank you for your order</h2>
</asp:Content>
```

Here is the code for \Views\CheckOut\FlowError.aspx:

```
<%@ Page Title="" Language="C#" MasterPageFile="~/Views/Shared/Site.Master"
    Inherits="System.Web.Mvc.ViewPage" %>

<asp:Content ID="Content1" ContentPlaceHolderID="TitleContent" runat="server">
    FlowError
</asp:Content>

<asp:Content ID="Content2" ContentPlaceHolderID="MainContent" runat="server">
    <h2>You are trying to hack into the flow.</h2>
</asp:Content>
```

5. Now, run the application, browse to /CheckOut/Confirm, and click OK. You'll go to the page that thanks you for the order.

6. If you instead try to execute the action that processes the order, CheckOut/ExecuteOrder, you'll see the FlowError view page.

How It Works

You just developed a very easy implementation of a Web workflow that has the following pipeline:

1. The Confirm action is the one that shows all the information on the order and renders the links that the user clicks to confirm or go back and edit the details.

2. The ExecuteOrder action processes the order.

3. Finally, the ThankYou page is rendered after the order has been processed.

This workflow is defined by using the custom RequiredStep attribute, which marks an action as required and allows the developer to specify the previous step in the workflow. To specify that the ExecuteOrder action can only be accessed if the user comes from the Confirm page, you have to use the following syntax:

```
[RequiredStep (PreviousStep = "Confirm")]
public ActionResult ExecuteOrder() { ... }
```

The custom action filter implements the two action-related methods:

❑   OnActionExecuted — After the action has been executed, the name of the action is stored in TempData.

❑   OnActionExecuting — If the action is not the first step and if the name of the previous step is different from the one specified with the attribute, the execution of the action is canceled and the action result is changed to display an error view.

Canceling the action and changing the action result is done by setting the `Result` property of the context:

```
filterContext.Result = new ViewResult()
                       {
                              ViewName = "FlowError"
                       };
```

When you access the `Confirm` action, the `PreviousStep` value in the `TempData` is set; when you then click OK, the flow goes to `ExecuteOrder`. At this point, the action filter confirms that the value stored in the `TempData` (the name of the previous action) is the same as in the required previous step and lets the flow go on.

When you try to go directly to the `ExecuteOrder` action, the action filter sees that it's not the first step of the flow and that there is no previous step stored in `TempData`, so it stops the execution of the action and renders the `FlowError` view.

Adding More Data for the View

Another scenario in which action filters are useful is when the view you are going to render either is included in a master page or contains some partial views that need their own data.

Supplying Data to a Master Page

The first, simple scenario is when you want to declaratively set the footer of the page in a situation that is similar to the one that is provided by the ASP.NET MVC project template: All the views are included in a master page, and the footer of the page is set into the master page.

```
<div id="footer"><%= Html.Encode(ViewData["Footer"]) %></div>
```

Setting the footer in every single action is pretty boring and error prone:

```
ViewData["Footer"] = "Sample Wrox Application";
```

A less boring and more declarative way of doing this, shown in Listing 11-9, is to use a custom action filter that implements only the `OnActionExecuted` method and adds the `Footer` key to the `ViewData` collection.

Listing 11-9: FooterFilterAttribute

```
namespace Footer
{
    public class FooterFilterAttribute: ActionFilterAttribute
    {
        public String Footer { get; set; }

        public override void OnActionExecuted(
            ActionExecutedContext filterContext)
        {
            ViewResult result = filterContext.Result as ViewResult;
```

Continued

Listing 11-9: FooterFilterAttribute *(continued)*

```
            if(result!=null)
                result.ViewData["Footer"] = Footer;
        }
    }
}
```

With this action filter, you can now define the footer of the view with an attribute, which is easier to read and less repetitive:

```
[FooterFilter(Footer = "Sample Wrox Application - About Page")]
public ActionResult About()
{
    return View();
}
```

Generating Data for a Partial View

In Chapter 10, you saw that one of the ways to encapsulate a portion of a view is to use a partial view. But if the partial view is reused in many other views, there could be a problem: All the actions must generate the data needed by the partial view. To avoid repeating the same code in all the actions, you can encapsulate the data retrieval process by using an action filter.

The concepts behind this process are no different from the ones you have already learned:

❑   Partial views (which you learned about in the previous chapter)

❑   The OnActionExecuted method of action filters

❑   The ubiquitous ViewData collection

In the next Try It Out, you build an application that uses the three aforementioned concepts.

Try It Out   **Action Filter for PartialView**

In this example, you develop a sample blog page with the category's list implemented as a partial view.

1.   Start by creating a new ASP.NET MVC application without the unit-testing project.

2.   In the Models folder, add a class file named BlogPage.cs with the code shown in Listing 11-10.

Listing 11-10: The View Model object

```
using System.Collections.Generic;

namespace PartialViewSample.Models
{
    public class BlogPage
    {
        public IList<Post> Posts { get; set; }
        public IList<Category> Categories { get; set; }
    }

    public class Category
```

```
    {
        public string Name { get; set; }

        public static IList<Category> Create10Categories(
            IList<Category> categories)
        {
            if (categories == null)
                categories = new List<Category>();
            for (int i = 0; i < 10; i++)
            {
                categories.Add(new Category(){Name = "Category "+ i});
            }
            return categories;
        }
    }

    public class Post
    {
        public int Id { get; set; }
        public string Title { get; set; }
        public string Body { get; set; }
    }
}
```

3. Next, clear the content of the `Controllers\HomeController.cs` file, and add the code from Listing 11-11. (Don't worry about any error messages you might get; they will be fixed in the next step.)

Listing 11-11: HomeController

```
using System.Collections.Generic;
using System.Web.Mvc;
using PartialViewSample.Actions;
using PartialViewSample.Models;

namespace PartialViewSample.Controllers
{
    [HandleError]
    public class HomeController : Controller
    {
        [AddCategoriesFilter]
        public ActionResult Index()
        {
            BlogPage page = new BlogPage();
            page.Posts = new List<Post>();
            for (int i = 1; i <= 10; i++)
            {
                page.Posts.Add(new Post()
                              {
                                  Id = i,
                                  Title = "Title " + i,
                                  Body = GetBigBody(i)
                              });
```

Continued

Listing 11-11: HomeController *(continued)*

```
        }

        return View(page);
    }

    [AddCategoriesFilter]
    public ActionResult Post(int id)
    {
        ViewData["Title"] = "Post Title "+ id;

        BlogPage page = new BlogPage();
        page.Posts = new List<Post>();
        page.Posts.Add(new Post() {
            Title = "Title "+ id,
            Body = GetBigBody(id)
            });
        return View(page);
    }

    private static string GetBigBody(int i)
    {
        string bigBody = string.Empty;
        for (int j = 0; j < 30; j++)
        {
            bigBody += " Body " + i;
        }
        return bigBody;
    }
    }
}
```

4. Add the action from Listing 11-12 in the file named `AddCategoriesFilterAttribute.cs` inside the `Actions` folder.

Listing 11-12: The Action filter

```
using System.Web.Mvc;
using PartialViewSample.Models;

namespace PartialViewSample.Actions
{
    public class AddCategoriesFilterAttribute: ActionFilterAttribute
    {
        public override void OnActionExecuted(
            ActionExecutedContext filterContext)
        {
            if (!filterContext.Canceled)
            {
                ViewResult result = filterContext.Result as ViewResult;
                if(result!=null)
                {
                    BlogPage page = result.ViewData.Model as BlogPage;
                    if(page!=null)
```

```
                    {
                        page.Categories = Category.Create10Categories(
                            page.Categories);
                    }
                }
            }
        }
    }
}
```

5. Finally, add the view pages, as shown in Listings 11-13, 11-14, and 11-15.

Listing 11-13: Index view

```
<%@ Page Language="C#" MasterPageFile="~/Views/Shared/Site.Master"
Inherits="System.Web.Mvc.ViewPage<BlogPage>" %>
<%@ Import Namespace="PartialViewSample.Models"%>

<asp:Content ID="indexTitle" ContentPlaceHolderID="TitleContent" runat="server">
    Home Page
</asp:Content>

<asp:Content ID="indexContent" ContentPlaceHolderID="MainContent" runat="server">
    <div style="float:right; width:80%">
    <% foreach (var post in Model.Posts)
    { %>
        <h3><%= Html.ActionLink(post.Title,"post",
            new {id = post.Id}) %></h3>
        <p><%=post.Body%></p>
    <% } %>
    </div>
    <div style="float:left; width:20%">
    <% Html.RenderPartial("Categories", Model.Categories); %>
    </div>
    <br class="clear" />
</asp:Content>
```

Listing 11-14: Post view

```
<%@ Page Language="C#" MasterPageFile="~/Views/Shared/Site.Master"
Inherits="System.Web.Mvc.ViewPage<BlogPage>" %>
<%@ Import Namespace="PartialViewSample.Models"%>

<asp:Content ID="Content1" ContentPlaceHolderID="TitleContent" runat="server">
        <%= ViewData["Title"] %>
</asp:Content>

<asp:Content ID="Content1" ContentPlaceHolderID="MainContent" runat="server">
<div style="float:left; width:80%">
        <h2><%= Model.Posts[0].Title%></h2>
        <p><%= Model.Posts[0].Body%></p>
</div>
<div style="float:right; width:20%">
```

Continued

253

Listing 11-14: Post view *(continued)*

```
<% Html.RenderPartial("Categories", Model.Categories); %>
</div>
<br class="clear" />
</asp:Content>
```

Listing 11-15: Categories partial view

```
<%@ Control Language="C#"
Inherits="System.Web.Mvc.ViewUserControl<IList<Category>>" %>
<%@ Import Namespace="PartialViewSample.Models"%>

<div style="border: 1px solid red">
<ul>
<% foreach (var category in Model)
    { %>
        <li><%= category.Name %></li>
    <% } %>
    </ul>
</div>
```

6. Now compile and run the code. The home page opens with the list of all posts on the right and categories on the left, as shown in Figure 11-9.

7. Click a title to see the post on the left and categories on the right.

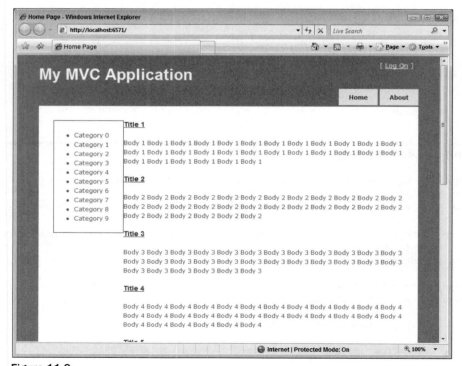

Figure 11-9

How It Works

This example involved a little bit of environmental code, so in this section you read about only the important things to remember about this usage scenario and not about all the rest of code.

In step 3, you created the controller with two actions: one that retrieves the list of posts and the other that gets the post by ID (in the example, they don't actually go to the database but just build the objects themselves, using some helper functions to reduce code duplication). Notice that the two actions don't do anything about categories. Notice also that these two methods are annotated with the AddCategoriesFilter attribute.

Step 4 is where the action filter is coded. First, the OnActionExecuted method verifies whether some other action filter canceled the execution because there is no point in augmenting the ViewData if no view is going to be rendered. This is done by checking the Canceled property of the context. Then some more checks are done to verify that everything is the way you expect it to be (it accesses the custom presentation object with the Model property of the ViewData), and finally the list of categories is retrieved and added to the object that is sent to the view.

Among the many lines of code added during step 5, focus on the HTML helper that renders the partial view:

```
Html.RenderPartial("Categories", Model.Categories);
```

You already read about partial views in the previous chapter, but now you are using this helper method to provide to the control the object that was created by the action filter. In this case, the object supplied becomes the Model property in the partial view.

Summary

Even if ASP.NET MVC removes the concepts of Web controls and user controls, you can still componentize the logic of your application by using action filters. Through them you can push the separation of concerns principle even further, and take out from your actions anything that is not specific to them and that could be reused also by other actions in other controllers.

In this chapter, you learned:

❑ How to use the four types of filters: authorization filters, exception filters, action filters, and result filters. The framework itself comes with a standard filter for each of these four categories.

❑ How to handle exceptions in a centralized way, using the HandleError attribute

❑ How you can still cache portions of your pages, using the OutputCache filter

❑ How to implement your own custom action filters

❑ How to write controller-scoped filters

❑ How to work with the tricky order of execution of filters

❑ How you cancel the execution of an action with an action filter

❑ How you supply data to a partial view without repeating yourself in all the actions used to render the view

Remember, don't over-engineer your application. First, write the logic in the action, and move it in an action filter only if it needs to be reused somewhere else or if that logic isn't sound inside the action.

In the next chapter, you learn to use AJAX inside an ASP.NET MVC view, but before moving on please take a moment to test the knowledge you acquired in this chapter by doing the following exercises.

Exercises

1. Start with an easy exercise: How would you trap an error that happens during the execution of a SQL statement?

2. Write an action filter that blocks the request if the user comes from an IP that is blacklisted.

3. Write another filter that simply changes the `Message` key of the `ViewData` dictionary to "Modified by the filter." Make sure that the message is not changed when an exception happens or when the IP is blocked.

AJAX

Since the beginning, building Web applications has consisted of two aspects: server-side development and client-side development. The server-side development is the part that deals with dynamic execution of program logic on the server and returns the appropriate HTML code to clients. The client-side development is the part that deals with anything that happens in a user's browser, such as the generation of a user interface and any script that may run on a user's machine.

Two main processes are occurring on the client machine: rendering the markup code (HTML/XHTML/CSS) to present the Web page's user interface that is returned from the server, and the execution of client-side scripts such as JavaScript that enable some client-side logic and processes to happen. Usually, such JavaScript code helps to refine the user interface and to simplify user interactions.

As you already know, ASP.NET MVC is intended to be a server-side technology, providing great features for Web developers to build powerful applications. But client-side development is an integral aspect of development, and it has been shown to be of equal importance in the past few years. Therefore, the ASP.NET team has put a huge effort into enabling client-side integration of features and simplifying the process of client-side development in conjunction with ASP.NET WebForms and ASP.NET MVC.

Besides the great features for Web standards and code markup integration that have been a part of ASP.NET since its infancy and have been enhanced significantly in the past two years, there was talk about enabling AJAX and AJAX capabilities in ASP.NET Web applications before the release of ASP.NET 2.0. I talk about the concept of AJAX and its applications in the body of this chapter, but, in a nutshell, AJAX is a concept that refers to some techniques that use JavaScript in conjunction with server-side code execution to have the best of both worlds: client-side interaction and server-side logic executing together. You can implement AJAX in your applications in various ways, from built-in AJAX technologies in server-side applications to handmade implementations, but they all have the same basis.

ASP.NET and ASP.NET MVC include a built-in AJAX mechanism that you can easily use to bring AJAX to your applications, and it's also possible to use other AJAX technologies rather than this built-in implementation. One advantage of the built-in AJAX technology in ASP.NET is that it almost eliminates the requirement to have any knowledge of JavaScript to be able to use the technology.

Though it isn't possible to discuss all the principles of AJAX in this chapter or even all the aspects of ASP.NET AJAX and jQuery, the chapter discusses the basics of what you need to know to use AJAX in your ASP.NET MVC applications. Note that a background in AJAX principles as well as ASP.NET AJAX are requirements for following this chapter. Even so, the chapter also gives a quick overview of AJAX and ASP.NET AJAX. This should help give you perspective if you are an AJAX novice and should help you decide if you want to explore this topic further.

Therefore, the main topics of this chapter are:

❑   What is AJAX?
❑   ASP.NET AJAX
❑   jQuery
❑   AJAX in ASP.NET MVC
❑   How to use AJAX with ASP.NET MVC

Let's get started with an introduction to AJAX.

What Is AJAX?

AJAX stands for *Asynchronous JavaScript and XML,* and is a concept in Web development that refers to a series of methods and techniques that enable partial rendering of Web pages to improve the user experience, usability, and speed of execution. AJAX is one of the high points in the range of technologies that have been trying to bring richness to Web applications. The goal of this revolution in Web development is to improve the quality of Web applications and the user experience.

In fact, AJAX applies XML and another format called JSON (JavaScript Object Notation) to send a request to the server and retrieve the updated portion of a Web page to avoid having to render the whole page again. Therefore, in AJAX you use JavaScript to send requests to the application server and retrieve data and apply DHTML to regenerate a part of a Web page that should be updated. This saves users from having to download the whole page again. They just download the part of the page that should be updated. This speeds up the rendering of pages and greatly improves usability.

As a direct result, AJAX helps Web applications provide a behavior similar to that provided by desktop applications, which is a desirable goal for end-users. On one hand, users like to have the high level of usability in desktop applications, and on the other hand, they like the portability of Web applications that can be viewed by a Web browser without installing any other software. By speeding up the usability of Web applications, AJAX tries to give the users the best of both worlds. So far, AJAX has been able to achieve this goal to a great extent, and the creation of Rich Internet Applications (RIAs) such as Silverlight has helped this progress significantly because such applications work with AJAX techniques to fill in some gaps.

The basis of AJAX is an object called `XmlHttpRequest`, which was first created by the Microsoft Exchange Server team to communicate with the server and render a part of a page. Soon other browsers joined Internet Explorer to include an enhanced version of this object. These days all the modern browsers support this object out-of-the-box, and it plays a key role in support of AJAX-based scenarios.

`XmlHttpRequest` enables a functionality that allows browsers to communicate with the Web server and send requests to receive a part of the data that should be updated. Behind the scenes, a lot of this is done by Web browsers to save you from having to do extra work.

But let me discuss what developers need to know about AJAX. Although AJAX is a general concept, various implementations of AJAX for Web developers are offered for different server-side technologies. Although work still needs to be done to enable AJAX implementations in a server-side technology, fortunately many developers and companies have tried to build good implementations for the public, and at the moment rich AJAX implementations exist for different technologies. PHP, Ruby on Rails, and ASP.NET each have their own AJAX libraries, but this chapter focuses on ASP.NET.

Since the beginning of widespread interest in AJAX implementations (which was contemporaneous with the birth of ASP.NET), some ASP.NET developers tried to bring its functionality to ASP.NET, so some implementations came into being as open source projects. Later the high demand for AJAX by ASP.NET developers persuaded the Microsoft ASP.NET team to work on their own implementation as an integrated part of the technology, and ASP.NET AJAX was introduced after the birth of ASP.NET 2.0. Since then Microsoft has improved ASP.NET AJAX with newer versions, while community projects are still active.

ASP.NET AJAX

ASP.NET AJAX is Microsoft's built-in implementation of AJAX functionality for ASP.NET, which has a generic framework for AJAX development. It includes a rich set of JavaScript libraries to simulate the main aspects of ASP.NET through the JavaScript API on the client side. In other words, ASP.NET AJAX implements some main parts of the ASP.NET server API on the client side, so you can use JavaScript code to access some classes and methods in ASP.NET namespaces.

It also contains a set of basic controls to work with this library in ASP.NET server applications that are the basis of other controls that you can build for your own.

There is also a shared source library named the ASP.NET AJAX Control Toolkit. It contains useful controls that are built based on the script framework. Some of the helpful controls for common applications in this toolkit include an AJAX calendar, auto-complete textbox, pop-up dialog, and many other controls that you can use easily in your applications.

To wrap up the content, ASP.NET AJAX consists of three main elements:

❑   A rich JavaScript framework for generic purposes that simulates the functionality of some .NET and ASP.NET classes on the client side through a set of JavaScript libraries that work in conjunction with Web services.

❑   A set of .NET classes and ASP.NET server controls to connect the rich AJAX framework to .NET classes in order to save developers from doing any direct work with JavaScript.

❑   A set of ASP.NET AJAX server controls, called the ASP.NET AJAX Control Toolkit, for various purposes that work based on the preceding elements. Many controls are included, such as Accordion, AutoComplete, ModalPopup, Slider, and Tabs.

If you really want to immerse yourself deeply in ASP.NET AJAX, I recommend that you read Professional ASP.NET 3.5 AJAX (ISBN: 978-0-470-39217-1) from Wrox, which can give you information about this JavaScript framework and its communication with ASP.NET.

Moreover, Visual Studio 2008 includes JavaScript IntelliSense, which can help developers work with JavaScript much more easily. Later you will see that this functionality has helped Microsoft to include a version of the jQuery library within ASP.NET MVC that has rich documentation and help.

An important consideration is that AJAX technologies work according to some principles that may have different implementations in different server technologies. Generally, AJAX applications work based on a JavaScript library that works in a client-side browser and applies RESTful services to pass data to a server and receive content with the appropriate response in XML or JSON formats. ASP.NET AJAX also works on top of this workflow.

The ASP.NET AJAX script framework is deployed to client browsers and handles requests. It sends requests to specific Web service methods on the server that are available as a part of the ASP.NET AJAX server implementation, and then it receives the appropriate content and updates the page.

By default, ASP.NET AJAX works with .ASMX Web services that have been a part of the .NET Framework since the early days, but it's also possible to replace these services with Windows Communication Foundation (WCF) services that are faster and safer. You need to know this because it is likely that an increasing number of .NET developers will replace .ASMX Web services with WCF services on the server side over time. To get more information on this topic, check out a tutorial on MSDN (http://msdn.microsoft.com/en-us/library/bb412167.aspx).

There is a security note about all AJAX implementations in general and ASP.NET AJAX in particular. Because ASP.NET AJAX uses Web services over the HTTP protocol to communicate with the server, it's possible for malicious users to grab the content and view it.

Therefore, all ASP.NET developers are discouraged from passing sensitive data (such as e-mail, password, and personal information) with their AJAX applications, and you need to take care about that. Some methods exist to secure your applications (such as the usage of HTTPS protocol), but they are beyond the scope of this book. You can get more information from MSDN (http://msdn.microsoft.com/ en-us/magazine/cc793961.aspx).

Figure 12-1 shows the request workflow in a normal ASP.NET WebForm application in which any request from the browser is sent to the Web server, and it returns HTML data as the response. In this case, the whole Web page will be loaded again.

Figure 12-2 is the request workflow in an ASP.NET AJAX application. There are different types of requests. Though older request types are still available, asynchronous requests have been added and the server returns JSON or XML as a response. In this case, only the necessary parts of the page will be updated.

Having provided this background about AJAX, ASP.NET AJAX, and related principles, let me extend the discussion to the topics related to ASP.NET MVC and AJAX scenarios in this new technology, but first let's start with jQuery, which is a library that you'll often hear about when working with AJAX scenarios in ASP.NET MVC.

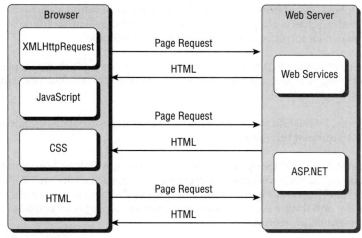

Figure 12-1

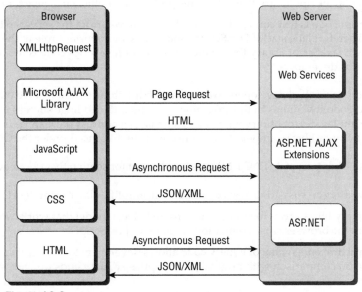

Figure 12-2

jQuery

Since the beginning of ASP.NET MVC, both Microsoft and community developers have used jQuery to implement AJAX scenarios in their applications, and this was a good reason for Microsoft to adapt jQuery and include it in its new server-side technology.

Therefore, in October 2008, Microsoft and the jQuery team announced a partnership that allows the ASP.NET team to ship jQuery as a part of ASP.NET MVC. Microsoft also announced that it supports jQuery IntelliSense in its software development IDE, Visual Studio.

jQuery is a JavaScript library that has had extensive success among Web developers in the past couple of years, and many big sites and companies are using it heavily as an alternative for the traditional way that JavaScript is developed.

To introduce jQuery, let me talk about the three main challenges for Web developers and designers when they write traditional JavaScript code:

❑ An integral part of JavaScript development is dealing with the Document Object Model (DOM) and accessing various objects in the client's browser, such as the browser object, windows, and many other elements. Original JavaScript features don't offer you a good means of working with DOM, and there have been several attempts to write JavaScript libraries that simplify this and supplement JavaScript.

❑ Different browsers exhibit different behaviors for the same JavaScript code, and some circumstances require you to write different code that works on a particular browser. Supplying a cross-browser JavaScript library that solves this problem is another challenge for JavaScript developers.

❑ JavaScript code is text content that must be transferred from the server to the client, at least once. Therefore, the size of JavaScript codes plays an important role in the speed of Web pages. Having a JavaScript library that reduces the size of JavaScript code is the third challenge for JavaScript developers.

These three goals compelled developers to build JavaScript libraries that resolve the issues. Although there have been good inventions in this area, none of them attained huge success until John Resig developed a lightweight JavaScript library named jQuery that can address these three issues. jQuery has become a very popular library among developers and is dual-licensed under the GNU and MIT licenses.

jQuery, which ships as part of ASP.NET MVC, is best known for solving these previously mentioned issues:

❑ jQuery offers an easy-to-use object model that simplifies JavaScript development significantly.

❑ The jQuery library tries to offer a standardized object model that works on all browsers and resolves the browser cross-compatibility issues of JavaScript.

❑ The structure and syntax of jQuery code allows developers to accomplish a goal in fewer lines of code (in comparison with original JavaScript), so jQuery ends up with smaller files.

In addition, jQuery provides the flexibility to perform some tasks that are difficult with JavaScript, such as event handling, animation, and AJAX interactions.

Note that jQuery is not a replacement for JavaScript. It's just a library written on top of JavaScript to simplify it and resolve some issues with traditional JavaScript development.

To use jQuery with your applications, you must reference its single library file as a part of your markup. This file is small, but it's required to have it on the client machine to be able to develop client-side scripts with jQuery. Note that a main part of the power of jQuery is in its plug-ins. Developers have built various plug-ins for jQuery that can be added to it as separate files, so in some cases you also need to reference these plug-in files.

Learning jQuery syntax and techniques requires some time and effort. A great book about jQuery is *jQuery in Action* (Bibeault, Katz, Resig, ISBN: 978-1933988351).

AJAX in ASP.NET MVC

Like any other server technology, including its predecessor, ASP.NET WebForms, ASP.NET MVC requires a good set of features that enable AJAX interactions within its Web applications.

Also as with other server technologies, you're able to apply any AJAX technology to use within your ASP.NET MVC applications, but depending on the specific AJAX technology, you may be required to do a significant amount of work to integrate everything. However, like ASP.NET WebForms, ASP.NET MVC offers you an option out-of-the-box, and that is a set of AJAX features integrated with ASP.NET MVC.

ASP.NET MVC also distributes a small helper library called MicrosoftMvcAjax as a part of the software that helps with AJAX interactions. Moreover, ASP.NET MVC includes the jQuery library as a library convenient for AJAX development with ASP.NET MVC.

Adding AJAX References

Before you can effectively use AJAX in ASP.NET MVC, you have to add the appropriate script references for it.

As you see in Figure 12-3, ASP.NET MVC projects come with a `Scripts` folder out-of-the-box that includes a series of script files and libraries that keep the necessary scripts for AJAX features in ASP.NET MVC and jQuery.

Two groups of files are available in this folder: One is for debugging purposes and the other is for production. Debugging files are larger and more readable, so they are preferred for debugging purposes. Note that you can simply replace debugging files with production files by changing the names of files in your references.

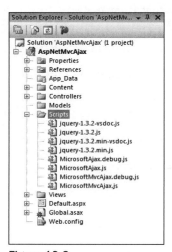

Figure 12-3

Chapter 12: AJAX

Obviously, the first step in adding AJAX functionality to your Web applications is adding appropriate JavaScript references. You need to add two references to your ASP.NET MVC applications. One is for the Microsoft AJAX script library and the other is for AJAX integration in ASP.NET MVC. The code for this purpose is something constant that you can simply add to your master page files. However, it's left to you to decide where to add the references. For example, you can add the references to the header section of your HTML.

In Listing 12-1 I add these two references to my master file (highlighted code). Here, I reference the `MicrosoftAjax.debug.js` and `MicrosoftMvcAjax.debug.js` libraries.

Listing 12-1: Add debug AJAX script references

```
<%@ Master Language="C#" Inherits="System.Web.Mvc.ViewMasterPage" %>

<!DOCTYPE html PUBLIC "-//W3C//DTD XHTML 1.0 Strict//EN"
 "http://www.w3.org/TR/xhtml1/DTD/xhtml1-strict.dtd">
<html xmlns="http://www.w3.org/1999/xhtml">
<head runat="server">
    <title>
        <asp:ContentPlaceHolder ID="TitleContent" runat="server" />
    </title>
    <script src="<%= Url.Content("~/Scripts/MicrosoftAjax.debug.js") %>"
     type="text/javascript"></script>
    <script src="<%= Url.Content("~/Scripts/MicrosoftMvcAjax.debug.js") %>"
     type="text/javascript"></script>
    <link href="../../Content/Site.css" rel="stylesheet" type="text/css" />
</head>
<body>
    <div class="page">
        <div id="header">
            <div id="title">
                <h1>
                    AJAX in ASP.NET MVC</h1>
            </div>
            <div id="menucontainer">
                <ul id="menu">
                    <li>
                        <%= Html.ActionLink("Home", "Index", "Home")%></li>
                    <li>
                        <%= Html.ActionLink("Sum", "Sum", "Home")%></li>
                </ul>
            </div>
        </div>
        <div id="main">
            <asp:ContentPlaceHolder ID="MainContent" runat="server" />
            <div id="footer">
                Wrox Press &copy; 2009
            </div>
        </div>
    </div>
</body>
</html>
```

As you see, here I have referenced the debug scripts that are the recommended options for development purposes. However, these debug scripts are so large that they can make your applications slower, so you need to replace them with production scripts when deploying your application to a server. Listing 12-2 is the updated version of Listing 12-1 that references production scripts.

Listing 12-2: Add production AJAX script references

```
<%@ Master Language="C#" Inherits="System.Web.Mvc.ViewMasterPage" %>

<!DOCTYPE html PUBLIC "-//W3C//DTD XHTML 1.0 Strict//EN"
 "http://www.w3.org/TR/xhtml1/DTD/xhtml1-strict.dtd">
<html xmlns="http://www.w3.org/1999/xhtml">
<head runat="server">
    <title>
        <asp:ContentPlaceHolder ID="TitleContent" runat="server" />
    </title>
    <script src="<%= Url.Content("~/Scripts/MicrosoftAjax.js") %>"
     type="text/javascript"></script>
    <script src="<%= Url.Content("~/Scripts/MicrosoftMvcAjax.js") %>"
     type="text/javascript"></script>
    <link href="../../Content/Site.css" rel="stylesheet" type="text/css" />
</head>
<body>
    <div class="page">
        <div id="header">
            <div id="title">
                <h1>
                    AJAX in ASP.NET MVC</h1>
            </div>
            <div id="menucontainer">
                <ul id="menu">
                    <li>
                        <%= Html.ActionLink("Home", "Index", "Home")%></li>
                    <li>
                        <%= Html.ActionLink("Sum", "Sum", "Home")%></li>
                </ul>
            </div>
        </div>
        <div id="main">
            <asp:ContentPlaceHolder ID="MainContent" runat="server" />
            <div id="footer">
                Wrox Press &copy; 2009
            </div>
        </div>
    </div>
</body>
</html>
```

The rest of this chapter shows you how to add AJAX functionality to your ASP.NET MVC applications, but before that, I have to point out that you shouldn't expect something as classical as ASP.NET AJAX development with ASP.NET WebForms in ASP.NET MVC. Like many other aspects of ASP.NET MVC that have a manual and more involved development process than ASP.NET WebForms, AJAX development in ASP.NET MVC may take more effort. But again, like all the other aspects of ASP.NET MVC, it offers you a higher level of flexibility and control over everything in your application. ASP.NET AJAX in WebForms was very limited to server controls, but now you have a powerful fundamental tool to use in building your own AJAX scenarios.

Principles of AJAX Development in ASP.NET MVC Applications

The AJAX development process for ASP.NET MVC applications is quite different from ASP.NET WebForms applications. In ASP.NET WebForms, you can drag and drop several controls and work with their properties, methods, and events to accomplish AJAX interactions. This is a fairly easy process, but in ASP.NET MVC you have to deal with lower-level APIs.

After adding the appropriate references to JavaScript libraries (as described in the previous section), you need to do several things. You need to add code to your views and masters to enable AJAX interactions in which you use some built-in extension methods (such as `BeginForm`) in ASP.NET MVC that pass data on specific client-side events to your controllers and corresponding methods. In controllers, you need to define specific functions that return the updated value of a portion of a view. This must be declared based on what you have already defined in your views and the names that you've used. For example, if you have declared `GetUpdatedSection` in a view, you might well need to define `GetUpdatedSection` in your controller. Likewise, you can use the `JsonResult` class in your ASP.NET MVC applications to update a part of a page with JSON format. You see an exercise for this method at the end of the chapter. There are also some other options that are not as common as these two. The preference of one option to another is completely based on your requirements and the development effort, but JSON format is comparatively more relevant for AJAX scenarios because it represents the hierarchy of data in the shortest possible length that can improve the speed of communications between the client and server.

Generally, the JSON format is the common way to communicate data between the client and server in AJAX interactions because it provides a short representation of data in such a way that their structure is maintained. Therefore, not only do you accomplish using less data to communicate AJAX interactions, but you also have the ability to communicate more complex data types without problems.

In AJAX development in ASP.NET MVC, a class located in the `System.Web.Mvc` namespace plays the key role in your AJAX development, especially in views and masters. It's actually a placeholder where developers can attach their own extension methods to it and use it wherever appropriate.

ASP.NET MVC has three classes called `ViewMasterPage`, `ViewPage`, and `ViewUserControl` that represent master pages, views, and user controls, respectively, and all these classes have a property named `Ajax`. This `Ajax` property is of the `AjaxHelper` type located in the `System.Web.Mvc` namespace, which enables AJAX interactions in your masters, views, and user controls. You see how the `Ajax` property is used throughout the rest of this chapter.

The following three classes play the main role in AJAX scenarios:

❑ `AjaxHelper` — This class represents the fundamental mechanism to render HTML through AJAX scenarios. This is the most common class that you use in your AJAX development in ASP.NET MVC.

❑   AjaxOptions — This class provides some important information about the client-side events and properties related to the client request that can be used in AJAX interactions. AjaxOptions is a class suitable for customized AJAX development, which is beyond the scope of this chapter, but generally, this class helps you define additional options for AJAX use.

❑   AjaxExtensions — This class provides a set of extension methods that allow you to connect your AJAX regions in views to controller methods that will return the updated code for that portion based on the appropriate client-side event. As a developer, you don't deal with this class directly.

Here are steps that you need to follow to add AJAX features to your ASP.NET MVC applications:

1.   Choose your AJAX interactions method (links, forms, or route links) and use the appropriate class to define the region in your masters, views, or user control.

2.   Set the appropriate parameters for AjaxExtensions methods that connect your views to controller methods and fire them on specific client-side events.

3.   Set the name of the HTML region in the views that should be updated.

4.   Add a corresponding function to your controllers that can get data from your views and return a value that will be used to update a part of your page.

Putting these elements together, you may wonder how ASP.NET MVC enables AJAX interactions through these steps. You generally have two choices for implementing AJAX in ASP.NET MVC.

In the first method, you submit forms asynchronously just like posting forms, as you already have done with ASP.NET MVC in other chapters. But here you update the portion inside the <form /> tag rather than the whole page.

In the second method, you add hyperlinks to your pages, and users can click them to send an asynchronous request to the server. Then the response from the server can be interpreted in several ways to update a part of the page.

You examine both methods more closely in the next section.

Putting It into Action: Using AJAX in ASP.NET MVC

This example puts to use the theoretical concepts that were reviewed throughout this chapter to this point.

In this example, you build an application that showcases AJAX in ASP.NET MVC in two ways: The user can click a link to see the updated portion of a page without reloading the whole page, and the user can also enter two numeric values in textboxes and click to see their sum. The first part of the example showcases a very basic AJAX interaction, and the second part exhibits an example of AJAX with forms.

In the home page of the site, the user can check the current time and click a link to update it through an AJAX interaction, and on another page, he can enter two integers in textboxes to get their sum, again through an AJAX interaction.

Try It Out   ActionLink

Here, you create the link to update the time.

1.   First you create the controller class with one action method for each page presented in
      Listing 12-3. Later you update this controller class.

Listing 12-3: HomeController

```
using System.Web.Mvc;

namespace AspNetMvcAjax.Controllers
{
    [HandleError]
    public class HomeController : Controller
    {
        public ActionResult Index()
        {
            return View();
        }
    }
}
```

2.   The next step is to create a view page. This view page uses the master page file presented in
      Listing 12-1. Listing 12-4 shows the code for this view page. It uses AJAX in ASP.NET MVC
      (see the highlighted code).

Listing 12-4: Index view

```
<%@ Page Language="C#" MasterPageFile="~/Views/Shared/Site.Master"
Inherits="System.Web.Mvc.ViewPage" %>

<%@ Import Namespace="AspNetMvcAjax.Controllers" %>
<asp:Content ID="indexTitle" ContentPlaceHolderID="TitleContent" runat="server">
    AJAX via ActionLink
</asp:Content>
<asp:Content ID="indexContent" ContentPlaceHolderID="MainContent" runat="server">
    <span id="time"></span>
    <br />
    <%= Ajax.ActionLink("Get Time", "GetTime",
            new AjaxOptions { UpdateTargetId = "time" })%>
</asp:Content>
```

3.   Now, you should add an action method to your controller class named GetTime, which returns
      a string value (see Listing 12-5). This string value will be inserted in the page. Note that you
      can also use ActionResult as your return type for your function.

Listing 12-5: Add GetTime action method to HomeController

```
using System;
using System.Web.Mvc;

namespace AspNetMvcAjax.Controllers
```

```
{
    [HandleError]
    public class HomeController : Controller
    {
        public ActionResult Index()
        {
            return View();
        }

        public string GetTime()
        {
            return string.Format("Current time is {0}",
                DateTime.Now.ToShortTimeString());
        }
    }
}
```

4.   Figures 12-4 and 12-5 show the output of this page. Of course, the figures in this book cannot represent the AJAX nature of the page, but you can download the source code package to check it yourself.

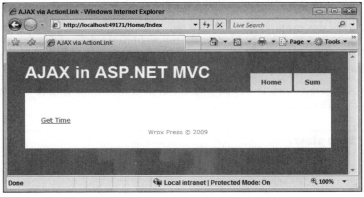

Figure 12-4

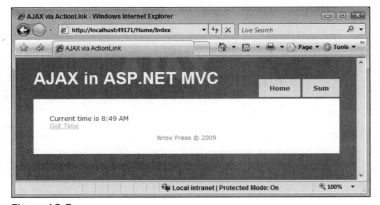

Figure 12-5

How It Works

As you see, there is a span with an `id` attribute set to `time`, which is used to display the current time in the page. There is also a call to the `Ajax.ActionLink` extension method, which renders an AJAX link in the page based on the parameters passed to it. `ActionLink` has several overloads, but here you used the simplest one with three parameters in which you passed the text value for the link, the action method name (in your controller), and an instance of the `AjaxOptions` object. You also used a simple structure to declare this `AjaxOptions` instance and passed the name of your target HTML element to it in step 2. This is a simple example that demonstrates basic principles. With a little creativity, you could easily extend this functionality to reload a part of your pages without reloading the whole page in some scenarios like an online tracking service or feed aggregator.

Try It Out   **BeginForm**

The other type of AJAX scenario occurs when you want to add your elements to a form with the dynamic control to be updated. This case is more common in today's AJAX development. This is also possible with AJAX features in ASP.NET MVC, and you can accomplish this with the `Ajax.BeginForm` extension method.

In the second part of this example, you create a new view that simulates a calculator that calculates the sum of two integer numbers. This page includes two textboxes where the user can enter numbers and click a button, and then ASP.NET MVC calculates the sum and displays the result in a part of the page without reloading the whole page.

1. First, you create a new view page with the code shown in Listing 12-6. Note the highlighted code where the main work is done.

Listing 12-6: Sum view

```
<%@ Page Title="" Language="C#" MasterPageFile="~/Views/Shared/Site.Master"
Inherits="System.Web.Mvc.ViewPage" %>

<%@ Import Namespace="AspNetMvcAjax.Controllers" %>
<asp:Content ID="Content1" ContentPlaceHolderID="TitleContent" runat="server">
    AJAX via BeginForm
</asp:Content>
<asp:Content ID="Content2" ContentPlaceHolderID="MainContent" runat="server">
    <% using (Ajax.BeginForm("SumForm", new AjaxOptions
{ UpdateTargetId = "sum" }))
        { %>
    Enter the first number:
    <br />
    <%= Html.TextBox("txtFirstNumber")%>
    <br />
    Enter the second number:
    <br />
    <%= Html.TextBox("txtSecondNumber")%>
    <br />
```

```
            <input type="submit" value="Submit" />
            <br />
            <span id="sum"></span>
            <% } %>
    </asp:Content>
```

2. Now you can guess what's next. You update your controller with a new action method called SumForm, which has two integer parameters with the same names as the textboxes (see Listing 12-7). In this action method, you can calculate the sum of the incoming numbers and return the result as a string value.

Listing 12-7: Add SumForm action method to HomeController

```csharp
using System;
using System.Web.Mvc;

namespace AspNetMvcAjax.Controllers
{
    [HandleError]
    public class HomeController : Controller
    {
        public ActionResult Index()
        {
            return View();
        }

        public string GetTime()
        {
            return string.Format("Current time is {0}",
                DateTime.Now.ToShortTimeString());
        }

        public ActionResult Sum()
        {
            return View();
        }

        public string SumForm(int txtFirstNumber, int txtSecondNumber)
        {
            int sum = txtFirstNumber + txtSecondNumber;

            return string.Format("Sum = {0}", sum.ToString());
        }
    }
}
```

3. When you run this page, you get the results shown in Figures 12-6 and 12-7.

    Notice the addition of a reference to AspNetMvcAjax.Controllers *in the view pages because it's required to enable your AJAX functionalities.*

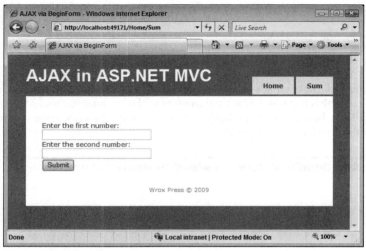

Figure 12-6

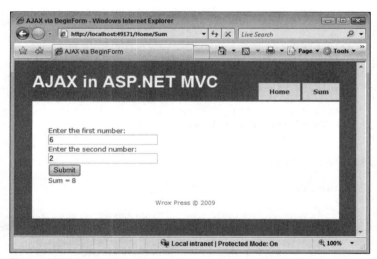

Figure 12-7

How It Works

Here the code uses `Ajax.BeginForm` to define the AJAX form. Like `Ajax.ActionLink`, it also has several overloads, but you used a simple one that gets an action method name and an instance of the `AjaxOptions` object with the name of target element ID.

You also declared two textboxes in your code in step 1, as well as a Submit button and a `<span />` element to display the result. Note that the values of these textboxes will be passed to your action method as its integer parameters automatically. This is a simple example that demonstrates basic principles. With a little creativity, you could easily extend this functionality to submit a contact form and show the message without reloading the page, or to simulate a Twitter-like status textbox that submits the status in place.

Summary

The topic of this chapter was AJAX — one of the most important concepts in modern Web development to improve the usability of Web sites.

This chapter started with an introduction to AJAX, its main concepts, and its advantages, and then followed that with a discussion of AJAX in ASP.NET, especially ASP.NET WebForms with an emphasis on ASP.NET AJAX, its structure, and its workflow. The next part of the chapter was an introduction to AJAX in ASP.NET MVC, including jQuery.

After getting this background, you took a look at the principles of AJAX in ASP.NET MVC and the classes that play the main role in AJAX development with ASP.NET MVC. After that, an example covered theories in two real-world scenarios, showing what can be done with AJAX features in ASP.NET MVC.

However, AJAX development in ASP.NET MVC requires more effort than in ASP.NET WebForms, basically because in ASP.NET WebForms you have access to server controls and a classic form of development that usually doesn't require much knowledge for many scenarios, but in ASP.NET MVC you have access to some basic tools that need to be expanded by your creativity and experience. AJAX development with ASP.NET MVC is something that should be learned with a pragmatic approach, so I strongly recommend you check out some sample applications and try to explore this further. Two good sample open source applications are NerdDinner (discovered by the author of *Wrox Professional ASP.NET MVC 1.0* [John Wiley & Sons, Inc.] and available under an open license) and Kigg (an ASP.NET MVC implementation of a Digg-like community that is open source).

Before heading to the next chapter, take some time to work on the following exercises.

Exercises

1. Instead of using the string action methods to return the updated portion of a page, use the `JsonResult` type to do this, and write an example to showcase this option.

2. Using `BeginForm`, implement a contact form in ASP.NET MVC with AJAX that accepts some parameters such as the name, e-mail address, subject, and the body of the e-mail. Moreover, try to show an animated icon that represents the progress that is being made. Note that there is a `LoadingElementId` property for `AjaxOptions` that you can use to implement this animated icon.

Deployment

The process of developing software consists of some predefined stages that are documented and taught to many developers. Based on the scale of the software and investments, some of these stages may be ignored and some may be restricted. However, you should be at least generally knowledgeable about some stages, such as planning, estimation, development, testing, deployment, and maintenance.

This chapter focuses mainly on one of these steps, deployment, for ASP.NET MVC applications. Here, you discover different ways to deploy an ASP.NET MVC application, and decide which one is the best option for your applications.

As Web applications, ASP.NET MVC projects are usually harder to install than Windows desktop applications, but in the past few years, there has been a significant improvement in the way that you can deploy Web applications.

Thankfully, ASP.NET MVC offers better deployment options than ASP.NET WebForms and also makes it easier and more flexible to deploy applications on servers and hosts. Moreover, Microsoft has been working on new tools such as the Web Platform Installer, which makes it pretty easy to configure a Web server and deploy a Web application to it.

Obviously, this chapter doesn't have any code to offer, but it gives you a good guide to deploying your ASP.NET MVC application based on the situation and your requirements. The following are the main topics covered in this chapter:

- ❑ A quick overview of deployment
- ❑ ASP.NET MVC hosting options
- ❑ Prerequisites to hosting an ASP.NET MVC application
- ❑ Using the Web Platform Installer to configure your IIS server
- ❑ The .NET security policy and its restrictions for hosting
- ❑ Building and deploying an ASP.NET MVC application with Visual Studio

ASP.NET Deployment Overview

Deployment is the process of preparing software to be used by end-users. Naturally, software consists of several components that work together to accomplish a goal, and obviously it's built from code and other pieces. (For example, some applications have dependencies on other resources such as databases or file systems, and some applications have prerequisite software that must be installed on a machine.)

The people who develop the applications try to make them easy for users to install and use. They try to make sure that their application works without problems, so deployment is a very crucial stage in software development and requires special attention from developers. Fortunately, deploying .NET applications in general and ASP.NET applications in particular is easier than deploying many other technologies out there.

As you might expect, all .NET applications rely on the installation of the appropriate .NET Framework version on the installation machine. Therefore, if you have an application written with .NET Framework 3.5, this version must be installed on any machine that hosts your application.

> *You might be curious about the installation of .NET applications on other platforms such as Mac or Linux. Fortunately, there is an open source project called Mono that enables the deployment of .NET projects on Linux. You can check out the Mono site to learn more about it at* `http://mono-project.com`.

The best way to deploy a .NET application (whether a desktop application or a Web application) is to build a Windows setup installer that encapsulates everything in a few steps that can be performed by any user. Although this is the most common method of deploying desktop applications, difficulties exist for Web applications because not all Web application users have access to their servers to run the installer, so alternatives have been created.

Usually, professional Web application products are available with two separate installation packages: one as a Windows setup installer and another as binary files to be deployed onto the server by hand. In this chapter, I show you how to deploy your applications with the latter method.

> *One point that is not related to your deployment process is trying to reduce the dependencies of your Web applications while you're developing them. This is something that you should consider during your application's infancy and during development to make your application easier to install and configure. By nature, ASP.NET MVC ameliorates your work in this area because the MVC pattern assists you in reducing some types of dependencies.*

ASP.NET MVC Hosting Options

Fortunately, ASP.NET MVC is built on top of a great infrastructure that abates its dependencies on the Common Language Runtime (CLR) versioning and allows you to host and deploy ASP.NET MVC applications as a specific ASP.NET application type with some references to a few additional assemblies. This is important because it allows you to host an application in an environment that doesn't have ASP.NET MVC installed, but only the .NET Framework.

Essentially, ASP.NET MVC is a set of libraries that are built to work on top of .NET Framework 3.5 (with or without Service Pack 1), and when you develop an ASP.NET MVC application, you're actually referencing assemblies that include ASP.NET MVC libraries. Other ASP.NET MVC resources are regular Web resources such as text or multimedia files. Therefore, all you need to host your ASP.NET MVC application is an installation of .NET Framework 3.5 (or .NET Framework 3.5 Service Pack 1) plus a version of IIS (as is discussed in the next section).

Having this background, you can understand that ASP.NET MVC applications are easier to deploy for everyone, and this has been a goal of the Microsoft ASP.NET MVC team as well.

Microsoft offers two options for installing and hosting your ASP.NET MVC applications: GAC installation and assembly deployment.

GAC Installation

As a .NET developer, you should know about the Global Assembly Cache (GAC), but if you don't know, in essence it is a global storage system that keeps assemblies that can be used by various applications and can be shared among them. You can register any strongly-named assembly in the GAC, but by default Microsoft registers some common assemblies in the GAC, such as those related to configuration or interoperability.

Microsoft ASP.NET MVC has a Windows installer that can be used to install it on any machine. When installed, it registers the appropriate assemblies into the GAC and allows you to host any ASP.NET MVC application on that machine.

This method has some advantages and disadvantages: for hosted environments, your host administrator must install ASP.NET MVC in order to allow you to use this option, because you don't have access to the server. On the other hand, GAC installation makes it possible to get the most recent updates via Windows updates and stay up-to-date with latest changes and security patches.

On your development machine, you must install ASP.NET MVC by running the installer, so obviously all the assemblies are automatically registered in the GAC.

Assembly Deployment

The other possible option for hosting is deploying ASP.NET MVC assemblies onto your servers. As stated earlier in this chapter, ASP.NET MVC consists of a set of libraries, which are encapsulated in a few assemblies, and you can deploy those assemblies along with other files onto any server that has the .NET Framework 3.5 installed.

If you're going to deploy these binaries to a server that is running .NET Framework 3.5 without Service Pack 1, you need to deploy more assemblies, but if you're using a host environment with .NET 3.5 Service Pack 1 installed, your job is easier because you can deploy fewer binaries. Phil Haack (ASP.NET MVC Program Manager) has described the instructions for both cases here: http://haacked.com/archive/2008/11/03/bin-deploy-aspnetmvc.aspx.

This option is suitable for hosted environments where your host won't install ASP.NET MVC for you.

Like the GAC option, this option has some advantages and disadvantages: Deployment of your projects is easier and is independent from the installation of ASP.NET MVC on the server, but you miss the option of automatic Windows updates.

In short, I'd recommend you to use the assembly deployment option only if you're in a hosted environment and if your host will not install ASP.NET MVC for you. Many hosts do offer this option to attract more clients, though!

Hosting Prerequisites

Some prerequisites are required for installing any application on a machine. Some of these prerequisites are related to the platform on which the application is developed, and others are related to the nature of the application and how it is developed.

When hosting ASP.NET applications (including ASP.NET MVC applications), you need to have a relevant operating system. Most ASP.NET applications are hosted on the Windows operating system, but it's also possible to host ASP.NET applications on other platforms. Of course, you may face some restrictions with the latter option. However, ASP.NET and Windows are recommended and widely used together.

In addition to the relevant operating system, you need to have a Web server application that can host ASP.NET applications. There are various Web servers out there, but the most common Web server for the Windows operating system is IIS.

> *Note that some small Web server applications are available to work with local requests such as a built-in Visual Studio server that works on local ports and is derived from the Cassini Web server, but such Web servers are not appropriate for production because they don't offer professional features and cannot work with remote requests.*

Internet Information Services (IIS) is a built-in Web server that comes with many of the editions of the Windows operating system as a part of the Windows server. IIS cannot be installed as a separate package and must be a part of your operating system. Also, it's not possible to upgrade from one major version to another (that is, from 6.0 to 7.0). At the moment, versions 6.0 and 7.0 are very common among developers.

In addition to an appropriate operating system and a Web server application, you also need an installation of the .NET Framework that is compatible with your Web application. For ASP.NET MVC, you need to have the .NET Framework 3.5 (as stated previously, with or without Service Pack 1) installed. Moreover, the appropriate ASP.NET version must be enabled and registered on your IIS Web server in order to host your applications, and this is accomplished by running the following command:

```
aspnet_regiis -i
```

This command installs the current version of ASP.NET on your IIS Web server. For other versions, you need to use other command switches. (To view the available switches, use the `aspnet_regiis /?` command.)

There may be some prerequisites for your particular application. For example, you may have used file operations in your project, and this requires you to grant write access to the appropriate folders for appropriate ASP.NET users. It's also common to use databases with your applications, so you need to have an installation of your database on your server (or on a remote server with the appropriate security settings). Many applications require configuration as well, so you may need to set the connection string for the database or a file path. All these cases are common, but they are not essential or within the scope of our deployment discussion, and they are also often dependent on your specific circumstances. Therefore, I leave it to you to explore them. You can find such information in resources about Windows and database administration at `http://iis.net`.

The .NET Security Policy

Many beginning developers don't know much about the .NET security policy and its impact on ASP .NET hosting, especially on hosted environments. If you're going to host your application in such environments, you are highly likely to face difficulties with .NET security policies.

This is a topic that you need to consider during the early stages of your development. If you don't attend to it early, this can create problems during the hosting and deployment stages of your applications.

Since .NET Framework 2.0, Microsoft has added a major new feature to the framework that provides huge improvements in the security level of .NET applications, mostly because there were some new features in this version that had the potential to be used as holes for security attacks.

In .NET 2.0, Microsoft introduced security policies as a set of mechanisms that improve security levels. This set of policies prevents security attacks through dangerous .NET APIs (such as network APIs), and some of the policies allow administrators to restrict access to portions of the API that have the potential to be used to attack the applications and the server (such as a DNS attack through a hosted ASP.NET application).

The .NET security policy is a broad topic that can't be covered here in depth. I will give you a short overview of the .NET security policy's impact on ASP.NET.

There is a set of policies categorized into groups based on which API they target. For example, there is a group of policies for file access and another group for network access. There are different trust levels, such as Full, High, Medium, and Low, that have a predefined set of policies for these groups. For example, at the Full trust level everything is allowed, but at the High trust level many of the operations are allowed and a limited set of very dangerous operations are disallowed. At the Medium trust level, the majority of operations are disallowed, but some of them are still open. Microsoft has defined these policies based on common applications and has documented their usage very well at `http://msdn.microsoft.com/en-us/library/ms998326.aspx`. For example, Microsoft recommends that hosting administrators use the Medium trust level in shared hosting environments. Additionally, there is a Custom trust level that you can define from scratch, based on your requirements or by modifying one of these policies.

It's also possible to define these policies at the machine level to enforce them for all applications or override the machine-level configuration in your applications. However, it's also possible to prevent child applications from overriding the generic configurations, and this is usually done by shared hosting administrators.

This topic is very crucial for shared hosting environments because they are usually running on Medium level or a modified version of this level, and some restrictions exist for applications such as the usage of network APIs or OLE databases, and occasionally you may also be restricted from using the file system APIs. If you're running on your own servers, this wouldn't be a big deal.

All in all, if you're going to host your application in an environment with such restrictions, you should consider these limitations during the earliest stages of your application's development in order to use alternatives (if possible) for your application. Microsoft has documented a set of practices that you can use to choose alternative methods for your development. These alternatives are available on MSDN, but it's not always possible to get rid of these restrictions.

The Web Platform Installer

Prior to the advent of the Web Platform Installer, the process of configuring a Web server to host applications required more effort and took time for administrators to accomplish. Configuration of IIS for hosting different applications was not a quick task either. You had to perform a number of manual steps to accomplish it. In Windows Server 2008 Microsoft tried to simplify this process with several wizards and also added new features to enable administrators to distribute one configuration and use it on multiple servers without wasting time performing the same steps on other servers.

Microsoft has been transitioning from manual steps to short wizards, so it also started new projects to simplify the process of IIS configuration and Web application hosting and released them at the same time as the ASP.NET MVC release.

The Web Platform Installer is an application that allows you to configure your IIS server based on your needs and technologies. For example, with a few clicks it helps you configure IIS for ASP.NET development, and it can also help you configure it for other Web technologies, such as PHP hosting.

In addition, this installer helps you install and configure some popular ASP.NET Web applications on your servers quickly and easily. Some applications such as DotNetNuke, Subtext, and BlogEngine.NET are included.

The Web Platform Installer is available as a free product that you can download and install on your machine. It is available at `http://www.microsoft.com/Web/downloads/platform.aspx`.

The Web Platform Installer consists of predefined templates that you can use as a starting point for common tasks. For example, it has a template for ASP.NET developers that you can use to configure IIS for ASP.NET development.

After downloading the small Web Platform Installer package, you can click the file to initiate the application. (The Web Platform Installer itself doesn't require installation on the machine.) Note that you must be an administrator to run the application. At start up, this installer downloads some basic files to run, so you need to be connected to the Internet in order to use the Web Platform Installer.

Note that this chapter is written for the Beta version of Web Platform Installer 2.0. At the time of this writing, Web Platform Installer 1.0 is in the stable stage, but the newer version has significant changes, and here we use the Beta version. Subsequent revisions should have the same major features and structures.

When you start this installer, it opens up with two or three options in the left pane. The number of options varies depending on your environment's settings and installed packages.

The default home tab is What's New (Figure 13-1), in which you see a list of available extensions that you can install using the Web Platform Installer. The installer connects to the Internet to load this list, and you can install the latest updates on your machine.

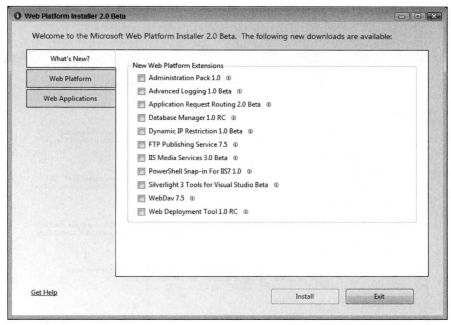

Figure 13-1

The second option is Web Platform (Figure 13-2), which is the option that we explore here. Using this option, you can configure your server for different purposes.

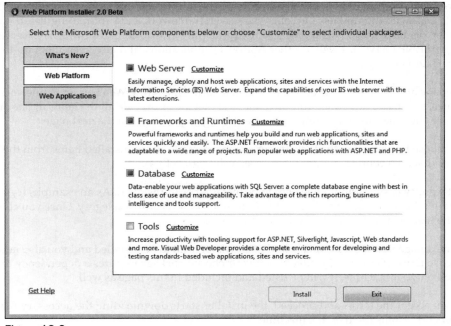

Figure 13-2

The third and last option is Web Applications (Figure 13-3), which allows you to install some common Web applications in a few clicks.

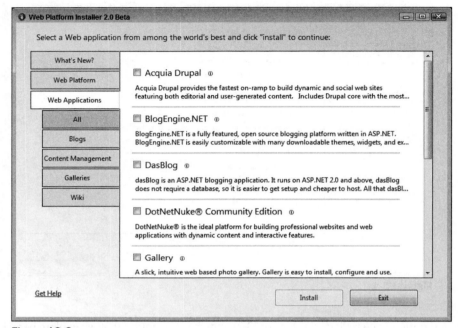

Figure 13-3

Let's focus on the Web Platform tab here. This option allows you to configure and install the possible packages and updates for your Web server, framework and runtime engines, databases, and other available tools. This is a very simple and quick way to configure your Web servers for hosting ASP.NET MVC (as well as other ASP.NET) applications, and also keep them up-to-date with the latest changes.

In this pane all the items are grouped in four categories, including Web Server, Frameworks and Runtimes, Database, and Tools. You can choose to include or exclude all the items in one of these categories or click the Customize link to choose a sub-group of items in the next page.

If you choose to customize the Web Server group, you see a list of installed items from the Web Server category that are grouped in subcategories as well (Figure 13-4).

Here it's pretty easy to choose one item to be installed or uninstalled. As an example, try to install Application Request Routing 1.0 from the Common HTTP Features category. Once you choose an item, the Install button activates and you can proceed.

In the next page you see a summary of the items that need to be installed and you also need to accept the license terms (Figure 13-5). Note that if your chosen package requires a dependency that is not installed on your machine, it will be listed and included in this page as well.

Once you accept the terms and proceed, the installer starts downloading the necessary files from the Internet and installs them on the machine.

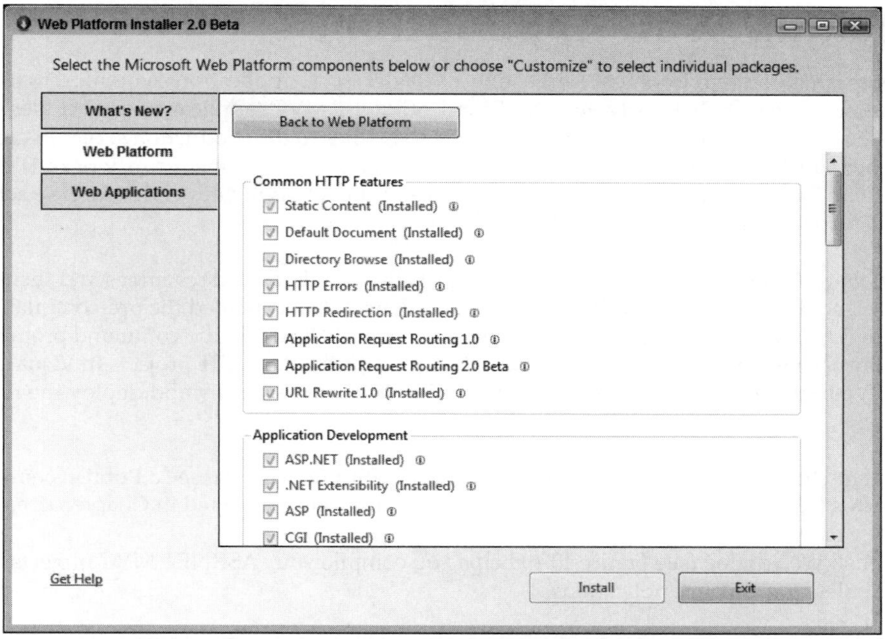

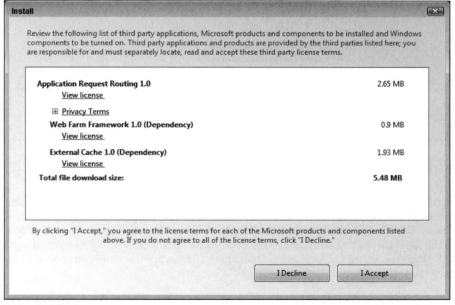

Figure 13-4

Figure 13-5

As you see, Web Platform Installer is a great way to set up, maintain, and update your Web server settings. The same installation process can be applied to other items in the installer list as well.

Publishing Web Applications

After preparing your environment for hosting ASP.NET MVC applications, you need to pack your applications to be installed easily. ASP.NET (and ASP.NET MVC) application project files consist of the original code, by default. You can simply copy all these files to the production server in order to start using your site, but this is not recommended because doing so has some security risks. (For example, anyone who has access to your files on the server can find details of your code and take actions that could disturb your application.)

Instead, you should compile your ASP.NET projects in assemblies and resources and then put them on the server, so source code files will not be included. This process is called the pre-compilation of the ASP .NET project, and it is originally done with the assistance of Visual Studio command prompt instructions. But it may become difficult to deal with command prompts, so ASP.NET projects in Visual Studio have a Publish Web dialog that allows you to perform this task automatically and deploy the result files efficiently.

If you right-click your ASP.NET MVC project in Visual Studio, you can see a Publish command that enables this feature. Here, I try to publish the project that was developed in Chapter 12 as the example.

The Publish Web dialog (see Figure 13-6) helps you compile your ASP.NET MVC projects and get all the required files to run your applications.

Figure 13-6

Clicking the ellipsis button in the Publish Web dialog displays the Open Web Site dialog, where you can choose your destination. Using this dialog, you can build and compile your projects and then deploy your files to your desired path. This dialog provides four options for your deployment: deployment to the local file system, local IIS, FTP server, and a remote server that has FrontPage Extensions installed. However, using the local file system and FTP sites are the more common options, and I discuss them here.

> *I always use the local file system because it lets me check and manipulate the files before deployment. I can always use my FTP client tools to deploy files from the local file system to the local or remote server. However, this is a personal preference, and you can use your own approach.*

The first option is File System, and you can choose the folder in which you want your project files to be deployed (see Figure 13-7).

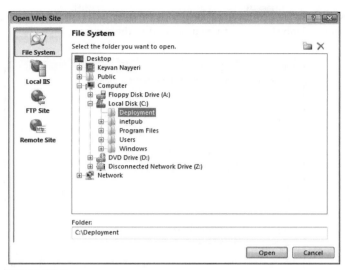

Figure 13-7

The other commonly used option is to select the FTP Site button, which is the third option on the left side of the screen (see Figure 13-8). In this pane you're able to enter your FTP server settings, so Visual Studio connects to your server and automatically uploads generated files for you.

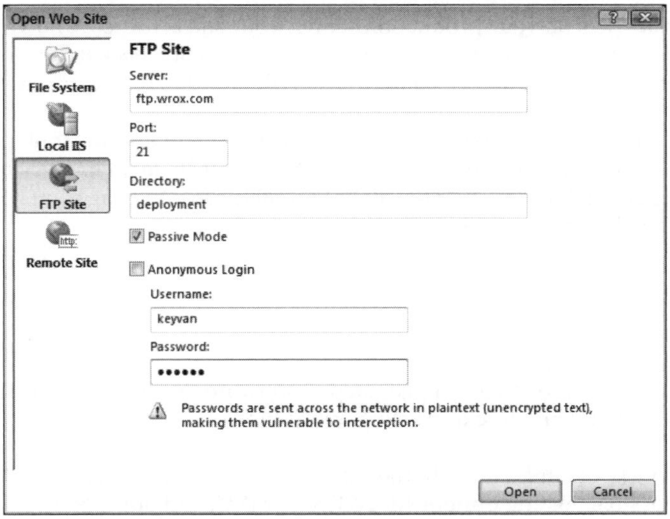

Figure 13-8

I prefer to use the local file system, so select a folder and return to the first dialog (see Figure 13-9). Here, you can choose to replace or delete existing files in the destination. You also need to be careful about selecting the copy option for your project files. You have three options, which are to generate the fewest files needed to run the application (without the source code), to copy all the project files, or even to copy all the files in the project folder. The first option (Only files needed to run this application) is recommended, especially for production, because it's the only option that doesn't include source code files and it generates a clean structure to be uploaded to the server.

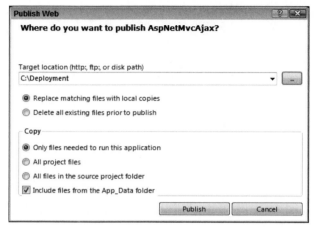

Figure 13-9

After performing these steps, you can click the Publish button to start publishing your project files. This may take from a few seconds to some minutes to complete, depending on your deployment option and the size of your project. (FTP publishing generally tends to be slower.)

With the appropriate files on your production server, your site is hosted, and you can check it. But before that, you often need to apply your own configuration and check its settings. For example, one common configuration is an update to configuration files for database connection strings.

At this point, you can navigate to your site's URL to test it. If you are confronted with an error, don't worry. Just check the instructions to resolve it. The Microsoft IIS team has a rich community (available at `http://iis.net`) that has documented all the possible error messages on IIS along with their solutions, so you can resolve errors quickly.

Summary

This chapter was about deployment, a major step in software development that usually doesn't deal with code but plays an integral role in creating applications.

After a quick overview of deployment in the software world in general and in ASP.NET in particular, I discussed two possible hosting options for ASP.NET MVC, and outlined their advantages and disadvantages. The next section was about hosting prerequisites for an ASP.NET application, and using the .NET security policy for hosting applications on shared environments.

The Web Platform Installer is a recent application that helps you configure your IIS Web servers to host different Web applications, especially ASP.NET applications. After a discussion of its usage, you explored the Publish Web dialog in Visual Studio as a widely popular option for building and deploying Web applications to production servers.

Leveraging ASP.NET WebForm Features

Throughout the previous chapters of this book, you have gotten familiar with many major topics related to ASP.NET MVC, and you have learned how to build your own ASP.NET MVC applications. However, some common topics not yet covered are necessary to understand when you implement a project.

Like ASP.NET WebForms, ASP.NET MVC is a Web development technology that is designed to provide a means for building Web applications, and each of them is built to address specific requirements. ASP.NET WebForms treats these requirements in its own way based on its infrastructure and development model (which is based on controls and events), but in ASP.NET MVC these concepts are implemented in a different form (which gives you a greater separation of concerns). You see an example in Chapter 15, which talks about authentication and authorization, where many of the concepts are constant between these two technologies.

The two technologies have some topics in common because as we discovered, both are using some constant parts of ASP.NET core API. However, even these similarities may have slightly different implementations in higher levels in each technology. So we can classify the differences between these two technologies into two groups:

❑ Some ASP.NET concepts and techniques that are available in ASP.NET MVC that have only minor differences between their implementation in ASP.NET WebForms and their implementation in ASP.NET MVC

❑ Some Web development techniques and concepts that have their own implementations in ASP.NET MVC

This chapter emphasizes some techniques that come in handy when you build an ASP.NET MVC Web application and want to consider the features that you might be familiar with from ASP.NET WebForms.

For example, one vital part of Web development with ASP.NET MVC (and any Web development technology) discussed in this chapter is caching. Caching is an inherent task in Web development and is easy to integrate with ASP.NET WebForms projects, but in ASP.NET MVC caching is presented in a completely new manner.

Another topic covered here is form and field validation in ASP.NET MVC. Validation is easy in ASP.NET WebForms (using built-in validation controls), but it is implemented at a lower level in ASP.NET MVC.

Master pages are another helpful feature included in ASP.NET WebForms since version 2.0 and ASP.NET MVC provides a similar mechanism out-of-the-box. This feature, which is pretty simple to use, is covered in this chapter as well.

Finally, this chapter offers a short overview and comparison of some features — such as sitemaps, profiling, health monitoring, and server controls — available in ASP.NET WebForms and shows how to adapt or use them in ASP.NET MVC.

Having a background in these topics in ASP.NET WebForms can help you understand the basic concepts and differences involved. Even so, their implementations in ASP.NET MVC are very different from ASP.NET WebForms.

Caching

Caching is a common Web development technique that helps improve the performance and speed of a Web application while simultaneously reducing its resource usage. Caching employs storage systems to store the data that is accessed by several requests, and load it without extra processing for later requests. In other words, when your application accesses a part of data for many requests, you can process the data for the first request and cache it on disk; then, for future requests, you can simply load the data from the storage system. This saves your application from processing the data for each and every request. As you can guess, caching can have a significant effect on resource usage, performance, and the speed of your applications, and the more requests your applications receive and the higher the loads, the more you will notice the influence of caching!

Let me give an example of caching for a common real-world situation to clarify the concept of caching. Suppose that you have a site that displays news publicly and editors publish news items on a regular basis, say one item per hour. Your site has visitors who check your homepage, which contains a list of the latest new stories. You have more than 50,000 requests for this page per hour. In the normal form, you implement an application that queries your storage system (that is, SQL Server database), retrieves the list of latest new stories, and then displays them in response to every single request, but it puts a huge load on your servers to call the database and retrieve data while this data is constant! Caching helps you query your database only one time and store the data on disk for a specific amount of time (in seconds, minutes, hours, or days) to be able to load data from this repository and save your resources and speed up your application.

Like PHP, Ruby on Rails, and other Web development technologies, ASP.NET and its derivations (WebForms and MVC) provide a great, flexible caching mechanism out-of-the-box that can be extended easily and quickly. However, the developer-level implementation of caching is different between ASP.NET WebForms and ASP.NET MVC, so I'm going to talk about this topic in the following sections.

> *Caching is a good technique for experienced developers to use to improve the performance of their applications, but it can also be a dangerous weapon in some cases, so it's necessary to learn different aspects of caching and study some examples to understand when, where, and how to use caching in a Web application. This is beyond the scope of this book and is left to you to explore.*

Caching in ASP.NET

ASP.NET provides a built-in caching mechanism that can be used easily by setting some properties. ASP.NET caching is really powerful and is widely used by Web developers. Of course, this is the simplest (and in many cases the most suitable) use of caching, but in many situations you need to have a higher level of caching than is provided by caching APIs in ASP.NET. Moreover, this caching mechanism is written to work on single servers and you can use it only when your application is running on a single server. If you have an enterprise Web application that runs on multiple servers, you need to use a third-party enterprise distributed caching product. Some commercial caching products cover the single-server environment to provide more professional features. Microsoft has its own solution, called Velocity, but it is still under development.

ASP.NET caching is built on top of an infrastructure that is governed by certain principles, and knowing these principles is an inherent part of your skill in caching.

To start with, ASP.NET caching is based on certain parameters. For example, the time parameter specifies how long a resource should be kept in the cache and is usually defined by a time span or an end time. The variance parameter of the cache is based on the request properties. For example, data for a request could vary by query string parameters or by data in a field. A third parameter in ASP.NET caching is the dependency between a resource and the data kept in the cache. For example, if you wanted to cache the contents of a configuration file or load its data to memory, you would prefer to reload your data whenever this file is updated, so you need a dependency between this file (the resource) and caching. In ASP.NET this is called *cache dependency*.

By default, ASP.NET stores its cached data in memory, but you can extend it to use alternative storage systems such as XML files or databases. However, the default implementation is the main focus of this chapter and is most likely what you will use in your applications.

ASP.NET WebForms contains some page headers that allow you to cache the output of a master page, Web page, or user control based on common properties, and it includes, of course, all the fundamental APIs that allow you to work at a lower level.

The next section talks about caching in ASP.NET MVC and the way that caching is brought to ASP.NET MVC applications. Principles, concepts, and many of the techniques used are constant between WebForms and MVC applications, but there are some techniques you need to learn to use caching in ASP.NET MVC.

If you have difficulty with understanding the concepts of some of the principles in ASP.NET caching (such as cache dependency), you can read online articles or other books to learn more about them. Appendix A contains useful resources.

Caching in ASP.NET MVC

Caching in ASP.NET MVC relies on the same principles as mentioned in the previous section about ASP.NET WebForms but is implemented in a different way. In ASP.NET WebForms you can cache the output of a master page, Web page, user control, or the output of the response easily, but in ASP.NET MVC you can cache the response of a controller using action filters. Of course, you still have the option to use lower-level APIs to cache your objects in memory.

As you read in Chapter 11, the OutputCache action filter allows you to cache the response of a controller based on several parameters. These parameters are identical to what you have in ASP.NET WebForms for an output cache.

You need to keep in mind that the basis of caching in ASP.NET MVC is the controller, and it's a matter of fact that many operations are done in the controller component in the MVC pattern. However, there is a drawback to this method and that is the fact that you cannot manage the caching for a portion of your view or your output. The ASP.NET MVC team has tried to provide some means to resolve this problem to some extent and to let you manage the caching for a partial view or output.

The OutputCache Action Filter

The OutputCache action filter plays the key role in caching in ASP.NET MVC. You can add this action filter to a controller class or to specific action methods, but it works the same in both cases and caches the response of all the action methods in a controller or those specific methods, respectively.

OutputCache can be used with no parameters, although it is more likely to have several parameters. The way that you use this action filter is very similar to the way that you use the OutputCache header in ASP.NET WebForms for pages, controls, and master pages.

> To maintain security when developing ASP.NET MVC applications, never cache the content of a controller that is protected from public users or specific users by authentication and authorization elements because those pages may be requested by other users, and this sensitive data may be rendered to them when they shouldn't see anything.

Listing 14-1 shows the source code for an action method that passes the current time to its view but whose content is cached into the memory for one minute.

Listing 14-1: Action method to cache the current time

```
[OutputCache(Duration = 60, VaryByParam = "None")]
public ActionResult Index()
{
    ViewData["Message"] = "Caching in ASP.NET MVC";
    ViewData["CurrentTime"] = DateTime.Now.ToString();

    return View();
}
```

The view page for this action method displays the time in the page (see Listing 14-2).

Listing 14-2: View page to display the time

```
<%@ Page Language="C#" MasterPageFile="~/Views/Shared/Site.Master"
Inherits="System.Web.Mvc.ViewPage" %>

<asp:Content ID="indexTitle" ContentPlaceHolderID="TitleContent" runat="server">
    ASP.NET MVC Caching
</asp:Content>
```

```
<asp:Content ID="indexContent" ContentPlaceHolderID="MainContent" runat="server">
    <h2>
        <%= Html.Encode(ViewData["Message"]) %></h2>
    <p>
        Current Time:
        <br />
        <%= Html.Encode(ViewData["CurrentTime"]) %>
    </p>
</asp:Content>
```

When you run this page, you get the current time (see Figure 14-1), but if you refresh the page, the value for the current time doesn't change for 60 seconds because the whole result of the controller is cached in memory.

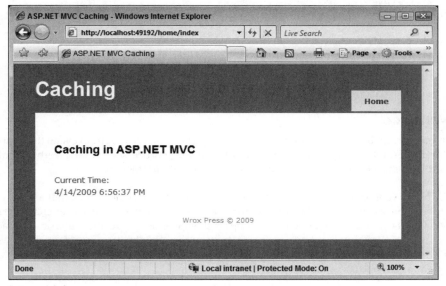

Figure 14-1

If you've read any ASP.NET WebForms books or articles about caching, you may wonder why you wouldn't display the exact current time along with the cached time in the same page to let you compare their values. The answer is that ASP.NET MVC provides a caching mechanism to allow you to cache the value of a controller, so even if you insert the exact time value in the view, it is kept in the cache by ASP.NET MVC.

This example showed the simplest form of the OutputCache *action filter. You have several other ways to customize the behavior of caching using the parameters that you pass to this filter.*

Duration is the most common parameter for the OutputCache filter. It accepts integer values that specify the time in seconds that the cache should keep the value of the controller response. Listing 14-1 sets the duration to 60 seconds. What the right value is for this parameter depends on your application requirements and your own experience. If you choose a lower value than what you need, you're not going to have an effective cache, and if you choose a value that is too high, there is a great chance that it will affect the quality of your content.

Default ASP.NET caching can take place at client-side, server-side, or downstream locations, or a combination of these. Using the `Location` parameter for the `OutputCache` action filter, you can modify this location with `OutputCacheLocation` enumerator values that are located in the System.Web.UI namespace. The default value for the `Location` parameter is `Any`.

Listing 14-3 is the modified version of Listing 14-1 that enforces ASP.NET caching to use "downstream" as the cache location.

Listing 14-3: Use the Location parameter to customize caching

```
[OutputCache(Duration = 60,
    Location = OutputCacheLocation.Downstream,
    VaryByParam = "None")]
public ActionResult Index()
{
    ViewData["Message"] = "Caching in ASP.NET MVC";
    ViewData["CurrentTime"] = DateTime.Now.ToString();

    return View();
}
```

Cache Variance

You can use parameters to vary your caches. For example, you may want to cache the content of a controller for all POST verb requests and have a different value processed for GET verbs. Similarly, you may want to cache a controller response based on different parameters.

Like ASP.NET WebForms, ASP.NET MVC offers a set of cache variance types that allows you to have a dependency between your cache and common requests, responses, and server characteristics. At a lower level, you can use cache dependency objects to enable other specific scenarios for cache variance.

ASP.NET MVC offers four types of cache variance parameters, including `VaryByParam`, `VaryByHeader`, `VaryByContentEncoding`, and `VaryByCustom`.

VaryByParam

Your cache can vary by different HTTP verb parameters, so you can enter a semicolon-separated list of values for the `VaryByParam` parameter in the `OutputCache` filter. Though you can set this parameter to the relevant values, you can also use the wildcard character (*) to refer to all the parameters or the `None` value to refer to no parameters.

Listing 14-4 updates the sample action method to cache its response based on all parameters.

Listing 14-4: Use the VaryByParam parameter to customize caching

```
[OutputCache(Duration = 60, VaryByParam = "*")]
public ActionResult Index()
{
    ViewData["Message"] = "Caching in ASP.NET MVC";
```

```
        ViewData["CurrentTime"] = DateTime.Now.ToString();

        return View();
    }
```

VaryByHeader

Another common scenario in caching variance is invalidating your cache value based on HTTP header parameters. For example, you may want to reprocess your pages when the `Accept-Language` parameter is changed, so you can render your pages with the appropriate language for the end-user. In such cases, you can use the `VaryByHeader` parameter, which accepts a semicolon-separated list of HTTP header properties.

Listing 14-5 provides an example of this parameter in action.

Listing 14-5: Use the VaryByHeader parameter to customize caching

```
[OutputCache(Duration = 60,
    VaryByParam = "*",
    VaryByHeader = "Accept-Language")]
public ActionResult Index()
{
    ViewData["Message"] = "Caching in ASP.NET MVC";
    ViewData["CurrentTime"] = DateTime.Now.ToString();

    return View();
}
```

VaryByContentEncoding

You can also use the cache variance option for content encoding using the `VarByContentEncoding` parameter, which takes a semicolon-separated list of encoding values. In fact, it uses the `Content-Encoding` header parameter behind the scenes. The usage of this parameter is shown in Listing 14-6.

Listing 14-6: Use the VaryByEncoding parameter to customize caching

```
[OutputCache(Duration = 60, VaryByContentEncoding = "gzip")]
public ActionResult Index()
{
    ViewData["Message"] = "Caching in ASP.NET MVC";
    ViewData["CurrentTime"] = DateTime.Now.ToString();

    return View();
}
```

VaryByCustom

`VaryByCustom` is a type of variance available for those who cannot find a relevant variance type among the other options and want to build their custom cache variance. Of course, this type of cache variance requires your own implementation based on some extensibility points, and it's beyond the scope of our Beginning book series, but you can search online resources to access the many articles that describe how to use this type of cache variance.

The Cache Profile

In many circumstances, you want to have consistency among your cache settings for various controller classes and action methods so that different parts of your application behave similarly. In such cases, you need to declare the same cache settings for all these parts of your application. One possible solution is to declare all these settings manually with the same values for all action methods. Obviously, this method has some drawbacks. For example, it requires a lot of your time and makes it hard to customize cache settings in the future (because this requires modifying of all the settings again).

To provide a solution for this common problem, Microsoft offers a cache profile mechanism that allows you to declare the cache settings in the Web configuration file and then refer to them in your code, so if you want to modify them, you can simply change your values in Web.config.

One of the OutputCache parameters is the CacheProfile, which can be set to the string name of cache profile element that you have defined in your Web.config file. ASP.NET automatically loads cache settings from that element and applies them to your controller class or action method.

In the Web.config file, you can add a <caching /> element inside <system.web /> that accepts <outputCacheSettings /> as one of its children. This element has an <outputCacheProfiles /> element that holds the cache profiles. You can add your cache profiles with a string name and some attributes that are identical to OutputCache parameters. Listing 14-7 shows the configuration for the Wrox cache profile.

Listing 14-7: Wrox cache profile configuration

```
<caching>
  <outputCacheSettings>
    <outputCacheProfiles>
      <add name="Wrox" duration="90" varyByParam="None" />
    </outputCacheProfiles>
  </outputCacheSettings>
</caching>
```

Listing 14-8 shows how simple it is to use this cache profile in your code.

Listing 14-8: Use Wrox cache profile

```
[OutputCache(CacheProfile = "Wrox")]
public ActionResult Index()
{
    ViewData["Message"] = "Caching in ASP.NET MVC";
    ViewData["CurrentTime"] = DateTime.Now.ToString();

    return View();
}
```

Cache Dependency

In some cases, you need to update your cached data (for example, in XML configuration files) with the latest changes. In fact, many cases exist where such dependencies come into the play, and you need to deal with them to guarantee that your software works properly.

Cache dependency is a general technique in ASP.NET caching that allows you to define a dependency between cache resources and their corresponding data source. This data source can be a file or a data table in a database.

In essence, cache dependency helps you update your cached data when the original resource is changed and hence it's necessary to update your cached data. For example, in a configuration file if you do not update your cached data with the latest changes, the system works with the old configuration and this disrupts your software and can produce errors.

The core part of cache dependency in ASP.NET caching is the CacheDependency object, which has several constructors that allow you to bind your caching to a file resource with several options. Though this is the main part of cache dependency, which has been part of the product since the beginning, in ASP.NET 2.0 Microsoft introduced a new concept called SQL cache dependency that is implemented in the SqlCacheDependency class, which is derived directly from CacheDependency.

SQL cache dependency helps you bind your cached data to database tables and update them whenever data is updated in the original table. This is a significant change that enhances the performance of your application to a great extent, because by using this object you can reduce your database calls to those that are absolutely necessary and avoid extra calls to retrieve the same old data.

Like ASP.NET WebForms, ASP.NET MVC supports cache dependency objects out-of-the-box. Even SQL cache dependency is supported, through a parameter for the OutputCache action filter, and you can set the SqlDependency parameter to the SQL cache dependency name defined in your configuration file followed by your table name. Before implementing SQL cache dependency for a table, you must register notification services for that table, using the command prompt.

Cache dependency is an advanced technique in ASP.NET caching; it is more appropriate for higher-level discussion and is outside the scope of this book.

Validation

One of the most common requirements in Web development and design is the validation of user input to ensure that input data is in the expected format or range and to prevent unexpected exceptions in the inner layers of the application.

In ASP.NET WebForms, validation was mainly implemented as a set of server controls that could be integrated with the client-side through JavaScript code and allowed you to validate user input based on several templates. You could, for example, use a RequiredFieldValidator control to make sure that a user had entered a value in your textbox, and you could also use a RegularExpressionValidator to make sure that a user had entered a valid Internet URL or e-mail address. In this way, validation was quite simple with ASP.NET WebForms and required little effort from you as a developer or a designer.

However, ASP.NET MVC doesn't come with any server-side control and doesn't have such a simple form validation mechanism in the same level. Most of the work is done by hand, and it requires you to write your own code to handle validation on the client- and server- sides.

As you'll see, two methods of validation exist in ASP.NET MVC. You can implement a very powerful and fail-safe validation mechanism in your models, which is much better than ASP.NET WebForms validation, but there is also a second mechanism that can be compared to ASP.NET WebForms validation, and you can argue that in that sense ASP.NET WebForms are easier to use.

Because this is the bad news, the good news is that the community has put great effort into this area and has released some third-party open source components to simplify the process and save you from writing a lot of code. Though I'm going to discuss the basic implementation in ASP.NET MVC with core APIs, I recommend that you first check out these tools and components before writing your own code. One of the several implementations that I can introduce is xVal, which is a powerful validation framework that integrates very well with client-side and is available on CodePlex at `http://xval.codeplex.com`.

Validation in ASP.NET MVC

ASP.NET MVC has no control, no event, and no viewstate for maintaining form data on the fly, so validation is a process that requires a special effort. Validation is a technique that is implemented in a lower level in ASP.NET MVC, and this of course means that there can be several approaches to validation that work on top of this lower API, which means that you have more powerful validation in ASP.NET MVC. Therefore, there isn't a single way to document validation in ASP.NET MVC, but there is an official main solution that is described in this section. Implementing a great validation system requires some effort, and the techniques go beyond the topic of this chapter. So, although it's better to find implementations in open source projects, the basic infrastructure of most of these implementations revolves around two general concepts:

❑   **Model State** — This is a feature that connects controllers and views to let controllers pass validation data to views using `ViewData.ModelState`. This approach is easier than the second approach (model binders), and we focus on it.

❑   **Model Binders** — Model binding is covered in Chapter 5 and has extensive applications, including validation. Validation with model binders needs more coding, but some of the current validation implementations are based solely on model-binding techniques. In this case (which is outside the scope of this discussion), you define your custom model binder. The ASP.NET MVC runtime calls your binder to grab values for model objects. Here, you can check the correctness of data with declarations on the model-binding side. This approach is very powerful and can ensure the correctness of data in a very low level.

In a moment, you examine the first method, but for now I should note that the best validation method is a method that addresses some important factors:

❑   All model objects ensure the correctness of their data in lower levels. In other words, when you need a higher level of validation (in the controller or UI, for example), you should try to bind your model objects in lower levels to handle any unforeseen cases. This is more likely to happen with the model binder approach than with the model state approach.

❑   Validation should cover all possible situations and data formats, so you need to think about all possible cases that may happen. For example, you should catch all the valid e-mail address formats when a field is accepting e-mail addresses. I've seen some e-mail formats that can't match valid e-mail addresses (that is, with localized domain names).

❑   It's convenient to have client-side validation along with server-side validation to display error messages before a user posts data to the server. Of course, this may be a little tricky in ASP.NET MVC, but there are some techniques you can apply.

Validation with Model State

The most relevant method of form validation is using model state. Model state is a feature included in ASP.NET MVC to pass model state data including validation error messages to the view, so it's the basic validation technique in the framework.

As a quick overview of the validation process with model state, you build controllers that accept POST verb requests that are ostensibly sent by end-users to update a form. You then check the correctness of input data in your controller code and use the `ModelState` object to add relevant error messages to corresponding elements. If there is no validation error, you can perform your operation and, for example, save your data in a database. Otherwise, you return the form with the entered data and error messages. On the view side, you can use built-in HTML Helper methods to display error messages for each element and show a summary of errors.

In the following Try It Out you work on a real-world example that can clarify the theoretical discussions to a great extent.

Try It Out   Building a Contact Form with Validation

Building a contact form and implementing its validation process is a great example of form validation in ASP.NET MVC because it covers several common types of validation. In this part of the chapter, you build a contact form that gets some parameters such as name, e-mail, subject, and the body of the e-mail. The form validates the input and then sends an e-mail to a recipient if the input data is valid.

In the first step, you create a `ContactController` class with two action methods called `Contact` but with different overloads. The first overload takes no parameter, accepts the GET verb requests, and serves to direct requests to the page, and the second overload takes four string parameters as e-mail properties and accepts POST verb requests from submitted requests from the page. Listing 14-9 shows the source code for this controller class.

Listing 14-9: ContactController

```
using System.Net.Mail;
using System.Text.RegularExpressions;
using System.Web.Mvc;

namespace Validation.Controllers
{
    public class ContactController : Controller
    {
        [AcceptVerbs(HttpVerbs.Get)]
        public ActionResult Contact()
        {
            return View();
        }
```

Continued

Listing 14-9: ContactController *(continued)*

```
[AcceptVerbs(HttpVerbs.Post)]
public ActionResult Contact(string name, string email,
    string subject, string body)
{
    // Validate Name
    if (string.IsNullOrEmpty(name))
        ModelState.AddModelError("name", "You must enter your name.");

    // Validate Email
    if (string.IsNullOrEmpty(email))
        ModelState.AddModelError("email", "You must enter your email.");
    else
    {
        Regex regex = new Regex
            (@"\w+([-+.']\w+)*@\w+([-.]\w+)*\.\w+([-.]\w+)*",
            RegexOptions.IgnoreCase);

        if (!regex.IsMatch(email))
            ModelState.AddModelError("email", "You must enter a valid
email.");
    }

    // Validate Subject
    if (string.IsNullOrEmpty(subject))
        ModelState.AddModelError("subject", "You must enter a subject.");

    // Validate Body
    if (string.IsNullOrEmpty(body))
        ModelState.AddModelError("body", "You must enter the body text.");

    // Send Email
    if (ViewData.ModelState.IsValid)
    {
        MailAddress from = new MailAddress(email, name);
        MailAddress to = new MailAddress("keyvan@wrox.com");

        MailMessage mail = new MailMessage(from, to);
        mail.Subject = subject;
        mail.Body = body;

        SmtpClient smtp = new SmtpClient("mail.wrox.com");
        smtp.DeliveryMethod = SmtpDeliveryMethod.Network;
        smtp.Send(mail);

        return RedirectToAction("Index", "Home");
    }

    // There is an error, so we display the form with error messages
    return View();
    }
  }
}
```

The other stage of validation is in the views. You create a `Contact` view (see Listing 14-10) that is responsible for the contact form rendering.

Listing 14-10: Contact view

```
<%@ Page Title="" Language="C#" MasterPageFile="~/Views/Shared/Site.Master"
 Inherits="System.Web.Mvc.ViewPage" %>

<asp:Content ID="Content1" ContentPlaceHolderID="TitleContent" runat="server">
    Contact Form
</asp:Content>
<asp:Content ID="Content2" ContentPlaceHolderID="MainContent" runat="server">
    <h2>
        Contact Form</h2>
    <p>
        You can use this form to contact us.
    </p>
    <%= Html.ValidationSummary() %>
    <% using (Html.BeginForm())
       { %>
    <div>
        <table>
            <tr>
                <td>
                    Name:
                </td>
                <td>
                    <%= Html.TextBox("name") %>
                    <%= Html.ValidationMessage("name")%>
                </td>
            </tr>
            <tr>
                <td>
                    Email:
                </td>
                <td>
                    <%= Html.TextBox("email") %>
                    <%= Html.ValidationMessage("email") %>
                </td>
            </tr>
            <tr>
                <td>
                    Subject:
                </td>
                <td>
                    <%= Html.TextBox("subject")%>
                    <%= Html.ValidationMessage("subject")%>
                </td>
            </tr>
            <tr>
                <td>
                    Body:
                </td>
```

Continued

Listing 14-10: Contact view *(continued)*

```
                <td>
                    <%= Html.TextArea("body") %>
                    <%= Html.ValidationMessage("body")%>
                </td>
            </tr>
            <tr>
                <td>
                </td>
                <td>
                    <input type="submit" value="Send" />
                </td>
            </tr>
        </table>
    </div>
    <% } %>
</asp:Content>
```

Now you can run your application and test this contact form. If you enter invalid data, the form displays the relevant error messages and highlights the appropriate textboxes (see Figure 14-2).

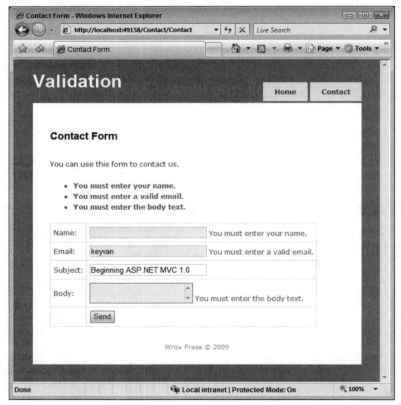

Figure 14-2

You see that the `Html.ValidateMessage` helper methods automatically highlight their corresponding boxes and notify the user of the error.

How It Works

The first `Contact` action method is pretty straightforward; the main part of our discussion is about the second overload. Here, you can consider the method as two main sections: a section that validates input values and a section that sends an e-mail. The emphasis is on the first section, where a few `if` conditions check the correctness of the input data with built-in string methods and regular expressions. If the input is invalid, the `ModelState.AddModelError` method lets you pass the appropriate error message to the view. It passes the name of the validation message key along with an error message.

After validating the input values, the `ViewData.ModelState.IsValid` property is checked to see if there is a validation error. If there isn't an error, the code creates the e-mail and sends it with the SMTP objects. If the form has invalid fields, the current input values will be returned to the form along with the errors to ask the user to correct them.

```
[AcceptVerbs(HttpVerbs.Post)]
public ActionResult Contact(string name, string email,
    string subject, string body)
{
    // Validate Name
    if (string.IsNullOrEmpty(name))
        ModelState.AddModelError("name", "You must enter your name.");

    // Validate Email
    if (string.IsNullOrEmpty(email))
        ModelState.AddModelError("email", "You must enter your email.");
    else
    {
        Regex regex = new Regex
            (@"\w+([-+.']\w+)*@\w+([-.]\w+)*\.\w+([-.]\w+)*",
            RegexOptions.IgnoreCase);

        if (!regex.IsMatch(email))
            ModelState.AddModelError("email", "You must enter a valid email.");
    }

    // Validate Subject
    if (string.IsNullOrEmpty(subject))
        ModelState.AddModelError("subject", "You must enter a subject.");

    // Validate Body
    if (string.IsNullOrEmpty(body))
        ModelState.AddModelError("body", "You must enter the body text.");

    // Send Email
    if (ViewData.ModelState.IsValid)
    {
        MailAddress from = new MailAddress(email, name);
        MailAddress to = new MailAddress("keyvan@wrox.com");

        MailMessage mail = new MailMessage(from, to);
        mail.Subject = subject;
```

```
            mail.Body = body;

            SmtpClient smtp = new SmtpClient("mail.wrox.com");
            smtp.DeliveryMethod = SmtpDeliveryMethod.Network;
            smtp.Send(mail);

            return RedirectToAction("Index", "Home");
        }

        // There is an error, so we display the form with error messages
        return View();
    }
```

The main part of the view is a normal form that renders some textboxes with a button to enter data, but there are some additions for validation in this code. First, there is an `Html.ValidationSummary` helper method that renders a list of all validation errors in a page, so it will be visible when your form has a validation error. The other addition is a few `Html.ValidateMessage` helper methods that get a string parameter that is the name of the textbox that you want to show error messages for (this string name is also in controller actions to refer to them). These helper methods display error messages as well.

```
<%= Html.ValidationSummary() %>
<% using (Html.BeginForm())
    { %>
<div>
    <table>
        <tr>
            <td>
                Name:
            </td>
            <td>
                <%= Html.TextBox("name") %>
                <%= Html.ValidationMessage("name")%>
            </td>
        </tr>
        <tr>
            <td>
                Email:
            </td>
            <td>
                <%= Html.TextBox("email") %>
                <%= Html.ValidationMessage("email") %>
            </td>
        </tr>
        <tr>
            <td>
                Subject:
            </td>
            <td>
                <%= Html.TextBox("subject")%>
                <%= Html.ValidationMessage("subject")%>
            </td>
        </tr>
        <tr>
            <td>
```

```
            Body:
        </td>
        <td>
            <%= Html.TextArea("body") %>
            <%= Html.ValidationMessage("body")%>
        </td>
    </tr>
    <tr>
        <td>
        </td>
        <td>
            <input type="submit" value="Send" />
        </td>
    </tr>
    </table>
</div>
<% } %>
```

As another example of validation, you can check out the source code for the registration systems in the project template generated for ASP.NET MVC by Visual Studio.

Master Pages

The idea of a shared user interface is commonplace for all Web applications, and I cannot think of a single Web application that doesn't require this feature. Master pages have been a very popular built-in feature in ASP.NET WebForms that allows you to easily share a consistent look-and-feel among all the pages in a Web application. ASP.NET MVC includes master pages as well, and their usage and implementation are very similar to ASP.NET WebForms. Therefore, this chapter doesn't include a long discussion; it just notes a few points relevant for an ASP.NET MVC developer.

Master pages have the same .master extension in ASP.NET MVC, and you can add them to your projects from the Add New Item dialog available in Visual Studio. You should know that you need to add master pages to the Shared subfolder inside the Views folder in your project to be able to share them in all the views in your application.

Similarly, ASP.NET WebForms master pages contain ContentPlaceHolder sections that act as holders for dynamic content in pages that apply them. Here, ContentPlaceHolder has the exact same characteristics as in ASP.NET WebForms.

As in ASP.NET WebForms, master pages in ASP.NET MVC are relevant for declaring the layout of your pages, setting HTML header elements, and adding your JavaScript resources.

You can also refer to view data in your master pages by using the ViewData collection, and you can use HTML Helper methods in your master pages. However, you should take care when using such elements, especially ViewData items, because they mandate that all derived views must have the exact same item provided in their controllers. For example, if you're going to refer to ViewData["Message"] in your master pages, then all controllers that use a view that has applied the master page should set this parameter.

You can create a master page easily and quickly. The main point of interest in the creation of master pages in ASP.NET MVC is the location in which they should be added. Listing 14-11 shows a simple master page with common characteristics.

Listing 14-11: Sample master page

```
<%@ Master Language="C#" Inherits="System.Web.Mvc.ViewMasterPage" %>

<!DOCTYPE html PUBLIC "-//W3C//DTD XHTML 1.0 Strict//EN"
 "http://www.w3.org/TR/xhtml1/DTD/xhtml1-strict.dtd">
<html xmlns="http://www.w3.org/1999/xhtml">
<head runat="server">
    <title>
        <asp:ContentPlaceHolder ID="TitleContent" runat="server" />
    </title>
    <script src="../../Scripts/MicrosoftAjax.js" type="text/javascript"></script>
    <script src="../../Scripts/MicrosoftMvcAjax.js" type="text/javascript">
    </script>
    <link href="../../Content/Site.css" rel="stylesheet" type="text/css" />
</head>
<body>
    <div class="page">
        <div id="header">
            <div id="title">
                <h1>
                    Master Pages</h1>
            </div>
            <div id="logindisplay">
                <% Html.RenderPartial("LogOnUserControl"); %>
            </div>
        <div id="menucontainer">
            <ul id="menu">
                <li>
                    <%= Html.ActionLink("Home", "Index", "Home")%></li>
                <li>
                    <%= Html.ActionLink("About", "About", "Home")%></li>
            </ul>
        </div>
        </div>
        <div id="main">
            <asp:ContentPlaceHolder ID="MainContent" runat="server" />
            <div id="footer">
                Wrox Press © 2009
            </div>
        </div>
    </div>
</body>
</html>
```

When you add a view to your application, a dialog appears and you can simply choose the master page for your view (along with some other options, such as its strongly typed class and the ID of ContentPlaceHolder that should be filled). This dialog is shown in Figure 14-3.

This dialog also helps you automatically generate a view that has set the placeholder names and values. Listing 14-12 shows the code for a view that uses the master page presented in Listing 14-11. The key points are to set the proper value for the ContentPlaceHolderID attributes and to add the Content section to the view code.

Figure 14-3

Listing 14-12: CustomView

```
<%@ Page Title="" Language="C#" MasterPageFile="~/Views/Shared/Site.Master"
Inherits="System.Web.Mvc.ViewPage" %>

<asp:Content ID="Content1" ContentPlaceHolderID="TitleContent" runat="server">
    Custom
</asp:Content>
<asp:Content ID="Content2" ContentPlaceHolderID="MainContent" runat="server">
    <h2>
        Custom View</h2>
</asp:Content>
```

Other Features

So far I have discussed some common Web development scenarios shared between ASP.NET WebForms and ASP.NET MVC, but some other, less common features are worth pointing out in this section.

Sitemaps

ASP.NET sitemaps help you manage the URLs and navigation of your site. ASP.NET WebForms provides an XML provider for sitemaps and supports an extensible provider model for other storage systems. Some APIs and controls also ease your job when working with navigation and URLs.

But the XML sitemap provider and its controls don't work with ASP.NET MVC. You need to use the provider extensibility points to implement your own provider for ASP.NET MVC and use its API to integrate your application with the new system.

Fortunately, such an XML sitemap provider is implemented for ASP.NET MVC, and you can save time by searching on Google to find existing implementations.

The Profile System

There has been a built-in profile system with an integrated provider model available in ASP.NET since version 2.0. Fortunately, this feature is available in ASP.NET MVC without any change, and you can use it in exactly the same way as in ASP.NET WebForms.

Health Monitoring

Like the profile system, health monitoring is a feature available in ASP.NET with an integrated provider model that is implemented for SQL Server by default and can be extended for other storage methods. This system allows you to log events and errors that occur in your application with all the details in a storage system. Health monitoring is helpful for developers and Webmasters for keeping track of their application diagnoses and resolving any possible issues on their sites.

ASP.NET MVC can work with this health-monitoring system as well, and there isn't any change that stops you from applying your knowledge from ASP.NET WebForms in ASP.NET MVC.

Server Controls

Most likely the biggest advantage of ASP.NET WebForms over ASP.NET MVC is the rich set of built-in, commercial, and free open source controls available for it, which can be used easily and declaratively. ASP.NET MVC doesn't support such controls.

However, many of these controls work based on state persistence and event mechanisms that are available in ASP.NET WebForms but are not included in ASP.NET MVC, so you need to write your code to present such user interface elements, and most of the time this requires much more effort on your part.

Community members and commercial software vendors are working hard to release different sets of options for user interface elements to save your time and simplify this process. Although it is currently difficult to produce the sophisticated visual experience users expect and rapid development with ASP.NET WebForms controls, this is likely to change in the future.

Summary

This chapter covered a wide range of topics, mainly about leveraging common Web development techniques and concepts of ASP.NET WebForms in ASP.NET MVC.

The first and most important concept covered was caching, because it's a very handy and common technique used for improving the performance of a Web application. The fundamentals of caching are common to ASP.NET WebForms and ASP.NET MVC, but caching's implementation is different in ASP .NET MVC, where you can cache your controllers and action methods based on the same parameters you use in ASP.NET WebForms pages, master pages, or user controls.

Validation in ASP.NET MVC is completely different, and you no longer can enjoy the ease and convenience of ASP.NET WebForms validation with simple controls. This chapter provided a quick overview of the validation options and introduced two main methods to apply validation. It then discussed the basic, easier way to perform validation, using the `ModelState` object.

The chapter also included a short discussion of master pages in ASP.NET MVC. The use of master pages is very similar to their use in ASP.NET WebForms both in structure and in implementation and there are only a few points to consider about them. The chapter wrapped up by pointing to some other features available in WebForms and how similar results can be achieved in ASP.NET MVC.

Although the topic of this chapter is extensive and could include many other aspects of Web development and ASP.NET WebForms as well, the main focus was on common features that you'll deal with in your daily development.

Exercises

1. Modify the caching example in this chapter to cache data for 90 seconds on the server side, and change it to vary according to HTTP referral values.

2. Modify the contact form validation example in this chapter to get the user's site URL and validate its value as well.

Authentication and Authorization

Security is one of the biggest concerns for all software systems in the world, and it includes many topics. But the common concern when first learning how to implement security can be divided into two main parts:

❑   Ensuring that only authorized users with the required permissions are allowed to access a resource

❑   Preventing any illegal access to sensitive data with techniques that improve the security level of a system

The latter aspect of security is mostly taken care of by Microsoft in its Web server and development technologies. ASP.NET, IIS, and SQL Server all have a great security level that restricts illegal access to resources even if developers don't know much about security settings. Fortunately, this aspect of security in Microsoft technologies is proven, and comparative statistics support this assertion.

The first aspect of security is something you should consider during the main stage of developing a software system because it is important to determine who has legal to access to your resources or which resources should be restricted from public access.

Here, two main concepts come into play: *authentication* and *authorization*. These concepts are found in all software development technologies, including ASP.NET MVC.

Authentication is the mechanism by which you distinguish registered users from anonymous users. For example, you may have a page that displays internal company news to employees, and you want to allow only registered (and maybe confirmed) users to have access to it. This process is authentication, which restricts public access to resources on a site and allows only authenticated users (those who are signed in) to access them.

The second concept in software security is authorization. Authorization restricts even generally authenticated users from accessing a specific resource, reserving access to special authorized users on a site. Authorization is a concept that is applied after authentication, at the next level, and supplements it. For example, consider the previous example for authentication within your company. While there are some users who have logged in to your site, you still may want to restrict the access to read pages with specific reports because those reports are for managers only. In this case, you need a new mechanism, called authorization, that allows you to restrict the access of specific users (or groups of users) to a page.

This chapter focuses on the practical aspects of authentication and authorization, showing you the methods, concepts, and techniques you need to know to implement these concepts. Fortunately, authentication and authorization in ASP.NET MVC are built on the same principles and APIs as ASP.NET WebForms, and actually they're both using a part of the core ASP.NET API, so you can extend your knowledge in ASP.NET WebForms for these topics to ASP.NET MVC as well.

Therefore, this chapter covers the following topics:

- ❑ Principles of authentication and authorization
- ❑ Authentication and authorization in ASP.NET
- ❑ Authentication and authorization in ASP.NET MVC
- ❑ How to configure an ASP.NET MVC application to support authentication and authorization
- ❑ How to use ASP.NET membership and role providers with ASP.NET MVC
- ❑ How to enable forms authentication with ASP.NET MVC

Of course, authentication, authorization, and other security matters encompass many possibilities, and entire books are written to address such topics. But with the core principles discussed in this chapter, you will have a solid foundation to build on if you want to explore security further.

Principles of Authentication and Authorization

First of all, you need to know some principles about authentication and authorization that already may be familiar to some readers.

Authentication is the process of distinguishing anonymous users from registered users, in which users employ some mechanisms to show their identity to the system. This mechanism is called signing in (or logging in). It consists of a step that gets the user's identity and password to validate them. If the user is valid, they will be authenticated and some specific characteristics will be assigned to them by the system. In essence, authentication can be understood as the step where the user logs in to the site, and it blocks public access to some resources. As is obvious, authentication requires mechanisms to build the login pages, validate users, and restrict some specific resources from public access.

Authorization supplements authentication and goes even further, by trying to restrict authenticated users from accessing specific resources. In this case, it allows you to give permissions to specific users or groups of users to access a particular resource. Like authentication, authorization requires certain mechanisms, such as a system to define user groups and to configure it to restrict particular users from accessing a page.

As stated, authorization can be declared per user or per group. In the former case, you configure your system based on the user identities (which are usually identical to the username), and in the latter case you use the concept of roles to group users and then grant access to those roles.

Authentication and Authorization in ASP.NET

ASP.NET comes with great and easy-to-use features to support authentication and authorization out-of-the-box. These features are built on top of a configuration system and a set of APIs that allow Web developers to easily enable authentication and authorization in their applications.

ASP.NET supports three authentication options out-of-the-box:

❑ **Forms authentication** — This is the most common option among developers, and what you probably have used on Internet sites so far. This method of authentication applies cookies to authenticate the user on a site. This is the option that this section focuses on.

❑ **Windows authentication** — This option, which is common for local portals, uses the same credentials as local Windows users over the network, so users can enter the same username and password to work with sites. This type of authentication works in conjunction with IIS authentication mechanisms such as the anonymous, digest, basic, and integrated authentication systems.

❑ **Passport authentication** — Considered to be an extinct option, this type of authentication works with the Microsoft Passport system to authenticate a user across several sites. The usage of this method has been challenged by open identities and Microsoft is transiting to its Live ID as an OpenID provider.

These days OpenIDs, universal identifiers for Internet users, are becoming common on the Web. Such identifiers (which are supported by Google, Microsoft, Yahoo!, and other software companies) allow you to use a constant username and password to log in to several sites. These sites use a secure connection to connect to the central OpenID provider to authenticate your user.

ASP.NET developers have integrated these open identifiers with ASP.NET applications through forms authentication, and great open source components and controls have been implemented and are available to you (such as DotNetOpenID at `http://code.google.com/p/dotnetopenid`*).*

Although great controls are available to work with authentication and authorization features in the ASP.NET WebForms, they can't be used in ASP.NET MVC as is, so this section doesn't focus on them. Instead, it discusses membership and role providers in ASP.NET because they're used in ASP.NET MVC, too.

In the latest version of the .NET Framework, Microsoft has included a set of built-in providers as one of the main parts of its development framework specifically for ASP.NET. These providers are supposed to provide a set of constant mechanisms to deal with common development scenarios, and smooth them out. Using these providers, Microsoft wants to maintain independence between data storage systems and the high-level APIs. Microsoft has introduced these providers with some default implementations for Microsoft database systems such as SQL Server, and also offers extensible APIs that could be used to implement these providers for other storage systems such as Oracle or MySql. Of course, community members have implemented these providers for other database systems and used them extensively.

Microsoft offers several provider systems in different portions of the .NET Framework whenever it is necessary to deal with a storage system, so developers can switch between storage options and maintain consistency in their applications.

Here, the main focus is on two provider systems that are known as membership and role providers, and both are a part of ASP.NET.

The Membership Provider

The ASP.NET membership provider offers a configurable system to keep track of a list of users with some of their essential properties in a data storage system, and a set of APIs that helps developers to deal with these users and their properties and, most importantly, to validate their credentials when necessary. The membership provider performs many tasks behind the scenes and saves developers from having to write a lot of code to achieve similar goals. The membership provider is also integrated with membership controls in ASP.NET WebForms to offer the simplest way of working with authentication.

In fact, the membership provider offers some features in the area of authentication and keeps track of some user properties such as the username, password, e-mail, last login time, and last failed login time. Moreover, it works in conjunction with .NET cryptography classes to offer several methods to store user passwords in a secure way.

The ASP.NET membership provider can be used with any storage system, but some default implementations for Microsoft SQL Server and Microsoft Access are available. By the way, it's mostly used with SQL Server in the backend.

The Role Provider

Like the membership provider, the built-in role provider comes with a set of features that are integrated with ASP.NET in order to enable some features that allow developers to work with authorization and manage user and role permissions. The role provider integrates with the membership provider to connect users to their roles and permissions. It also works according to a configuration system and can be used with different data storage methods.

In essence, the role provider offers some features to deal with authorization, and its configuration system helps you restrict access to any page in your application for specific users or roles.

Membership and role providers can be used with any storage system through their extensible model, but the default installation of the .NET Framework copies some SQL script files that can be used to set up ASP.NET tables in your SQL Server databases manually. Alternatively, you can run the aspnet_regsql *command in the Visual Studio command prompt in order to run the same scripts on your database using a friendly wizard.*

Authentication and Authorization in ASP.NET MVC

ASP.NET MVC, like ASP.NET WebForms, is a portion of the more general ASP.NET technology, and inherits some features from its parent and applies the ASP.NET core API. Authentication and authorization are features that are mostly inherited from ASP.NET and are used in ASP.NET MVC, ASP.NET WebForms, and ASP.NET Dynamic Data.

ASP.NET MVC uses the same configuration system as well as membership and role APIs as ASP.NET WebForms does, and can also apply membership and role providers easily.

Configuring Your Application to Use Authorization and Authentication

The most common and basic step in enabling authentication and authorization in an ASP.NET application is configuring the application to use them. You may be familiar with the configuration from your knowledge of ASP.NET WebForms because there is no significant difference between ASP.NET MVC and ASP.NET WebForms in this area.

Generally, four configuration sections can be added to your applications to enable authentication and authorization, but based on your requirements you may need none of them, some of them, or all of them:

❑   If you don't want to use authentication and authorization in your system, you don't need to add any configuration sections to your application.

❑   If you want to use authentication only, you just need to add the `<authentication />` element to your `Web.config`.

❑   If you want to restrict access to some resources in your application for users or roles (authorization), you can add one or more `<authorization />` elements to your `Web.config`.

❑   If you're interested in using ASP.NET membership and/role providers in your application, you can add `<membership />` and/or `<roleManager />` elements to your `Web.config`.

Note that all these configuration sections appear within the `<system.web />` *element in* `Web.config` *files.*

<authentication />

The most common element in authentication configuration is the `<authentication />` element, which allows you to define the type of authentication that you want to use as well as the settings that you need.

This element has a `mode` attribute, which gets one of the Forms, None, Passport, or Windows values to enable one of these authentication types in your application. Moreover, it can have two subelements including `<forms />` and `<passport />` that enable further configuration of these systems. This section focuses on the `<forms />` element.

The `<forms />` element is one of the common elements in ASP.NET configuration. It allows you to configure a forms authentication system for your applications, and set it up with some common attributes. We leave it to you to read and learn about all the possible attributes for this element as well as its only subelement, `<credentials />`, but here we try to give a short discussion about the main attributes that you usually need to configure.

This element has a `name` attribute that specifies the name of the cookie that should be used with your site. It also has a `loginUrl` attribute that gets the virtual path of the login page that you have implemented for your application. You need to set this attribute to the appropriate URL based on your implementation and routing. Moreover, there is a `defaultUrl` attribute that gets the URL of the page where users will automatically be redirected after logging in. `timeout` is the last common attribute. It gets the time in minutes when the cookie expires.

An example of a common configuration for the `<authentication />` element is shown in Listing 15-1.

Listing 15-1: A common implementation of the `<authentication />` element

```
<authentication mode="Forms">
  <forms name=".WROXASPNETMVC"
         loginUrl="~/Login"
         defaultUrl="~/Home"
         timeout="1440" />
</authentication>
```

Here, the cookie name is set to `.WROXASPNETMVC` and uses `/Login` as the login page. The home page is the default URL for users after successful login. The timeout of the cookie is set to 1440 minutes (24 hours), so users must log in to the site again after this time.

<authorization />

The `<authorization />` element enables you to allow or deny access to specific resources on your site for particular users, roles, or HTTP verbs. First, you need to define a `<location />` element in your `Web.config` that is a direct child of the root `<configuration />` element (and not `<system.web />`). Then you need to add a `<system.web />` element within this `<location />` element. `<location />` has a `path` attribute that allows you to define the path of the resource that you want to restrict access to. It also has an `allowOverride` attribute that helps you override this restriction for subfolders and resources. However, you mainly rely on the `path` attribute in most real-world implementations.

> *Note that In ASP.NET MVC you have two common options to define authorization and authentication rules. In this section, you see the configuration option that is used in ASP.NET WebForms; later in this chapter you see a new option specific to ASP.NET MVC that uses a declarative approach by applying action filters to accomplish the same goals. These two options are available and you can use them based on your requirements, but the action filter approach seems to be more common among developers.*

Within the newly defined `<system.web />` element, you can add your `<authorization />` element, which doesn't have any attributes but can access the `<allow />` or `<deny />` elements as its children. Using these two elements, you can configure authorization in your application.

Both `<allow />` and `<deny />` elements accept three common attributes that help you when setting up your authorization:

❑ `roles` — Allows or denies access to the resource for one or more roles

❑ `users` — Allows or denies access to the resource for particular users (based on their username)

❑ `verbs` — Allows or denies access to the resource for one or more HTTP verbs (GET, POST, PUT, and so on)

As their names suggest, the `<allow />` element allows access to the resource, and the `<deny />` element denies access to a resource, but they can be configured similarly. You also can use wildcards such as ? or * to configure your authorization elements in order to allow or deny access to all or some users or roles. * represents all authenticated users, and ? represents all anonymous users.

You also need to learn about the two common authorization types: file authorization and URL authorization. In file authorization, ASP.NET checks a user's access rights to a particular file on the system based on User Access Control (UAC), and in URL authorization, it checks the user's access rights to URLs.

Listing 15-2 is a sample configuration that reflects a common implementation of authorization in ASP.NET applications.

Listing 15-2: A common implementation of the `<authorization />` element

```
<location path="profile">
  <system.web>
    <authorization>
      <deny users="?"/>
      <allow users="*"/>
    </authorization>
  </system.web>
</location>

<location path="storage/files">
  <system.web>
    <authorization>
      <deny users="?" />
      <allow users="*" />
    </authorization>
  </system.web>
</location>

<location path="admin">
  <system.web>
    <authorization>
      <allow roles="Admin"/>
      <deny users="?"/>
      <deny roles="User"/>
    </authorization>
  </system.web>
</location>
```

In this configuration file, three `<location />` elements are defined. In the first part of the code, public access is restricted to the /profile path, where users can edit their profiles. Obviously, this page must be limited to authenticated users only. The `<deny />` and `<allow />` elements restrict access for all anonymous users and allow access for all authenticated users, respectively.

In the second part, access to all physical files on the system is restricted inside the /storage/files path, and the same authorization configuration allows only authenticated users to download files.

In the third part, access to /admin path is restricted; this is the path that administrative users use to perform specific tasks. This path must be protected not only from public users but also from normal authenticated users, so first you grant access to the Admin role through an `<allow />` element, and then you deny access for all anonymous users and normal users (users with a User role) through a `<deny />` element.

Although this is the common part of working with authorization configuration in ASP.NET applications, you may still need to take a look at more configuration examples to be able to find your proper configuration. Various open source sample applications are available on the Internet, especially on the CodePlex community, both for ASP.NET MVC and ASP.NET WebForms.

<membership />

Although using the ASP.NET membership provider in your applications is optional, developers usually prefer to build their applications on top of this membership to ease their development effort and extend it only for necessary changes in their applications. To be honest, ASP.NET membership is a great choice for many of the scenarios and can be used without any change. Of course, the power of this membership is in its complete integration with ASP.NET WebForms server controls and features, so you may not notice part of its power in ASP.NET MVC.

However, you're still able to use ASP.NET membership in ASP.NET MVC. The first step is configuring your application to use this membership provider, which is the same in ASP.NET WebForms and ASP.NET MVC.

To configure the ASP.NET membership provider, you need to add a `<membership />` element within your `<system.web />` element. `<membership />` accepts a single `<providers />` element as its child, and `<providers />` holds a list of different ASP.NET membership providers that you can declare. It can have one or more of the `<add />`, `<clear />`, and `<remove />` elements. These element names are fairly self-explanatory, especially for `<clear />` and `<remove />`, which are used to clear the list and remove a provider, respectively. `<clear />` and `<remove />` have a few simple attributes that require no further elaboration.

`<add />` is used to add a new provider to the list of available providers and set some common properties for it.

Talking about all these attributes of the `<add />` element is beyond the scope of this chapter, and you can find a full discussion on many online resources. In essence, two groups of attributes are associated with this element: essential attributes to configure the provider (such as name, type, connectingString, and applicationName) and attributes that manage the settings of the provider and its functioning (such as requiresQuestionAndAnswer, requiresUniqueEmail, and passwordFormat).

The .NET Framework comes with some built-in implementations of its providers, and there is a SQL Server database provider for membership available in the System.Web.Security.SqlMembershipProvider namespace. Moreover, generic extensibility points such as abstract classes and interfaces are available that you can use to write your own provider for different storage systems.

The ASP.NET MVC project template generates a configuration file that contains a default setting for a SQL Server ASP.NET membership provider with some common settings that work with a local SQL Express database. As mentioned earlier in the chapter, you can set up the appropriate database schema and objects for ASP.NET providers (membership, role, and health monitoring) by running the `aspnet_regsql` command at the Visual Studio command prompt and following the instructions in the wizard.

Listing 15-3 shows this generated configuration. It is applicable for many applications.

Listing 15-3: ASP.NET MVC membership provider configuration

```
<membership>
  <providers>
    <clear/>
    <add name="AspNetSqlMembershipProvider"
         type="System.Web.Security.SqlMembershipProvider, System.Web,
Version=2.0.0.0, Culture=neutral, PublicKeyToken=b03f5f7f11d50a3a"
         connectionStringName="ApplicationServices"
         enablePasswordRetrieval="false"
         enablePasswordReset="true"
         requiresQuestionAndAnswer="false"
         requiresUniqueEmail="false"
         passwordFormat="Hashed"
         maxInvalidPasswordAttempts="5"
         minRequiredPasswordLength="6"
         minRequiredNonalphanumericCharacters="0"
         passwordAttemptWindow="10"
         passwordStrengthRegularExpression=""
         applicationName="/"
         />
  </providers>
</membership>
```

This piece of code adds a SQL Server ASP.NET membership provider, named `AspNetSqlMembershipProvider`, to the ASP.NET MVC application. It also sets the type that implements this provider and set the name of the connection string to the defined SQL Server database in connection strings list. The rest are settings for the functionality of the provider such as password type and conditions. Finally, it also sets the name associated with the application.

<roleManager />

Another built-in provider in ASP.NET associated with authorization is the role provider, which can be defined in `Web.config` with the `<roleManager />` element. Like `<membership />`, this element can have a `<providers />` child element, which has a set of `<add />`, `<clear />`, and `<remove />` elements of its own, and its configuration is similar to that of the membership provider.

The ASP.NET MVC project template generates a default configuration for the role provider as well, but this provider is disabled by default. Listing 15-4 represents this default implementation, which adds two providers to the system: a SQL Server role provider and a Windows tokens role provider (which works based on Windows user groups and roles). These two providers are disabled in the default generated application, but they can be enabled easily.

Listing 15-4: ASP.NET MVC role provider configuration

```
<roleManager enabled="false">
  <providers>
    <clear />
    <add connectionStringName="ApplicationServices"
         name="AspNetSqlRoleProvider"
         type="System.Web.Security.SqlRoleProvider, System.Web, Version=2.0.0.0,
Culture=neutral, PublicKeyToken=b03f5f7f11d50a3a"
         applicationName="/"
         />
    <add applicationName="/"
         name="AspNetWindowsTokenRoleProvider"
         type="System.Web.Security.WindowsTokenRoleProvider, System.Web,
Version=2.0.0.0, Culture=neutral, PublicKeyToken=b03f5f7f11d50a3a"
         />
  </providers>
</roleManager>
```

Here, there is an `AspNetSqlRoleProvider` that works with the SQL Server database and is connected to the appropriate database through its `connectionStringName` attribute. There is also a Windows token role provider that works just with users and roles.

As stated previously, this configuration is disabled by default, and you can enable the role provider by changing the value of the `enabled` *attribute for the* `<roleManager />` *element to* `true`.

Custom Membership and Role Providers

One of the questions that might come to your mind is about the possibility of using a completely different membership and/or role provider in an ASP.NET MVC application. This is possible, and you're able to build your own databases and write your own code with its very own membership or role provider. You can use some extensibility points to connect your own providers to the ASP.NET authentication and authorization systems. However, this is beyond the scope of this book.

By the way, the best way to apply your own providers is to implement ASP.NET membership and role providers for your application's requirements, which is possible through abstract base classes.

Limiting Access to Resources with the Authorize Action Filter

In ASP.NET MVC, you can limit access to a resource by limiting access to its controller, and here action filters come into play. As introduced in Chapter 11, there is an `Authorize` action filter that you can use to deny access to a particular controller for users or roles.

The `Authorize` action filter accepts two types of parameters called `Roles` and `Users`, which allow you to pass the name of the roles and/or users that can access an action method. All other users or roles cannot access that particular action method.

If you only set an `Authorize` action filter for an action method without any role or user associated with it, that method will be available to all authenticated users and only anonymous users will be blocked. Similarly, you can set the `Authorize` filter for a controller class, which applies the authorization settings to all action methods defined in that class.

Listing 15-5 gives an example of this action filter being used to restrict access to the `ChangePassword` action method and grant access only to users in the Admin role as well as two specific users (Keyvan and Simone) to load it.

Listing 15-5: Authorize action filter

```
[Authorize(Roles = "Admin", Users = "Keyvan, Simone")]
public ActionResult ChangePassword()
{
    ViewData["PasswordLength"] = MembershipService.MinPasswordLength;

    return View();
}
```

Note that you can use one or both of the `Roles` or `Users` parameters with the `Authorize` action filter.

You may compare the list of possible elements inside the `<authorization />` element in `Web.config` and wonder how you can restrict access to an action filter for specific HTTP verbs. Here another action filter, called `AcceptVerbs`, can help you choose the list of allowed HTTP verbs.

Two other action filters play more professional roles in ASP.NET MVC security that are called `ValidateInputAttribute` *and* `ValidateAntiForgeryTokenAttribute`. *The first one marks an action method to validate its input values, and the second one is used to determine if a request is manipulated to prevent cross-site security attacks. We don't elaborate on them further because it's beyond the scope of this book.*

Authentication and Authorization in Action in ASP.NET MVC

As you can see, most of the theoretical concepts behind authorization and authentication are constant between ASP.NET WebForms and ASP.NET MVC. What you need now are some techniques to apply these concepts in the ASP.NET MVC development model. Therefore, it's worthwhile to take a look at an example that leverages these techniques. Fortunately, ASP.NET MVC generates a project template that has all the means to manage authorization and authentication based on ASP.NET membership and role providers, and here we can just walk through this existing implementation and describe it for clarification.

You have already seen how to configure the application to use membership and role providers, so we will try to cover the rest of the process and mainly emphasize registration, login, and changing the password for the user. To do this, we will focus mainly on `AccountController` and its views.

The Principles of Using AccountController

Generally, `AccountController` has a public constructor that gets two instances of the `IFormsAuthentication` and the `IMembershipService` interfaces and sets the appropriate properties with their values.

`IFormsAuthentication` is an interface defined by the ASP.NET MVC team and included in the project because the `FormsAuthentication` class in the ASP.NET code API is a sealed class with static members, which can make it difficult to work with when unit testing in ASP.NET MVC. `IFormsAuthentication` resolves this issue by acting as a proxy. There is also a `FormsAuthenticationService` class that is the default implementation of the `IFormsAuthentication` interface, and they're both included as a part of the `AccountController` module file (see Listing 15-6).

Listing 15-6: IFormsAuthentication and FormsAuthenticationWrapper

```
public interface IFormsAuthentication
{
    void SignIn(string userName, bool createPersistentCookie);
    void SignOut();
}

public class FormsAuthenticationService : IFormsAuthentication
{
    public void SignIn(string userName, bool createPersistentCookie)
    {
        FormsAuthentication.SetAuthCookie(userName, createPersistentCookie);
    }
    public void SignOut()
    {
        FormsAuthentication.SignOut();
    }
}
```

As you can see, `IFormsAuthentication` defines the `SetAuthCookie()` and `SignOut()` methods to simulate main methods in the `FormsAuthentication` class.

For the exact same reasons (the ease of unit testing for the membership API), the ASP.NET MVC team has included an `IMembershipService` interface with a default implementation called `AccountMembershipService` with some common methods for the membership provider (Listing 15-7).

Listing 15-7: IMembershipService and AccountMembershipService

```
public interface IMembershipService
{
    int MinPasswordLength { get; }

    bool ValidateUser(string userName, string password);
```

```
    MembershipCreateStatus CreateUser(string userName, string password, string
email);
    bool ChangePassword(string userName, string oldPassword, string newPassword);
}

public class AccountMembershipService : IMembershipService
{
    private MembershipProvider _provider;

    public AccountMembershipService()
        : this(null)
    {
    }

    public AccountMembershipService(MembershipProvider provider)
    {
        _provider = provider ?? Membership.Provider;
    }

    public int MinPasswordLength
    {
        get
        {
            return _provider.MinRequiredPasswordLength;
        }
    }

    public bool ValidateUser(string userName, string password)
    {
        return _provider.ValidateUser(userName, password);
    }

    public MembershipCreateStatus CreateUser(string userName, string password,
string email)
    {
        MembershipCreateStatus status;
        _provider.CreateUser(userName, password, email, null, null, true, null, out
status);
        return status;
    }

    public bool ChangePassword(string userName, string oldPassword, string
newPassword)
    {
        MembershipUser currentUser = _provider.GetUser(userName, true /*
userIsOnline */);
        return currentUser.ChangePassword(oldPassword, newPassword);
    }
}
```

AccountController has a main constructor that gets an instance of IFormsAuthentication and an instance of IMembershipService to set the appropriate properties. Later, these two properties will be used by action methods frequently (see Listing 15-8).

Listing 15-8: AccountController constructors and properties

```
public AccountController()
    : this(null, null)
{
}

public AccountController(IFormsAuthentication formsAuth, IMembershipService
service)
{
    FormsAuth = formsAuth ?? new FormsAuthenticationService();
    MembershipService = service ?? new AccountMembershipService();
}

public IFormsAuthentication FormsAuth
{
    get;
    private set;
}

public IMembershipService MembershipService
{
    get;
    private set;
}
```

Setting Up Registration

In this example, registration is accomplished through `Register` action methods. `AccountController` has two `Register` action methods. One is the regular action method that receives direct requests for a registration page, and the other is for HTTP POST requests that are sent by users to submit their registration information to add new users to the system.

Listing 15-9 shows these two `Register` action methods.

Listing 15-9: Register action methods

```
public ActionResult Register()
{
    ViewData["PasswordLength"] = MembershipService.MinPasswordLength;

    return View();
}

[AcceptVerbs(HttpVerbs.Post)]
public ActionResult Register(string userName, string email, string password, string
confirmPassword)
{
    ViewData["PasswordLength"] = MembershipService.MinPasswordLength;

    if (ValidateRegistration(userName, email, password, confirmPassword))
    {
        // Attempt to register the user
```

```
        MembershipCreateStatus createStatus = MembershipService.
CreateUser(userName, password, email);

        if (createStatus == MembershipCreateStatus.Success)
        {
            FormsAuth.SignIn(userName, false /* createPersistentCookie */);
            return RedirectToAction("Index", "Home");
        }
        else
        {
            ModelState.AddModelError("_FORM", ErrorCodeToString(createStatus));
        }
    }

    // If we got this far, something failed, redisplay form
    return View();
}
```

The first action method just passes the minimum requirement for password length. Most likely you remember that this value was a part of the `IMembershipService` interface.

The second `Register` action method does much more than the first one and is the subject of our main discussion for the registration process. It receives four string values from the view for user registration: username, e-mail, password, and password confirmation; these are entered by the user in textboxes (as you see in a moment).

First, like the first `Register` action method, it passes the minimum length of accepted passwords to the view. Then it validates the entered information using the `ValidateRegistration` helper function.

If these inputs are valid, it proceeds and adds a new user to the system. Here, the `MembershipService` property (of `IMembershipService` type) is used to call the `CreateUser` function, pass it the appropriate parameters, and create a new user.

If the `CreateUser` function is successful, it logs the user in using the `FormsAuth.SetAuthCookie` method. Otherwise, an error is reflected in the `MembershipCreateStatus` enumerator, and its string error can be extracted from the helper `ErrorCodeToString`.

As you see, two helper functions play important roles in the internal workings of `Register` action methods. The first one is `ValidateRegistration` (Listing 15-10), which gets the inputs values by users and validates the correctness of data, otherwise it displays the errors to the view.

Listing 15-10: ValidateRegistration helper function

```
private bool ValidateRegistration(string userName, string email, string password,
string confirmPassword)
{
    if (String.IsNullOrEmpty(userName))
    {
        ModelState.AddModelError("username", "You must specify a username.");
    }
    if (String.IsNullOrEmpty(email))
```

Continued

323

Listing 15-10: ValidateRegistration helper function *(continued)*

```
    {
        ModelState.AddModelError("email", "You must specify an email address.");
    }
    if (password == null || password.Length < MembershipService.MinPasswordLength)
    {
        ModelState.AddModelError("password",
            String.Format(CultureInfo.CurrentCulture,
                "You must specify a password of {0} or more characters.",
                MembershipService.MinPasswordLength));
    }
    if (!String.Equals(password, confirmPassword, StringComparison.Ordinal))
    {
        ModelState.AddModelError("_FORM", "The new password and confirmation
password do not match.");
    }
    return ModelState.IsValid;
}
```

The second helper function is `ErrorCodeToString` (Listing 15-11), which gets a
`MembershipCreateStatus` enumerator value and returns the appropriate text message to be displayed
in the view.

Listing 15-11: ErrorCodeToString helper function

```
private static string ErrorCodeToString(MembershipCreateStatus createStatus)
{
    // See http://msdn.microsoft.com/en-us/library/system.web.security.
membershipcreatestatus.aspx for
    // a full list of status codes.
    switch (createStatus)
    {
        case MembershipCreateStatus.DuplicateUserName:
            return "Username already exists. Please enter a different user name.";

        case MembershipCreateStatus.DuplicateEmail:
            return "A username for that e-mail address already exists. Please enter
a different e-mail address.";

        case MembershipCreateStatus.InvalidPassword:
            return "The password provided is invalid. Please enter a valid password
value.";

        case MembershipCreateStatus.InvalidEmail:
            return "The e-mail address provided is invalid. Please check the value
and try again.";

        case MembershipCreateStatus.InvalidAnswer:
            return "The password retrieval answer provided is invalid. Please check
the value and try again.";

        case MembershipCreateStatus.InvalidQuestion:
```

```
        return "The password retrieval question provided is invalid. Please
check the value and try again.";

        case MembershipCreateStatus.InvalidUserName:
            return "The user name provided is invalid. Please check the value and
try again.";

        case MembershipCreateStatus.ProviderError:
            return "The authentication provider returned an error. Please verify
your entry and try again. If the problem persists, please contact your system
administrator.";

        case MembershipCreateStatus.UserRejected:
            return "The user creation request has been canceled. Please verify
your entry and try again. If the problem persists, please contact your system
administrator.";

        default:
            return "An unknown error occurred. Please verify your entry and try
again. If the problem persists, please contact your system administrator.";
    }
}
```

The rest is nothing but the user interface code done in the Register view (see Listing 15-12), which renders some textboxes and a button for registration.

Listing 15-12: Register view

```
<%@ Page Language="C#" MasterPageFile="~/Views/Shared/Site.Master"
Inherits="System.Web.Mvc.ViewPage" %>

<asp:Content ID="registerTitle" ContentPlaceHolderID="TitleContent" runat="server">
    Register
</asp:Content>
<asp:Content ID="registerContent" ContentPlaceHolderID="MainContent"
runat="server">
    <h2>
        Create a New Account</h2>
    <p>
        Use the form below to create a new account.
    </p>
    <p>
        Passwords are required to be a minimum of
        <%=Html.Encode(ViewData["PasswordLength"])%>
        characters in length.
    </p>
    <%= Html.ValidationSummary("Account creation was unsuccessful. Please correct
the errors and try again.") %>
    <% using (Html.BeginForm())
        { %>
    <div>
        <fieldset>
            <legend>Account Information</legend>
```

Continued

Listing 15-12: Register view *(continued)*

```
            <p>
                <label for="username">
                    Username:</label>
                <%= Html.TextBox("username") %>
                <%= Html.ValidationMessage("username") %>
            </p>
            <p>
                <label for="email">
                    Email:</label>
                <%= Html.TextBox("email") %>
                <%= Html.ValidationMessage("email") %>
            </p>
            <p>
                <label for="password">
                    Password:</label>
                <%= Html.Password("password") %>
                <%= Html.ValidationMessage("password") %>
            </p>
            <p>
                <label for="confirmPassword">
                    Confirm password:</label>
                <%= Html.Password("confirmPassword") %>
                <%= Html.ValidationMessage("confirmPassword") %>
            </p>
            <p>
                <input type="submit" value="Register" />
            </p>
        </fieldset>
    </div>
    <% } %>
</asp:Content>
```

Now you can run the application and navigate to the registration page to add a user, as shown in Figure 15-1. After successful registration, it logs you in and redirects you to the home page.

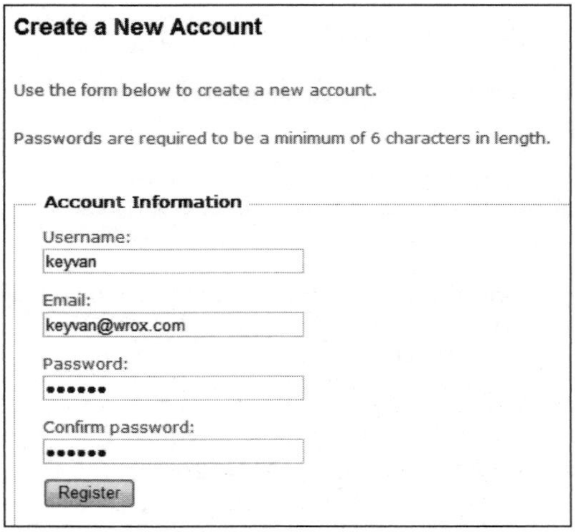

Create a New Account

Use the form below to create a new account.

Passwords are required to be a minimum of 6 characters in length.

Account Information

Username:
keyvan

Email:
keyvan@wrox.com

Password:
●●●●●●

Confirm password:
●●●●●●

Register

Figure 15-1

Handling Logons

The other part of the `AccountController` is related to login and logout tasks that are encapsulated in multiple `Logon` methods and a single `LogOff` action method.

Listing 15-13 represents two `Logon` methods that are responsible for handling direct requests to the logon page and submitted logon requests by users, respectively.

Listing 15-13: Logon action method

```
public ActionResult LogOn()
{
    return View();
}

[AcceptVerbs(HttpVerbs.Post)]
[System.Diagnostics.CodeAnalysis.SuppressMessage("Microsoft.Design", "CA1054:UriPar
ametersShouldNotBeStrings",
    Justification = "Needs to take same parameter type as Controller.Redirect()")]
public ActionResult LogOn(string userName, string password, bool rememberMe, string
returnUrl)
{
    if (!ValidateLogOn(userName, password))
    {
        return View();
    }

    FormsAuth.SignIn(userName, rememberMe);
    if (!String.IsNullOrEmpty(returnUrl))
    {
        return Redirect(returnUrl);
    }
    else
    {
        return RedirectToAction("Index", "Home");
    }
}
```

The first method is pretty straightforward because it only displays the view. The second method uses three steps to get its job done. It gets four parameters (username, password, cookie persistence values, and a return URL). Then it validates these values to make sure that they can be processed. This is done with the help of the `ValidateLogOn` function. The next steps are signing the user in and probably redirecting them to the preferred URL.

Listing 15-14 displays the source code for the `ValidateLogOn` helper function that gets usernames and passwords and determines if the user is valid to be signed in. It mainly relies on the `ValidateUser` method of the `MembershipService` property.

Listing 15-14: ValidateLogOn helper method

```
private bool ValidateLogOn(string userName, string password)
{
    if (String.IsNullOrEmpty(userName))
    {
        ModelState.AddModelError("username", "You must specify a username.");
    }
    if (String.IsNullOrEmpty(password))
    {
        ModelState.AddModelError("password", "You must specify a password.");
    }
    if (!MembershipService.ValidateUser(userName, password))
    {
        ModelState.AddModelError("_FORM", "The username or password provided is
incorrect.");
    }

    return ModelState.IsValid;
}
```

Listing 15-15 is the simple code for the LogOff action method, which simply calls FormsAuth.SignOut to log the user out.

Listing 15-15: LogOff action method

```
public ActionResult LogOff()
{
    FormsAuth.SignOut();

    return RedirectToAction("Index", "Home");
}
```

Listing 15-16 is the LogOn view, which renders a few textboxes, a checkbox, and a button to ask for the user's credentials, and passes them to the LogOn action method.

Listing 15-16: LogOn view

```
<%@ Page Language="C#" MasterPageFile="~/Views/Shared/Site.Master"
Inherits="System.Web.Mvc.ViewPage" %>

<asp:Content ID="loginTitle" ContentPlaceHolderID="TitleContent" runat="server">
    Log On
</asp:Content>

<asp:Content ID="loginContent" ContentPlaceHolderID="MainContent" runat="server">
    <h2>Log On</h2>
    <p>
        Please enter your username and password. <%= Html.ActionLink("Register",
"Register") %> if you don't have an account.
    </p>
```

```
<%= Html.ValidationSummary("Login was unsuccessful. Please correct the errors
and try again.") %>

<% using (Html.BeginForm()) { %>
    <div>
        <fieldset>
            <legend>Account Information</legend>
            <p>
                <label for="username">Username:</label>
                <%= Html.TextBox("username") %>
                <%= Html.ValidationMessage("username") %>
            </p>
            <p>
                <label for="password">Password:</label>
                <%= Html.Password("password") %>
                <%= Html.ValidationMessage("password") %>
            </p>
            <p>
                <%= Html.CheckBox("rememberMe") %> <label class="inline"
for="rememberMe">Remember me?</label>
            </p>
            <p>
                <input type="submit" value="Log On" />
            </p>
        </fieldset>
    </div>
<% } %>
</asp:Content>
```

Running the application and navigating to the logon page, you can enter the credentials and sign in to the application (see Figure 15-2).

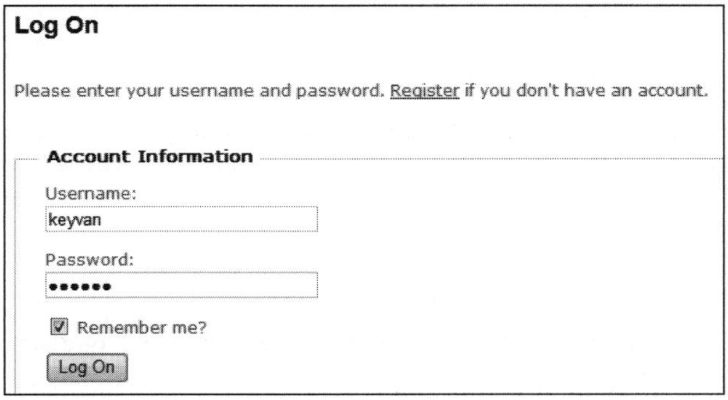

Figure 15-2

Changing the Password

That last portion of `AccountController` deals with changing the password for users. This change is accomplished through two `ChangePassword` action methods and a `ChangePasswordSuccessful` method that displays only a message.

The `ChangePassword` action methods are shown in Listing 15-17.

Listing 15-17: ChangePassword action methods

```
public ActionResult ChangePassword()
{
    ViewData["PasswordLength"] = MembershipService.MinPasswordLength;

    return View();
}

[Authorize]
[AcceptVerbs(HttpVerbs.Post)]
[System.Diagnostics.CodeAnalysis.SuppressMessage("Microsoft.Design", "CA1031:DoNotC
atchGeneralExceptionTypes",
    Justification = "Exceptions result in password not being changed.")]
public ActionResult ChangePassword(string currentPassword, string newPassword,
string confirmPassword)
{
    ViewData["PasswordLength"] = MembershipService.MinPasswordLength;

    if (!ValidateChangePassword(currentPassword, newPassword, confirmPassword))
    {
        return View();
    }

    try
    {
        if (MembershipService.ChangePassword(User.Identity.Name, currentPassword,
newPassword))
        {
            return RedirectToAction("ChangePasswordSuccess");
        }
        else
        {
            ModelState.AddModelError("_FORM", "The current password is incorrect or
the new password is invalid.");
            return View();
        }
    }
    catch
    {
        ModelState.AddModelError("_FORM", "The current password is incorrect or the
new password is invalid.");
        return View();
    }
}
```

The second method is what this section focuses on. First, note the usage of the `Authorize` action filter, which allows only authenticated users to change their passwords.

This action method receives the current password of the user as well as the new password and its confirmation. First it passes the minimum password length requirement to the view to be displayed. Then it uses the `ValidateChangePassword` helper function to validate these values and make sure that they can be used as input. In the next step, it calls the `ChangePassword` function of the `MembershipService` property to change the password for the current user. Note that `User.Identity.Name` is a string property that returns the username for the current user.

`ValidateChangePassword` is a helper function that gets user inputs and determines whether or not a password can be replaced (Listing 15-18).

Listing 15-18: ChangePasswordSuccess action method

```
private bool ValidateChangePassword(string currentPassword, string newPassword,
string confirmPassword)
{
    if (String.IsNullOrEmpty(currentPassword))
    {
        ModelState.AddModelError("currentPassword", "You must specify a current
password.");
    }
    if (newPassword == null || newPassword.Length < MembershipService.
MinPasswordLength)
    {
        ModelState.AddModelError("newPassword",
            String.Format(CultureInfo.CurrentCulture,
                "You must specify a new password of {0} or more characters.",
                MembershipService.MinPasswordLength));
    }

    if (!String.Equals(newPassword, confirmPassword, StringComparison.Ordinal))
    {
        ModelState.AddModelError("_FORM", "The new password and confirmation
password do not match.");
    }

    return ModelState.IsValid;
}
```

If a user changes their password successfully, they will be redirected to a new page where they will see a message. `ChangePasswordSuccess` is the action method that handles this page (see Listing 15-19).

Listing 15-19: ChangePasswordSuccess action method

```
public ActionResult ChangePasswordSuccess()
{
    return View();
}
```

As in the previous sections, there is a `ChangePassword` view that renders a few textboxes and a button to ask for the user's current and new passwords (see Listing 15-20).

Listing 15-20: ChangePassword view

```
<%@ Page Language="C#" MasterPageFile="~/Views/Shared/Site.Master"
Inherits="System.Web.Mvc.ViewPage" %>

<asp:Content ID="changePasswordTitle" ContentPlaceHolderID="TitleContent"
runat="server">
    Change Password
</asp:Content>
<asp:Content ID="changePasswordContent" ContentPlaceHolderID="MainContent"
runat="server">
    <h2>
        Change Password</h2>
    <p>
        Use the form below to change your password.
    </p>
    <p>
        New passwords are required to be a minimum of
        <%=Html.Encode(ViewData["PasswordLength"])%>
        characters in length.
    </p>
    <%= Html.ValidationSummary("Password change was unsuccessful. Please correct
the errors and try again.")%>
    <% using (Html.BeginForm())
       { %>
    <div>
        <fieldset>
            <legend>Account Information</legend>
            <p>
                <label for="currentPassword">
                    Current password:</label>
                <%= Html.Password("currentPassword") %>
                <%= Html.ValidationMessage("currentPassword") %>
            </p>
            <p>
                <label for="newPassword">
                    New password:</label>
                <%= Html.Password("newPassword") %>
                <%= Html.ValidationMessage("newPassword") %>
            </p>
            <p>
                <label for="confirmPassword">
                    Confirm new password:</label>
                <%= Html.Password("confirmPassword") %>
                <%= Html.ValidationMessage("confirmPassword") %>
            </p>
            <p>
                <input type="submit" value="Change Password" />
            </p>
        </fieldset>
    </div>
    <% } %>
</asp:Content>
```

A user can simply change their password by navigating to this page and entering their current and new passwords (see Figure 15-3).

Figure 15-3

Summary

The topic of this chapter was the implementation of two common security concepts in ASP.NET MVC: authentication and authorization.

This chapter started with a brief introduction to authentication and authorization and their principles, followed by the implementation of these concepts in ASP.NET. We then extended the discussion to ASP.NET MVC.

After the background information, you learned about the essential configurations used to enable authentication and authorization in your ASP.NET MVC applications. The next, short topic was the usage of custom membership and role providers in ASP.NET MVC, which was followed by a discussion about the usage of the `Authorize` action filter to restrict access to action methods.

You then walked through the authorization and authentication mechanism implemented in the default generated code for ASP.NET MVC by its project template.

Exercises

1. Modify the example in this chapter to restrict access to the change password page to a particular user by using an action filter.

2. Modify the example in this chapter to restrict access to the change password page to a particular role by using the configuration file.

Figure 15-2

Summary

Exercises

Extending ASP.NET MVC

At this point in the book, you have explored all the major features of the ASP.NET MVC framework. You've looked at components and action filters. You've explored routing, controllers, and views, and you might have noticed that almost any part of the framework can be replaced; if you don't like something, you can replace it with your own implementation of it. That's because the other big architectural guideline followed by the ASP.NET MVC team was to allow maximum extensibility.

This chapter shows you how to exploit that extensibility for your project. You see:

❑ What the main extensibility points are

❑ How to customize the main aspects of the framework (routing, action execution, view engines)

❑ How to use these custom implementations

❑ What the open source project MvcContrib is

❑ What some of the alternative view engines offer

This chapter is a bit more advanced than the other ones, because it delves into some of the internals of the framework. If you don't feel confident yet, I suggest you go back and review the chapters about routing, controllers, views, and unit testing.

Introduction to Extensibility

What is *extensibility*? This may seem like a simple question to answer, but before diving into this long chapter, it's better to make sure that we are on the same page about the meaning of the word. The Merriam-Webster dictionary says that extensibility is the "capability of being extended."

Transferred to computing science, extensibility is the quality of a software system that allows future expansion without the need to change and recompile the original source code. This concept is also referred to as the *open/closed principle* from a famous essay by Bertrand Meyer about object-oriented programming (*Object-Oriented Software Construction*, 1988, Prentice Hall, ISBN

0136290493): "Software entities (classes, modules, functions, etc.) should be open for extension, but closed for modification."

❑   *Open for extension* means that the entity can be made to behave in different ways from the original requirements and that new requirements can be added.

❑   *Closed for modification* means that the code of such an entity must not be changed once it is declared completed.

Without extensibility that meets these criteria, a system can become difficult to maintain, and this can quickly lead to obsolescence.

Extensibility is also key to testability, as you saw in Chapter 8. To do unit testing and to really isolate the code, the framework needs to be extensible to allow the injection of test-specific implementations of dependencies.

The standard ASP.NET WebForm programming model was somewhat extensible, thanks to the broad usage of the provider model, but ASP.NET MVC is more extensible, and you can even extend the internals of the framework.

Areas of Extensibility

The main areas where you decide to extend the ASP.NET MVC framework to inject your own logic are:

❑   **Route Handlers** — Changing the route handler allows you to process the incoming request through a different pipeline. Use this if you don't want a specific request to go into the MVC framework but need it to be handled by your own handler or even as a standard WebForm request.

❑   **Controller Factories** — The *controller factory* is the component that is responsible for selecting the controller and invoking the action to execute in order to process the request.

❑   **View Engines** — Finally, the *view engine* is the component that takes in the data retrieved by the actions, parses the code in the view, and produces the output that will be sent back to the end user.

Besides these areas, the framework is full of extensibility points. Just to name a few, you can customize how the TempData is stored, how the controller base class works, and how an action is invoked; you can also create your own ActionResult. And because most of the methods of the internal components are marked as virtual, you can inherit from the default components and personalize just one specific behavior without touching the rest. Most components inherit from either an abstract base class or an interface and can be replaced in their entirety as well.

In the next sections, you read about the three main areas of extensibility and about how to customize how the TempData collection is stored.

The first area you explore is *route handlers*.

Route Handlers

In Chapter 7, you read about the routing engine. You learned that you can specify a different route handler for each route and that you can use it with WebForm pages, too. Now let's see how this is achieved.

The routing engine is part of the ASP.NET 3.5 SP1, not part of the ASP.NET MVC framework. Nevertheless, because routing is a fundamental part of the processing pipeline, this section talks about how to extend it.

Writing a Custom Route Handler

A route handler is nothing but a simple class that inherits from the interface `IRouteHandler` and implements its only method, `GetHttpHandler`, whose signature is:

```
public IHttpHandler GetHttpHandler(RequestContext requestContext)
```

This method receives an instance of the request context object as a parameter. It contains the current HTTP context and the `RouteData` object, which contains, among the other things, a `RouteValueDictionary` (in the `Values` property) with all the URL parameters retrieved from the URL. This method processes the URL parameters and returns an instance of an `IHttpHandler`.

A usual scenario that needs a custom route handler is one in which you want to handle the request using a standard WebForm, but still want to keep the coolness and RESTfulness of the ASP.NET MVC-like URLs. This turns out to be pretty easy. If you are unaware of it, a standard WebForm page, which inherits from `System.Web.UI.Page`, is already an instance of an `IHttpHandler`.

Try It Out   Creating a Custom Route Handler

In this example you handle the requests for all the URLs that start with "photo" by using a standard WebForm:

1. After creating a new ASP.NET MVC project, add a standard WebForm to the root of the site, and name it **Gallery.aspx**.

2. Add two lines of code in the markup of the file, so that it looks like this:

```
<%@ Page Language="C#" AutoEventWireup="true"
CodeBehind="Gallery.aspx.cs"
Inherits="RoutingHandler.Gallery" %>

<!DOCTYPE html PUBLIC "-//W3C//DTD XHTML 1.0 Transitional//EN"
"http://www.w3.org/TR/xhtml1/DTD/xhtml1-transitional.dtd">

<html xmlns="http://www.w3.org/1999/xhtml" >
<head runat="server">
    <title></title>
    <link href="Content/Site.css" rel="stylesheet" type="text/css" />
</head>
<body>
    <form id="form1" runat="server">
```

```
    <div id="main">
    Gallery Name: <asp:Label runat="server" ID="lblGalleryName" /><br />
    Photo Title: <asp:Label runat="server" ID="lblPhotoTitle" />
    </div>
    </form>
</body>
</html>
```

3. Then, in the code-behind add two properties and the following `Page_Load`:

```
public partial class Gallery : Page
{
    public string GalleryName { get; set; }
    public string PhotoTitle { get; set; }

    protected void Page_Load(object sender, EventArgs e)
    {
        lblGalleryName.Text = GalleryName;
        lblPhotoTitle.Text = PhotoTitle;
    }
}
```

4. Now, open up the `Global.asax.cs` file, and add a new class to the file:

```
internal class CustomRouteHandler : IRouteHandler
{
    public IHttpHandler GetHttpHandler(RequestContext requestContext)
    {
        Gallery page = BuildManager
            .CreateInstanceFromVirtualPath("~/Gallery.aspx",
            typeof(Gallery)) as Gallery;

        page.GalleryName =
            requestContext.RouteData.Values["gallery"].ToString();
        page.PhotoTitle =
            requestContext.RouteData.Values["title"].ToString();

        return page;
    }
}
```

5. Finally, register the route inside the `RegisterRoutes` method:

```
Route routeWithCustomHandler = new Route(
    "photos/{gallery}/{title}",
    new CustomRouteHandler());

routes.Add(routeWithCustomHandler);
```

6. Now if you launch the Web application and browse to the URL `/Photos/MyClimbingTrips/OnTheGlacier`, you'll see the screen shown in Figure 16-1:

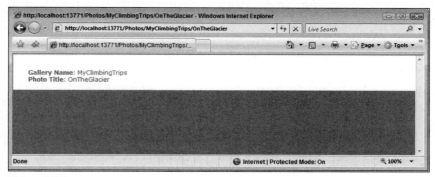

Figure 16-1

How It Works

As you might have noticed, implementing a custom route handler that lets you handle RESTful URLs using a WebForm is very easy. Everything rotates around one line of code (added in step 4):

```
Gallery page = BuildManager
    .CreateInstanceFromVirtualPath("~/Gallery.aspx",
    typeof(Gallery)) as Gallery;
```

This method parses a file from a virtual path and creates an instance of the page. This way, you can compile and create an instance of the Gallery page so that later you can set the value of the properties from the URL parameters retrieved from the URL, getting them from the `requestContext` `.RouteData.Values` dictionary.

```
page.GalleryName =
    requestContext.RouteData.Values["gallery"].ToString();
page.PhotoTitle =
    requestContext.RouteData.Values["title"].ToString();
```

Finally, because a `Page` is also an `IHttpHandler`, you can just return it from the `GetHttpHandler` method of the route handler. Easy, isn't it?

The WebForm that handles the request is the same as any other WebForm, except that it uses the properties set by the route handler instead of getting the values from the query string of the page.

Once the route handler is ready, you just have to register it inside the route you want it to handle. You cannot use the `MapRoute` helper method, because it always registers the `MvcRouteHandler`; you have to create an instance of the `Route` and then add it directly to the `routes` collection (which is what you did in step 5).

A Generic WebFormRouteHandler

Routing a request to a WebForm is probably the most common scenario you will face, so Listing 16-1 is a generic route handler that you can reuse in your applications.

Listing 16-1: WebFormRouteHandler

```
public class WebFormRouteHandler: IRouteHandler
{
    public string VirtualPath { get; set; }

    public WebFormRouteHandler(string virtualPath)
    {
        VirtualPath = virtualPath;
    }

    public IHttpHandler GetHttpHandler(RequestContext requestContext)
    {
        foreach (KeyValuePair<string, object> token in
            requestContext.RouteData.Values)
        {
            requestContext.HttpContext.Items.Add(token.Key, token.Value);
        }
        foreach (KeyValuePair<string, object> token in
            requestContext.RouteData.DataTokens)
        {
            requestContext.HttpContext.Items.Add(token.Key, token.Value);
        }
        IHttpHandler result = BuildManager
            .CreateInstanceFromVirtualPath(VirtualPath,
            typeof(Page)) as IHttpHandler;
        return result;
    }
}
```

The difference between this handler and the one from the Try It Out example is that this one doesn't know about the properties of the page. It just copies all the URL parameters and data tokens inside the current HTTP context so that the WebForm can get them.

To access the parameters in the WebForm, all you need to do is use their name. To obtain the same result as in the previous Try It Out section, the Page_Load of the Gallery.aspx page should be:

```
protected void Page_Load(object sender, EventArgs e)
{
    lblGalleryName.Text = Context.Items["gallery"].ToString();
    lblPhotoTitle.Text = Context.Items["title"].ToString();
}
```

Also, the route registration is a bit different; because this handler allows you to map to any WebForm of your Web application, you have to specify its virtual path in the constructor:

```
Route routeWithCustomHandler = new Route(
    "photos/{gallery}/{title}",
    new WebFormRouteHandler("~/Gallery.aspx"));
routes.Add(routeWithCustomHandler);
```

This approach has advantages and disadvantages, however: The generic WebFormRouteHandler eliminates the need for you to write a handler for each WebForm you want to use, but you lose the compile-time check and the IntelliSense of the properties.

The Controller Factory

The second big extensibility point is the component that is responsible for finding the controller that handles the request and creates an instance of it.

The controller factory that comes with the framework is pretty simple. It looks in the current application domain for a class that implements the interface IController and whose name is the name of the requested controller plus "Controller." When such a class is found, its controller factory creates an instance of it, calling the parameter-less constructor.

One of the main reasons you might want to use a custom controller factory is because you want to use Dependency Injection. You don't want to hard-code the name of the dependencies inside the constructor of the controller, but want them to be "injected" from the outside to allow the reconfiguration of the application without the need to change code and recompile it (remember the open/closed principle). To accomplish this, you need to have the IoC Container create the controller instead of instantiating it directly. If you are not familiar with Dependency Injection and Inversion of Control, go back to Chapters 8 and 9, which cover these two concepts in detail.

Anatomy of a Controller Factory

A controller factory is a class that implements the IControllerFactory interface and its two methods:

```
IController CreateController(RequestContext requestContext,
    string controllerName);
void ReleaseController(IController controller);
```

The first method is responsible for finding the right controller and returning an instance of it, and the second one is responsible for destroying the controller.

As an example of what a custom controller factory looks like, Listing 16-2 shows the code for the factory that creates a controller using Ninject, which was discussed in Chapter 8 and can be downloaded from http://ninject.org/. This code is part of the Extra package of MvcContrib, a community open source project that contains many utilities and many small projects to connect the "official" ASP.NET MVC framework to various other open source projects. You can download it from its page on CodePlex at http://MvcContrib.org.

Listing 16-2: NinjectControllerFactory

```
namespace MvcContrib.Ninject
{
    public class NinjectControllerFactory : IControllerFactory
    {
        public IController CreateController(RequestContext context,
            string controllerName)
        {
            return NinjectKernel.Kernel.Get<IController>(
                With.Parameters.ContextVariable(
                    "controllerName", controllerName));
        }
```

Continued

341

Listing 16-2: NinjectControllerFactory *(continued)*

```
            public void ReleaseController(IController controller)
            {
                var disposable = controller as IDisposable;
                if (disposable != null)
                {
                    disposable.Dispose();
                }
            }
        }
    }
```

The controller is constructed by just one line of "real" code, the one that asks the Ninject's kernel to create an instance of the controller and adds a context variable with the name of the controller that must be returned.

MvcContrib contains, in its Extra package, a controller factory for all the most popular IoC Containers available on the .NET platform:

- ❏ CastleWindsor
- ❏ Ninject
- ❏ Microsoft p&p ObjectBuilder
- ❏ Spring.NET
- ❏ StructureMap
- ❏ Microsoft p&p Unity

Besides the MvcContrib project, if you read the blogs you'll find lots of samples and ideas on how to extend the framework.

Using the Ninject Custom Controller Factory

Once you have a custom controller factory, which either you developed yourself or you got from an external source (as in the case of MvcContrib), you have to instruct the ASP.NET MVC framework to use yours instead of the default one. This is pretty trivial, and it's done by setting the controller factory used by the current application (there can be only one controller factory per application).

If you want to use the `NinjectControllerFactory`, the line of code is:

```
ControllerBuilder.Current.SetControllerFactory(
    typeof (Ninject.NinjectControllerFactory));
```

Remember that MvcContrib is just the glue between ASP.NET MVC and the other third-party frameworks, so to use any of its "connectors," you have to reference inside your project both the MvcContrib assembly and the assembly or assemblies of the external components you want to integrate.

Then, obviously, you have to configure the IoC Container so that it supplies the correct instances when needed.

In the next section you see how to use the Ninject controller factory that comes with MvcContrib, which is still based on Ninject v1.0. Even if it is not the latest version of Ninject, we think that going through the steps required to use this version will help you have a better understanding of what is needed to use an IoC Container with the ASP.NET MVC framework because, even if the syntax is different, the same concepts apply to all the other IoC Containers.

Later you read how to use Ninject v2.0, which puts a level of abstraction on top of all these steps. This makes using it a lot easier, but it doesn't demonstrate the functionality as clearly as the version that comes with MvcContrib.

Using the Controller Factory that Comes with MvcContrib

For this example to work, you have to add a reference to two of the many assemblies from which Ninject v1.0 is made: the core `Ninject.Core.dll` and the `Ninject.Conditions.dll`.

If you remember, in Chapter 8 there was a sample of a mathematical library that calls an external Web service to get the current value of pi. The example used here is the same, but the role performed by the MathLib will now be performed by a `MathController`.

The first thing you have to do to IoC-enable the application is write the external component so that it implements a known interface. Because the external component is a Web service, it cannot implement an interface because it's an auto-generated proxy (`PiService.PiService`, which is the type generated by Visual Studio when you add the reference to the Web service), so you need a wrapper to encapsulate the call. (See Listing 16-3.)

Listing 16-3: PiWebService

```
namespace NinjectMVC.Models
{
    public class PiWebServiceWrapper : IPiWebService
    {
        public float GetPi()
        {
            PiService.PiService service = new PiService.PiService();
            return service.GetPi();
        }
    }

    public interface IPiWebService
    {
        float GetPi();
    }
}
```

The controller must have a constructor that accepts the external component as a parameter, referenced only through its interface. This constructor is marked with the Ninject-specific attribute `[Inject]`, as shown in Listing 16-4.

Listing 16-4: MathController

```
namespace NinjectMVC.Controllers
{
    public class MathController : Controller
    {
        IPiWebService _ws;

        [Inject]
        public MathController(IPiWebService ws)
        {
            _ws = ws;
        }

        public ActionResult ComputeCircumference(float radius)
        {
            float pi = _ws.GetPi();
            float circ = 2 * pi * radius;
            ViewData["Circumference"] = circ.ToString();
            return View();
        }
    }
}
```

Now you need the module that tells Ninject which implementation of the IPiWebService interface to use, as shown in Listing 16-5.

Listing 16-5: ServiceModule

```
namespace NinjectMVC.Modules
{
    internal class ServiceModule : StandardModule
    {
        public override void Load()
        {
            Bind<IPiWebService>().To<PiWebServiceWrapper>();
        }
    }
}
```

To separate the registration of the controllers from the registration of the external services, it's better to create two modules. Listing 16-6 shows how to create the module that instructs Ninject to return an instance of MathController already set up with the correct implementation of the PiWebService.

Listing 16-6: ControllerModule

```
namespace NinjectMVC.Modules
{
    internal class ControllerModule : StandardModule
    {
        public override void Load()
        {
```

```
Bind<IController>().To<HomeController>()
    .Only(When.Context.Variable("controllerName")
        .EqualTo("Home"));

Bind<IController>().To<MathController>()
    .Only(When.Context.Variable("controllerName")
        .EqualTo("Math"));
        }
    }
}
```

This module is a bit more complex than the one before, but because it uses a fluent API, it should be easy to understand what it does just by reading the code: It says "When someone asks for the IController interface, send him the HomeController only when the value of the context variable named controllerName is equal to Home."

Then you have to configure the container, supply the two modules, and finally tell ASP.NET MVC to use the NinjectControllerFactory to load the controllers. (See Listing 16-7.)

Listing 16-7: Global.asax

```
public class MvcApplication : System.Web.HttpApplication
{
    public static void RegisterRoutes(RouteCollection routes)
    {
        //Route registration
    }

    protected void Application_Start()
    {
        InitializeNinject();
        RegisterRoutes(RouteTable.Routes);
    }

    private static void InitializeNinject()
    {
        NinjectKernel.Initialize(
            new ControllerModule(),
            new ServiceModule()
            );

        ControllerBuilder.Current.SetControllerFactory(
            typeof(NinjectControllerFactory));
    }
}
```

Configuring the IoC Container for each controller can become a big pain if your application grows, so in Ninject v2.0 Nate Kohari released an MVC-specific configuration module that automatically binds all the controllers available in the current assembly.

In the next section you see how the new version of Ninject makes the integration with ASP.NET MVC a lot easier.

Using the Controller Factory that Comes with Ninject v2.0

First, you don't need to use the `ControllerModule` any more, because it will be replaced by the `RegisterAllControllersIn` method. Second, you don't have to register the custom controller factory yourself, because this will be done by the integration library. Listing 16-8 shows how the `Global.asax` `.cs` file looks using the `Ninject.Framework.Mvc` assembly that comes with Ninject 1.5.

Listing 16-8: Global.asax using the Ninject integration library for ASP.NET MVC

```
public class MvcApplication : NinjectHttpApplication
{
    protected void RegisterRoutes(RouteCollection routes)
    {
        //Route registration
    }

    protected override void OnApplicationStarted()
    {
        RegisterRoutes(RouteTable.Routes);
        RegisterAllControllersIn(Assembly.GetExecutingAssembly());
    }

    protected override IKernel CreateKernel()
    {
        return new StandardKernel(new ServiceModule());
    }
}
```

The differences from the previous versions are highlighted in grey: It doesn't inherit from the standard `System.Web.HttpApplication` class but from Ninject's `Ninject.Web.Mvc` `.NinjectHttpApplication`. It provides two extension points to allow you to set up your application at startup time and configure the kernel (the `OnApplicationStarted` and the `CreateKernel` method are overrides of the abstract ones defined in the base class). Also, notice the usage of the `RegisterAllControllersIn` method. Internally, it loops through all the `IContoller` classes defined in the specified assembly, relieving you from hand-coding the module to do the binding.

View Engines

The last, and probably most important, extensibility point of ASP.NET MVC is the view engine. It is responsible for parsing the view code, executing it, and rendering the final HTML sent to the browser. The default view engine that ships with the framework is the `WebFormViewEngine`, which was covered in detail in Chapter 6.

But what if you don't want to deal with WebForms anymore? Or what if you have to render a PDF instead of an HTML file? You can build your own view engine.

Actually, you don't really have to because there are already a few alternative view engines you can use, both inside MvcContrib and as standalone packages. Some of them are quite popular, and you read more about them later. But first you see how to write a custom view engine.

Writing a Custom View Engine

Writing a custom view engine is a bit more complex than writing a routing engine and a controller factory. Instead of implementing an interface with just one method, here you have to implement two interfaces, with a total of three methods.

The two interfaces that you have to implement are:

❑   IView

❑   IViewEngine

IView

The object that implements the IView interface is the one that will be responsible for rendering the actual view to the browser. Its only method is:

```
void Render(ViewContext viewContext, TextWriter writer);
```

The parameters it accepts are viewContext and writer. The first parameter contains the ViewData and TempData collections so that the view can use the data collected in the controller to render the HTML. The second, writer, is a simple TextWriter object that the framework will populate with the Response.Output object, which is rendered directly to the HTTP stream.

IViewEngine

To keep a clearer separation between rendering the view and finding the view to render, another interface exists. It's called IViewEngine, and the classes that implement it are the ones responsible for finding the views, both full and partial.

The methods that you need to write to implement this interface are:

❑   ViewEngineResult FindPartialView(ControllerContext controllerContext, string partialViewName)

❑   ViewEngineResult FindView(ControllerContext controllerContext, string viewName, string masterName)

❑   void ReleaseView(ControllerContext controllerContext, IView view)

The first two methods do very similar tasks: They look for the view based on the controller and the view names, and they return an instance of either a view or a partial view. (Actually, the view object is encapsulated inside the ViewEngineResult object, which also contains information needed to give an explanatory error message in case the view cannot be found.) The difference between the two is that one searches for only partial views, which are typically used to render only a portion of a view, whereas the other locates regular views. The third method is only there in case your view needs to be disposed of.

The framework comes with a handy implementation of IViewEngine that probably solves most of the scenarios: VirtualPathProviderViewEngine. This view locator looks for the files needed using the virtual path provider that comes with ASP.NET, so if your views are stored on the file system under the application root, you don't need to implement the whole IViewEngine interface. You just inherit from this base class and override the two abstract methods that, given the virtual path of the file, return the corresponding IView. These two methods are CreateView and CreatePartialView.

You need to implement the full interface only if your views are not stored on the file system but are stored on a database or inside a zip file or in any other exotic source.

Creating a Simple Custom View Engine

In this section you see how to create a custom view engine.

Step 1 — Choose Your Syntax

The first thing you have to understand is what you want to achieve with the new view engine. Most of the time you will want to use a different syntax or render a different type of output. This simple custom view engine does not support code execution; it is only a templating engine that renders as a string the values stored in the ViewData collection.

The placeholder inside the template is w[*key*].

Step 2 — Implement the Parser and Rendering Engine

The second step is to implement the IView's Render method:

```
public void Render(ViewContext viewContext, TextWriter writer)
{
    Stream virtualFileStream = VPP.GetFile(ViewPath).Open();
    StreamReader reader = new StreamReader(virtualFileStream);
    string template = reader.ReadToEnd();
    foreach (KeyValuePair<string, object> valuePair in viewContext.ViewData)
    {
        template = template.Replace("w[" + valuePair.Key + "]",
            valuePair.Value.ToString());
    }
    writer.Write(template);
}
```

This method simply puts the values contained inside the ViewData into the template, in the positions where the placeholders were.

Notice that the path that is provided is not a physical path but is the virtual path. (For the Index view, it will be ~/Views/Home/Index.wrox.) So, you need to use the VirtualPathProvider in order to get the file, which could be located on the disk but could also be somewhere else, retrieved by a custom VirtualPathProvider.

Two other pieces of code need to be added: the constructors of the view and the properties that hold the path of the template file:

```
public string ViewPath { get; private set; }
public string MasterPath { get; private set; }

public WroxView(string viewPath) : this(viewPath, null)
{
}

public WroxView(string viewPath, string masterPath)
```

```
{
    ViewPath = viewPath;
    MasterPath = masterPath;
}
```

Then, to make it possible to test the view engine without the dependency on the file system, you need to add a public property to inject a fake virtual path provider during the tests:

```
private VirtualPathProvider _vpp;

public VirtualPathProvider VPP
{
    get
    {
        if (_vpp == null)
        {
            _vpp = HostingEnvironment.VirtualPathProvider;
        }
        return _vpp;
    }
    set
    {
        _vpp = value;
    }
}
```

Step 3 — Implement the View Factory

The next step is to create the view factory. It will be responsible for looking for the view, based on the view name and controller name, and for creating an instance of the view.

In case you want to look for the view in the virtual directory where the Web application lives, instead of implementing the IViewEngine interfaces you can extend and override the VirtualPathProviderViewEngine. To do so, you must first set the location that needs to be searched. You do this in the constructor of the view factory. In this example, you are just changing the extensions of the view.

```
public WroxViewFactory()
{
    base.MasterLocationFormats = new string[] {
        "~/Views/{1}/{0}.wmaster",
        "~/Views/Shared/{0}.wmaster"
    };
    base.ViewLocationFormats = new string[] {
        "~/Views/{1}/{0}.wrox",
        "~/Views/Shared/{0}.wrox"
    };
    base.PartialViewLocationFormats = new string[] {
        "~/Views/{1}/{0}.wroxc",
        "~/Views/Shared/{0}.wroxc"
    };
}
```

Three location lists must be set, one for each type of view: master pages, normal views, and partial views. Notice that you are not setting a real location but just a format for the location: The placeholder {1} will be replaced with the name of the controller, and {0} will be replaced with the view name.

Next, you need to implement the two methods that are in charge of instantiating the views: CreateView and CreatePartialView:

```
protected override IView CreatePartialView(
    ControllerContext controllerContext, string partialVirtualPath)
{
    return new WroxView(partialVirtualPath);
}

protected override IView CreateView(
    ControllerContext controllerContext, string viewVirtualPath,
    string masterVirtualPath)
{
    return new WroxView(viewVirtualPath, masterVirtualPath);
}
```

This scenario is pretty simple. All you need to do is to create an instance of the view given the virtual path of the files. The virtual to physical path is performed by the WroxView class. In a more complex scenario, you probably need to compile and cache the template to improve performance and allow code execution inside the template (which is not possible in this simple view).

Step 4 — Custom View Syntax

Now that everything has been implemented, you need to write a view using the new syntax and the new naming convention. The file must be named /View/Home/Index.wrox:

```
<html>
<head>
<title>w[Title]</title>
</head>
<body>
    <h2>w[Message]</h2>
    <p>
        . . .
    </p>
</body>
</html>
```

Step 5 — Test the View Engine

The final step is writing the tests for your view engine, and especially the implementation of IView, because it is the one that contains the logic to parse and render the view and so is the most likely to change and break.

This is made possible by the fact that the Render method accepts an output writer as a parameter, so for the purposes of testing you pass a simple StringWriter.

```
[TestMethod()]
public void RenderTest()
{
```

```
WroxView view = new WroxView("~/Views/Home/Index.wrox ");
string virtualFile = "<html>...</html>";
view.VPP = new FakeVPP(virtualFile);

ViewDataDictionary ViewData = new ViewDataDictionary();
ViewData["Title"] = "Home Page From Wrox View";
ViewData["Message"] = "Welcome to the Wrox View Engine!";

ViewContext context = CreateFakeViewContext(ViewData, view);

StringWriter writer = new StringWriter();
view.Render(context, writer);

string rendered = writer.ToString();
string expected = "<html>...</html>";

Assert.AreEqual(expected, rendered);
}
```

First the test creates the instance of the view, passing the local path as a parameter, and it creates the ViewData collection with the values that need to be tested.

Then it creates the two parameters for the Render method: ViewContext (using the CreateFakeViewContext helper method) and StringWriter, which will contain the output of the view.

The method is then executed and the contents of the writer flushed to a string are then verified against the expected result.

Before moving to the next topic, here is the code for the CreateFakeViewContext method. It sets up the dependencies needed by ViewContext, even using a fake implementation of the HTTP context.

```
private static ViewContext CreateFakeViewContext(
    ViewDataDictionary ViewData, WroxView view)
{
    RouteData routeData = new RouteData();
    ControllerContext controllerContext = new ControllerContext(
        new FakeHttpContextBase(), routeData, new HomeController());
    return new ViewContext(controllerContext,view, ViewData, new
TempDataDictionary());
}
internal class FakeHttpContextBase : HttpContextBase { }
```

The previous test also makes use of another fake object, FakeVPP, which removes the dependency on the real VirtualFileProvider. Explaining how this was implemented will take you a little away from the central topic, but to give you all the information, here is the code for the fake object. First is the FakeVPP, which inherits from the base abstract class VirtualFileProvider:

```
internal class FakeVPP : VirtualPathProvider
{
    private string _fakeFile;
    public FakeVPP(string fakeFile)
    {
        _fakeFile = fakeFile;
```

```
        }

        public override VirtualFile GetFile(string virtualPath)
        {
            return new FakeVirtualFile(virtualPath, _fakeFile);
        }
    }
```

Next is the `FakeVirtualFile`, which inherits from `VirtualFile` and is the class responsible for actually streaming the file to the client:

```
internal class FakeVirtualFile : VirtualFile
{
    private string _fakeFile;
    public FakeVirtualFile(string file, string fakeFile)
        : base(file)
    {
        _fakeFile = fakeFile;
    }

    public override Stream Open()
    {
        return new MemoryStream(ASCIIEncoding.Default.GetBytes(_fakeFile));
    }
}
```

Notice that the `Open` method doesn't look at the file system but just streams the string that was provided during the test.

You just created a view engine, with its own syntax and its own naming convention, and it's even tested. In the next sections, you learn how to inject it into your application and how to use some of the other alternative view engines.

Using a Custom View Engine

Adding the custom view engine to the application is pretty easy. It needs to be done during the application startup by adding the new view engine to the list of possible view engines to use.

```
ViewEngines.Engines.Add(new WroxViewFactory());
```

When the framework looks for a view, it cycles through all the available view engines and returns the first view it finds. The `WebFormViewEngine` is automatically added to the collection of view engines as the first element, so if a WebForm view exists, it will always be returned.

Alternative View Engines

As alternatives to the `WebFormViewEngine`, the community created a few others. Some are part of MvcContrib; others were released as autonomous projects. They have been developed to overcome the limitations of the syntax of WebForms or even HTML. In the following pages, you get a taste of the main view engines so that you can decide if you still want to use the WebForm one or if you like an alternative one better.

To put the focus on the syntax and how to set up the view engines, the examples all render a list of cycling routes, so the model and controller part will always be the same.

Here is the code for the shared parts. Listing 16-9 is the `Route` class.

Listing 16-9: Models.Route

```
namespace CyclingRoutes.Models
{
    public class Route
    {
        public string Name { get; set; }
        public DifficutlyLevel Difficutly { get; set; }
        public double Length { get; set; }
        public double Gain { get; set; }
        public double AverageGrade { get; set; }
    }

    public enum DifficutlyLevel
    {
        Easy,
        Medium,
        Hard,
        Strenuous,
        ArmstrongLevel
    }
}
```

Listing 16-10 is the `RouteList` class, which is a strongly typed list of routes.

Listing 16-10: Models.RouteList

```
namespace CyclingRoutes.Models
{
    public class RouteList : List<Route>
    {
        public RouteList()
        {
        }

        public RouteList(IEnumerable<Route> collection) : base(collection)
        {
        }
    }
}
```

Next you need an in-memory repository of routes, as shown in Listing 16-11, with two methods: one that returns the list of routes ordered by name and another one that searches for a specific route. In a real-world scenario, this would have been a data access class, but for the purposes of the examples, the in-memory one is enough.

Listing 16-11: Models.RouteRepository

```
namespace CyclingRoutes.Models
{
    public class RouteRepository
    {
        private List<Route> _routes;
        public RouteRepository()
        {
            _routes = new List<Route>();

            _routes.Add(new Route()
                    {
                        Name = "Passo dello Stelvio",
                        Length = 24.3,
                        AverageGrade = 7.4,
                        Gain = 1808,
                        Difficutly = DifficutlyLevel.Hard
                    }
                );

            _routes.Add(new Route()
                    {
                        Name = "Mont Ventoux",
                        Length = 21.2,
                        AverageGrade = 7.2,
                        Gain = 1532,
                        Difficutly = DifficutlyLevel.Medium
                    }
                );

            _routes.Add(new Route()
                    {
                        Name = "Mortirolo",
                        Length = 12.4,
                        AverageGrade = 10.5,
                        Gain = 1300,
                        Difficutly = DifficutlyLevel.Strenuous
                    }
                );

            _routes.Add(new Route()
                    {
                        Name = "Mount Washington",
                        Length = 12.4,
                        AverageGrade = 11.5,
                        Gain = 1420,
                        Difficutly = DifficutlyLevel.ArmstrongLevel
                    }
                );

            _routes.Add(new Route()
```

```
                        {
                            Name = "Brinzio",
                            Length = 8.28,
                            AverageGrade = 3.5,
                            Gain = 292,
                            Difficutly = DifficutlyLevel.Easy
                        }
                    );
            }

            public RouteList GetTopRoutes()
            {
                var query = from r in _routes
                            orderby r.Name
                            select r;
                return new RouteList(query);
            }

            public Route GetRoute(string name)
            {
                var route = from r in _routes
                            where r.Name == name
                            select r;
                return route.First();
            }
        }
    }
```

And, finally, Listing 16-12 is the controller that manages the retrieval of data. For the purposes of the example, only the list of routes will be rendered as a view.

Listing 16-12: Controllers.RouteController

```
namespace CyclingRoutes.Controllers
{
    public class RouteController : Controller
    {
        private RouteRepository _repository;
        public RouteController()
        {
            _repository=new RouteRepository();
        }

        public ActionResult List()
        {
            var routes = _repository.GetTopRoutes();
            return View(routes);
        }
    }
}
```

Listing 16-13 shows how the List view looks using the WebFormViewEngine.

Listing 16-13: List view

```
<%@ Page Title="" Language="C#" MasterPageFile="~/Views/Shared/Site.Master"
Inherits=" System.Web.Mvc.ViewPage<RouteList> " %>
<%@ Import Namespace="CyclingRoutes.Models"%>

<asp:Content ID="Content1"
    ContentPlaceHolderID="MainContent" runat="server">
    <table>
        <tr>
            <th>Name</th>
            <th>Length</th>
            <th>Gain</th>
            <th>Grade</th>
            <th>Difficutly</th>
        </tr>
        <%foreach (var route in Model) { %>
        <tr>
            <td><%= route.Name %></td>
            <td><%= route.Length %> Km</td>
            <td><%= route.Gain %> m</td>
            <td><%= route.AverageGrade %>%</td>
            <td><%= route.Difficutly %></td>
        </tr>
    <% } %>
    </table>
</asp:Content>
```

This view is included in the usual Site.Master page that comes from the project template, as shown in Figure 16-2.

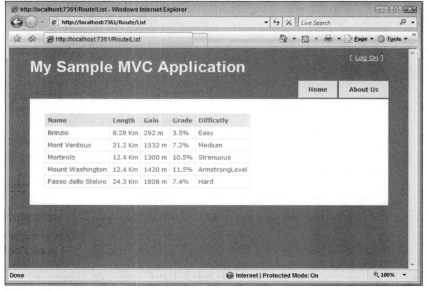

Figure 16-2

Now you can compare this view with the ones that are developed with the other view engines.

The Brail View Engine

Brail is one of the view engines of Castle MonoRail. It was developed by Oren Eini (aka Ayende), and it uses Boo as language. The integration library with ASP.NET MVC is part of MvcContrib.

Setting Up the Brail View Engine

For all view engines that come with MvcContrib, you have to add at least three references to the project:

❑   The MvcContrib assembly

❑   The assemblies of the view engine used

❑   The specific MvcContrib integration assembly (which is part of the Extra package)

Adding Brail References

In order to have the Brail View engine work, you need to download Castle MonoRail (`www`
`.castleproject.org/castle/download.html`) and get the relevant assemblies. All in all,
you have to add the following references to the project:

❑   `MvcContrib.dll`

❑   `MvcContrib.BrailViewEngine.dll`

❑   `Boo.Lang.dll`

❑   `Boo.Lang.Compiler.dll`

❑   `Boo.Lang.Extensions.dll`

❑   `Boo.Lang.Parser.dll`

Adding to Web.Config

Brail requires also a little bit of configuration inside the `web.config` file. Add the configuration section definition at the top of the file, inside the `<configsections>` section:

```
<section name="brail"
   type="MvcContrib.BrailViewEngine.BrailConfigurationSection,
   MvcContrib.BrailViewEngine"/>
```

And then add the real configuration:

```
<brail debug="true" saveToDisk="false" batch="false"
  commonScriptsDirectory="CommonScripts" saveDirectory="CompiledViews">
  <import namespace="Boo.Lang.Builtins"/>
  <import namespace="System"/>
</brail>
```

Registering the Brail View Engine

Before doing anything, you need to register the view engine with ASP.NET MVC:

```
ViewEngines.Engines.Add(new BrailViewFactory());
```

Brail's View Syntax

The Brail view engine supports master pages just like the WebForm view engine. Instead of being inside any possible view folder, with the `.master` extension, a Brail master page must be inside a folder named `Layouts` and the extension must be `.brail`. The placeholder for the real content page is `${childOutput}`. (See Listing 16-14.)

Listing 16-14: MasterPage in brail — site.brail

```
<!DOCTYPE html PUBLIC "-//W3C//DTD XHTML 1.0 Strict//EN"
    "http://www.w3.org/TR/xhtml1/DTD/xhtml1-strict.dtd">

<html xmlns="http://www.w3.org/1999/xhtml">
<head runat="server">
    <meta http-equiv="Content-Type"
        content="text/html; charset=iso-8859-1" />
    <title>Brail View Engine</title>
    <link href="${siteRoot}Content/Site.css"
        rel="stylesheet" type="text/css"  />
</head>

<body>
    <div class="page">

        <div id="header">
            <div id="title">
                <h1>My Sample MVC Application</h1>
            </div>

            <div id="logindisplay">
                <% html.RenderPartial("LogOnUserControl") %>
            </div>

            <div id="menucontainer">

                <ul id="menu">
                    <li>${html.ActionLink("Home", "Index", "Home")}</li>
                    <li>${html.ActionLink("About Us", "About", "Home")}</li>
                </ul>

            </div>
        </div>

        <div id="main">
            ${childOutput}

            <div id="footer">
            </div>
        </div>
    </div>
</body>
</html>
```

Besides the content placeholder, in this sample code you can find two other reserved variables for Brail: ${siteroot} contains the URL of the root of the site, and html contains the reference to the HtmlHelper class.

With the HtmlHelper class, you can also render partial views with a different view engine. In this example with the RenderPartial method, you ask the framework to render a partial view named LoginUserControl. Because the WebFormViewEngine is already registered by default and the partial view is an .ascx file, it will be rendered with the WebForm view engine. This way you can mix and match different view engines and reuse "components" written in other view engines.

The content page shown in Listing 16-15 is not different: It's just the fragment of code you want to be added to the view. The conventions are the usual ones: The view must be in a folder named like the controller and the extension of the file must be .brail.

Listing 16-15: List.brail view

```
<table>
    <tr>
        <th>Name</th>
        <th>Length</th>
        <th>Gain</th>
        <th>Grade</th>
        <th>Difficutly</th>
    </tr>
    <%
        for route in viewData.Model:
            output "<tr>"
            output "<td>${route.Name}</td>"
            output "<td>${route.Length} Km</td>"
            output "<td>${route.Gain} m</td>"
            output "<td>${route.AverageGrade}%</td>"
            output "<td>${route.Difficutly}</td>"
            output "</tr>"
        end
    %>
</table>
```

As you might have already noticed, the code block delimiters inside the template are the same as the WebForm view engine (<% %>). Anything surrounded by ${...} will automatically be evaluated and its result rendered in the HTML page.

In this example, the code accesses the Model property of the view data. If you want to access a value that has been put into the ViewData hashtable, you simply have to use its name. For example, ${Title} will access something added with ViewData["Title"].

Notice that, unlike the WebForm engine, the view knows nothing about the master page that will be included. To render a view inside a master page, you have to explicitly state this in the controller:

```
return View("List","site",routes);
```

Accessing Brail Resources

You can learn more about the syntax and configuration options of the Brail view engine on MonoRail's documentation site (www.castleproject.org/MonoRail/documentation/trunk/viewengines/brail/index.html) and about Boo on its official Web site (http://boo.codehaus.org/).

NVelocity

This is another view engine from MonoRail, and it's a port of the popular Velocity templating engine for Java. Hamilton "Hammett" Verissimo, the founder of Castle, also wrote the integration library, which is now part of MvcContrib.

Setting Up the NVelocity View Engine

You can download NVelocity together with MonoRail from the Castle project Web site (www.castleproject.org). Make sure that you don't download the NVelocity project, which is found on SourceForge, because this is a dead project.

NVelocity References

After you take the assembly out of the MonoRail installation folder, you have to add it as reference to your application. This results in your having to add three references:

- ❑ MvcContrib.dll
- ❑ MvcContrib.ViewEngines.NVelocity.dll (where the integration between NVelocity and ASP.NET MVC is)
- ❑ NVelocity.dll

Changing Web.Config

This view engine, unlike the BrailViewEngine and the other engines that follow, doesn't need anything placed inside the web.config file.

Registering the NVelocity View Engine

The registration is done, as usual, by adding this piece of code in the Application_Start method of the global.asax.cs file:

```
ViewEngines.Engines.Add(new NVelocityViewFactory());
```

The NVelocity View Syntax

Like Brail, NVelocity supports master pages, and they need to be put in a specific folder named Masters, inside the Views folder. The extension of the master page, as well as the one for any view, must be .vm. Listing 16-16 contains the code of the master page for the site.

Listing 16-16: MasterPage in NVelocity — site.vm

```
<!DOCTYPE html PUBLIC "-//W3C//DTD XHTML 1.0 Strict//EN"
    "http://www.w3.org/TR/xhtml1/DTD/xhtml1-strict.dtd">

<html xmlns="http://www.w3.org/1999/xhtml">
<head runat="server">
    <meta http-equiv="Content-Type"
      content="text/html; charset=iso-8859-1" />
    <title>NVelocity View Engine</title>
    <link href="$Url.Content('~/Content/Site.css')"
      rel="stylesheet" type="text/css"  />
</head>

<body>
    <div class="page">

        <div id="header">
            <div id="title">
                <h1>My Sample MVC Application</h1>
            </div>

            <div id="logindisplay">
                $html.RenderPartial("LogOnUserControl")
            </div>

            <div id="menucontainer">
                <ul id="menu">
                    <li>$html.ActionLink("Home", "Index", "Home")</li>
                    <li>$html.ActionLink("About Us", "About", "Home")</li>
                </ul>

            </div>
        </div>

        <div id="main">
            #parse($childContent)

            <div id="footer">
            </div>
        </div>
    </div>
</body>
</html>
```

The syntax here is a bit different from that in the Brail view. The variables are still referenced using the dollar sign ($), but there is the new concept of *directives*, which are Velocity-specific constructs (like the one used to render the content page, #parse). Because all the directives start with the hash sign (#), there is no need for code block delimiters as with the WebForm and Brail views. In that case, if a directive needs to surround a portion of code, it must have an end directive, for example, the `foreach` loop:

```
#foreach($route in $Viewdata.Model)
    ...
#end
```

Then the content page (see Listing 16-17) is just the fragment, as it is with Brail and unlike the WebForm (which also needs some surrounding markup).

Listing 16-17: List.vm

```
#foreach($route in $Viewdata.Model)
#beforeall
    <table>
        <tr>
            <th>Name</th>
            <th>Length</th>
            <th>Gain</th>
            <th>Grade</th>
            <th>Difficutly</th>
        </tr>
#before
        <tr>
#each
        <td>$route.Name</td>
        <td>$route.Length Km</td>
        <td>$route.Gain m</td>
        <td>$route.AverageGrade%</td>
        <td>$route.Difficutly</td>
#after
        </tr>
#afterall
    </table>
#end
```

Of course, you could have done the same looping through the collection of routes and manually writing the table, but using NVelocity directives the code is clearer.

Something that shows the power of these directives even more is the built-in support for alternating rows. If you replace the `#before` directive with the following ones, you'll get a nice "zebra-striped" table, as shown in Figure 16-3.

```
#odd
        <tr style='background:lightgrey'>
#even
        <tr style='background:white'>
```

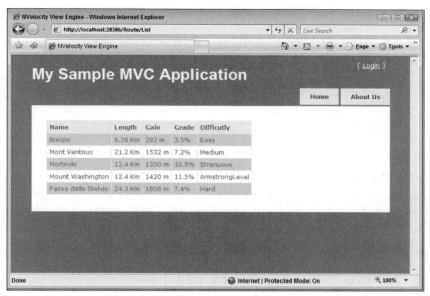

Figure 16-3

To achieve the same result with WebForms, you would have needed to write a custom HTML extension method (as you did at the end of Chapter 6) or other code mixed with markup.

One last thing before moving on to the next view engine: As with Brail, the content page knows nothing about its master page, so it must be explicitly set inside the controller:

```
return View("List","site",routes);
```

Accessing NVelocity Resources

Because this view engine is a port of the popular Java Velocity templating engine, you can read about its syntax on the Apache Velocity Web site (http://velocity.apache.org).

Spark

One of the latest view engines to appear is Spark (http://sparkviewengine.com). It's a completely new view engine written by Lou DeJardin (http://whereslou.com) with the idea that "HTML should dominate the flow and that the code should fit seamlessly."

Setting Up the Spark View Engine

You can download the view engine from its project's Web site http://sparkviewengine.com/download. The download package also contains quite a few samples, the documentation, and an installer that will enable IntelliSense support and color syntax highlighting inside Spark views (as shown in Figure 16-4).

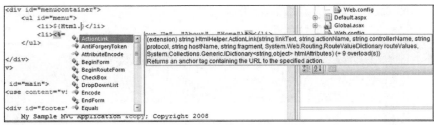

Figure 16-4

Adding Spark References

This view engine contains everything you need to run an ASP.NET MVC application, so just download the Spark engine and add it, together with a reference to the MVC-specific assembly. This results in your having the following assemblies added as references:

❑   Spark.dll

❑   Spark.Web.Mvc.dll

Changing Web.Config

Spark requires a bit of configuration inside the web.config file. First, you need to add the configuration section inside the <configSection> section:

```
<section name="spark"
      type="Spark.Configuration.SparkSectionHandler, Spark"/>
```

and then add the real configuration. It can be anything from the simple debug=true to a more elaborate one that contains additional assemblies used to compile the views:

```
<spark>
  <compilation debug="true"/>
  <pages>
    <namespaces>
      <add namespace="System.Web.Mvc.Html"/>
    </namespaces>
  </pages>
</spark>
```

Registering the Spark View Engine

You use the usual view engine registration:

```
ViewEngines.Engines.Add(new SparkViewFactory());
```

If you don't like using the web.config to configure the view engine, you can do it during the registration of the engine in the global.asax.cs file:

```
var settings = new SparkSettings();
settings.Debug = true;
```

```
settings.AddNamespace("System.Web.Mvc.Html");

ViewEngines.Engines.Add(new SparkViewFactory(settings));
```

The Spark View Syntax

Unlike the previous view engines that use their own syntax, Spark uses C# as the language of choice, so there is no need to learn another new scripting language.

To find the location of the master pages, Spark uses a conventions-based approach. It looks for the master page inside the Layouts folder and then in the Shared folder. If the controller doesn't specify a master page, it will look for the default one, named application.spark. Listing 16-18 contains the code for that default master page.

Listing 16-18: Application.spark master page

```
<!DOCTYPE html PUBLIC "-//W3C//DTD XHTML 1.0 Strict//EN"
    "http://www.w3.org/TR/xhtml1/DTD/xhtml1-strict.dtd">

<html xmlns="http://www.w3.org/1999/xhtml">
<head runat="server">
    <meta http-equiv="Content-Type"
        content="text/html; charset=iso-8859-1" />
    <title><use content="title"/></title>
    <link href="~/Content/Site.css" rel="stylesheet" type="text/css"/>
</head>

<body>
    <div class="page">

        <div id="header">
            <div id="title">
                <h1>My Sample MVC Application</h1>
            </div>

            <div id="logindisplay">
                <% Html.RenderPartial("LogOnUserControl"); %>
            </div>

            <div id="menucontainer">
                <ul id="menu">
                    <li>${Html.ActionLink("Home", "Index", "Home")}</li>
                    <li><%=Html.ActionLink("About Us",
                        "About", "Home")%></li>
                </ul>

            </div>
        </div>

        <div id="main">
            <use:view />
```

Continued

Listing 16-18: Application.spark master page *(continued)*

```
            <div id="footer">
            </div>
        </div>
    </div>
</body>
</html>
```

The syntax of Spark is the most similar to WebForms. As you can see, you can use either the WebForm's `<%= ... %>` or `${...}` to delimit code that will directly render to HTML. Also, the content placeholder is the custom tag `<use:view/>`. At runtime this will be replaced with the content page.

Unlike the previous two view engines, which allowed only one content area per master page, Spark takes back the WebForm's concept of named content placeholders. If the content page contains more than one content area, you can name it and reference it using a variation of the `<use>` tag (like it happens for the title placeholder):

```
<use content="title"/>
```

If you want to take advantage of this feature, instead of just being an HTML fragment, the views have to group contents inside a `<content>` tag, as you see in the next listing.

Listing 16-19 shows the content page that lists the cycling routes.

Listing 16-19: List.spark view

```
<viewdata model="CyclingRoutes.Models.RouteList"/>

<content name="title">
Spark View Engine
</content>

<table>
  <tr>
    <th>Name</th>
    <th>Length</th>
    <th>Gain</th>
    <th>Grade</th>
    <th>Difficutly</th>
  </tr>
  <tr each='var route in ViewData.Model'>
    <td>${route.Name}</td>
    <td>${route.Length} Km</td>
    <td>${route.Gain} m</td>
    <td>${route.AverageGrade}%</td>
    <td>${route.Difficutly}</td>
  </tr>
</table>
```

The first thing worth noticing is that the `foreach` loop is embedded directly inside the HTML tag that needs to be repeated. This is what the author of the view engine meant when he said "HTML should dominate the flow."

Then the `viewdata` tag is used to declare the type of each of the elements that are part of the `ViewData` collection. In this case, the model attribute is used to inform the page of the type of the model object stored inside the `viewdata`. If you want to use a value that is stored using the hashtable, you have to do it like this:

```
<viewdata Title="string"/>
```

And then access it simply by accessing the `Title` variable `${Title}`.

Just to give you another taste of the syntax of the view engine, here is how you can create an `if-then-else` decision with Spark:

```
<if condition='!user.IsLoggedIn()'>
  <p>Here's a login form</p>
</if>
<else if='user.HasRole(RoleType.Administrator)'>
  <p>Hello - you're an admin</p>
</else>
<else>
  <p>I have no idea what type of person you are.</p>
</else>
```

Accessing Spark Resources

But Spark has many other features. It has intrinsic partial views, support for generics, and more. The place to get more information on this view engine is the official Spark Web site (`http://sparkviewengine.com/`).

The NHaml View Engine

If you think Spark is revolutionary, it's because you have never seen a view written with NHaml; it's a port of the Ruby on Rails Haml view engine by New Zealander Andrew Peters. If you don't like the "angle-bracket syntax" of HTML, you'll find yourself liking this view engine. It supports C#, and also Boo (like Brail) and even IronRuby (the Microsoft version of Ruby).

The philosophy behind NHaml is that:

❑ Markup should be beautiful.

❑ Markup should be DRY ("don't repeat yourself").

❑ Markup should be well indented.

❑ The XHTML structure should be clear.

Setting Up the NHaml View Engine

This view engine was first included in the MvcContrib project, but it was later moved to its own space, on Google Code (`http://code.google.com/p/nhaml/`). To download the view engine, go to the aforementioned site and get version 2.0 (which is the one these samples are built with).

Setting NHaml References

Because this view engine is not part of MvcContrib, all you need to reference are the NHaml assemblies. If you don't want to write your views with Boo or IronRuby, you need to reference these three assemblies:

❑   NHaml.dll

❑   NHaml.Web.Mvc.dll

❑   Microsoft.Web.Mvc.dll

Changing Web.Config

With NHaml it's possible to switch between production and debugging mode via a configuration attribute in the web.config. This is done via the autorecompile attribute. When you are in production, it's a good idea to set the attribute to false, so that once compiled, the views are cached to increase performance. But when you are still developing, you want to see immediately every change you make to the view, so it's better to set the autoRecompile attribute to true.

As with the other view engines, first you have to add the configuration definition inside the <configSection> element:

```
<section name="nhaml"
    type="NHaml.Configuration.NHamlConfigurationSection, NHaml"/>
```

And then the configuration section:

```
<nhaml autoRecompile="true" >
  <assemblies>
    <add assembly="CyclingRoutes"/>
  </assemblies>
  <namespaces>
    <add namespace="CyclingRoutes.Models"/>
  </namespaces>
</nhaml>
```

Also, the configuration section is useful for specifying which assemblies and namespaces need to be referenced by the view compiler.

Registering the NHaml View Engine

Finally, you have to register the view engine in the Application_Start method:

```
ViewEngines.Engines.Add(new NHamlViewFactory());
```

The NHaml View Syntax

Now, are you ready to be shocked? Listing 16-20 is the master page written in NHaml.

Listing 16-20: site.haml master page

```
!!!
%html{xmlns="http://www.w3.org/1999/xhtml"}
  %head
    %meta{http-equiv="Content-Type" content="text/html; charset=iso-8859-1"}
    %title NHaml View Engine
    %link{href="../../Content/Site.css" rel="stylesheet" type="text/css"}
  %body
    .page
      #header
        #title
          %h1 My Sample MVC Application
        #logindisplay
          - Html.RenderPartial("LogOnUserControl")
        #menucontainer
          %ul#menu
            %li
              = Html.ActionLink("Home", "Index", "Home")
            %li
              = Html.ActionLink("About Us", "About", "Home")
      #main

        _

        #footer
```

Now take a deep breath, and let's start with the explanations. The view location conventions of NHaml are the same as the WebForm view engine except for the extension of the file, which is .haml. The placeholder instead is a bit different: It's the line highlighted in grey, the one with only the "_" underscore character.

This is not the only strange characteristic of the view:

❑   !!! is the doctype definition.

❑   % precedes a tag (%li is converted to <li>).

❑   . (the dot) indentifies the text that follows a CSS class name, and if used alone without following a tag, it defaults to a div tag (.page is converted to <div class="page">, and %span .page is converted to <span class="page">).

❑   # (the hash sign) is the same as the dot, but is applied to id instead of CSS classes (#header is converted to <div id="header">).

❑   = (the equal character) means that everything that follows on the line will be evaluated and rendered in the page.

❑   – (the dash character) marks the line as containing "silent" code, which means that the execution of it doesn't return a string directly rendered (RenderPartial does render a string, but by putting it directly in the output string).

Notice that there are no closing tags. That's because NHaml relies on indentation. Nested elements are two spaces more to the right than their ancestors, and the enclosing "tag" is closed where there is another element at its same level of indentation. When the end of the file is reached, all the open tags are automatically closed.

Now on to the content page, as shown in Listing 16-21.

Listing 16-21: List.haml content view

```
%table
  %tr
    %th
      Name
    %th
      Length
    %th
      Gain
    %th
      Grade
    %th
      Difficutly
- foreach (var route in ViewData.Model)
  %tr
    %td
      = route.Name
    %td
      = (route.Length + " Km")
    %td
      = (route.Gain + " m" )
    %td
      = (route.AverageGrade + "%")
    %td
      = route.Difficutly
```

In this view the "-" (dash) sign is used to mark the line that contains the `foreach` loop.

As with the other view engines, because the view doesn't know anything about the master page it should use, the controller must always explicitly specify the master page name:

```
return View("List","site",routes);
```

As you see, it's a complete break with everything that came before. More than a markup language, NHaml can be seen as a DSL for writing XHTML.

Its main disadvantages are that it relies on whitespaces, and we are now used to writing code that ignores how many whitespaces or tabs you use. Also, there is no support inside Visual Studio, meaning no code highlighting and no IntelliSense (but this is common to all the other view engines except Spark).

Accessing HNaml Resources

The primary source of information about the view engine is the post in which Andrew announced it: `http://andrewpeters.net/2007/12/19/introducing-nhaml-an-aspnet-mvc-view-engine`. You can find more information and updates regarding the project on the project's site as well (`http://code.google.com/p/nhaml`) and on the site of the original Ruby version: `http://haml.hamptoncatlin.com`.

Minor Extensibility Points

Besides these three big areas of extensibility (route handlers, controller factories, and view engines), the ASP.NET MVC framework can be extended in many other points. In the following sections you see several of the possibilities.

ActionMethodSelectorAttribute

In Chapter 5 you learned that action methods are selected based on their method name and by evaluating other attributes like the `AcceptVerbs` and the `NonAction` attributes. But if you want a more granular control over how an action is selected, you can write your own selection attribute by writing a class that inherits from the base class `ActionMethodSelectorAttribute`.

The only method you have to implement is `IsValidForRequest`, which returns `true` if the action is valid for the current request or `false` if it's not. The two attributes — `NonActionAttribute` and `AcceptVerbsAttribute` — are two implementations of this base class.

Listing 16-22 shows the code for a custom attribute that validates the action based on the preferred language set in the user's browser.

Listing 16-22: AcceptLanguagesAttribute

```
using System;
using System.Collections.Generic;
using System.Collections.ObjectModel;
using System.Linq;
using System.Reflection;
using System.Web.Mvc;

namespace Attributes_for_Actions.Controllers
{
    public class AcceptsLanguagesAttribute: ActionMethodSelectorAttribute
    {
        public ICollection<string> Languages { get; private set; }

        public AcceptsLanguagesAttribute(params string[] languages)
        {
            this.Languages = new ReadOnlyCollection<string>(languages);
        }

        public override bool IsValidForRequest(
                ControllerContext controllerContext, MethodInfo methodInfo)
        {
        string lang = controllerContext.HttpContext.Request.UserLanguages[0];
        return Languages.Contains<string>(lang,
                                        StringComparer.OrdinalIgnoreCase);
        }
    }
}
```

The `IsValidForRequest` method implemented in this attribute just verifies whether the language preferred by the user is among the ones that are considered valid by the action.

The following action is invoked only if the user's browser is configured to have Italian or United States English as the preferred language:

```
[AcceptsLanguages("it-IT","en-us")]
public ActionResult Language()
{
    //Process language-specific procedures
    return View();
}
```

TempDataProvider

The `TempData` object is the collection that is used to store values that need to be passed to an action on the next request. The `TempData` provider supplied with the framework stores the values inside the `Session` object tied to the current user. This means that you have to enable the session state.

If you don't want to enable the session state or you want to store `TempData` on a database or in any other location, you have to implement a custom `TempDataProvider`. You can do this by implementing the `ITempDataProvider` interface. It contains two methods:

❑ `LoadTempData`

❑ `SaveTempData`

They both work on two parameters: a `Dictionary<String, Object>` of values, which is the list of all the values that have to be saved/retrieved, and a `ControllerContext` object.

In Listing 16-23, the `TempData` collection is stored in the ASP.NET Cache.

Listing 16-23: CacheTempDataProvider

```
public class CacheTempDataProvider: ITempDataProvider
{
    private const string keyName = "__TempData";
    public IDictionary<string, object> LoadTempData(
        ControllerContext controllerContext)
    {
        string cacheKey = GetCacheKey(controllerContext.HttpContext);
        Dictionary<string, object> tempData =
            controllerContext.HttpContext.Cache[cacheKey]
            as Dictionary<string, object>;
        if(tempData!=null)
        {
            controllerContext.HttpContext.Cache.Remove(keyName);
            return tempData;
        }
```

```
        return new Dictionary<string, object>();
    }

    public void SaveTempData(ControllerContext controllerContext,
        IDictionary<string, object> values)
    {
        string cacheKey = GetCacheKey(controllerContext.HttpContext);
        controllerContext.HttpContext.Cache.Insert(cacheKey, values);
    }

    private string GetCacheKey(HttpContextBase httpContext)
    {
        string uniqueIdentifier = httpContext.Request.UserHostAddress;
        return String.Format("{0}[{1}]",keyName, uniqueIdentifier);
    }
}
```

This implementation is pretty simple. One method gets the values and stores them in the cache; the other checks for their existence and returns them to the caller.

Also notice that because you are not using SessionState, you have to find a way to uniquely identify a user's session. In the example, the user's IP address is used, but this is not an optimal solution because more than one user can come from a single IP address (imagine offices that access the Internet through a firewall). A possible solution might be generating a unique identifier and storing it inside a client-side cookie.

Now that the custom provider is ready, you need to inject it into the controller. If you need it for just one controller, you can just instantiate it in the constructor of the controller.

```
public HomeController()
{
    TempDataProvider = new CacheTempDataProvider();
}
```

Otherwise, you can create your own base controller, instantiate the TempData provider in its Initialize method, and then have all your controllers inherit from it instead of from System.Web .Mvc.Controller:

```
public class CacheTempDataController: Controller
{
    protected override void Initialize(
        System.Web.Routing.RequestContext requestContext)
    {
        base.Initialize(requestContext);
        TempDataProvider = new CacheTempDataProvider();
    }}
public class HomeController : CacheTempDataController { … }
```

Having a custom base class is also one of the other extensibility points that the framework allows. This way, you can add helper methods used in all your controllers or slightly change the behavior of the standard controller class.

Custom ActionResult

Another micro-extension you can make is a custom `ActionResult` class. If you remember from Chapter 5, an action result is the class that contains all the logic to return the result back to the browser. The framework already provides a lot of action results to cover almost every need, but if you want to write a specific one, you can do it by inheriting from `System.Web.Mvc.ActionResult` and overriding the `ExecuteResult` method, which accepts the `ControllerContext` as a parameter.

Try It Out   Building a Custom ActionResult

In this example, you address an issue typical in blogging engines: The URL contains the title of the post, which is then passed as a parameter to the action method. If the post is not in the database, the engine cannot just return a "post not found" message; otherwise, it will fool search engines. It needs to return a proper "Page Not Found" page with the correct HTTP status. In this Try It Out, you build an action result for that.

1.   Start as usual by creating an ASP.NET MVC Web application project without testing the project.

2.   Add a folder named `Code`, create a new class file named `PageNotFoundResult.cs`, and add the following code to it:

```
public class PageNotFoundResult: ActionResult
{
    public string Path { get; set; }

    public PageNotFoundResult(string path)
    {
        Path = path;
    }

    public override void ExecuteResult(ControllerContext context)
    {
        if (context == null)
        {
            throw new ArgumentNullException("context");
        }
        context.HttpContext.Response.StatusCode = 404;
        Controller controller = context.Controller as Controller;
        context.HttpContext.Response.WriteFile(
            controller.Url.Content(Path));
    }
}
```

3.   Add to the `Content` folder an HTML file named `PageNotFound.html`.

```
<!DOCTYPE html PUBLIC "-//W3C//DTD XHTML 1.0 Transitional//EN"
    "http://www.w3.org/TR/xhtml1/DTD/xhtml1-transitional.dtd">
<html xmlns="http://www.w3.org/1999/xhtml" >
<head>
    <title>Page not found</title>
</head>
<body>
    <h1>Page Not Found</h1>
</body>
</html>
```

4. Then, open the `Controllers\HomeController.cs` file and modify the `Action` method so that it matches the following code:

```
public ActionResult About()
{
    ViewData["Title"] = "About Page";
    return new PageNotFoundResult("~/Content/PageNotFound.html");
}
```

5. Now compile and run the code, and go to `/Home/About`. Instead of the About page, you will see the page you just added as HTML, and the status code will be 404. In Figure 16-5 you see the "friendly error" that is shown by Internet Explorer.

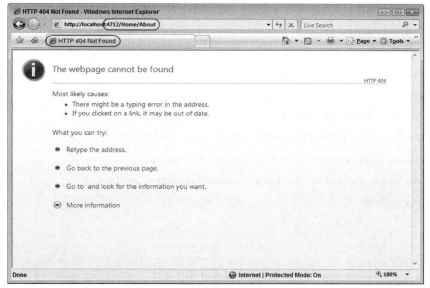

Figure 16-5

How It Works

Implementing an `ActionResult` is not difficult, and it's what you did in step 2 of the example. The method first checks whether the context parameter has really been supplied. Then it accesses the response output stream and writes the HTML file that has been passed in the constructor of the result. It also sets the `StatusCode` to 404, which is the code that browsers and search engine spiders recognize as "page not found."

Then you return the custom action result as the return value of the action (step 4). Notice that the URL displayed to the user in the browser is still the original one, because the user is not being redirected to another generic "Page Not Found" page.

Summary

The ASP.NET MVC framework is a complete Web application framework that you can use as is, but to completely exploit its power you can customize and extend it so that it fits all your needs and development style. In this long chapter, you learned a lot about the extension points of the framework, and you are ready now to embark in the development of your first real application.

But before moving forward, it's time to review what you learned in this chapter:

❑ What extensibility means

❑ How to use the three main areas of extensibility in the framework

    ❑ Route handler

    ❑ Controller factory

    ❑ View engine

❑ How to write a custom route handler that uses the WebForm model

❑ How a controller factory is made

❑ What the MvcContrib project is

❑ How to use the Ninject controller factory with ASP.NET MVC

❑ What steps are needed to write a custom view engine

❑ How to use some of the most popular alternative view engines:

    ❑ Brail

    ❑ NVelocity

    ❑ Spark

    ❑ NHaml

❑ How to implement a custom `TempData` provider

❑ How to create a custom `ActionResult`

A lot of content, isn't it? For this reason, this chapter has no exercises with clear solutions as there have been in some of the other chapters. But there are still some exercises, so take some time to review the chapter and do them before moving to the last theoretical chapter of the book, which is about the path to migrate from the "old" WebForm model to the new MVC approach. Then you'll finally be able to see some real code in the last two chapters, with case studies of two simple real-world applications.

Exercises

1. Try to think of other possible scenarios for which you might want to write a custom route handler.

2. Try to set up the sample Math MVC application, using another IoC Container of your choice.

3. Look at the documentation of the various view engines and try to form an opinion of which you like best.

4. Try to implement the other features of the WebForm view engine (partial views, HTML helpers), using the view engine you chose in the previous exercise.

5. Using as a starting point the `TempDataProvider` of Listing 16-23, write a provider that uses a client-side cookie to uniquely identify the current user session.

Migrating from ASP.NET WebForms

ASP.NET MVC is a new technology in comparison with many other Web development technologies available, especially those produced by Microsoft, so it looks like there will be a great demand for ASP.NET MVC in the coming years, and many companies will switch to the technology. At the moment, several enterprise applications that are built with ASP.NET WebForms require an implementation of the MVC pattern to perform better. The advent of ASP.NET MVC provides a good opportunity for companies to migrate their applications to ASP.NET MVC and enjoy its flexibility and testability features.

Besides, there should be a next generation of Web applications built with ASP.NET MVC rather than ASP.NET WebForms. There is a lot of excitement in the community about the idea of building future applications with this framework because it has some unique features that are not available in ASP.NET WebForms. We have already discussed the advantages of ASP.NET MVC over ASP.NET WebForms, particularly in Chapter 2 (as well as some advantages that ASP.NET WebForms have).

Though it is best to make a clear decision to use ASP.NET MVC or its alternatives before implementing a project, at times developers will want to migrate their existing projects from ASP.NET WebForms to ASP.NET MVC. This strongly depends on the type of project and its requirements, and no one can invent a step-by-step guide that would be consistently reliable for migrating all applications.

The purpose of this chapter is to provide an overview of the major steps that should be followed to migrate an ASP.NET WebForms application to ASP.NET MVC, based on a practical approach and with an example, but keep in mind that this chapter covers the basic ideas. It's not possible to introduce a unique solution for all scenarios. Your solution depends on your project and your knowledge. The deeper your knowledge of ASP.NET WebForms and ASP.NET MVC, the better you can migrate from one to another.

This chapter is organized into the following main topics:

❑   Reasons to migrate and deciding whether to do so

❑   An overview of the migration process from ASP.NET WebForms to ASP.NET MVC

❑   Fundamental differences between ASP.NET WebForms and ASP.NET MVC and what you should consider

❑   Finding alternatives for ASP.NET WebForms server controls in ASP.NET MVC

❑   A practical example of the migration of code from ASP.NET WebForms to ASP.NET MVC

Why Migrate?

Before anything else, we should talk about something that is much more important than the migration itself, and that is the necessity to migrate an ASP.NET WebForms application to ASP.NET MVC.

Many developers who will convert their applications probably shouldn't do so because it won't bring any value to their projects. To be honest, some developers are hot to use new technologies and try to apply them whether or not it's a good option for them.

Unless you seriously need to have a high level of testability in your existing Web projects and/or a deeper level of access to everything to have control over your project elements, ASP.NET MVC probably won't add much value to what you already have. There are many advantages to ASP.NET MVC over ASP.NET WebForms and vice versa. Some major points can encourage someone to prefer ASP.NET MVC over ASP.NET WebForms, but if they're not applicable to your situation, you should avoid converting. The level of testability, the level of control on project elements, the implementation of the MVC pattern with great separation of concerns, and the capability to replace different components of a project with the least effort possible are all major points that can move you to use ASP.NET MVC.

Although ASP.NET MVC has some unique features that are not available in ASP.NET WebForms (such as the ones just described, which we discuss in detail throughout the book), ASP.NET WebForms have many advantages as well. Therefore, if you have developed an ASP.NET WebForms application and deployed to production, there is no need to switch to ASP.NET MVC and put more effort into building an MVC application, which naturally takes more resources and time!

Think about your application requirements and decide whether ASP.NET MVC can add something to your project. Then evaluate the value of this addition and compare it with the money and effort that you must put into a migration process.

ASP.NET MVC may add something to your project and improve its quality and testability, but the downside is the effort that it takes to build it, so you should keep a balance between effort and outcome. ASP.NET MVC is an independent server technology of its own, and despite some similarities with ASP.NET WebForms, it mustn't be considered as a part of it. ASP.NET MVC is something independent like Ruby on Rails or PHP, so there isn't a clear path to convert your Web applications to ASP.NET MVC. However, ASP.NET WebForms and ASP.NET MVC are a part of the .NET Framework and more particularly of the ASP.NET stack, and some techniques can facilitate the migration process for you. Moreover, it's possible to use them both in a single project, and we discuss this further, shortly.

Do not forget that software development involves the art of balancing several factors: meeting your goals, satisfying your client's requirements, creating a quality application, completing the development process, and of course, keeping the cost of development within a target range, which is always a very important factor.

Overview of the Migration Process

If you decide to migrate a Web application from ASP.NET WebForms to ASP.NET MVC, you are entering into a new world where there isn't a direct course to follow for migration.

You may expect to see a step-by-step guide or even a simple classic wizard (like the Upgrade Wizard for converting ASP.NET 1.*x* applications to ASP.NET 2.0) to migrate your application from WebForms to MVC, but unfortunately such options are not available and are unlikely to be built in the future. Though ASP.NET WebForms and ASP.NET MVC share several aspects in common with their parent ASP.NET technology, they also have major fundamental differences that outweigh their similarities in the area of migration, so it's not possible to automate a direct migration path for developers.

A good migration depends on your existing WebForms application, its architecture, and your development model, requirements, and goals. Your migration path will vary according to these factors. Knowing them is helpful for designing a smooth migration.

Migration may look like a difficult task, especially when you're dealing with large-scale applications or with some architectures that don't have a good separation between layers. But this shouldn't distract you because even if migration is not a straightforward task, it isn't impossible or necessarily arduous. Luckily, working with an application that is built on top of an *n*-tier application is much easier than an application that has tight components.

Your migration process might consist of a number of steps that can be classified into two main groups:

❑ **Common steps** — These steps are common to all migrations and deal with fundamental differences between ASP.NET WebForms and ASP.NET MVC, such as replacing your server controls in ASP.NET MVC.

❑ **Uncommon steps** — The second group consists of steps that may be specific to your project and are not shared by all applications, such as rebuilding your data layer to be compatible with the MVC pattern or finding a user interface element to replace your custom ASP.NET server control in your WebForms application.

Understanding the fundamental similarities and differences between ASP.NET WebForms and ASP .NET MVC should be the basis of a successful migration, so the next two sections discuss these briefly. Of course, most of these concepts are already covered throughout the chapters of this book, but it's worth having a brief overview with an emphasis on migration here.

> *This chapter focuses on the main similarities and differences when migrating between ASP.NET WebForms and ASP.NET MVC. Depending on your specific circumstances, there may be other factors that affect migration not covered in this discussion. (For example, you might have followed a specific development pattern and there should be specific steps to convert that code to MVC, or you might have used a third-party tool for managing your profile systems in ASP.NET WebForms that needs to be replaced in ASP.NET MVC.)*

Fundamental Similarities between ASP.NET WebForms and ASP.NET MVC

ASP.NET WebForms and ASP.NET MVC share some commonalities even though the number of these similarities is not as large as the number of differences. Fortunately, ASP.NET 4.0 is supposed to include more features that are already a part of ASP.NET MVC, so you can expect a better future for migration from ASP.NET WebForms to ASP.NET MVC.

The interesting news is that you're allowed to use ASP.NET WebForms and ASP.NET MVC in the same application, which is a very important advantage if you are seeking a smooth migration. With this capability, you're able to run your application using both technologies concurrently and gradually migrate WebForm parts to MVC. Phil Haack has a very nice blog post at `http://haacked.com/archive/2008/03/11/using-routing-with-webforms.aspx` where he shows you how to use `IRouteHandler` as an extensibility point in ASP.NET MVC to modify routing and run ASP.NET WebForms pages along with ASP.NET MVC.

Let's take a look at the major similarities between ASP.NET WebForms and ASP.NET MVC that can save you time when implementing a migration process. These features are actually a part of the general ASP.NET concept that includes ASP.NET WebForms, ASP.NET MVC, and ASP.NET Dynamic Data as parts of its main body.

Authentication and Authorization Similarities

As discussed in Chapter 15, ASP.NET MVC inherits the same authentication and authorization mechanisms as ASP.NET WebForms; however, some minor higher-level differences exist between the implementations. The main difference is in the area of applying security roles. In WebForms you generally use `<location />` elements to define rules, but in ASP.NET MVC you primarily apply security settings to the objects and action methods.

Generally, you don't need to do much work with authentication and authorization to import your applications from ASP.NET WebForms to ASP.NET MVC.

Provider Similarities

ASP.NET MVC applies the same providers as ASP.NET WebForms, and you can use membership, role, profile, and health monitoring providers with ASP.NET MVC as well. Fortunately, many of these providers can be used without any change in ASP.NET MVC, but minor tweaks may be required to port some providers in some cases.

HttpModule and HttpHandler

Two of the most common parts of ASP.NET Web applications are `HttpModules` and `HttpHandlers`. These have not been covered because they have the exact same implementation and development model as ASP.NET WebForms, so you can apply your knowledge from WebForms in MVC.

No changes are required to import `HttpModules` and `HttpHandlers` in general, but some fundamental server and client objects are changed in ASP.NET MVC, so you may need to apply minor tweaks to integrate your code.

Also note that in ASP.NET MVC new derivations of these components are introduced that provide better features specific for ASP.NET MVC. Though the parent components work fine, you may consider using these derivations as well.

Fundamental Differences between ASP.NET WebForms and ASP.NET MVC

The number of fundamental differences between ASP.NET WebForms and ASP.NET MVC is larger than their similarities specifically in the context of migration. ASP.NET WebForms are built on top of some basic structures such as `ViewState`, server controls, various events, and separation of HTML code from code-behind logic files, but ASP.NET MVC changes all these principles and provides a different development process that deals with a lower level of request and response workflow. This model usually takes a little more effort from developers to build an application in comparison to ASP.NET WebForms.

The ViewState Difference

ASP.NET MVC doesn't maintain state via `ViewState`. Although this is one of the major changes that many developers liked, by its very nature it creates difficulties for developing Web applications because it requires you to duplicate the effort that you put into building applications.

Without `ViewState` you cannot use most ASP.NET WebForms server controls (as you read in a moment), and you need to write your own code to maintain the state of your forms between requests. This is one of the common tasks you need to perform when you port a WebForms application to ASP.NET MVC.

Maintaining the state of your forms is covered further in Chapter 5 and Chapter 14.

Differences in Using Server Controls

As you have seen, ASP.NET MVC doesn't have any support for `ViewState`; this means that you cannot use most ASP.NET WebForms server controls anymore. Server controls are one of the great advantages of using ASP.NET WebForms. The lack of them requires that you implement alternative options.

Later in this chapter, there is a brief discussion of finding alternative options for ASP.NET WebForms server controls, but you will no doubt need to rewrite a lot of code to use these alternative options in your ported applications.

Code Model Differences

ASP.NET WebForms offers two coding model options: using code inline (usually for pages with less business code) and using code-behind (for many scenarios). This requires the storage of up to three different files for a single page, which is not an efficient practice.

ASP.NET MVC replaces this model with the MVC pattern, which moves your handling logic to controllers. An example of this change is covered later in this chapter when you explore an example of the migration process.

If you have developed your WebForms applications with a good separation of business, data, and user interface code, migration will be easier because you can move the separate layers, with some tweaks to components. However, if your WebForms application doesn't have a good separation, you should prepare yourself for a longer migration process. ASP.NET MVC has, however, reduced the need for multiple files for pages and views.

Event Model Differences

Another major change in ASP.NET MVC is the replacement of page, control, and client events with controllers, which is related to the replacement of the WebForms code model with the MVC pattern.

In ASP.NET MVC, you implement your handling logic in the model and controllers, as opposed to handling the logic in events. To do this, you use different HTTP verbs to achieve your goals and handle requests in the controllers, as you saw in Chapter 5.

The implementation of the event-handling mechanism also depends heavily on your existing WebForms application and how well its layers are separated, but generally you need to move your event-handling logic to controllers in order to port your applications.

Differences in Using URLs

ASP.NET MVC replaces the URL system in ASP.NET WebForms with RESTful URLs that are routed to controllers, so some significant changes in this area require your special attention when importing a WebForms application. For more information about URL routing, check Chapter 7.

Most of ASP.NET WebForms applications are built on .aspx pages that appear in their URLs and make these URLs dependent on the server technology extension. But ASP.NET MVC has a RESTful URL structure without such extensions (that is a very good advantage for this technology).

It's necessary to keep all your old URLs valid and redirect them to the new corresponding resource in your MVC application after migration.

To do so, you need to use URL redirection techniques, which are mostly constant between ASP.NET WebForms and ASP.NET MVC. In WebForms you have several options offered by Microsoft, third-party companies, and open source projects that all rely on very similar structures and basics. You can use them to redirect those old URLs to the new ones in ASP.NET MVC, which you do in the same way as you do in WebForms in general.

Fortunately, ASP.NET 4.0 will use the same routing mechanism as ASP.NET MVC, so it can simplify the conversion for future versions of ASP.NET WebForms.

Differences in the Separation of Resources

ASP.NET MVC creates default project templates with special folder structures to separate view, controller, model, and content files. All developers are strongly encouraged to take advantage of this separation.

ASP.NET WebForms doesn't have such a default or recommended structure, and there is a high probability that you need to work on this area as well. For more information about the recommended structure of ASP.NET MVC project folders, read Chapter 3.

Validation Differences

Chapter 14 provides an in-depth discussion of validation in ASP.NET MVC along with discussing the basic differences between ASP.NET MVC and simple ASP.NET WebForms validation.

ASP.NET WebForms validation consists of a set of server controls that apply JavaScript to provide validation on the client- and server-sides, but ASP.NET MVC doesn't offer that kind of solution and mandates that you write more code to achieve it with better flexibility. Chapter 14 contains a common validation process along with an introduction to some other techniques and methods that you can use to enable validation in your applications.

Differences in Support for AJAX

Chapter 12 discussed AJAX in ASP.NET MVC in detail and showed that AJAX scenarios are completely different in ASP.NET MVC from ASP.NET WebForms.

Existing AJAX implementations in ASP.NET WebForms are built with ASP.NET AJAX and its various server controls, but ASP.NET MVC doesn't support that model, so you need to follow a new pattern. Instead, ASP.NET MVC offers its own implementation of AJAX and integrates well with jQuery, and you may need to apply this nice JavaScript technology in your Web applications. If your WebForms application is heavily dependent on ASP.NET AJAX controls and scenarios, you should prepare yourself for a lot of work to change your code.

Replacing Controls During Migration to ASP.NET MVC

One of the most common concerns when moving from ASP.NET WebForms to ASP.NET MVC is its lack of various easy-to-use server controls, which may discourage some developers because it requires a more involved development process on their side.

Generally, developers must embrace this reality as a part of their job with ASP.NET MVC because none of the current or future solutions is likely to result in the high level of simplicity and declarative model of ASP.NET WebForms controls. However, there is an advantage for this model in ASP.NET MVC and it's the intention of the way that these features are developed. With ASP.NET MVC you have more control over the user interface elements and can manipulate them, which is not easily done with ASP.NET WebForms.

Generally, ASP.NET MVC has two groups of replacements for server controls:

❏ **HtmlHelpers** — You already know about `HtmlHelpers` and different applications that they have. One of the most important and common applications of `HtmlHelpers` is to provide alternative options for rendering user interface elements like textboxes. At the time of writing, there are some `HtmlHelpers` that render some elements, and most likely there will be many open source `HtmlHelpers` to simulate common ASP.NET WebForms server controls in the near future.

❏ **jQuery Plug-ins** — The other group of alternative options for server controls is nothing but jQuery plug-ins. jQuery is a great JavaScript library that integrates very well with ASP.NET MVC, and it has an extensible model that allows developers to build helpful plug-ins for it. Many great plug-ins have been written for jQuery that can be used with ASP.NET MVC to simulate the behavior of ASP.NET server controls, specifically some complex controls that require some interactions on the client-side. For example, the jQuery Grid plug-in can be used to replace ASP.NET's GridView control or the jQuery Date Picker plug-in can be used in place of the Calendar server control.

Migrating a Simple WebForms Application

In this section you look at how to write a very simple ASP.NET WebForms application and migrate it from WebForms to ASP.NET MVC to exhibit some common steps in migration. Of course, this is not a real-world example, just a sample demonstration. Of course, in the real world, many situation-specific factors would also come into consideration, but the core principles learned here provide a solid foundation that can be tailored to specific situations.

The example uses a WebForms application that retrieves a list of people from an XML file, displays them in a form, and allows you to add new values via a textbox. In the second part, you see how to convert this project to an MVC application.

WebForms Implementation

This section creates an ASP.NET WebForms application with a single page that displays the list of people and asks for new names in a textbox. Listing 17-1 shows the `.aspx` code file for this page. When the user enters a value in the textbox and clicks the button, the new value will be added to storage.

Listing 17-1: ASPX code file

```
<%@ Page Language="C#" AutoEventWireup="true" CodeBehind="Default.aspx.cs"
Inherits="MigrationWebForms._Default" %>

<!DOCTYPE html PUBLIC "-//W3C//DTD XHTML 1.0 Transitional//EN"
 "http://www.w3.org/TR/xhtml1/DTD/xhtml1-transitional.dtd">
<html xmlns="http://www.w3.org/1999/xhtml">
<head runat="server">
    <title></title>
</head>
<body>
    <form id="form1" runat="server">
    <div>
```

```
        <asp:BulletedList ID="peopleList" runat="server">
        </asp:BulletedList>
        Enter Name:<br />
        <asp:TextBox ID="txtName" runat="server"></asp:TextBox>
        <br />
        <asp:Button ID="btnSubmit" runat="server" Text="Submit" OnClick="btnSubmit_
Click" />
    </div>
    </form>
</body>
</html>
```

Note that validation of the textbox value is necessary to make sure that a value is entered, but it is omitted here for simplicity.

The code-behind file for this page is presented in Listing 17-2. In the load event of the Web page, a list of names is loaded from an XML file, using the LINQ to XML API, and in the button click event, the same API is used to add a new value to the system.

Listing 17-2: Code-behind

```csharp
using System;
using System.Linq;
using System.Xml.Linq;

namespace MigrationWebForms
{
    public partial class _Default : System.Web.UI.Page
    {
        private string _filePath = string.Empty;

        protected void Page_Load(object sender, EventArgs e)
        {
            this.Title = "People (WebForms)";

            this._filePath = Server.MapPath("~/app_data/people.xml");

            if (!IsPostBack)
            {
                XDocument doc = XDocument.Load(this._filePath);

                var people = from person in doc.Element("People").Elements()
                             select person.Value;

                this.peopleList.DataSource = people;
                this.peopleList.DataBind();
            }
        }

        protected void btnSubmit_Click(object sender, EventArgs e)
        {
            XDocument doc = XDocument.Load(this._filePath);
```

Continued

Listing 17-2: Code-behind *(continued)*

```
            doc.Element("People").Add
                (new XElement("Person", this.txtName.Text));

            doc.Save(this._filePath);
        }
    }
}
```

As you see, this code loads the list of people from the XML file using the LINQ to XML API and binds the bulleted list control to the list of people. It also uses the LINQ to XML API to add a new person to the XML list whenever the user clicks the button.

Figure 17-1 shows this Web page in action.

- Keyvan Nayyeri
- Simone Chiaretta
- Scott Guthrie
- Scott Hanselman
- Phil Haack
- Rob Conery

Enter Name:

Steven Smith

Submit

Figure 17-1

The MVC Implementation

Now you learn how to convert this basic WebForms application to MVC, using some commonplace steps and techniques.

Try It Out   Separating the Project's Components

The first step in the conversion process is separating the different components of the project. The original WebForms project applies a data access process in the same place that it applies business logic and user interface code.

You may wonder why this is the first step. The answer comes from the nature of software development. Choosing the software development pattern precedes the implementation, so here you also need to move everything to the MVC pattern and separate components.

Now you should choose a strategy for your separation so that you end up with an MVC pattern, and then implement it in the next step. Obviously, you should create a model class for your data interactions and move your data code to that class, where you also implement the main part of your business logic, and create a controllers class where you handle the requests to send or receive data to or from views and connect them to the data model. You also need to write your user interface code (the view) to display data because there isn't any data binding in ASP.NET MVC in the sense of what you have in ASP.NET WebForms.

1.   Creating the Data Model

You create a `PeopleContext` class in your `Model` folder to implement your data model code, as shown in Listing 17-3.

Listing 17-3: PeopleContext data model

```
using System.Collections.Generic;
using System.Linq;
using System.Web;
using System.Xml.Linq;

namespace MigrationMvc.Models
{
    public class PeopleContext
    {
        private string _filePath = string.Empty;

        public PeopleContext()
        {
            this._filePath = HttpContext.Current.Server.MapPath
                ("~/app_data/people.xml");
        }

        public List<string> GetNames()
        {
            XDocument doc = XDocument.Load(this._filePath);

            var people = from person in doc.Element("People").Elements()
                        select person.Value;

            return people.ToList<string>();
        }

        public void AddName(string name)
        {
            XDocument doc = XDocument.Load(this._filePath);

            doc.Element("People").Add
                (new XElement("Person", name));

            doc.Save(this._filePath);
        }
    }
}
```

As you can see, the core uses the same code used for the WebForms application with some minor tweaks to make it compatible with the MVC pattern. It has two methods: `GetNames` loads and returns the list of names, and `AddName` gets a name and adds it to the XML file.

2. Building the Controller

The next step is building a controller class called `PeopleController`, which contains two action methods, as shown in Listing 17-4.

Listing 17-4: PeopleController

```
using System.Web.Mvc;
using MigrationMvc.Models;

namespace MigrationMvc.Controllers
{
    public class PeopleController : Controller
    {
        [AcceptVerbs(HttpVerbs.Get)]
        public ActionResult List()
        {
            ViewData["Title"] = "People (MVC)";

            PeopleContext context = new PeopleContext();
            ViewData["List"] = context.GetNames();

            return View();
        }

        [AcceptVerbs(HttpVerbs.Post)]
        public ActionResult List(string name)
        {
            ViewData["Title"] = "People (MVC)";

            PeopleContext context = new PeopleContext();
            context.AddName(name);

            ViewData["List"] = context.GetNames();

            return View();
        }
    }
}
```

One of the action methods is responsible for receiving HTTP GET verb requests to list the data, and the other is responsible for receiving HTTP POST verb requests to add data to the system. First, the List action method can be considered a replacement for your page load event in WebForms, and the second action method can be considered as a replacement for the button click event handler.

Both action methods use PeopleContext to retrieve or store data, and you can see that the original ASP.NET WebForms page without a good separation of concerns is being converted to an MVC application with clearly distinguished components that work together.

3.   Adding the Page View

The last main step in the conversion is adding a view for this page. Because the example WebForms application doesn't use master pages, you don't use any master page for your MVC application. You put everything in a single view file called List, as shown in Listing 17-5.

Fortunately the development and usage of master pages is constant between ASP.NET WebForms and ASP.NET MVC (despite major differences in their internal workings) so you can apply your knowledge from WebForms to MVC easily. Further information about handling your master pages in ASP.NET MVC is discussed in Chapter 14.

Listing 17-5: List view

```
<%@ Page Language="C#" Inherits="System.Web.Mvc.ViewPage" %>

<!DOCTYPE html PUBLIC "-//W3C//DTD XHTML 1.0 Transitional//EN"
 "http://www.w3.org/TR/xhtml1/DTD/xhtml1-transitional.dtd">
<html xmlns="http://www.w3.org/1999/xhtml">
<head id="Head1" runat="server">
    <title>
        <%= Html.Encode(ViewData["Title"])%></title>
</head>
<body>
    <div>
        <% using (Html.BeginForm())
           { %>
        <ul>
            <% List<string> names = ViewData["List"] as List<string>; %>
            <% foreach (string name in names)
               { %>
            <li>
                <%= Html.Encode(name) %></li>
            <% } %>
        </ul>
        Enter Name:
        <br />
        <%= Html.TextBox("name") %>
        <br />
        <input type="submit" value="Submit" />
        <% } %>
    </div>
</body>
</html>
```

As you can see, there is no data binding in ASP.NET MVC, so you use a `for` loop to iterate through all items in the list of names that is passed from the controller by retrieving the values from the model. Here you use HtmlHelpers to replace the ASP.NET server controls.

How It Works

When you run this application, you see the result shown in Figure 17-2.

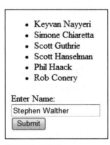

Figure 17-2

Do you notice any difference? Although there are no differences in this example, most of time this is not the case, and a complete conversion without any differences is difficult because ASP.NET WebForms and ASP.NET MVC have such different natures.

To notice one of the changes, just try to view the source code of the generated page both in WebForms and MVC samples. Listing 17-6 shows the code for the WebForms application.

Listing 17-6: Generated HTML code for the WebForms sample

```
<!DOCTYPE html PUBLIC "-//W3C//DTD XHTML 1.0 Transitional//EN"
 "http://www.w3.org/TR/xhtml1/DTD/xhtml1-transitional.dtd">
<html xmlns="http://www.w3.org/1999/xhtml">
<head><title>
        People (WebForms)
</title></head>
 <body>
    <form name="form1" method="post" action="default.aspx" id="form1">
<div>
<input type="hidden" name="__VIEWSTATE" id="__VIEWSTATE" value="/
wEPDwUKLTI5NTA3NzQ4NQ9kFgICAw9kFgICAQ8QDxYCHgtfIURhdGFCb3VuZGdkEBUHDktleXZhbiBOY
Xl5ZXJpEFNpbW9uZSBDaGlhcmV0dGENU2NvdHQgR3V0aHJpZQ9TY290dCBIYW5zZWxtYW4KUGhpbCBI
YWFjawpSb2IgQ29uZXJ5DFN0ZXZlbiBTbWl0aBTbWl0aBUHDktleXZhbiBOYXl5ZXJpEFNpbW9uZSBDaGlhcm
V0dGENU2NvdHQgR3V0aHJpZQ9TY290dCBIYW5zZWxtYW4KUGhpbCBIYWFjawpSb2IgQ29uZXJ5DFN0
ZXZlbiBTbWl0aBQrAwdnZ2dnZFgkZFLJc4P4J4nIWtDOVlWC/OTd9nqE" />
</div>

    <div>
        <ul id="peopleList">
        <li>Keyvan Nayyeri</li><li>Simone Chiaretta</li><li>Scott Guthrie</li>
<li>Scott Hanselman</li><li>Phil Haack</li><li>Rob Conery</li><li>Steven Smith</li>
</ul>
        Enter Name:<br />
        <input name="txtName" type="text" id="txtName" />
        <br />
        <input type="submit" name="btnSubmit" value="Submit" id="btnSubmit" />
    </div>

<div>

        <input type="hidden" name="__EVENTVALIDATION" id="__EVENTVALIDATION"
value="/wEWAwLZtf/nDALEhISFCwLCi9reA8RL3k2u0/jXb9ZHknSSO6qH0pJe" />
</div></form>
</body>
</html>
```

As you can see from the highlights, ASP.NET WebForms applications generate long and ugly HTML codes for you, and you usually cannot have a high level of control over them. They generate hidden fields and ViewState code that can make your pages larger, and they also generate long and unreadable IDs for HTML elements.

Listing 17-7 shows the source code for the MVC implementation in which you see a very simple and readable output without the abovementioned issues.

Listing 17-7: Generated HTML code for the MVC sample

```html
<!DOCTYPE html PUBLIC "-//W3C//DTD XHTML 1.0 Transitional//EN"
"http://www.w3.org/TR/xhtml1/DTD/xhtml1-transitional.dtd">
<html xmlns="http://www.w3.org/1999/xhtml">
<head id="Head1"><title>

        People (MVC)
</title></head>
<body>
    <div>
        <form action="/People/List" method="post">
        <ul>

            <li>
                Keyvan Nayyeri</li>

            <li>
                Simone Chiaretta</li>

            <li>
                Scott Guthrie</li>

            <li>
                Scott Hanselman</li>

            <li>
                Phil Haack</li>

            <li>
                Rob Conery</li>

            <li>
                Stephen Walther</li>

        </ul>
        Enter Name:
        <br />
        <input id="name" name="name" type="text" value="" />
        <br />
        <input type="submit" value="Submit" />
        </form>
    </div>
</body>
</html>
```

Here you put things together after importing them from your WebForms application.

When the request is routed to the `PeopleController` and its action methods, they call the `PeopleContext` in the model to apply data operations. Then they pass the appropriate data to the view to render the output.

You can contrast this with the scenario in WebForms applications when a request was accessing the content of a page. The load event of that page loads data from data storage to set it in server controls. Then when the user submits a new value, the appropriate button click event is called to apply data manipulation and add the new item.

393

Summary

This chapter talked about migrating ASP.NET WebForms applications to ASP.NET MVC, which is not easily done. There isn't a clear path for such a migration, and ASP.NET MVC should be treated as a completely separate technology. Switching from ASP.NET WebForms to ASP.NET MVC isn't an easy task.

However, this chapter covered some general topics and techniques to guide you when migrating your applications from ASP.NET WebForms to ASP.NET MVC. The chapter started with the most important step of migration, which is asking about the necessity of migration and thinking carefully about it because, in many circumstances, migration is not required at all.

The second main topic of the chapter provided an overview of the migration process from a general perspective and discussed the basics. The next two topics talked about the major similarities and differences between ASP.NET WebForms and ASP.NET MVC and what you need to know about them to import your applications. Introducing some techniques to replace ASP.NET WebForms server controls was the next topic, which is an important concern for Web developers.

Finally, you looked at a very simple example of a process that you can follow to migrate your applications from WebForms to MVC.

Exercise

This exercise can help you understand the level of flexibility and power of ASP.NET MVC in comparison to ASP.NET WebForms. In Chapter 14 you saw the implementation of a sample ASP.NET MVC application used to validate the input data for a contact form. As an exercise, implement the same scenario using ASP.NET WebForms, and check the source code HTML of the generated output and compare the output for ASP.NET MVC and ASP.NET WebForms.

Case Study 1

At this point, you're done reading the main content of this book. The first 17 chapters covered the principles of ASP.NET MVC. But of course, ASP.NET MVC is much bigger and more extensive than what we have discussed in the book, and it's not possible to cover everything in a single book.

We think that the best complement to this book is a good sample application that deals with a real-world case study. So this chapter and Chapter 19 present two real-world case studies developed specifically for this book that complement the other chapters and supplement each other. In this chapter, we walk through the development process of a sample application, so you can see how to apply many of the techniques covered in this book. This chapter focuses on more principles of MVC development, and Chapter 19 goes further and covers more advanced topics and techniques; therefore, you get a thorough understanding and knowledge from this book.

Throughout the book, we didn't give complete sample code of a real-world application, so you could focus on the concepts; therefore, most of the samples in the chapters are rudimentary (but key) examples that appear frequently as a basis of real-world situations. But in these final two chapters we're going to provide real-world examples that address many questions you may have and, more importantly, prepare you to be able to start developing an ASP.NET MVC application from scratch.

The sample case study for this chapter is a blog engine powered by ASP.NET MVC. The application offers some common blogging features and uses SQL Server as its database. LINQ to SQL is used to implement data interaction, and the rest of the application showcases some common ASP.NET MVC development procedures and techniques as well as design for testability practices.

In this chapter, we provide the full implementation of public parts of the application but leave it to you to implement the backend control panel to allow editors and authors to publish and edit content; however, the database schema is ready to accept your users without using the ASP.NET membership provider. The implementation of the backend is a great supplement of this chapter. By implementing it yourself, you will learn a lot about working with ASP.NET MVC. In addition, at the end of the chapter are some good exercises for unit testing this application so you can work on your skills in this part as well.

You can learn many things from this chapter by reviewing the available download code for it. Because Beginning books focus on concepts and principles rather than techniques and hacks, many more advanced techniques could not be covered in the earlier chapters. Examining the available code can help build on your current knowledge and discover more ASP.NET MVC possibilities.

In this chapter we assume that you've carefully examined the previous chapters of this book, and have learned all the basics, so we don't repeat them here, and just try to demonstrate many of them as an example. Remember, to be a good developer, you need to read and examine code.

This chapter (like Chapter 19) is important for the following reasons:

❑ The first advantage of this chapter is that you see and learn the whole development process of a real-world application. Many new developers have problems with starting a project, developing it, and finally deploying it, mostly because they don't have enough experience and such tasks require a higher level of experience. These case studies help you develop that level of knowledge and experience.

❑ When developing ASP.NET MVC applications, there are many techniques that you can learn. Some of the more advanced techniques are outside the scope of this book. However, this real-world example can help you start to explore these techniques more easily and quickly.

❑ Developing in ASP.NET MVC requires integrating HTML code with your views and importing professional user interface elements to your projects. This is a tricky task that cannot be documented easily but in this chapter, we import a free, real-world template with some common user interface elements to teach you such tricks.

❑ Using third-party tools and components for several purposes can be an important part of MVC development specifically in ASP.NET MVC. While teaching you core ASP.NET MVC principles, most of the samples of this book didn't require that level of development, but you use such tools in these two case studies actively.

The other point worth mentioning here is the usage of the Dependency Injection approach in developing WroxBlog. This has some benefits such as the ease of unit testing and providing more flexible code for further development. For this case study we use the Ninject framework for Dependency Injection. You can read Chapter 16 to learn about using this framework with ASP.NET MVC.

WroxBlog is a simple blogging engine that is developed in this chapter. We know that there are some WroxBlog examples in other Wrox titles but we think it's worth having a new one with a new technology and implementation!

> *Don't forget to follow the thread after reading this chapter. In this book you are being grounded in the fundamentals, and there are still a lot of ASP.NET MVC techniques for you to discover! There are more techniques involved in ASP.NET MVC development (specifically in ASP.NET MVC as a technology that comes with many customization options, third-party tools, and components) that are beyond the scope of a Beginning series book, but you may want to learn them from other resources such as Professional ASP.NET MVC 1.0, open source projects, and blog posts.*

The WroxBlog Overview

Understanding WroxBlog is a mandatory step in learning its structure. A blog engine is a general type of Web application (such as forums or wikis) that allows one or more authors to publish individual items as their content (which is called a post). This content may vary from general diaries to very technical details, but the type of content doesn't have any influence on the technical structure of the blog software. A typical blog displays the most recent items in its home page, allows users to view individual items on their unique URLs, leave comments on the posts, search in the items, and view them by category or monthly archive. Of course, some more professional features for blog engines are available that we ignore here. At the time of writing, there are great .NET-powered blogging engines such as Community Server, Graffiti, Subtext, BlogEngine.NET, and DasBlog that you can use to provide your content, and they differ in their level, scale, features, license, and storage systems. Also, there is an open source ASP.NET MVC powered CMS written by Microsoft called Oxite (available at `http://oxite.codeplex.com`) that can act as a blog engine. You may want to explore it after this chapter.

WroxBlog is a simple implementation of a blog engine with a few common features because we want to keep it simple. WroxBlog displays a list of posts, and each post has an author and a single category. End-users can view an individual post with a URL that is made unique by using the post ID in the database. They also can leave comments on each post to be displayed under the post. They can also check the posts in each category by navigating to a unique URL for each category. In addition, there is an About page that, unlike the post system, retrieves its content from an XML file.

As stated in the introduction, we don't implement the backend control panel for this blog because it mostly relies on authentication techniques that are covered in the case study for Chapter 19. Instead, we focus on some basics that are not elaborated there. However, note that you can use the existing database to build a control panel to allow authenticated users to add, edit, or delete the posts and categories.

The main storage system behind the blog is SQL Server, and LINQ to SQL is used to build the model component of the ASP.NET MVC application.

Unlike all the examples in this book that use the default generated template for ASP.NET MVC projects, WroxBlog uses a very beautiful theme that is ported to the system. This theme is a free open source template provided by Styleshout (`http://styleshout.com`) for public use. Styleshout is one of the best free template providers on the Web.

The following sections describe different components of WroxBlog in the order of models (and services), controllers, views, and routing. Additionally, they provide some common techniques and practices that can improve your development quality to a good extent.

The WroxBlog Models

The model component of WroxBlog consists of two distinct storage providers: The first storage provider is a simple model that applies LINQ to XML to load the data for the About page from an XML file, and the second one is a LINQ to SQL model that deals with the main data of the blog such as users, categories, posts, and comments.

These two models are included in a series of services that are implemented as general interfaces and their corresponding implementations. This way, you take an important step in design for testability that improves the quality of your code to a great extent. These repositories provide the better level of encapsulation and design for testability experience.

The WroxBlog Database Structure

WroxBlog has a simple database structure that consists of four tables that hold data for users, categories, posts, and comments. This simple structure and the relationships between data tables is shown in Figure 18-1 and is discussed in the following list.

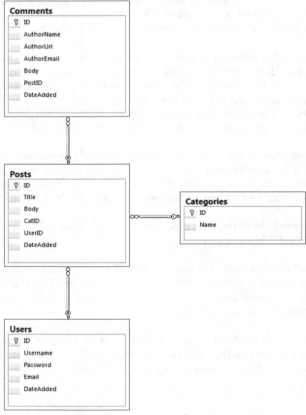

Figure 18-1

❑ **The Users table** — This table keeps data for users such as their username, password, e-mail, and the date that they were added to the system. Each post is related to a user as its author, but we don't deal with this table very much, and its role is bolder in the control panel backend.

❑ **The Categories table** — Each post is related to a single category, and categories are stored in the Categories table with their unique name.

❑ **The Posts table** — This is the main table of WroxBlog, where post data is stored. Each post is related to a category and a user, and consists of some fields such as its title, body, category ID, author ID, and the date that it is added.

❑ **The Comments table** — The Comments table holds data for comments. Each comment is connected to its corresponding post through its ID. This table has some fields such as author name, author URL, author e-mail, body, post ID, and the addition date, but some of the fields are optional.

The LINQ to SQL Model

With the correct database structure and relationships in place, you can use LINQ to SQL to build the data model. You don't need to do much; all you need to do is drag and drop your tables from Server Explorer to the LINQ to SQL designer. The rest is done by the LINQ to SQL provider to generate entities, methods, and necessary objects for you.

Figure 18-2 shows the LINQ to SQL diagram for WroxBlog in Visual Studio.

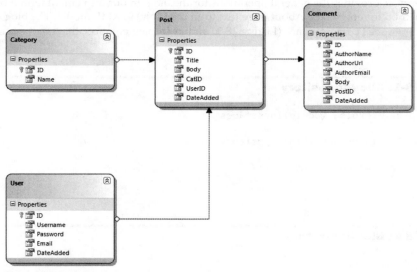

Figure 18-2

The Services

As stated at the beginning of this section, we encapsulate the model implementation of WroxBlog in some services (repositories). Here we build some interfaces and implement them with our data storage methods in order to improve the level of testability, extensibility, and maintainability of our code.

In this section we build four services that are designed specifically for general blog operations, posts, categories, and comments. Figure 18-3 shows the relationship between the four interfaces representing these services along with their implementation classes.

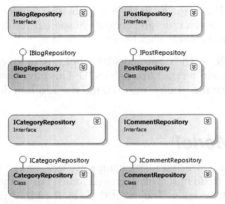

Figure 18-3

The Blog Service

The blog service provides the general operations for the blog. In our implementation it only provides a single method to retrieve the About page text from the LINQ to XML model. The blog service is built as the `IBlogRepository` interface (Listing 18-1) and its implementation, the `BlogRepository` class (Listing 18-2).

Listing 18-1: IBlogRepository

```
namespace WroxBlog.Models.Interfaces
{
    public interface IBlogRepository
    {
        string GetAboutText();
    }
}
```

Listing 18-2: BlogRepository

```
using System.Web;
using System.Xml.Linq;
using WroxBlog.Models.Interfaces;

namespace WroxBlog.Models.Implementations
{
    public class BlogRepository : IBlogRepository
    {
        #region IBlogRepository Members

        public string GetAboutText()
        {
            var doc = XDocument.Load(HttpContext.Current.Server.MapPath
                ("~/app_data/about.xml"));

            return doc.Element("About").Value;
```

```
        }

            #endregion
    }
}
```

This service has a pretty easy implementation that loads the value of the `<About />` element from the XML file using the LINQ to XML API. This is actually the LINQ to XML part of our data model.

The Post Service

The second service that provides the main functionality of the blog engine data model is the post service, which is responsible for operations related to posts such as retrieving recent posts, posts in a specific category, or single posts.

The post service consists of the `IPostRepository` interface (Listing 18-3) and the `PostRepository` class (Listing 18-4).

Listing 18-3: IPostRepository

```
namespace WroxBlog.Models.Interfaces
{
    public interface IPostRepository
    {
        PostCollection GetRecentPosts(int count);
        PostCollection GetPostsInCategory(string categoryName);
        Post GetPost(int id);
    }
}
```

Listing 18-4: PostRepository

```
using System.Collections.Generic;
using System.Linq;
using WroxBlog.Models.Interfaces;

namespace WroxBlog.Models.Implementations
{
    public class PostRepository : IPostRepository
    {
        #region IPostRepository Members

        public PostCollection GetRecentPosts(int count)
        {
            WroxBlogDataContext context = new WroxBlogDataContext();

            List<Post> posts = context.Posts.Take(count).OrderByDescending
                        (p => p.DateAdded).ToList();

            return GetPostCollection(posts);
        }

        public PostCollection GetPostsInCategory(string categoryName)
```

Continued

Listing 18-4: PostRepository *(continued)*

```
            {
                WroxBlogDataContext context = new WroxBlogDataContext();

                var postsInCategory = from post in context.Posts
                                      where post.Category.Name.ToLower() ==
      categoryName.ToLower()
                                      select post;

                List<Post> posts = postsInCategory.OrderByDescending
                    (p => p.DateAdded).ToList();

                return GetPostCollection(posts);
            }

            public Post GetPost(int id)
            {
                WroxBlogDataContext context = new WroxBlogDataContext();

                var selectedPost = (from post in context.Posts
                                    where post.ID == id
                                    select post).Single();

                return selectedPost;
            }

            #endregion

            #region Private Methods

            private PostCollection GetPostCollection(List<Post> posts)
            {
                PostCollection collection = new PostCollection();
                collection.AddRange(posts);
                return collection;
            }

            #endregion
        }
    }
```

This implementation consists of three functions that all work based on some LINQ operations that retrieve data from the LINQ to SQL data model. You've seen a good discussion of such models in Chapter 4.

The Category Service

We also need a service for category management and operations. Our implementation of this service consists of a single GetCategories method that returns a collection of categories. The category service consists of the ICategoryRepository interface (Listing 18-5) and the CategoryRepository class (Listing 18-6).

Listing 18-5: ICategoryRepository

```
namespace WroxBlog.Models.Interfaces
{
    public interface ICategoryRepository
    {
        CategoryCollection GetCategories();
    }
}
```

Listing 18-6: CategoryRepository

```
using System.Collections.Generic;
using System.Linq;
using WroxBlog.Models.Interfaces;

namespace WroxBlog.Models.Implementations
{
    public class CategoryRepository : ICategoryRepository
    {
        #region ICategoryRepository Members

        public CategoryCollection GetCategories()
        {
            WroxBlogDataContext context = new WroxBlogDataContext();

            List<Category> categories = context.Categories.ToList<Category>();

            return GetCategoriesCollection(categories);
        }

        #endregion

        #region Private Methods

        private CategoryCollection GetCategoriesCollection
            (List<Category> categories)
        {
            CategoryCollection collection = new CategoryCollection();
            collection.AddRange(categories);
            return collection;
        }

        #endregion
    }
}
```

As you see, this service applies LINQ to SQL operations to retrieve a list of categories from the data model and has a very similar structure to the post service.

The Comment Service

The last service that logically would be a part of the system is the comment service, which provides some operations to retrieve the list of comments for a specific post or add a new comment to a post.

This service is implemented as the `ICommentRepository` interface (Listing 18-7) and the `CommentRepository` class (Listing 18-8).

Listing 18-7: ICommentRepository

```
namespace WroxBlog.Models.Interfaces
{
    public interface ICommentRepository
    {
        CommentCollection GetComments(int postID);
        void AddComment(Comment comment);
    }
}
```

Listing 18-8: CommentRepository

```
using System;
using System.Collections.Generic;
using System.Linq;
using WroxBlog.Models.Interfaces;

namespace WroxBlog.Models.Implementations
{
    public class CommentRepository : ICommentRepository
    {
        #region ICommentRepository Members

        public CommentCollection GetComments(int postID)
        {
            WroxBlogDataContext context = new WroxBlogDataContext();

            var selectedPost = (from post in context.Posts
                                where post.ID == postID
                                select post).Single();

            List<Comment> comments = selectedPost.Comments.ToList<Comment>();

            return GetCommentsCollection(comments);
        }

        public void AddComment(Comment comment)
        {
            comment.DateAdded = DateTime.Now;

            WroxBlogDataContext context = new WroxBlogDataContext();
```

```
        context.Comments.InsertOnSubmit(comment);

        context.SubmitChanges();
    }

    #endregion

    #region Private Methods

    private CommentCollection GetCommentsCollection(List<Comment> comments)
    {
        CommentCollection collection = new CommentCollection();
        collection.AddRange(comments);
        return collection;
    }

    #endregion
    }
}
```

Again, this is a piece of LINQ to SQL code that retrieves or adds data for comments to or from the database.

The Collection Classes

In the preceding implementations of services we used three collection classes (PostCollection, CategoryCollection, and CommentCollection) as public types to carry the list of Post, Category, and Comment objects (presented in Listings 18-9, 18-10, and 18-11).

Listing 18-9: PostCollection

```
using System.Collections.Generic;

namespace WroxBlog.Models
{
    public class PostCollection : List<Post>
    {
    }
}
```

Listing 18-10: CategoryCollection

```
using System.Collections.Generic;

namespace WroxBlog.Models
{
    public class CategoryCollection : List<Category>
    {
    }
}
```

Listing 18-11: CommentCollection

```
using System.Collections.Generic;

namespace WroxBlog.Models
{
    public class CommentCollection : List<Comment>
    {
    }
}
```

These classes are derived from the list of the objects and don't add anything to them. The reason for using this technique is providing the space for any future expansion of the collection objects without breaking the existing code. Also, usage of generic lists in public APIs is not a recommended practice and can be avoided with this simple technique.

Binding the Services

For WroxBlog we use Ninject framework as our Dependency Injection tool, so we need to bind the abovementioned services. In this step we need to bind service interfaces to their corresponding implementation classes in a Ninject module (Listing 18-12).

Listing 18-12: RepositoriesModule

```
using Ninject.Modules;
using WroxBlog.Models.Implementations;
using WroxBlog.Models.Interfaces;

namespace WroxBlog.BindingModules
{
    public class RepositoriesModule : NinjectModule
    {
        public override void Load()
        {
            Bind<IBlogRepository>()
                .To<BlogRepository>();

            Bind<IPostRepository>()
                .To<PostRepository>();

            Bind<ICategoryRepository>()
                .To<CategoryRepository>();

            Bind<ICommentRepository>()
                .To<CommentRepository>();
        }
    }
}
```

Four bindings are added to the overridden Load method of the module. Later this module is used to create the kernel in Ninject.

The WroxBlog Controllers

As is taught throughout the book, the controller is where you connect your views to models, so it's important to have a good separation of business logic when you build your MVC applications.

WroxBlog has three controller classes. Thank to the services and the level of encapsulation that they provide, here we have an easy job of building our controllers with simple code. As a general note, you have to keep in mind that later we pass instances of our repository objects to controller constructors through the Ninject framework.

Implementing HomeController

HomeController is responsible for handling requests for index and About pages. It consists of two action methods for these two pages. HomeController is shown in Listing 18-13.

Listing 18-13: HomeController

```
using System.Web.Mvc;
using WroxBlog.Models.Interfaces;

namespace WroxBlog.Controllers
{
    public class HomeController : Controller
    {
        private IBlogRepository _blogRepository;
        private IPostRepository _postRepository;
        private ICategoryRepository _categoryRepository;

        public HomeController(IBlogRepository blogRepository,
            IPostRepository postRepository, ICategoryRepository categoryRepository)
        {
            this._blogRepository = blogRepository;
            this._postRepository = postRepository;
            this._categoryRepository = categoryRepository;
        }

        public ActionResult Index()
        {
            ViewData["Categories"] = this._categoryRepository.GetCategories();
            ViewData["Posts"] = this._postRepository.GetRecentPosts(10);

            return View();
        }

        public ActionResult About()
        {
            ViewData["AboutText"] = this._blogRepository.GetAboutText();

            return View();
        }
    }
}
```

This controller gets three instances of IBlogRepository, IPostRepository, and ICategoryRepository in its constructor to perform operations with the data model and provides two action methods. These methods simply call service functions to load data from the model and pass it to views.

Here you can notice the beautiful separation of concerns in a real-world application and how well these components are connected to work together without any dependency, which makes their maintenance all the easier.

Implementing PostController

The longest controller in WroxBlog is PostController, which handles POST and GET requests for individual posts using two IndividualPost action methods. Listing 18-14 is the source code of PostController.

Listing 18-14: PostController

```
using System.Web.Mvc;
using WroxBlog.Models;
using WroxBlog.Models.Interfaces;

namespace WroxBlog.Controllers
{
    public class PostController : Controller
    {
        private IPostRepository _postRepository;
        private ICategoryRepository _categoryRepository;
        private ICommentRepository _commentRepository;

        public PostController(IPostRepository postRepository,
            ICategoryRepository categoryRepository, ICommentRepository
commentRepository)
        {
            this._postRepository = postRepository;
            this._categoryRepository = categoryRepository;
            this._commentRepository = commentRepository;
        }

        [AcceptVerbs(HttpVerbs.Get)]
        public ActionResult IndividualPost(int id)
        {
            Post post = this._postRepository.GetPost(id);

            ViewData["Title"] = post.Title;

            ViewData["Categories"] = this._categoryRepository.GetCategories();
            ViewData["Post"] = post;
            ViewData["Comments"] = this._commentRepository.GetComments(id);

            return View();
        }

        [AcceptVerbs(HttpVerbs.Post)]
```

```
        public ActionResult IndividualPost(int id, Comment comment)
        {
            comment.PostID = id;

            this._commentRepository.AddComment(comment);

            return RedirectToAction("IndividualPost");
        }
    }
}
```

Like `HomeController`, `PostController` gets instances of `IPostRepository`, `ICategoryRepository`, and `ICommentRepository` to use them for data operations.

There are two `IndividualPost` action methods. The first one handles direct requests to display the post and its comment list; therefore, it loads the data from the model by calling the functions from the service objects and passes it to the view.

The second action method does more and handles POST verb requests to add comments to the system. The logic of this method can be divided into three main steps: In the first step it gets user inputs as a `Comment` object, in the second step it adds a new comment to the system using the `ICommentRepository` methods, and in the third step it does the same job as the first `IndividualPost` action method by redirecting to that action method to load data.

Implementing CategoryController

The last controller of WroxBlog — `CategoryController` — contains a single action method, which handles requests for category index pages to load all posts in a specified category and pass them to view, as shown in Listing 18-15.

Listing 18-15: CategoryController

```
using System.Web.Mvc;
using WroxBlog.Models.Interfaces;

namespace WroxBlog.Controllers
{
    public class CategoryController : Controller
    {
        private IPostRepository _postRepository;
        private ICategoryRepository _categoryRepository;

        public CategoryController(IPostRepository postRepository,
            ICategoryRepository categoryRepository)
        {
            this._postRepository = postRepository;
            this._categoryRepository = categoryRepository;
        }

        public ActionResult CategoryIndex(string name)
```

Continued

Listing 18-15: CategoryController *(continued)*

```
        {
            ViewData["Title"] = name;
            ViewData["Posts"] = this._postRepository.GetPostsInCategory(name);
            ViewData["Categories"] = this._categoryRepository.GetCategories();

            return View();
        }
    }
}
```

This controller is a little shorter and gets `IPostRepository` and `ICategoryRepository` instances via its constructor.

The only action method in `CategoryController` uses service methods in order to load data in a specified category (whose name is passed to the method via parameter) and then passes the data to view items.

The WroxBlog Views

With the data model and controllers ready, you can build your views and user interface elements. WroxBlog uses the built-in ASP.NET MVC view engine and ports a free beautiful blog template. For WroxBlog we use a master page, two user controls, and four views, which we describe one-by-one in the same order.

The Site Master

The basic layout of all pages is added to a single master page that is a bit longer than the master page that Visual Studio generates for you, and is more similar to real-world master pages.

This master page defines the HTML header elements of the page and defines the title as a placeholder that can be set in child views. It also defines a header with some menu items that link to the home page and the About page. The main part of the template consists of the main body, which you replace with a placeholder, and a sidebar that keeps a short About text along with a categories list, and some links. The list of categories is also implemented as an ASP.NET MVC user control that is discussed later. Finally, a footer shows the copyright notice and a few links. The code for `SiteMaster` is shown in Listing 18-16.

Listing 18-16: SiteMaster

```
<%@ Master Language="C#" Inherits="System.Web.Mvc.ViewMasterPage" %>

<!DOCTYPE html PUBLIC "-//W3C//DTD XHTML 1.0 Strict//EN"
"http://www.w3.org/TR/xhtml1/DTD/xhtml1-strict.dtd">
<html xmlns="http://www.w3.org/1999/xhtml">
<head id="Head1" runat="server">
    <title>
```

```
            <asp:ContentPlaceHolder ID="TitleContent" runat="server" />
    </title>
    <meta http-equiv="content-type" content="application/xhtml+xml; charset=UTF-8"
/>
    <meta name="description" content="An ASP.NET MVC Powered Blog..." />
    <meta name="keywords" content=".NET, ASP.NET MVC, Wiley, Wrox, C#, Keyvan
Nayyeri, Simone Chiaretta" />
    <meta name="robots" content="index, follow, noarchive" />
    <meta name="googlebot" content="noarchive" />
    <link rel="stylesheet" href="/content/VectorLover.css" type="text/css" />
</head>
<body>
    <!-- wrap starts here -->
    <div id="wrap">
        <!--header -->
        <div id="header">
            <h1 id="logo-text">
                <%= Html.ActionLink("Wrox Blog", "Index", "Home")%></h1>
            <p id="slogan">
                An ASP.NET MVC Powered Blog...</p>
            <!--header ends-->
        </div>
        <!-- navigation starts-->
        <div id="nav">
            <ul>
                <li>
                    <%= Html.ActionLink("Home", "Index", "Home")%></li>
                <li>
                    <%= Html.ActionLink("About", "About", "Home")%></li>
            </ul>
            <!-- navigation ends-->
        </div>
        <!-- content starts -->
        <div id="content">
            <div id="main">
                <asp:ContentPlaceHolder ID="MainContent" runat="server" />
            </div>
            <div id="sidebar">
                <h3>
                    About</h3>
                <p>
                    <a href="index.html">
                        <img src="/content/images/gravatar.jpg" width="40"
height="40" alt="image" class="float-left" /></a>
                    This is a sample blog engine powered by ASP.NET MVC 1.0 written
for Wrox Beginning
                    ASP.NET MVC 1.0 book authored by Simone Chiaretta and Keyvan
Nayyeri. You can read
                    a description about this blog engine in the chapters of the
book.
                </p>
                <% Html.RenderPartial("CategoriesControl"); %>
```

Continued

Listing 18-16: SiteMaster *(continued)*

```
                    <h3>
                        Links</h3>
                    <ul class="sidemenu">
                        <li><a href="http://nayyeri.net">Keyvan Nayyeri</a></li>
                        <li><a href="http://codeclimber.net.nz">Simone Chiaretta</a>
</li>

                        <li><a href="http://weblogs.asp.net/scottgu">Scott Guthrie</a>
</li>

                        <li><a href="http://www.hanselman.com/blog">Scott Hanselman</a>
</li>

                        <li><a href="http://haacked.com">Phil Haack</a></li>
                        <li><a href="http://blog.wekeroad.com">Rob Conery</a></li>
                    </ul>
                    <!-- sidebar ends -->
                </div>
                <!-- content ends-->
            </div>
            <!-- footer starts -->
            <div id="footer">
                <p>
                    Copyright &copy; Wrox Beginning ASP.NET MVC 1.0    Design
by : <a href="http://www.styleshout.com/">
                    styleshout</a> | Valid <a href="http://validator.w3.org/
check?uri=referer">XHTML</a>
                    | <a href="http://jigsaw.w3.org/css-validator/check/referer">CSS
</a>         
                    <%= Html.ActionLink("Home", "Index", "Home")%> 
                </p>
                <!-- footer ends-->
            </div>
            <!-- wrap ends here -->
        </div>
    </body>
</html>
```

Here it's important to compare the original HTML template code with what is imported to the master page in order to learn how to deal with HTML code in your ASP.NET MVC applications, and how to modularly split your user interface elements into logical parts. As has been discussed throughout this book, this clear separation of elements is one of the most significant advantages of ASP.NET MVC in the area of user interface design.

Adding the Categories Control

Displaying the list of categories is a common part of all pages, and a user control is used to show the list of categories along with the links to their index pages (see Listing 18-17). This user control is referenced in the sidebar in the master page to avoid repetition.

Listing 18-17: CategoriesControl

```
<%@ Control Language="C#" Inherits="System.Web.Mvc.ViewUserControl" %>
<%@ Import Namespace="WroxBlog.Models" %>
<h3>
    Categories</h3>
<ul class="sidemenu">
    <% CategoryCollection categories = ViewData["Categories"]
        as CategoryCollection; %>
    <% foreach (Category category in categories)
        { %>
    <li>
        <%= Html.ActionLink(category.Name, "CategoryIndex",
            new { controller = "Category", name = category.Name })%></li>
    <% } %>
</ul>
```

You see that the data for categories is passed through view data as a `CategoryCollection`. A list of action links is rendered to provide appropriate links to each category's index page.

Adding the Post Control

The other common user interface element is the blog post information, which is used in post lists and also in individual post pages. So it's a good idea to separate this part of user interface and put it in its own control (Listing 18-18).

Listing 18-18: PostControl

```
<%@ Control Language="C#" Inherits="System.Web.Mvc.ViewUserControl" %>
<%@ Import Namespace="WroxBlog.Models" %>
<% Post post = Model as Post; %>
<h2>
    <%= Html.ActionLink(post.Title, "IndividualPost",
        new { controller="Post", id = post.ID })%></h2>
<p class="post-info">
    <p class="post-info">
        Posted by
        <%= Html.Encode(post.User.Username) %>
    </p>
    <%= Html.Encode(post.Body) %>
    <p class="post-footer">
        <%= Html.ActionLink("Comments " + post.Comments.Count.ToString(),
        "IndividualPost", "Post", new { id = post.ID },
                new { @class="comments"}) %>
        | <span class="date">
            <%= Html.Encode(post.DateAdded.ToString("MMMM dd, yyyy")) %>
        </span>
    </p>
</p>
```

Note the way that programming code and markup HTML are combined to provide the best compatibility with the expected output code. Also note the way that different HTML elements are imported to the ASP.NET MVC application to render the exact same markup as we have in the pure HTML template.

Adding the Posts Control

The other common user interface element is the list of blog posts that must be shown in home page, and category index pages, so it's worth having a separate user control for posts as well. The source code for this control is presented in Listing 18-19.

Listing 18-19: PostsControl

```
<%@ Control Language="C#" Inherits="System.Web.Mvc.ViewUserControl" %>
<%@ Import Namespace="WroxBlog.Models" %>
<% PostCollection posts = ViewData["Posts"] as PostCollection; %>
<% foreach (Post post in posts)
   { %>
       <% Html.RenderPartial("PostControl", post); %>
<% } %>
```

Like the Categories control, this control iterates through all posts that are passed to it through view data as a PostCollection object, then applies PostControl (described in the previous section) to render each post. Note the highlighted code where PostControl is partially rendered by passing the appropriate Post object as its model.

Adding the Comment Control

Rendering the information for individual comments is another part of the user interface that can be encapsulated in its own control. CommentControl uses a set of many types of HTML elements to display the information for a single comment (Listing 18-20).

Listing 18-20: CommentControl

```
<%@ Control Language="C#" Inherits="System.Web.Mvc.ViewUserControl" %>
<%@ Import Namespace="WroxBlog.Models" %>
<% Comment comment = Model as Comment; %>
<li class="alt" id="comment-<%= Html.Encode(comment.ID.ToString())%>"><cite>
    <img alt="" src="/content/images/gravatar.jpg"
     class="avatar" height="40" width="40" />
    <a href="<%= Html.Encode(comment.AuthorUrl)%>">
        <%= Html.Encode(comment.AuthorName) %>
    </a>Says:
    <br />
    <span class="comment-data">
    <a href="#comment-<%= Html.Encode(comment.ID.ToString())%>"
        title="">
        <%= Html.Encode(comment.DateAdded.ToString("MMMM dd, yyyy"))%>
    </a>
    </span>
```

```
        </cite>
        <div class="comment-text">
            <p>
                <%= Html.Encode(comment.Body)%>
            </p>
        </div>
    </li>
```

Notice the highlighted code where we can easily combine the static information with the dynamic information retrieved from the model in order to set the link to the individual comment in a page. This is the power of ASP.NET MVC in letting you manipulate the HTML markup.

Adding the Comments Control

Displaying a single comment isn't what we want. It's just a part of the bigger scenario to display the list of comments for a post. So we can apply the CommentControl to show a list of comments for a specific post in the CommentsControl.

Listing 18-21: CommentsControl

```
<%@ Control Language="C#" Inherits="System.Web.Mvc.ViewUserControl" %>
<%@ Import Namespace="WroxBlog.Models" %>
<% CommentCollection comments = Model as CommentCollection; %>
<h3 id="comments">
    <%= Html.Encode(comments.Count.ToString())%>
    Responses</h3>
<ol class="commentlist">
    <% foreach (Comment comment in comments)
        { %>
            <% Html.RenderPartial("CommentControl", comment); %>
    <% } %>
</ol>
```

Notice the highlighted code and how CommentControl is occupied by passing the appropriate Comment object to its model.

Adding the CommentForm Control

The element of user interface that deals with comments is the comment form, where you define a form to let visitors leave their comments for blog authors. The CommentFormControl is presented in Listing 18-22.

Listing 18-22: CommentFormControl

```
<%@ Control Language="C#" Inherits="System.Web.Mvc.ViewUserControl" %>
<h3 id="respond">
    Leave a Reply</h3>
```

Continued

415

Listing 18-22: **CommentFormControl** *(continued)*

```
<% using (Html.BeginForm("IndividualPost", "Post"))
   { %>
<p>
   <label for="AuthorName">
      Name (required)</label><br />
   <%= Html.TextBox("AuthorName", null, new { tabindex = "1" })%>
</p>
<p>
   <label for="AuthorEmail">
      Email Address (required)</label><br />
   <%= Html.TextBox("AuthorEmail", null, new { tabindex = "2" })%>
</p>
<p>
   <label for="AuthorUrl">
      Website (required)</label><br />
   <%= Html.TextBox("AuthorUrl", null, new { tabindex = "3" })%>
</p>
<p>
   <label for="Body">
      Your Message (required)</label><br />
   <%= Html.TextArea("Body", new { rows = "10", cols = "20", tabindex = "4" })%>
</p>
<p class="no-border">
   <input class="button" type="submit" value="Publish" tabindex="5" />
</p>
<% } %>
```

This control doesn't deal with data and only submits the user input to the action methods in the controller. It consists of some static information as well as some textboxes.

Creating the Home View

A typical blog home page displays a list of most recent posts, say 10 recent posts, in reverse chronological order; therefore, the home page of WroxBlog applies the post control to display a list of most recent blog posts. Having a user control in hand, the final source code for this view is pretty simple (see Listing 18-23).

Listing 18-23: Home Index view

```
<%@ Page Language="C#" MasterPageFile="~/Views/Shared/Site.Master"
Inherits="System.Web.Mvc.ViewPage" %>

<asp:Content ID="indexTitle" ContentPlaceHolderID="TitleContent" runat="server">
   Home Page
</asp:Content>
<asp:Content ID="indexContent" ContentPlaceHolderID="MainContent" runat="server">
   <% Html.RenderPartial("PostsControl"); %>
</asp:Content>
```

You see that this view sets the static title of the home page and renders the `PostsControl` in two separate content sections. The simplicity that you see in this code (and the next views) is coming from the modular structure of our code and the separation of components. This is one of the very important practices and notable points that we're trying to show you in our case studies.

Adding the About View

There is also an About page for the blog that gives the biographies of authors or other information about the blog itself. You need a view for this page, which is shown in Listing 18-24. The code is not complicated. It just retrieves the About text from the view data collection.

Listing 18-24: About view

```
<%@ Page Language="C#" MasterPageFile="~/Views/Shared/Site.Master"
Inherits="System.Web.Mvc.ViewPage" %>

<asp:Content ID="aboutTitle" ContentPlaceHolderID="TitleContent" runat="server">
    About
</asp:Content>
<asp:Content ID="aboutContent" ContentPlaceHolderID="MainContent" runat="server">
    <h2>
        About Us</h2>
    <p>
        <%= Html.Encode(ViewData["AboutText"]) %></p>
</asp:Content>
```

Creating the IndividualPost View

One of the most important parts of any blog engine is the page where you show individual items, which is usually the page on which you also display a comments list, and allow visitors to enter their own comments. In WroxBlog all these functions are contained in a single view called `IndividualPost` that is presented in Listing 18-25.

Listing 18-25: IndividualPost view /

```
<%@ Page Title="" Language="C#" MasterPageFile="~/Views/Shared/Site.Master"
Inherits="System.Web.Mvc.ViewPage" %>

<asp:Content ID="Content1" ContentPlaceHolderID="TitleContent" runat="server">
    <%= ViewData["Title"] %>
</asp:Content>
<asp:Content ID="Content2" ContentPlaceHolderID="MainContent" runat="server">
    <% Html.RenderPartial("PostControl", ViewData["Post"]); %>
    <% Html.RenderPartial("CommentsControl", ViewData["Comments"]); %>
    <% Html.RenderPartial("CommentFormControl"); %>
</asp:Content>
```

You can code this view so simply because you already have seen the implementation of the controls that are used by it. ASP.NET MVC facilitates this modular structure of our user interface elements to help us achieve this simplicity. This view consists of three main parts: the original post, the comment lists, and the comment form.

In the first content section, the title of the page is set dynamically from the view data. The title is passed by the controller based on the title of the blog post.

But the main code is located inside the second content section where appropriate data is passed to the `Post` and `Comments` controls via model objects to render the post information and comments list respectively. The `CommentForm` control is also rendered to display the comment form to users.

Creating the CategoryIndex View

The last view in WroxBlog displays the list of posts in a certain category. Thanks to the `Posts` user control, the code for this view is clean and simple, as shown in Listing 18-26.

Listing 18-26: CategoryIndex view

```
<%@ Page Title="" Language="C#" MasterPageFile="~/Views/Shared/Site.Master"
Inherits="System.Web.Mvc.ViewPage" %>

<asp:Content ID="Content1" ContentPlaceHolderID="TitleContent" runat="server">
    <%= ViewData["Title"] %>
</asp:Content>
<asp:Content ID="Content2" ContentPlaceHolderID="MainContent" runat="server">
    <% Html.RenderPartial("PostsControl"); %>
</asp:Content>
```

This view is very similar to the home index and About views.

WroxBlog Routing

At this point WroxBlog is almost ready, but one major step remains, and that is the implementation of routing strategy for the application.

Here is a brief discussion of the URL patterns for WroxBlog:

❑ **Home page** — The home page is handled by `HomeController` and displays the list of the most recent posts.

❑ **/about** — The About page is also handled by `HomeController` and displays the About text.

❑ **/post/{id}** — Individual posts can be accessed in this pattern, where the `id` parameter is the ID of the post stored in the database. These requests are handled by `PostController`.

❑ **/category/{name}** — Category index pages can be accessed in this pattern, where the name parameter is the name of the category. These requests are handled by `CategoryController`.

Listing 18-27 is the source code of the application file where routing is implemented.

Listing 18-27: Global application class

```csharp
using System.Reflection;
using System.Web.Mvc;
using System.Web.Routing;
using Ninject;
using Ninject.Web.Mvc;
using WroxBlog.BindingModules;

namespace WroxBlog
{
    public class MvcApplication : NinjectHttpApplication
    {
        public static void RegisterRoutes(RouteCollection routes)
        {
            routes.IgnoreRoute("{resource}.axd/{*pathInfo}");

            routes.MapRoute(
                "Category",
                "category/{name}",
                new
                {
                    controller = "Category",
                    action = "CategoryIndex",
                    name = ""
                });

            routes.MapRoute(
                "Post",
                "post/{id}",
                new
                {
                    controller = "Post",
                    action = "IndividualPost",
                    id = ""
                });

            routes.MapRoute(
                "Default",
                "{controller}/{action}/{id}",
                new { controller = "Home", action = "Index", id = "" }
            );
        }

        protected override IKernel CreateKernel()
        {
            IKernel kernel = new StandardKernel(new RepositoriesModule());
            return kernel;
        }
```

Continued

419

Listing 18-27: Global application class *(continued)*

```
                    protected override void OnApplicationStarted()
                    {
                        RegisterRoutes(RouteTable.Routes);
                        RegisterAllControllersIn(Assembly.GetExecutingAssembly());
                    }
            }
    }
```

You quickly can see the difference between the regular ASP.NET MVC global application file and this one because it's derived from `NinjectHttpApplication`. We use the Ninject open source framework as our Dependency Injection framework for the WroxBlog project, so we need to apply some changes in this file.

Inside the `RegisterRoutes` method, you see the defining of routes just as you do it in any other ASP.NET MVC application so there isn't anything special to note about it.

We also have two additional methods that are overridden from the `NinjectHttpApplication` base class.

`CreateKernel` is a Ninject framework function that should return an instance of an `IKernel` object that will be used by the Dependency Injection framework. Inside the method we define an `IKernel` object as a `StandardKernel` by using the `RepositoriesModule` that we had defined earlier to bind our services.

`OnApplicationStarted` is another Ninject method that we override, and we use the `RegisterRoutes` method to register our routes table and also the `RegisterAllControllersIn` method to automatically detect all the controllers in our assembly and register them with the Ninject framework.

Check It Out

Now WroxBlog is ready, and you can test it to see what you have cooked! Figures 18-4, 18-5, 18-6, and 18-7 exhibit some main parts of WroxBlog in action.

Figure 18-4 shows the upper side of home page, which contains the header section, menu navigation, list of recent posts, and a short About section in the sidebar.

Figure 18-5 shows the lower side of home page, containing the list of categories, links, and the footer section.

Figure 18-6 shows the list of comments for one of the posts when an individual post is being viewed.

Figure 18-7 is the comment form when a visitor wants to leave a new comment for an individual post.

Figure 18-4

Figure 18-5

Figure 18-6

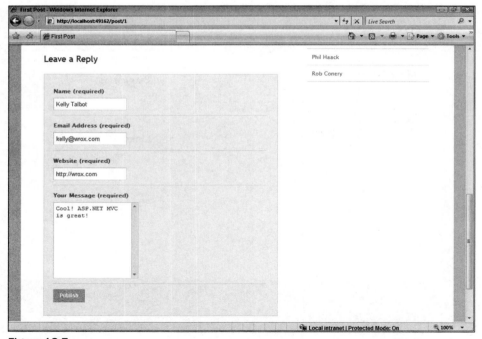

Figure 18-7

Summary

This chapter is a case study and a real-world example of ASP.NET MVC, where you walked through the implementation of a blog engine called WroxBlog. The example explained all the major stages in WroxBlog's development such as models, views, controllers, and the routing mechanism.

This chapter focused on a practical approach to train your skills and newly learned knowledge in the MVC pattern and ASP.NET MVC pattern with a common scenario.

We developed WroxBlog based on some approaches such as design for testability, separation of concerns, modularity, and integrity. All these concepts were connected together to present a very sweet development experience step-by-step.

Exercises

1. Modify WroxBlog with a form validation mechanism that validates user inputs for the comment form to make sure all fields (name, e-mail, URL, and body) are provided, and also that e-mail and URL values are in the valid format.

2. Apply the Rhino Mocks framework and write some unit tests for WroxBlog to test its functionality.

Case Study 2

In the previous chapter, you went through all the parts of a simple blog engine written on ASP.NET MVC, where you got a taste of what writing a full database-driven application involves. But it lacked some of the little utility components that are possible, thanks to the MVC framework and its many extensibility points.

This case study covers the missing points and does it while developing a photo gallery, which takes it contents not from a local storage, but from Flickr (http://flickr.com).

This case study addresses the following points:

- ❏ Using the TDD approach
- ❏ Designing for testability
- ❏ Using action filters
- ❏ Setting up authentication
- ❏ Using AJAX and jQuery

If you are not familiar with these topics, we encourage you to go back to the relevant chapters (chapters 8, 9, 11, 12 and 15) and give them a quick read.

Another issue we try to emphasize is the importance of using a clean HTML markup structure.

Let's get into the analysis of the WroxGallery application, starting from the first thing that a project should have: the requirements.

User Stories (aka Requirements)

Because WroxGallery adopts a Test Driven Development approach, the first thing you have to decide is what does the application have to do? In TDD jargon, the requirements are called User Stories.

This application has to:

❑ Allow any user to see the five most recent photos on the home page.

❑ Allow any user to see all the albums in a sidebar on the all the pages.

❑ Allow any user to search for photos based on their tags.

❑ Allow any user to see the five most recent photos of any given album.

❑ Allow any user to see a page with a description of the site owner (the About page).

❑ Allow the site administrator to log in to the backend of the site.

❑ Allow the administrator of the site to change the title of the gallery, the Flickr account the gallery connects to, and the contents of the About page.

The next natural step is to start writing the test to make the first requirement happen. But before you do that you must know what external libraries you are going to use in this application.

The WroxGallery External Libraries

This application makes use of three external libraries:

❑ **Rhino Mocks** — Used as a facilitator in creating mock objects for testing.

❑ **Ninject** — The Inversion of Control Container that you are going to use to inject the dependencies at runtime.

❑ **Flickr.NET** — A library that allows you to query the Flickr Web service in a strongly typed manner. You read more about this in a bit.

From earlier chapters, you already know everything about the first two, how to get them and how to use them, so this section focuses only on Flickr.NET.

Flickr.NET

Flickr is an online Web 2.0 service that stores the photos of millions of users around the world. You can interact with it also via its Web API. However, this Web API is difficult to deal with so someone developed Flickr.NET. It's an open source library that wraps the calls to these Web services and exposes them to the developer in a friendly manner. You can download it from its project page on CodePlex at http://www.codeplex.com/FlickrNet.

To connect to Flickr's Web services, you need to have an API key. To obtain this, just go the Flickr Services site and request a new one (http://www.flickr.com/services/api/keys). (See Figure 19-1.)

Just to have a quick taste of how using this library is, here is the code needed to get the latest pictures from a user:

```
Flickr _flickr = new Flickr(apiKey);
PhotoSearchOptions searchOptions = new PhotoSearchOptions();
```

```
searchOptions.UserId = username;
searchOptions.PerPage = 10;
Photos userPhotos = _flickr.PhotosSearch(searchOptions);
```

Figure 19-1

Using the TDD Approach

In a TDD approach, once you have your requirements and main architectural decisions, the tests come next. It's not possible to really put on paper the process needed to come out with the final version of the test (and code), but imagine that for each of the tests, you followed the Red/Green/Refactor approach you saw at the end of Chapter 9. And for the same reason, if you write all the tests before the implementation, you are not going to understand the architecture and the technical details of the application.

Listing 19-1 is one of the tests, the one that verifies that the Index action, which renders the home page, returns the Index view, and puts a list of five photos inside the ViewData. Some other tests are shown at the end of the chapter (and even more are available in the code).

Listing 19-1: HomePage_Contains_Five_Photos

```
[TestMethod]
public void HomeController_HomePage_Contains_List_Of_Five_Images()
{
    MockRepository mocks = new MockRepository();
    IConfigurationRepository configurationRepository =
        mocks.DynamicMock<IConfigurationRepository>();
    IGalleryRepository galleryRepository =
```

Continued

427

Listing 19-1: HomePage_Contains_Five_Photos *(continued)*

```
        mocks.DynamicMock<IGalleryRepository>();

    using (mocks.Record())
    {
        Expect.Call(galleryRepository.GetLatestPhoto(5))
            .Return(BuildFakePhotoList(5));
    }

    HomeController controller = new HomeController(
        configurationRepository,
        galleryRepository);

    using (mocks.Playback())
    {
        ViewResult result = controller.Index() as ViewResult;
        Assert.IsNotNull(result, "Not a view result");
        PhotoCollection model = result.ViewData.Model
            as PhotoCollection;
        Assert.AreEqual(5, model.Count);
        Assert.AreEqual("", result.ViewName);
    }
}
```

The `BuildFakePhotoList` method is just a helper method that builds a list of photos.

Building the WroxGallery Model

The first part of the application you are going to implement is the model, which conceptually consists of two parts: the data model, which contains the objects that represent the data handled and displayed by the gallery, and the services, which are the objects that operate on the data model.

Creating the Data Model

The data model of this application is pretty simple. It has only three classes:

❑ **GalleryConfiguration** — Holds the information about the configuration of the application.

❑ **Album** — Contains the details of an album of photos.

❑ **Photo** — The single photo

Figure 19-2 shows the relationships among the data model objects.

There is nothing complicated about the objects. They're just a series of automatic properties. Instead of having some generic collections, it's usually better to have a custom collection object. It's easier to read and understand, and it can be useful later if you want to add a method to your implementation of the collection. The data model object code is shown in Listing 19-2.

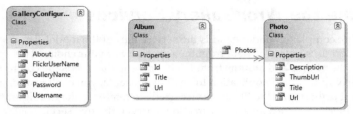

Figure 19-2

Listing 19-2: The data model objects

```csharp
public class GalleryConfiguration
{
    public string GalleryName { get; set; }
    public string FlickrUserName { get; set; }
    public string Username { get; set; }
    public string Password { get; set; }
    public string About { get; set; }
}

public class Photo
{
    public string Title { get; set; }
    public string Description { get; set; }
    public string Url { get; set; }
    public string ThumbUrl { get; set; }
}

public class PhotoCollection: List<Photo>
{

}

public class Album
{
    public string Title { get; set; }
    public string Url { get; set; }
    public string Id { get; set; }
    public PhotoCollection Photos { get; private set; }
}

public class AlbumCollection : List<Album>
{
    public AlbumCollection(IEnumerable<Album> collection)
        : base(collection) { }

    public AlbumCollection() { }
}
```

Implementing the WroxGallery Services

What is a bit more complex to understand is the service part of the model. The services are the objects that the application uses to get the data from the repository of your choice. This application needs one service that gets the photos and albums from Flickr and one that reads the configuration of the application. But because you want the application to be easily testable, you can't just reference the services from your controllers. Furthermore, the Flickr service needs to reference the Configuration Service to get the current user, so there must be a level of indirection between the two services as well.

> *At this point, before going on with the tour of the application, if you are not confident that you are following what we are saying, we recommend you go back to Chapters 8 and 9 and review the concepts about design for testability, Dependency Injection (DI), and Inversion of Control Containers (IoCCs).*

Figure 19-3 shows the services model.

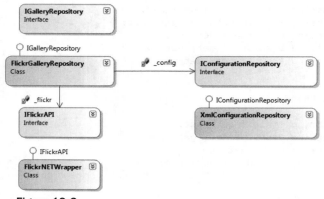

Figure 19-3

As you can see in Figure 19-3, there are three interfaces, one for the gallery repository, one for the wrapper to the Flickr library, and one for the configuration repository, and then the three concrete implementations. Notice also that, because the `FlickrGalleryRepository` needs to get the username from the configuration repository, it holds a reference to the interface instead of the concrete implementation. The same thing happens with the `IFlickrAPI` interface.

Listing 19-3 is the code of the `IConfigurationRepository` interface.

Listing 19-3: IConfigurationRepository

```
namespace WroxGallery.Models.Interfaces
{
    public interface IConfigurationRepository
    {
        GalleryConfiguration Config { get; set; }
```

```
            string GalleryName { get; }
            string FickerUserName { get; }
            string About { get; }
            bool ValidateUser(string username, string password);
            void Store();
        }
    }
```

Listing 19-4 is the code of the `IGalleryRepository` interface.

Listing 19-4: IGalleryRepository

```
namespace WroxGallery.Models.Interfaces
{
    public interface IGalleryRepository
    {
        PhotoCollection GetLatestPhoto(int num);
        AlbumCollection GetAlbums(int num);
        PhotoCollection GetPhotosInAlbum(string albumId, int num);
        PhotoCollection SearchPhotosByTag(string tag, int num);
        StringCollection TagList(string search);
    }
}
```

Listing 19-5 is the code of the `IFlickrAPI` interface.

Listing 19-5: IFlickrAPI

```
namespace WroxGallery.Models.Interfaces
{
    public interface IFlickrAPI
    {
        Photos PhotosSearch(string flickrUserName, int pageSize);
        Photos PhotosSearch(string flickrUserName,
            string tag, int pageSize);
        Photosets PhotosetsGetList(string flickrUserName);
        PhotoInfo PhotosGetInfo(string photoId);
        string APIKey { get; set; }
        Photoset PhotosetsGetPhotos(string photosetId, int pageSize);
        IEnumerable<string> GetTags(string userId);
    }
}
```

Let's first review the implementation of `IFlickrAPI`: This is just a wrapper used to decouple the gallery repository from the library that connects to Flickr. It helps during the tests because it allows you to test the logic inside the gallery repository without really connecting to the Flickr Web service. Listing 19-6 contains the code of it.

Listing 19-6: FlickrNETWrapper

```csharp
using System.Collections.Generic;
using System.Linq;
using FlickrNet;
using WroxGallery.Models.Interfaces;

namespace WroxGallery.Models.Implementations
{
    public class FlickrNETWrapper: IFlickrAPI
    {
        private Flickr _flickr;
        public FlickrNETWrapper()
        {
            _flickr= new Flickr();
        }

        public Photos PhotosSearch(string flickrUserName, int pageSize)
        {
            PhotoSearchOptions options = new PhotoSearchOptions(
                flickrUserName);
            options.PerPage = pageSize;
            return _flickr.PhotosSearch(options);
        }

        public Photos PhotosSearch(string flickrUserName,
            string tag, int pageSize)
        {
            PhotoSearchOptions options = new PhotoSearchOptions(
                flickrUserName);
            options.PerPage = pageSize;
            options.Tags = tag;
            options.TagMode = TagMode.AllTags;
            return _flickr.PhotosSearch(options);
        }

        public Photosets PhotosetsGetList(string flickrUserName)
        {
            return _flickr.PhotosetsGetList(flickrUserName);
        }

        public PhotoInfo PhotosGetInfo(string photoId)
        {
            return _flickr.PhotosGetInfo(photoId);
        }

        public IEnumerable<string> GetTags(string userId)
        {
            Tag[] tags = _flickr.TagsGetListUser(userId);
            return (from tag in tags
                    select tag.TagName);
        }
}
```

```
        public Photoset PhotosetsGetPhotos(string photoSetId, int pageSize)
        {
            return _flickr.PhotosetsGetPhotos(photoSetId, 1, pageSize);
        }

        public string APIKey
        {
            get { return _flickr.ApiKey; }
            set { _flickr.ApiKey = value; }
        }
    }
}
```

Now let's review the implementation of IGalleryRepository that relies on the Flickr wrapper to retrieve the photos and albums from the "cloud." In Listing 19-7, the lines that are about the injection of the dependency on the configuration repository and the Flickr wrapper are highlighted in grey.

As you read at the beginning of the chapter, you need an API to connect to the Flickr Web services. In the code that follows the API is represented by "xxxx . . . ." For the code work in your environment, you have to replace this with your own API key.

Listing 19-7: FlickrGalleryRepository

```
using System.Collections.Specialized;
using FlickrNet;
using System.Linq;
using WroxGallery.Models.Interfaces;

namespace WroxGallery.Models.Implementations
{
    public class FlickrGalleryRepository: IGalleryRepository
    {
        private IFlickrAPI _flickr;
        private IConfigurationRepository _config;

        public FlickrGalleryRepository(IConfigurationRepository config,
            IFlickrAPI flickr)
        {
            string apiKey = "xxxxxxxxxxxxxxxxxxxxxxxxxxxxxx";
            _config = config;
            _flickr = flickr;
            _flickr.APIKey = apiKey;
        }

        public PhotoCollection GetLatestPhoto(int num)
        {
            Photos userPhotos = _flickr.PhotosSearch(_config.FickerUserName,
                num);
            return GetPhotoCollection(userPhotos.PhotoCollection);
        }
```

Continued

433

Listing 19-7: FlickrGalleryRepository *(continued)*

```
public PhotoCollection GetPhotosInAlbum(string albumId, int size)
{
    Photoset photoset = _flickr.PhotosetsGetPhotos(albumId, size);
    return GetPhotoCollection(photoset.PhotoCollection);
}

public PhotoCollection SearchPhotosByTag(string tag, int size)
{
    Photos userPhotos = _flickr.PhotosSearch(_config.FickerUserName,
        tag, size);
    return GetPhotoCollection(userPhotos.PhotoCollection);
}

public AlbumCollection GetAlbums(int num)
{
    var photoSets = _flickr.PhotosetsGetList(
        _config.FickerUserName);
    var album = from ps in photoSets.PhotosetCollection
                orderby ps.PhotosetId descending
                select new Album
                    {
                        Title = ps.Title,
                        Id = ps.PhotosetId,
                        Url = ps.PhotosetSquareThumbnailUrl
                    };

    return new AlbumCollection(album.Take(num));
}

private PhotoCollection GetPhotoCollection(FlickrNet.Photo[] photos)
{
    PhotoCollection collection = new PhotoCollection();
    foreach (FlickrNet.Photo photo in photos)
    {
        Photo mvcPhoto = new Photo()
                    {
                        Title = photo.Title,
                        Description =
                            _flickr.PhotosGetInfo(photo.PhotoId)
                                .Description,
                        ThumbUrl = photo.SmallUrl,
                        Url = photo.MediumUrl
                    };
        collection.Add(mvcPhoto);
    }
    return collection;
}

public StringCollection TagList(string search)
```

```
                {
                    var tags = _flickr.GetTags(_config.FickerUserName);
                    var searched = from t in tags
                                   orderby t
                                   where t.StartsWith(search)
                                   select t;
                    var retVal = new StringCollection();
                    retVal.AddRange(searched.ToArray());
                    return retVal;
                }
        }
    }
```

And now for the implementation of the IConfigurationRepository, which is shown in Listing 19-8. In the sample, we decided to use an XML file and read from it using XML serialization.

Listing 19-8: XmlConfigurationRepository

```
using System.Xml;
using System.Xml.Serialization;
using WroxGallery.Models.Interfaces;

namespace WroxGallery.Models.Implementations
{
    public class XmlConfigurationRepository: IConfigurationRepository
    {
        private GalleryConfiguration configuration;
        private string _configfileName;

        public XmlConfigurationRepository(string configfileName)
        {
            _configfileName = configfileName;
            LoadConfig();
        }

        private void LoadConfig()
        {
            XmlSerializer serializer = new XmlSerializer(
                typeof(GalleryConfiguration));
            using (XmlReader reader = XmlReader.Create(_configfileName))
            {
                object deserialized = serializer.Deserialize(reader);
                if (deserialized != null)
                    configuration = deserialized as GalleryConfiguration;
                else
                {
                    configuration = new GalleryConfiguration();
                }
            }
        }
```

Continued

435

Listing 19-8: XmlConfigurationRepository *(continued)*

```
public void Store()
{
    XmlSerializer serializer = new XmlSerializer(
        typeof(GalleryConfiguration));
    using (XmlWriter writer = XmlWriter.Create(_configfileName))
    {
        serializer.Serialize(writer, configuration);
    }
    LoadConfig();
}

public string GalleryName
{
    get { return configuration.GalleryName; }
}

public string FickerUserName
{
    get { return configuration.FlickrUserName; }
}

public string About
{
    get { return configuration.About; }
}

public bool ValidateUser(string username, string password)
{
    if(username.Equals(configuration.Username)
        && password.Equals(configuration.Password))
        return true;
    return false;
}

public GalleryConfiguration Config
{
    get { return configuration; }
    set { configuration = value; }
}
    }
}
```

Usually, repositories like this one — that rely on a single resource, such as a file on the local file system — are implemented in a way that allows only one instance of the class to exist in the application (if you have knowledge of Design Patterns, we are talking about a *Singleton*). But this is not a singleton, because if you want to be able to easily test it, you will want to create an instance of the repository in every test. You see later how the singleton behavior can be obtained in production code.

The WroxGallery Controllers

Now that the model has been unveiled, let's see how the controllers have been designed.

The application has three areas, and each one has its own controller:

❑ **Home** — This is the main area of the application and contains the list of photos, the list of albums, and the About page, and enables searching based on tags.

❑ **Admin** — This is the backend of the application. It allows you to change the configuration of the gallery.

❑ **Account** — This powers the login screen. It's an extremely trimmed down version of what comes with the project template.

As with the model services, you want to be able to test the controllers in isolation, so we made use of IoCCs and DI in this part of the application as well. Figure 19-4 shows a bigger picture of the architecture.

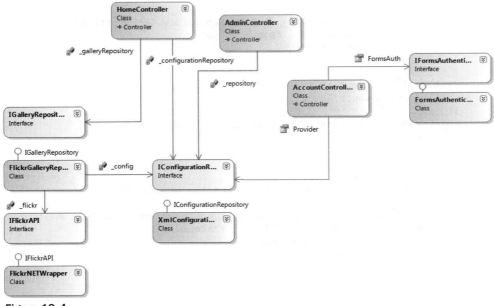

Figure 19-4

Let's see each of the controllers in detail.

The Home Controller

This controller is responsible for showing the list of photos in the home page and the list of albums in a sidebar of all the pages, and enabling searching by tag and rendering the About page.

Listing 19-9 shows the code.

Listing 19-9: HomeController

```
[HandleError]
public class HomeController : Controller
{
    private IConfigurationRepository _configurationRepository;
    private IGalleryRepository _galleryRepository;

    public HomeController(IConfigurationRepository configurationRepository,
        IGalleryRepository galleryRepository)
    {
        _configurationRepository = configurationRepository;
        _galleryRepository = galleryRepository;
    }

    [TitleFilter("Home")]
    public ActionResult Index()
    {
        PhotoCollection photos = _galleryRepository.GetLatestPhoto(5);
        ViewData["AlbumName"] = "Recent pics";
        return View(photos);
    }

    [TitleFilter("About")]
    public ActionResult About()
    {
        ViewData["AboutText"] = _configurationRepository.About;
        return View();
    }

    [TitleFilter("Album")]
    public ActionResult Album(string Id, string albumName)
    {
        PhotoCollection photos = _galleryRepository.GetPhotosInAlbum(Id, 5);
        ViewData["AlbumName"] = "Album " + albumName;
        ViewData["Title"] = albumName;
        return View("Index",photos);
    }

    public ActionResult Search(string search)
    {
        return RedirectToAction("Tag", new {Id = search});
    }

    [TitleFilter("Tag")]
    public ActionResult Tag(string Id)
    {
        PhotoCollection photos = _galleryRepository.SearchPhotosByTag(Id,
            5);
```

```
        ViewData["AlbumName"] = "Search result: " + Id;
        ViewData["Title"] = Id;
        return View("Index",photos);
    }
```

```
    protected override void OnActionExecuted(
        ActionExecutedContext filterContext)
    {
        ViewResult result = filterContext.Result as ViewResult;
        if (result != null)
        {
            result.ViewData["Albums"] = _galleryRepository.GetAlbums(5);
        }
    }
```

```
    public ActionResult Tags(string q)
    {
        StringCollection tags = _galleryRepository.TagList(q);
        StringBuilder builder = new StringBuilder();
        foreach (var s in tags)
        {
            builder.AppendLine(s);
        }
        string tagList = builder.ToString();
        tagList = tagList.TrimEnd('\r','\n');
        return Content(tagList);
    }
}
```

As you see later, each page shows its main contents, but also a series of surrounding details that is shared among all the pages: the sidebar with the list of albums and the title of the page, which contains the name of the gallery plus the name of the current page. The actions are pretty simple, because they all do their core activity: Index retrieves the list of the most recent photos, About gets the text with the description, Album shows the most recent photos in a given album, and finally, Tag shows the result of the search by tag. The Tags action returns a plain-text list of tags; this will be used by the jQuery plug-in used for the autocomplete.

All the other operations are done via action filters.

The Album Filter

Because this filter is only used to retrieve the data needed by the frontend and its views are all rendered as result of the actions in this controller, it has been implemented as a controller-specific filter.

It adds a new object to the ViewData dictionary so that it can be displayed in the master page.

The TitleFilter

The title of each page should contain both the current page and the name of the gallery, but the name of the gallery is in the configuration object. So, to avoid cluttering all the actions with requests that are not core for them, you implement it as an action filter. Because it's also going to be used in the other controllers, you put it in as an external class, as shown in Listing 19-10.

Listing 19-10: TitleFilterAttribute

```
public class TitleFilterAttribute : ActionFilterAttribute
{
    private IConfigurationRepository _repository;
    [Inject]
    public IConfigurationRepository Repository
    {
        get { return _repository; }
        set { _repository = value; }
    }
    public string Title { get; set; }

    public TitleFilterAttribute(string title)
    {
        Title = title;
    }

    public TitleFilterAttribute(string title,
        IConfigurationRepository repository)
    {
        _repository = repository;
        Title = title;
    }

    public override void OnActionExecuted(
            ActionExecutedContext filterContext)
    {
        ViewResult result = filterContext.Result as ViewResult;
        if (result != null)
        {
            string galleryName = _repository.GalleryName;
            result.ViewData["GalleryName"] = galleryName;
            if (result.ViewData["Title"] == null)
                result.ViewData["Title"] = "";
            else
                result.ViewData["Title"] += " - ";
            result.ViewData["Title"] += galleryName + " - " + Title;
        }
    }
}
```

As with everything else up to now, the dependency on the configuration repository is injected, via the constructor in the testing code and by the IoCC, through the Repository property (note that it's marked with the Inject attribute) in production code.

WroxGallery Account Controller

The account controller just handles the login and the logout from the backend. It's a trimmed down version of the AccountController that comes with the ASP.NET MVC project template. Because logging in and out with the FormAuthentication provider requires an HTTP context, for the same usual reason, testing, the real FormAuthentication provider is put inside a wrapper that implements an interface. This way, it can be mocked to be tested. (See Listing 19-11.)

Listing 19-11: AccountController

```
public class AccountController : Controller
{
    public AccountController(IFormsAuthentication formsAuth,
        IConfigurationRepository provider)
    {
        FormsAuth = formsAuth;
        Provider = provider;
    }

    public IFormsAuthentication FormsAuth
    {
        get;
        private set;
    }

    public IConfigurationRepository Provider
    {
        get;
        private set;
    }

    [TitleFilter("Login")]
    public ActionResult Login()
    {
        ViewData["Title"] = "Login";
        return View();
    }

    [AcceptVerbs(HttpVerbs.Post)]
    [TitleFilter("Login")]
    public ActionResult Login(string username, string password,
        bool rememberMe, string returnUrl)
    {
        if (!ValidateLogOn(userName, password))
        {
            return View();
        }

        FormsAuth.SignIn(userName, rememberMe);
        if (!String.IsNullOrEmpty(returnUrl))
        {
            return Redirect(returnUrl);
        }
        else
        {
            return RedirectToAction("Index", "Home");
        }
    }

    public ActionResult Logout()
    {
```

Continued

Listing 19-11: AccountController *(continued)*

```
        FormsAuth.SignOut();
        return RedirectToAction("Index", "Home");
    }

    private bool ValidateLogOn(string userName, string password)
    {
        if (String.IsNullOrEmpty(userName))
        {
            ModelState.AddModelError("username", "You must specify a username.");
        }
        if (String.IsNullOrEmpty(password))
        {
            ModelState.AddModelError("password", "You must specify a password.");
        }
        if (!Provider.ValidateUser(userName, password))
        {
            ModelState.AddModelError("_FORM",
              "The username or password provided is incorrect.");
        }

        return ModelState.IsValid;
    }
}


public interface IFormsAuthentication
{
    void SignIn(string userName, bool createPersistentCookie);
    void SignOut();
}


public class FormsAuthenticationService : IFormsAuthentication
{
    public void SignIn(string userName, bool createPersistentCookie)
    {
        FormsAuthentication.SetAuthCookie(userName, createPersistentCookie);
    }
    public void SignOut()
    {
        FormsAuthentication.SignOut();
    }
}
```

Other than the usual DI used to inject the IFormAuthentication and the IConfigurationRepository (which contains the method used to authorize the user), there is another element that you need to notice. There are two actions named Login: one that renders the login screen and another one that validates the input, verifies the user credentials, and, if everything is fine, redirects the user to the page he requested. Otherwise, it redisplays the login screen, adding errors to the ModelState bag. This is what we introduced as the PRG Pattern (Post, Redirect, Get). Also notice that the validation logic is extracted in an external method. This makes the controller action "thinner" and easier to understand.

Building the Admin Controller

This last controller doesn't introduce new contents, but it is needed to allow the user to change the values of the configuration, as shown in Listing 19-12.

Listing 19-12: AdminController

```
public class AdminController: Controller
{
    private IConfigurationRepository _repository;
    public AdminController(IConfigurationRepository repository)
    {
        _repository = repository;
    }

    [TitleFilter("Admin")]
    public ActionResult Index()
    {
        GalleryConfiguration config = _repository.Config;
        return View(config);
    }

    [TitleFilter("Admin")]
    [AcceptVerbs(HttpVerbs.Post)]
    public ActionResult Index(
        [Bind(Prefix = "")]
        GalleryConfiguration config)
    {
        if (ModelState.IsValid)
        {
            _repository.Config = config;
            _repository.Store();
            return RedirectToAction("Index");
        }
        return View();
    }
}
```

As the login screen, this implements the PRG pattern but handles the binding of data in a different way. It applies the Bind attribute to the parameter of the action so that the framework automatically populates the object with the values it takes from the form. This is cool, because you can add a field to the object without touching the controller class, just by adding a new textbox in the view.

Configuring the IoCC

The last piece that is needed to make everything work in production code is the configuration of the IoCC, in this case Ninject.

If you remember from the other chapters, two steps are needed to accomplish this. The first is the definition of the binding rules inside a module, as shown in Listing 19-13.

Listing 19-13: RepositoriesModule.cs

```
public class RepositoriesModule : NinjectModule
{
    public override void Load()
    {
        string configurationFilePath = HttpContext.Current.Server
            .MapPath(@"App_Data\ConfigurationFile.xml");

        Bind<IConfigurationRepository>()
            .To<XmlConfigurationRepository>().InSingletonScope()
            .WithConstructorArgument("configfileName",
                configurationFilePath);

        Bind<IGalleryRepository>()
            .To<FlickrGalleryRepository>();

        Bind<IFormsAuthentication>()
            .To<FormsAuthenticationService>();

        Bind<IFlickrAPI>()
            .To<FlickrNETWrapper>();
    }
}
```

The interesting thing here is the rule highlighted in grey. It does two things more than the usual bindings: First, it instructs the controller factory to pass a specific file location in the XmlConfigurationRepository. Then it tells the IoCC to treat it as a singleton. The first time an instance will be created, but all the other times the same instance will be used instead of creating a new one each time.

The second step is to instruct the framework to use the Ninject as a controller factory. (See Listing 19-14.)

Listing 19-14: Global.asax

```
namespace WroxGallery
{

    public class MvcApplication : NinjectHttpApplication
    {
        protected override void RegisterRoutes(RouteCollection routes)
        {
            routes.IgnoreRoute("{resource}.axd/{*pathInfo}");

            routes.MapRoute(
                "Default",
                "{controller}/{action}/{id}",
```

```
                    new { controller = "Home", action = "Index", id = "" }
                );
        }

        protected override void OnApplicationStarted()
        {
            RegisterRoutes(RouteTable.Routes);
            RegisterAllControllersIn(Assembly.GetExecutingAssembly());
        }

        protected override IKernel CreateKernel()
        {
            return new StandardKernel(new RepositoriesModule());
        }
    }

}
```

And now, it's time to have a look at the view pages.

Creating the WroxGallery Views

In this case study, we wanted to show how to design a clean grid with HTML. To accomplish this, we relied on the Yahoo! UI Library for CSS (`http://developer.yahoo.com/yui/grids`), which contains a set of ready-to-use CSS that help with starting with the design of a clean page layout. There are four style sheets:

❑   **Reset** — As the name implies, this style sheet resets to a common ground all the different default styles of the various browsers.

❑   **Base** — Sets the base styles foundation for all the HTML elements.

❑   **Fonts** — Equalizes the base font size on all the different browsers.

❑   **Grids** — Offers a set of classes to allow you to build a grid-based layout just by placing the correct IDs and class names on the HTML elements.

To help you build your own layout, there is grid builder tool shown in Figure 19-5 (`http://developer .yahoo.com/yui/grids/builder`), which generates a skeleton page with the correct HTML tags and style hooks.

Here is the HTML that you get from the grid builder:

```
<!DOCTYPE HTML PUBLIC "-//W3C//DTD HTML 4.01//EN"
 "http://www.w3.org/TR/html4/strict.dtd">
<html>
<head>
    <title>YUI Base Page</title>
    <link rel="stylesheet" href="reset-fonts-grids.css" type="text/css">
</head>
```

```
<body>
<div id="doc2" class="yui-t6">
   <div id="hd"><h1>YUI: CSS Grid Builder</h1></div>
   <div id="bd">
     <div id="yui-main">
        <div class="yui-b">
           <!-- YOUR DATA GOES HERE -->
        </div>
     </div>
     <div class="yui-b">
        <!-- YOUR NAVIGATION GOES HERE -->
     </div> .
   </div>
   <div id="ft">Footer is here.</div>
</div>
</body>
</html>
```

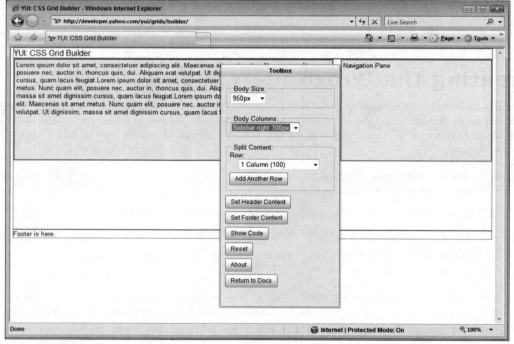

Figure 19-5

Creating the Master Pages

Based on this grid, we developed the following two master pages: one for the public site and one for the login and the administration site. These are shown in Listing 19-15.

Listing 19-15: Site.Master

```
<%@ Master Language="C#" AutoEventWireup="true" CodeBehind="Site.master.cs"
Inherits="WroxGallery.Views.Shared.Site" %>

<!DOCTYPE HTML PUBLIC "-//W3C//DTD HTML 4.01//EN"
    "http://www.w3.org/TR/html4/strict.dtd">

<html>
<head runat="server">
    <meta http-equiv="Content-Type"
        content="text/html; charset=iso-8859-1" />
    <title><%= Html.Encode(ViewData["Title"]) %></title>

    <link href="<%=Url.Content("~/Content/reset-fonts-grids.css")%>"
        rel="stylesheet" type="text/css" />
    <link href="<%=Url.Content("~/Content/base-min.css")%>"
        rel="stylesheet" type="text/css" />
    <link href="<%=Url.Content("~/Content/Site.css")%>"
        rel="stylesheet" type="text/css" />

    <link href="<%=Url.Content("~/Content/thickbox.css")%>"
        rel="stylesheet" type="text/css" />
    <link href="<%=Url.Content("~/Content/jquery.autocomplete.css")%>"
        rel="stylesheet" type="text/css" />
    <link href="<%=Url.Content("~/Content/jquery.lightbox-0.5.css")%>"
        rel="stylesheet" type="text/css" />

    <%if (false) {%><script src="../../Scripts/jquery-1.3.2.js"
        type="text/javascript"></script> <%}%>
    <script src="<%=Url.Content("~/Scripts/jquery-1.3.2.min.js") %>"
        type="text/javascript"></script>

    <script
    src="<%=Url.Content("~/Scripts/Autocomplete/thickbox-compressed.js") %>"
    type="text/javascript"></script>
    <script
    src="<%=Url.Content("~/Scripts/Autocomplete/jquery.bgiframe.min.js") %>"
    type="text/javascript"></script>
    <script
    src="<%=Url.Content("~/Scripts/Autocomplete/jquery.autocomplete.js") %>"
    type="text/javascript"></script>
    <script
    src="<%=Url.Content("~/Scripts/Autocomplete/jquery.ajaxQueue.js") %>"
    type="text/javascript"></script>

    <script src="<%=Url.Content("~/Scripts/jquery.lightbox-0.5.js") %>"
        type="text/javascript"></script>

    <script>
        $().ready(function() {
            $("#searchBox").autocomplete('<%= Url.Action("Tags") %>', {
```

Continued

Listing 19-15: Site.Master *(continued)*

```
                minChar: 2,
                max: 50
            });
            $("#searchBox").result(function(event, data, formatted) {
                $("form").submit();
            });
            $('a[rel=lightbox]').lightBox();
        });
    </script>
</head>

<body>
    <div id="doc2" class="yui-t6">
        <div id="hd">
            <div id="menucontainer">
                <ul>
                    <li>
                        <%= Html.ActionLink("Home", "Index", "Home")%></li>
                    <li>
                        <%= Html.ActionLink("About Us", "About",
                                "Home")%></li>
                    <li>
                        <% using (Html.BeginForm("Search", "Home"))
                            {%><input type="text" id="searchBox"
                                name="search" /></li>
                    <% } %>
                </ul>
            </div>
            <h1><%= Html.Encode(ViewData["GalleryName"]) %></h1>
        </div>
        <div id="bd">
            <div id="yui-main">
                <div class="yui-b" id="content">
                    <asp:ContentPlaceHolder ID="MainContent"
                        runat="server" />
                </div>
            </div>
            <div class="yui-b" id="right">
                <h2>
                    My Albums</h2>
                <% Html.RenderPartial("AlbumList", ViewData["Albums"]); %>
            </div>
        </div>
        <div id="ft">
            <p>
                Wrox Gallery &copy; Copyright 2008 -
                <% Html.RenderPartial("LogOnUserControl"); %></p>
        </div>
    </div>
</body>
</html>
```

The frontend layout is based on two columns: the main one, which contains the list of images or the generic main contents, and the left one, which contains the list of albums. Notice in the header of the file that three style sheets are included (two YUI ones and the one with the styles specific to the site). You then reference the jQuery library plug-ins needed for the cool AJAX features like the autocomplete and the photo slideshow, together with their style sheets.

The `Admin.Master` page is the same as this one, but with just one column, so we will not include it here, to save some trees. You can find it in the source code that comes with the book at `wrox.com`.

Adding the Content Pages

The content pages are pretty simple. The ones for the frontend pages are pretty basic; they just render a list of photos (and all the actions share the same view). (See Listing 19-16.)

Listing 19-16: Home\Index.aspx

```
<%@ Page Language="C#" MasterPageFile="~/Views/Shared/Site.Master"
Inherits="System.Web.Mvc.ViewPage<PhotoCollection>" %>
<%@ Import Namespace="WroxGallery.Models"%>

<asp:Content ID="indexContent"
    ContentPlaceHolderID="MainContent" runat="server">
<%foreach (Photo photo in Model)
    {%>
        <dl class="photo">
        <dt><a href="<%=photo.Url %>" rel="lightbox">
           <img src="<%=photo.ThumbUrl %>"
                alt="<%= Html.Encode(photo.Title) %>" /></a>
        </dt>
        <dd>
         <h3><%=Html.Encode(photo.Title) %></h3>
            <%=Html.Encode(photo.Description) %>
        </dd>            </dl>
    <%}%>

</asp:Content>
```

Notice here the use of the "*semantic*" tags `<dl>` (definition list), which fits well with the list of images and their titles. This view is also reused to show the list of photos in an album and the result of the search by tag. Also notice that the title and description have been HTML-encoded.

The login page is exactly the one provided by the ASP.NET MVC project template, so we'll skip it, also because the same concepts have been used in the administrative page, which is shown in Listing 19-17.

Listing 19-17: Admin\Index.aspx

```
<%@ Page Title="" Language="C#" MasterPageFile="~/Views/Shared/Admin.Master"
Inherits="WroxGallery.Views.Admin.Index" %>
<asp:Content ID="Content1" ContentPlaceHolderID="MainContent"
```

Continued

Listing 19-17: Admin\Index.aspx *(continued)*

```
                  runat="server">

<%= Html.ValidationSummary() %>

<%
     using (Html.BeginForm("Index","Admin"))
     {%>
     <fieldset>
         <legend> Flickr </legend>
         <label for="FlickrUserName">Flickr User Name</label>
         <%= Html.TextBox("FlickrUserName", null, new { @class = "text" })%>
         <%= Html.ValidationMessage("FlickrUserName")%><br class="clear" />
         <label for="GalleryName">Gallery Name</label>
         <%= Html.TextBox("GalleryName", null, new { @class = "text" })%>
         <%= Html.ValidationMessage("GalleryName")%>
     </fieldset>

     <fieldset>
     <legend>Admin Credentials</legend>
         <label for="Username">Admin Username</label>
         <%= Html.TextBox("Username", null, new { @class = "text" })%>
         <%= Html.ValidationMessage("Username")%><br class="clear" />
         <label for="Password">Admin Password</label>
         <%= Html.TextBox("Password", null, new { @class = "text" })%>
         <%= Html.ValidationMessage("Password")%>
     </fieldset>

     <fieldset>
     <legend>About <%= Html.ValidationMessage("About")%></legend>
     <div>
         <%= Html.TextArea("About", null, 7, 50, new { @class = "text" })%>
     </div>
     </fieldset>

     <input type="submit" class="button" value="Save"/>
     <%} %>

</asp:Content>
```

The validation messages automatically turn red when the action that handles the post detects errors. In this page, also notice the markup used: `fieldset`, `legend`, and `label` are all tags specifically used for writing HTML forms.

Using AJAX and jQuery

The case study makes use of two AJAX features obtained through the use of two jQuery plug-ins:

❑   The image gallery through a Lightbox plug-in

❑   The autocomplete textbox through one of the jQuery UI plug-ins

The complete code for both the plug-ins and how they integrate with the rest of the page is shown in Listing 19-15. The next two sections talk in detail about how the two AJAX features are implemented.

The Lightbox Plug-In

To set up the Lightbox plug-in, you need to download the jQuery-Lightbox plug-in, which is available at http://leandrovieira.com/projects/jquery/lightbox.

Then you need to reference the JavaScript file and its style sheet in the head section of the page:

```
<link href="<%=Url.Content("~/Content/jquery.lightbox-0.5.css")%>"
    rel="stylesheet" type="text/css" />
<script src="<%=Url.Content("~/Scripts/jquery.lightbox-0.5.js") %>"
    type="text/javascript"></script>
```

Finally, you need to activate it. To keep things simple, you can just add a rel tag to the links you want, and then select them using jQuery, inside the page's onload event.

```
$().ready(function() {
    $('a[rel=lightbox]').lightBox();
});
```

The HTML of the link is now as easy as the following one:

```
<a href="bigImage.jpg" rel="lightbox"><img src="thumb.jpg" /></a>
```

The Autocomplete Plug-In

Adding the autocomplete feature to the search requires a bit more work.

First, you need to download it from the jQuery site: http://docs.jquery.com/Plugins/Autocomplete

Then you have to add the script references. The plug-in makes use of other jQuery plug-ins, so the list of references is pretty long:

```
<link href="<%=Url.Content("~/Content/thickbox.css")%>"
    rel="stylesheet" type="text/css" />
<link href="<%=Url.Content("~/Content/jquery.autocomplete.css")%>"
    rel="stylesheet" type="text/css" />

<script
src="<%=Url.Content("~/Scripts/Autocomplete/thickbox-compressed.js") %>"
type="text/javascript"></script>
<script
src="<%=Url.Content("~/Scripts/Autocomplete/jquery.bgiframe.min.js") %>"
type="text/javascript"></script>
<script
src="<%=Url.Content("~/Scripts/Autocomplete/jquery.autocomplete.js") %>"
type="text/javascript"></script>
<script
src="<%=Url.Content("~/Scripts/Autocomplete/jquery.ajaxQueue.js") %>"
type="text/javascript"></script>
```

Finally, you have to bind the autocomplete feature to the search box of your choice. This is done inside the `onload` event of the page:

```
$().ready(function() {
    $("#searchBox").autocomplete('<%= Url.Action("Tags") %>', {
        minChar: 2,
        max: 50
    });
    $("#searchBox").result(function(event, data, formatted) {
        $("form").submit();
    });
});
```

And, as you see in the `HomeController`, there must be an action that returns a list of tags. It must be a plain-text list of tags, one per line:

```
public ActionResult Tags(string q)
{
    StringCollection tags = _galleryRepository.TagList(q);
    StringBuilder builder = new StringBuilder();
    foreach (var s in tags)
    {
        builder.AppendLine(s);
    }
    string tagList = builder.ToString();
    tagList = tagList.TrimEnd('\r','\n');
    return Content(tagList);
}
```

Running More Tests

Because this application has been developed with TDD, there are lots of tests, and there's no point putting them all in this book. The most interesting ones are shown in Listing 19-18 with the most interesting lines highlighted in grey.

Listing 19-18: AccountControllerTest

```
[TestClass()]
public class AccountControllerTest
{
    private MockRepository mocks;
    private IFormsAuthentication formsAuth;
    private IConfigurationRepository provider;

    [TestInitialize]
    public void SetupMocks()
    {
        mocks = new MockRepository();
        formsAuth = mocks.DynamicMock<IFormsAuthentication>();
        provider = mocks.DynamicMock<IConfigurationRepository>();
```

```
    }

    [TestMethod]
    public void Valid_Credentials_Redirects_To_Admin_Index_Page()
    {
        string username = "admin";
        string password = "admin";

        using (mocks.Record())
        {
            Expect.Call(provider.ValidateUser(username, password))
                .Return(true);
            Expect.Call(
                delegate { formsAuth.SignIn(username, false); });
        }

        AccountController controller = new AccountController(formsAuth,
            provider);

        using (mocks.Playback())
        {
            RedirectToRouteResult result = controller.Login(username,
                password, false,"") as RedirectToRouteResult;
            Assert.IsNotNull(result, "Not a redirect result");

            Assert.AreEqual("Index", result.RouteValues["Action"]);
            Assert.AreEqual("Admin", result.RouteValues["Controller"]);
        }
    }

    [TestMethod]
    public void Invalid_Credentials_RendersView_With_ModelError()
    {
        string username = "admin";
        string password = "admin";

        using (mocks.Record())
        {
            Expect.Call(provider.ValidateUser(username, password))
                .Return(false);
        }

        AccountController controller = new AccountController(formsAuth,
            provider);

        using (mocks.Playback())
        {
            ViewResult result = controller.Login(username, password,
                                        false, "") as ViewResult;
            Assert.IsNotNull(result, "Not a view result");

            Assert.AreEqual("",result.ViewName);
            Assert.IsNotNull(result.ViewData.ModelState["_FORM"]);
        }
    }
}
```

The first test sets an expectation on a method that returns void, so it's necessary to use the syntax with the delegate. If the SignIn method is not called, it means that something went wrong with the login procedure. The second test does an assertion on the contents of the ModelState bag; it must contain the _FORM key that identifies the login failure.

The other interesting test, shown in Listing 19-19, is the one that verifies the behavior of the ActionFilter.

Listing 19-19: TitleActionTest

```
[TestClass]
public class TitleActionTest
{
    private MockRepository mocks;
    private IConfigurationRepository configurationRepository;

    [TestInitialize]
    public void SetupController()
    {
        mocks = new MockRepository();
        configurationRepository = mocks.DynamicMock<IConfigurationRepository>();
    }

    [TestMethod]
    public void TitleActionFilter_Enriches_ViewData_With_GalleryName()
    {
        using (mocks.Record())
        {
            Expect.Call(repository.GalleryName)
                .Return("Gallery Name");
        }

        TitleFilterAttribute action = new TitleFilterAttribute("Home",
            configurationRepository);
        ViewDataDictionary viewData = new ViewDataDictionary();
        ActionExecutedContext context = ActionFiltersTestingHelper
            .GetActionExecutedContext(viewData);

        using (mocks.Playback())
        {
            action.OnActionExecuted(context);

            Assert.AreEqual("Gallery Name", viewData["GalleryName"]);
            Assert.AreEqual("Gallery Name - Home", viewData["Title"]);
        }
    }

    [TestMethod]
    public void TitleActionFilter_Keeps_Original_Title()
    {
```

```
                    using (mocks.Record())
                    {
                        Expect.Call(configurationRepository.GalleryName).
                            Return("Gallery Name");
                    }

                    TitleFilterAttribute action = new TitleFilterAttribute("Home",
                        configurationRepository);
                    ViewDataDictionary viewData = new ViewDataDictionary();
                    viewData["Title"] = "Album";
                    ActionExecutedContext context = ActionFiltersTestingHelper.
                        GetActionExecutedContext(viewData);

                    using (mocks.Playback())
                    {
                        action.OnActionExecuted(context);

                        Assert.AreEqual("Gallery Name", viewData["GalleryName"]);
                        Assert.AreEqual("Album - Gallery Name - Home",
                            viewData["Title"]);
                    }
                }
            }
        }

    public static class ActionFiltersTestingHelper
    {
        public static ActionExecutedContext GetActionExecutedContext(
            ViewDataDictionary viewdata)
        {
            RouteData routeData = new RouteData();
            ControllerContext controllerContext = new ControllerContext(
                new FakeHttpContextBase(), routeData, new FakeController());

            ActionExecutedContext context = new ActionExecutedContext(
                controllerContext, new FakeActionDescriptor(), false, null);

            ViewResult result = new ViewResult();
            result.ViewData = viewdata;
            context.Result = result;
            return context;
        }

        internal class FakeController : Controller
        {

        }

        internal class FakeHttpContextBase : HttpContextBase
        {

        }
```

Continued

Listing 19-19: TitleActionTest *(continued)*

```
internal class FakeActionDescriptor : ActionDescriptor
{
    public override object Execute(ControllerContext controllerContext,
        IDictionary<string, object> parameters)
    {
        throw new System.NotImplementedException();
    }

    public override ParameterDescriptor[] GetParameters()
    {
        throw new System.NotImplementedException();
    }

    public override string ActionName
    {
        get { throw new System.NotImplementedException(); }
    }

    public override ControllerDescriptor ControllerDescriptor
    {
        get { throw new System.NotImplementedException(); }
    }
}
}
```

Testing an action filter is something you didn't read about in the book. It's not different from any other test, but because an `ActionFilter` requires an `ActionExecutedContext` as a parameter, you need to create one, with the values expected by the action filter, and with the fake object for the portions of the context that the filter doesn't need.

The code contains 37 tests that cover pretty much of the complete codebase.

The WroxGallery in Action

To see how the application works, you can just run the code, but we want to put in the most interesting pieces of the UI.

On the home page of the application (shown in Figure 19-6), notice the menu and the search box overlaid over the header and the borders, all obtained with only CSS, applied to the pretty basic markup used on the master page.

If you click a thumbnail in the main part of the home page, the lightbox appears and allows you to navigate among all the pictures, as shown in Figure 19-7.

If you want to search for photos based on tags, just start typing some text on the search box, and a nice autocomplete drop-down will appear, as shown in Figure 19-8.

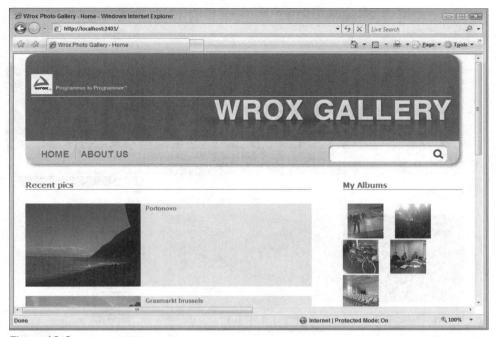

Figure 19-6

Figure 19-7

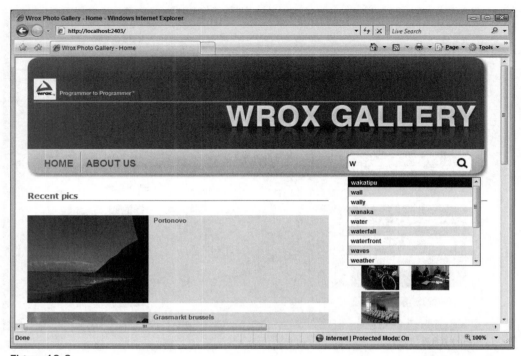

Figure 19-8

Summary

In this last chapter, you got a feeling for how to build an ASP.NET MVC application in a way that meets the quality requirements of a production-grade application.

You learned how to test every part of the application and how to write a clean semantic markup, making use of the external framework created on purpose for the task. Whenever you have to develop something, always search on the Web for something that can save you time and help you attain higher quality, as you did with the YUI Grids CSS and the two jQuery plug-ins.

The application is still not ready for production usage, however. Make sure that you take the time to do the last exercise in the book.

We hope you enjoyed reading the book as much as we enjoyed writing it.

Exercise

Relying on Flickr makes the site pretty slow, because for every request the application has to go to the Flickr Web site and get the values. As an exercise, try to add some caching to speed up the process.

Resources

Communities

- ❏ **ASP.NET Official Web site** — `http://asp.net`
- ❏ **ASP.NET MVC Home page** — `http://asp.net/mvc`
- ❏ **ASP.NET Workspace on CodePlex** — `http://codeplex.com/aspnet`
- ❏ **ASP.NET Forums** — `http://forums.asp.net`
- ❏ **ASP.NET Wiki** — `http://wiki.asp.net`
- ❏ **ASP Alliance** — `http://aspalliance.com`
- ❏ **4GuysFromRolla** — `http://4guysfromrolla.com`
- ❏ **CodeProject** — `http://codeproject.com`
- ❏ **CodePlex** — `http://codeplex.com`
- ❏ **DotNetSlackers** — `http://dotnetslackers.com`
- ❏ **CodeBetter** — `http://codebetter.com`
- ❏ **ASP.NET MVC Resources** — `http://aspdotnetmvc.com`

Blogs

- ❏ **Scott Guthrie** — `http://weblogs.asp.net/scottgu`
- ❏ **Scott Hanselman** — `http://hanselman.com`
- ❏ **Phil Haack** — `http://haacked.com`
- ❏ **Rob Conery** — `http://blog.wekeroad.com`
- ❏ **Keyvan Nayyeri** — `http://nayyeri.net`
- ❏ **Simone Chiaretta** — `http://codeclimber.net.nz`
- ❏ **Stephen Walther** — `http://weblogs.asp.net/stephenwalther`
- ❏ **Jeffrey Palermo** — `http://jeffreypalermo.com`
- ❏ **Steven Smith** — `http://stevesmithblog.com`
- ❏ **Roy Osherove** — `http://weblogs.asp.net/rosherove`
- ❏ **Oren Eini** — `http://ayende.com/blog`

Books

- ❏ *Professional ASP.NET MVC* (ISBN: 978-0-470-38461-9, Conery, Hanselman, Haack, Guthrie)
- ❏ *ASP.NET MVC Website Programming: Problem - Design - Solution* (ISBN: 978-0-470-41095-0, Berardi, Katawazi, Bellinaso)
- ❏ *Professional Visual Studio 2008* (ISBN: 978-0-470-22988-0, Randolph, Gardner)
- ❏ *Professional Visual Basic 2008* (ISBN: 978-0-470-19136-1, Evjen, Hollis, et al.)
- ❏ *Professional C# 2008* (ISBN: 978-0-470-19137-8, Robinson, Nagel, et al.)
- ❏ *Professional ASP.NET 3.5: in C# and VB* (ISBN: 978-0-470-18757-9, Evjen, Hanselman, Rader)
- ❏ *Professional ADO.NET 3.5 with LINQ and the Entity Framework* (ISBN: 978-0-470-18261-1, Jennings)
- ❏ *Professional LINQ* (ISBN: 978-0-470-04181-9, Klein)
- ❏ *Professional XML* (ISBN: 978-0-471-77777-9, Evjen, Sharkey, et al.)
- ❏ *jQuery in Action* (ISBN: 978-0-470-41095-0, Bibeault, Katz, Resig)
- ❏ *ASP.NET MVC in Action* (ISBN: 978-1-933-98862-7, Palermo, Scheirman, Boggard)
- ❏ *ASP.NET MVC Framework Unleashed* (ISBN: 978-0-672-32998-2, Walther)
- ❏ *Pro ASP.NET MVC Framework* (ISBN: 978-1-430-21007-8, Sanderson)

Tools

- ❏ **Subsonic** — http://subsonicproject.com
- ❏ **RhinoMocks** — http://ayende.com/projects/rhino-mocks.aspx
- ❏ **TypeMock** — http://typemock.com
- ❏ **Moq** — http://code.google.com/p/moq
- ❏ **MbUnit** — http://mbunit.com
- ❏ **NUnit** — http://nunit.org
- ❏ **xUnit.NET** — http://codeplex.com/xunit
- ❏ **Structure Map** — http://structuremap.sourceforge.net
- ❏ **Spring.NET** — http://springframework.net
- ❏ **Castle Windsor** — http://castleproject.org
- ❏ **Ninject** — http://ninject.org
- ❏ **Autofac** — http://code.google.com/p/autofac
- ❏ **Spark View Engine** — http://sparkviewengine.com/
- ❏ **MVCContrib** — http://mvccontrib.org/
- ❏ **nHaml** — http://code.google.com/p/nhaml/

Exercise Solutions

Chapter 1

Exercise 1 Solution

An application implemented following the MVC pattern is divided into three components:

- **Model** — This component's responsibility is to retrieve an object from the database and to apply domain-specific logic.
- **Controller** — This is the component that receives the user input, calls the model, and sends data to be displayed by the view.
- **View** — The view simply renders the data that it received from the controller.

Exercise 2 Solution

The Presentation Model is the part of the model that contains the objects that are used only with the purpose of sending data from the controller to the view. This contains the data ready to be rendered by the view without further transformations needed.

Exercise 3 Solution

The main differences between MVC and the MVP are:

- With the MVP pattern the requests first hit the view and then flow to the Presenter, whereas with the MVC, the first component being hit is the controller and the view is the last one.
- Using the MVC pattern, the various components are standard classes, and they are wired-up together by simple method calls. With the MVP pattern, each view must implement its own interface and must publish some events to which the Presenter must subscribe.

Chapter 2

Exercise 1 Solution

Migrating an ASP.NET WebForms application to an ASP.NET MVC application is a broad topic that is covered in Chapter 17. However, it's very helpful for you to think about migration at this point to prepare yourself to understand the similarities and differences between these two technologies.

Generally, you face some major issues when converting a WebForms application to MVC. First, by default there is no separation of concerns in your WebForms application. This requires you to put some extra work into converting your application to MVC. Second, there is no event model in ASP.NET MVC, and you need to replace all your page and control events in ASP.NET WebForms with controller action methods in ASP.NET MVC. Third, you need to replace your server controls with HTML helpers and other replacements in ASP.NET MVC. The other concern is the lack of a default development practice and project templates in ASP.NET WebForms that are enforced in ASP.NET MVC, but this shouldn't affect your working effort.

Though you can convert an ASP.NET WebForms application to ASP.NET MVC in many ways, they all depend on some basics that we outline here.

The data storage conversion to the model can vary significantly depending on your original implementation, but if you have followed a good development practice in development of your data interactions, you won't have major problems in converting them to a model component in ASP.NET MVC, and you usually can import them with very few changes. The most important point that reduces the effort is the level of encapsulation in your data components in ASP.NET WebForms applications that can make it much easier to import the model. Besides, based on your original architecture and implementation, you may need to move your business logic to the model component after conversion.

In ASP.NET MVC you don't have access to events, and you need to replace them with controller action methods. For example, to respond to a button click event, you need to create an action method that responds to HTTP POST verb requests on a specific URL that receives the user inputs as its parameters. Generally, this is the most convenient part of your work because the process is constant and you can gain the required experience by training.

Masters, views, and user controls can be converted to their similar components in ASP.NET MVC. Basically, their main structure wouldn't change, but you need to find replacements for ASP.NET server controls. This usually ends up with the usage of HTML helpers, jQuery plug-ins, or your own user interface implementations. Also, you'll need to replace some parts of server-side controls and data bindings with ASP.NET MVC inline coding to render data from the view data collection.

URLs should be replaced in ASP.NET MVC to use a routing system. Usually ASP.NET WebForms use physical files and URL rewriting mechanisms to accomplish URL organization, but this is completely different in ASP.NET MVC where you no longer need a physical page to handle a request. This is another area where you wouldn't have much work to do because routing definitions are simple.

Though these are the main parts of your work, you still need to have more specific replacements for some common requirements such as caching, form validation, authentication, authorization, and AJAX. All these techniques have different implementations in ASP.NET MVC. Some of the implementations are grounded in the same basics as ASP.NET WebForms and others are completely different, but all in all, they usually need you to define them from scratch.

Migrating an ASP.NET WebForms application to ASP.NET MVC can be a little overwhelming to try to think about as you are first getting started. Don't worry if you are still getting the hang of some of these concepts. As you progress through the book, you will see these concepts explored in more detail. By the time you get to Chapter 17, this will all feel a little more natural.

Chapter 3

Exercise 1 Solution

The solution to this exercise can exhibit very good points about the advantages of ASP.NET MVC in comparison with ASP.NET WebForms and also can give you good ideas about the way that a WebForms application and its components can be converted to the MVC pattern. Here we try to rewrite the application in a form that exhibits the order of MVC development and simulates as much as possible. (Obviously, variations exist on how you could implement such a WebForm, but we cover one of the more standard approaches here.)

First you need to create a new ASP.NET WebForms application and then your data repository. Here you create a LINQ to SQL model in the exact same way as your ASP.NET MVC application. The only difference is that you don't have a default folder structure so you can add your LINQ to SQL model to any physical place that you want.

Second, you need to import the template and CSS files from the MVC application. To do this, create a new folder called `Style` that keeps your `Site.css` file. As you see, ASP.NET WebForms doesn't mandate a default folder structure to keep your files including the CSS files. You also need to create a new master file and import the content of the MVC application master file.

```
<%@ Master Language="C#" AutoEventWireup="true" CodeBehind="Site.master.cs"
Inherits="StartWebForms.Site" %>

<!DOCTYPE html PUBLIC "-//W3C//DTD XHTML 1.0 Strict//EN"
 "http://www.w3.org/TR/xhtml1/DTD/xhtml1-strict.dtd">
<html xmlns="http://www.w3.org/1999/xhtml">
<head id="Head1" runat="server">
    <title>
        <asp:ContentPlaceHolder ID="TitleContent" runat="server" />
    </title>
    <link href="/Style/Site.css" rel="stylesheet" type="text/css" />
</head>
<body>
    <form id="form1" runat="server">
    <div class="page">
        <div id="header">
            <div id="title">
                <h1>
                    Getting Started</h1>
            </div>
            <div id="menucontainer">
                <ul id="menu">
                    <li><a href="/">Home</a> </li>
                </ul>
            </div>
```

```
            </div>
            <div id="main">
                <asp:ContentPlaceHolder ID="MainContent" runat="server" />
                <div id="footer">
                    Wrox Beginning ASP.NET MVC
                </div>
            </div>
        </div>
        </form>
    </body>
    </html>
```

There is only one major change (the highlighted code) where you convert the action link in ASP.NET MVC to a regular HTML link in ASP.NET WebForms.

Now you enter the main part of development. To have a similar structure as in an ASP.NET MVC application, you need to create a `Person` folder with a `Default.aspx` in it, and an `IndividualPerson` subfolder inside this `Person` folder. You also need to create a `Default.aspx` page in this subfolder. The first page in the `Person` folder handles the requests for `Persons` indexing (like the `Index` action method in ASP.NET MVC) and the second page handles requests for individual person info (like the `IndividualPerson` action method in ASP.NET MVC). But these two pages need to have separate implementations and use the master file.

The default page in the `Person` folder indexes the list of persons with links to the individual person profile. The ASPX code for this page is provided here:

```
<%@ Page Language="C#" AutoEventWireup="true" CodeBehind="Default.aspx.cs"
Inherits="StartWebForms.Person.Default" MasterPageFile="~/Site.Master" %>

<asp:Content ID="indexTitle" ContentPlaceHolderID="TitleContent" runat="server">
    Persons List
</asp:Content>
<asp:Content ID="indexContent" ContentPlaceHolderID="MainContent" runat="server">
    <h2>
        <asp:Literal ID="ltrMessage" runat="server"></asp:Literal></h2>
    <p>
        <ul>
            <asp:DataList ID="dlPersons" runat="server">
                <ItemTemplate>
                    <li><a href='/person/individualperson/id=
<%# DataBinder.Eval(Container.DataItem, "ID") %>'>
                        <%# DataBinder.Eval(Container.DataItem, "Name")%>
                    </a></li>
                </ItemTemplate>
            </asp:DataList>
        </ul>
    </p>
</asp:Content>
```

View data references are replaced with ASP.NET server controls (especially the `Literal` control) and instead of the inline code to iterate through items and rendering them, it uses a `DataList` control with ASP.NET data binding to display data passed from the code-behind.

This page has a code-behind as well. This part acts like a controller action method (with some major differences, of course).

```
using System;
using System.Linq;
using StartWebForms.Data;

namespace StartWebForms.Person
{
    public partial class Default : System.Web.UI.Page
    {
        protected void Page_Load(object sender, EventArgs e)
        {
            IndexPersons();
        }

        private void IndexPersons()
        {
            this.ltrMessage.Text = "Persons List";

            PersonsDataContext dataContext = new PersonsDataContext();
            this.dlPersons.DataSource = dataContext.Persons.ToList();
            this.dlPersons.DataBind();
        }
    }
}
```

Here, rather than setting the data view items by loading the data from storage, we set the values for ASP.NET server controls and use data binding techniques, which is a very different approach than in ASP.NET MVC. Of course, you can notice the flexibility and ease of development with ASP.NET MVC.

The next page is the default page in the `IndividualPerson` subfolder where you handle requests for individual person information.

```
<%@ Page Language="C#" AutoEventWireup="true" CodeBehind="Default.aspx.cs"
Inherits="StartWebForms.Person.IndividualPerson.Default"
    MasterPageFile="~/Site.Master" %>

<asp:Content ID="indexTitle" ContentPlaceHolderID="TitleContent" runat="server">
    <asp:Literal ID="ltrTitle" runat="server"></asp:Literal>
</asp:Content>
<asp:Content ID="indexContent" ContentPlaceHolderID="MainContent" runat="server">
    <h2>
        <asp:Literal ID="ltrPersonName" runat="server"></asp:Literal>
    </h2>
    <p>
        <p>
            Name:
            <asp:Literal ID="ltrName" runat="server"></asp:Literal>
        </p>
        <p>
            Date Added:
            <asp:Literal ID="ltrDateAdded" runat="server"></asp:Literal>
```

```
                </p>
            </p>
        </asp:Content>
```

Here references to view data items are replaced with ASP.NET `Literal` server controls. As you see, you need to repeat the user interface element, which adds to your work in code-behind while you could simply use a single reference in ASP.NET MVC views to view data items.

Finally, here is the source code of the code-behind file:

```csharp
using System;
using System.Linq;
using StartWebForms.Data;

namespace StartWebForms.Person.IndividualPerson
{
    public partial class Default : System.Web.UI.Page
    {
        protected void Page_Load(object sender, EventArgs e)
        {
            int personID = 0;

            if (!string.IsNullOrEmpty(Request["id"]))
            {
                int.TryParse(Request["id"], out personID);
                LoadPerson(personID);
            }
        }

        private void LoadPerson(int personID)
        {
            PersonsDataContext dataContext = new PersonsDataContext();

            Data.Person person = dataContext.Persons.Where
                (p => p.ID == personID).Single();

            this.ltrTitle.Text = person.Name;
            this.ltrName.Text = person.Name;
            this.ltrPersonName.Text = person.Name;
            this.ltrDateAdded.Text = person.DateAdded.ToString();
        }
    }
}
```

Here you see two major differences. The first one is in the `Page_Load` event where the person identifier is extracted from request query string items. This of course yields uglier URLs to replace the routing mechanism that could work with better URLs for your site.

The other difference is in the `LoadPerson` method where you replace view data value assignments with setting the values of server controls.

Exercise 2 Solution

All you need to do is modify the `Global.asax` file and update the routing definitions in the `RegisterRoutes` method. You need to change the pattern for the `IndividualPerson` route.

```
public static void RegisterRoutes(RouteCollection routes)
{
    routes.IgnoreRoute("{resource}.axd/{*pathInfo}");

    // Index
    routes.MapRoute(
        "Default",
        "",
        new { controller = "Person", action = "Index" }
        );

    // Individual Person
    routes.MapRoute(
        "IndividualPerson",
        "person/individual/{id}",
        new { controller = "Person", action = "IndividualPerson" }
        );
}
```

Chapter 4

Exercise 1 Solution

First of all, we need to define our business scenario for this example. We're going to extend the ADO.NET Data Objects sample in Chapter 4 (Iranian historical places) to use LINQ to SQL, and also use two tables with a relationship between them.

The user sees a list of provinces and can click them to list the historical places in that province. Then he can click on individual place items to see their details.

We create a new table called `Provinces` with two columns as `ID` and `Name`. Then we add a new column to the `Places` table called `ProvinceID` and add a relationship between this column and the `ID` column of the `Provinces` table.

In the next step we create a new LINQ to SQL model called `Places` and drag and drop these two tables to its designer. Now we add a new class called `IranPlacesDataContext` that encapsulates the main data operations in four static functions for us:

```
using System.Collections.Generic;
using System.Linq;

namespace RelationalLinqToSql.Models
{
    public class IranPlacesDataContext
    {
```

```
        public static IEnumerable<Province> GetProvinces()
        {
            PlacesDataContext dataContext = new PlacesDataContext();
            return dataContext.Provinces;
        }
```

```
        public static Province GetProvince(int provinceID)
        {
            PlacesDataContext dataContext = new PlacesDataContext();
            return dataContext.Provinces.Where
                (province => province.ID == provinceID).Single();
        }
```

```
        public static IEnumerable<Place> GetPlaces(int provinceID)
        {
            PlacesDataContext dataContext = new PlacesDataContext();
            return dataContext.Places.Where
                (place => place.ProvinceID == provinceID);
        }
```

```
        public static Place GetPlace(int placeID)
        {
            PlacesDataContext dataContext = new PlacesDataContext();
            return dataContext.Places.Where
                (place => place.ID == placeID).Single();
        }
    }
}
```

Here we just use the LINQ to SQL API in a very simple form to retrieve the data.

The next step is creating a PlacesController with three action methods:

```
using System.Web.Mvc;
using RelationalLinqToSql.Models;

namespace RelationalLinqToSql.Controllers
{
    public class PlacesController : Controller
    {
        public ActionResult Index()
        {
            ViewData["Provinces"] = IranPlacesDataContext.GetProvinces();

            return View();
        }
```

```
        public ActionResult Province(int id)
        {
            ViewData["Title"] = IranPlacesDataContext.GetProvince(id).Name;
            ViewData["Places"] = IranPlacesDataContext.GetPlaces(id);

            return View();
```

```
        }

        public ActionResult Place(int id)
        {
            Place place = IranPlacesDataContext.GetPlace(id);

            ViewData["Title"] = place.Name;
            ViewData["Place"] = place;

            return View();
        }
    }
}
```

The Index action method loads the list of all the provinces and passes them to the view to be displayed. The Province action method gets the ID of a province and loads the list of all the places in that province and passes them to the view. And finally, the Place action method gets the ID of a place and loads its data to pass the data to the view.

The last stage consists of building three views for these three operations.

The Index view gets the provinces list and renders them with links to the individual province places list:

```
<%@ Page Title="" Language="C#" MasterPageFile="~/Views/Shared/Site.Master"
Inherits="System.Web.Mvc.ViewPage" %>

<%@ Import Namespace="RelationalLinqToSql.Models" %>
<asp:Content ID="Content1" ContentPlaceHolderID="TitleContent" runat="server">
    Iranian Historical Places
</asp:Content>
<asp:Content ID="Content2" ContentPlaceHolderID="MainContent" runat="server">
    <h2>
        Provinces</h2>
    <div>
        <ul>
            <%foreach (Province province
                in this.ViewData["Provinces"] as IEnumerable<Province>)
             {%>
            <li>
                <%= Html.ActionLink(province.Name, "Province",
                    "Places", new { id = province.ID }, null)%></li>
            <%}%>
        </ul>
    </div>
</asp:Content>
```

The Province view displays the list of places in a specified province with links to their details:

```
<%@ Page Title="" Language="C#" MasterPageFile="~/Views/Shared/Site.Master"
Inherits="System.Web.Mvc.ViewPage" %>

<%@ Import Namespace="RelationalLinqToSql.Models" %>
<asp:Content ID="Content1" ContentPlaceHolderID="TitleContent" runat="server">
    <%= ViewData["Title"] %>
</asp:Content>
```

```
<asp:Content ID="Content2" ContentPlaceHolderID="MainContent" runat="server">
    <h2>
        <%= ViewData["Title"] %></h2>
    <div>
        <ul>
            <%foreach (Place place
                in this.ViewData["Places"] as IEnumerable<Place>)
               {%>
            <li>
                <%= Html.ActionLink(place.Name + " (" + place.City + ")" , "Place",
                    "Places", new { id = place.ID }, null)%></li>
            <%}%>
        </ul>
    </div>
</asp:Content>
```

Finally, the Place view shows the detailed information about a specified historical place in Iran:

```
<%@ Page Title="" Language="C#" MasterPageFile="~/Views/Shared/Site.Master"
Inherits="System.Web.Mvc.ViewPage" %>

<%@ Import Namespace="RelationalLinqToSql.Models" %>
<asp:Content ID="Content1" ContentPlaceHolderID="TitleContent" runat="server">
    <%= ViewData["Title"] %>
</asp:Content>
<asp:Content ID="Content2" ContentPlaceHolderID="MainContent" runat="server">
    <h2>
        <%= ViewData["Title"] %></h2>
    <% Place place = this.ViewData["Place"] as Place;%>
    Name: <a href="<%= Html.Encode(place.Url.ToString()) %>">
        <%=place.Name%></a>
    <br />
    City:
    <%= place.City %>
    <br />
    Province:
    <%= place.Province.Name %>
</asp:Content>
```

You also can download the source code package for this appendix to run this application and see it in action.

Chapter 5

Exercise 1 Solution

```
[ActionName("Content")]
public ActionResult ContentExec(string id)
{
    return View();
}
```

You need to specify the action name; otherwise, a method named `Content` will hide the method with the same name that already exists in every controller.

Exercise 2 Solution

First, you need to create a custom model class in the `Model` folder and name it `Image`:

```
using System;

namespace ExercisesResolution.Models
{
    public class Image
    {
        public string Title { get; set; }
        public string ImageUrl { get; set; }
        public DateTime CreationDate { get; set; }
        public string Description { get; set; }
    }
}
```

You have to change the `Content` action of the previous exercise to the following one:

```
[ActionName("Content")]
public ActionResult ContentExec(string id)
{
    Image image = new Image
      {
          CreationDate = DateTime.Now,
          Description = "Header Image for my blog",
          ImageUrl = "http://codeclimber.net.nz/.../header-logo.jpg",
          Title = "CodeClimber Header"
      };
    return View(image);
}
```

And then you have to create a view named `Content` with the following code:

```
<%@ Page Title="" Language="C#" MasterPageFile="~/Views/Shared/Site.Master"
Inherits="System.Web.Mvc.ViewPage<ExercisesResolution.Models.Image>" %>

<asp:Content ID="Content1" ContentPlaceHolderID="TitleContent" runat="server">
    Content
</asp:Content>

<asp:Content ID="Content2" ContentPlaceHolderID="MainContent" runat="server">

<p><b><%=TempData["Message"] %></b></p>
<h2><%= Model.Title %></h2>
<img src="<%= Model.ImageUrl %>" /><br />
<p><%= Model.Description %></p>
<p>Created on <%= Model.CreationDate.ToShortDateString() %></p>

</asp:Content>
```

Exercise 3 Solution

The action is just a simple method that renders the view:

```
public ActionResult Edit()
{
    return View();
}
```

Then you have to implement the `Edit` view:

```
<%@ Page Title="" Language="C#" MasterPageFile="~/Views/Shared/Site.Master"
Inherits="System.Web.Mvc.ViewPage" %>

<asp:Content ID="Content1" ContentPlaceHolderID="TitleContent" runat="server">
    Edit
</asp:Content>

<asp:Content ID="Content2" ContentPlaceHolderID="MainContent" runat="server">

<form action="/Home/Edit" method="post">
Title: <input type="text" name="title"
                id="image_title" /><br />
Image Url: <input type="text" name="ImageUrl"
                id="image_imageurl" /><br />
Description: <input type="text" name="description"
                id="image_description" /><br />
<input type="submit" value="Save" />
</form>

</asp:Content>
```

Remember that the names of the HTML controls must match the ones of the properties of the model object.

Exercise 4 Solution

This last exercise is built on top of all of the other three exercises. First, you have to create another `Edit` method, this time one that accepts only POST requests.

```
[AcceptVerbs("POST")]
public ActionResult Edit([Bind(Exclude = "CreationDate")] Image image)
{
    TempData["Message"] = "Image saved!";
    image.CreationDate = DateTime.Now;
    TempData["Image"] = image;
    return RedirectToAction("Content");
}
```

The HTML controls created in the previous exercise don't have the prefix `image`, so you need to specify an empty prefix, using the `Bind` attribute.

Then change the other `Edit`, adding the selection attribute on top:

```
[AcceptVerbs("GET")]
public ActionResult Edit()
{
    return View();
}
```

The last thing you have to change is the `Content` action to show the image that has been saved in the `TempData`:

```
[ActionName("Content")]
public ActionResult ContentExec(string id)
{
    Image image = new Image {Title = "No image selected"};
    if (TempData["Image"] != null)
        image = (Image) TempData["Image"];
    return View(image);
}
```

And to the "Image saved!" message you have to add to the `Content` view the following line of code:

```
<p><b><%=TempData["Message"] %></b></p>
```

Chapter 6

Exercise 1 Solution

The `Edit.aspx` view must be changed to match this:

```
<%@ Page Title="" Language="C#" MasterPageFile="~/Views/Shared/Site.Master"
Inherits="System.Web.Mvc.ViewPage" %>

<asp:Content ID="Content1" ContentPlaceHolderID="TitleContent" runat="server">
    Edit Image
</asp:Content>

<asp:Content ID="Content2" ContentPlaceHolderID="MainContent" runat="server">

    <h2>Edit Image</h2>

    <% using (Html.BeginForm()) { %>
    Title: <%= Html.TextBox("Image.Title") %><br />
    Image Url: <%= Html.TextBox("Image.ImageUrl")%><br />
    Description: <%= Html.TextBox("Image.Description")%><br />
    <input type="submit" value="Save" />
    <% } %>

</asp:Content>
```

Exercise 2 Solution

To resolve this exercise, you need to create two new classes and modify the `Image.cs` one.

Models\License.cs

```csharp
using System;

namespace ExercisesResolution.Models
{
    public class License
    {
        public int Id { get; set; }
        public String Name { get; set; }
    }
}
```

Models\ImageRepository.cs

```csharp
using System.Collections.Generic;
using System.Linq;

namespace ExercisesResolution.Models
{
    public class ImageRepository
    {
        private IList<License> _licenses;

        public ImageRepository()
        {
            _licenses = new List<License>();
            _licenses.Add(new License { Id = 1,
                Name = "All Right Reserved" });
            _licenses.Add(new License { Id = 2,
                Name = "Attribution CC" });
            _licenses.Add(new License { Id = 3,
                Name = "Attribution-ShareAlike CC" });
            _licenses.Add(new License { Id = 4,
                Name = "Attribution-NonCommercial CC" });
        }

        public IList<License> GetLicenseList()
        {

            return _licenses;
        }

    }
}
```

Models\Image.cs

```
using System;

namespace ExercisesResolution.Models
{
    public class Image
    {
        public string Title { get; set; }
        public string ImageUrl { get; set; }
        public DateTime CreationDate { get; set; }
        public string Description { get; set; }
        public License License { get; set; }
    }
}
```

Exercise 3 Solution

First, you need to create a `SelectList` object in the `Edit` action inside the `HomeController.cs` file and then add a drop-down list to the `Edit` view.

Here is the `Edit` action inside `Controllers\HomeController.cs`:

```
[AcceptVerbs("GET")]
public ActionResult Edit()
{
    SelectList select = new SelectList(
        new ImageRepository().GetLicenseList(),
        "Id",
        "Name");
    ViewData["AvailableLicenses"] = select;
    return View();
}
```

Here is the `Edit` view:

Views\Home\Edit.aspx

```
<%@ Page Title="" Language="C#" MasterPageFile="~/Views/Shared/Site.Master"
Inherits="System.Web.Mvc.ViewPage" %>

<asp:Content ID="Content1" ContentPlaceHolderID="TitleContent" runat="server">
    Edit Image
</asp:Content>

<asp:Content ID="Content2" ContentPlaceHolderID="MainContent" runat="server">

    <h2>Edit Image</h2>

    <% using (Html.BeginForm()) { %>
    Title: <%= Html.TextBox("Image.Title") %><br />
    Image Url: <%= Html.TextBox("Image.ImageUrl")%><br />
```

Continued

475

```
License: <%= Html.DropDownList("Image.License.Id",
    (SelectList)ViewData["AvailableLicenses"], "Select license...")%><br />
```

```
Description: <%= Html.TextBox("Image.Description")%><br />
<input type="submit" value="Save" />
<% } %>
```

```
</asp:Content>
```

Exercise 4 Solution

First, you need to add a new method to the ImageRepository to include a method that gets the license given its ID.

Models\ImageRepository.cs

```
using System.Collections.Generic;
using System.Linq;

namespace ExercisesResolution.Models
{
    public class ImageRepository
    {
        private IList<License> _licenses;

        public ImageRepository()
        {
            _licenses = new List<License>();
            _licenses.Add(new License { Id = 1,
                Name = "All Right Reserved" });
            _licenses.Add(new License { Id = 2,
                Name = "Attribution CC" });
            _licenses.Add(new License { Id = 3,
                Name = "Attribution-ShareAlike CC" });
            _licenses.Add(new License { Id = 4,
                Name = "Attribution-NonCommercial CC" });
        }

        public IList<License> GetLicenseList()
        {

            return _licenses;
        }

        public License GetLicenseById(int id)
        {
            return _licenses.Where(l => l.Id == id).Single();
        }

    }
}
```

Because now the only property of the license that is bound to the parameter is the `id`, in the controller you need to retrieve the full `License` object. To do this you have to modify the `Edit` action that takes the `Image` as parameter (the lines of code that are added are highlighted):

```
[AcceptVerbs("POST")]
public ActionResult Edit(Image image)
{
    TempData["Message"] = "Image saved!";
    if (image.License != null)
        image.License = new ImageRepository()
                        .GetLicenseById(image.License.Id);
    image.CreationDate = DateTime.Now;
    TempData["Image"] = image;
    return RedirectToAction("Content");
}
```

Finally, you add to the `Content` view:

View\Home\Content.aspx

```
<%@ Page Title="" Language="C#" MasterPageFile="~/Views/Shared/Site.Master"
    Inherits="System.Web.Mvc.ViewPage<ExercisesResolution.Models.Image>" %>

<asp:Content ID="Content1" ContentPlaceHolderID="TitleContent" runat="server">
    Content
</asp:Content>

<asp:Content ID="Content1" ContentPlaceHolderID="MainContent" runat="server">
<p><b><%=TempData["Message"] %></b></p>
<h2><%= Model.Title %></h2>
<img src="<%= Model.ImageUrl %>" /><br />
<p><%= Model.Description %></p>
<% if (Model.License != null)
    { %>
<p>Licensed under the <%= Model.License.Name %> license</p>
<% } %>
<p>Created on <%= Model.CreationDate.ToShortDateString() %></p>
</asp:Content>
```

Exercise 5 Solution

As you see in the previous example, there is too much mixing of HMTL and C# code, so you need to remove the only `if` used.

To do that, you have to add the code-behind file to the `Content` view. It's easier to delete the old file, create a new view as a standard WebForm page, and then change its base class to `ViewPage`.

In the code-behind, add the following helper method (`Views\Home\Content.aspx.cs`):

```
using System.Web.Mvc;
using ExercisesResolution.Models;

namespace ExercisesResolution.Views.Home
```

```
    {
        public partial class Content : ViewPage<Models.Image>
        {
            protected string WriteLicense(string licenseFormat, License license)
            {
                if (license == null)
                    return "";
                return string.Format(licenseFormat, license.Name);
            }
        }
    }
```

And finally in the markup (Views\Home\Content.aspx):

```
<%@ Page Title="" Language="C#" MasterPageFile="~/Views/Shared/Site.Master"
AutoEventWireup="true" CodeBehind="Content.aspx.cs"
Inherits="ExercisesResolution.Views.Home.Content" %>

<asp:Content ID="Content1" ContentPlaceHolderID="TitleContent" runat="server">
    Content
</asp:Content>
<asp:Content ID="Content2" ContentPlaceHolderID="MainContent" runat="server">

<p><b><%=TempData["Message"] %></b></p>
<h2><%= Model.Title %></h2>
<img src="<%= Model.ImageUrl %>" /><br />
<p><%= Model.Description %></p>
<p><%= WriteLicense("Licensed under the {0} license", Model.License)%></p>
<p>Created on <%= Model.CreationDate.ToShortDateString() %></p>

</asp:Content>
```

Chapter 7

Exercise 1 Solution

First, write a custom IRouteConstraint that checks whether the date supplied occurs in the past:

```
public class DateIsValidConstraint : IRouteConstraint
{
    public bool Match(HttpContextBase httpContext, Route route,
        string parameterName, RouteValueDictionary values,
        RouteDirection routeDirection)
    {
        try
        {
            DateTime date = new DateTime(
                Convert.ToInt32(values["year"]),
                Convert.ToInt32(values["month"]),
```

```
                            Convert.ToInt32(values["day"])
                            );
                    if(date.CompareTo(DateTime.Now)<=0)
                        return true;
                    else
                        return false;
                }
                catch
                {
                    return false;
                }
            }
        }
```

Then you have to add the route with the pattern, default values, and constraints to the route table:

```
routes.MapRoute(
    "BlogArchive",
    "archive/{year}/{month}/{day}",
    new
        {
            controller ="Home",
            action ="Index",
            year = "2008",
            month = "10",
            day = "05"
        },
    new
        {
            year =@"\d{4}",
            month =@"\d{2}",
            day = @"\d{2}",
            date = new DateIsValidConstraint()
        }
    );
```

Exercise 2 Solution

A valid release file name contains a name, the timestamp, and a version number. The regular expression for it is:

```
\w+-\d{8}-\d+\.\d+\.\d+\.\d+
```

It means:

- ❑ \w+- at least one (+) word characters (all letters, all numbers, plus the underscore) followed by the dash

- ❑ \d{8}- 8 digits followed by the dash

- ❑ \d+\. at least one digit followed by the dot (here escaped with the slash), then repeated four times

Exercise 3 Solution

There is no right or wrong solution here. The only thing that needs to be done is to register the route debugger to the `global.asax.cs` file and add the `RouteDebug.dll` as a reference:

```
protected void Application_Start()
{
    RouteTable.Routes.RouteExistingFiles = true;
    RegisterRoutes(RouteTable.Routes);
    RouteDebug.RouteDebugger.RewriteRoutesForTesting(RouteTable.Routes);
```

Chapter 8

Exercise 1 Solution

To cover all the possible outcomes of the method, you need to implement three tests: one for the standard scenario (I want to get the percent of 8 out of 10), one for the case where you pass 0 as total, and then one for when you want to get the percent of a value that is bigger than the total (10 out of 8). Here is the code:

```
[TestMethod]
public void CanComputePercent()
{
    float result = _lib.Percent(8, 10);
    Assert.AreEqual(80, result);
}

[TestMethod]
public void NegativeIsReturnedIfTotalLessThanPart()
{
    float result = _lib.Percent(10, 4);
    Assert.AreEqual(-1, result);
}

[TestMethod]
[ExpectedException(typeof(DivideByZeroException))]
public void DivideByZeroIsThrownWithZeroTotal()
{
    _lib.Percent(8, 0);
}
```

Exercise 2 Solution

Besides creating the new method, you need to expand the interface. Here is the resulting code:

```
namespace CalculatorLib
{
    public interface IPiWebService
    {
        float GetPi();
        float GetGravity(string location);
```

```
    }

    public class MathLib
    {

        IPiWebService _ws;

        public MathLib(IPiWebService ws)
        {
            _ws = ws;
        }

        public MathLib()
        {
            _ws = new PiWebService();
        }


        //Compute the circumference of a circle
        public float ComputeCircumference(float radius)
        {
            float pi = _ws.GetPi();
            return 2 * pi * radius;
        }

        //Compute the circumference of a circle
        public float CalculateMass(float weight, string location)
        {
            float gravity = _ws.GetGravity(location);
            return weight/gravity;
        }
    }
}
```

Exercise 3 Solution

Here's the code for the test using a stub object:

```
using CalculatorLib;
using Microsoft.VisualStudio.TestTools.UnitTesting;

namespace CalculatorLib.Test
{

    [TestClass]
    public class MathLibTestWithStub
    {

        private MathLib _lib;

        [TestInitialize]
        public void SetupLib()
        {
            StubPiWebService ws = new StubPiWebService();
            _lib = new MathLib(ws);
```

```
        }

        [TestMethod]
        public void CircumferenceIsComputedCorrectly()
        {
            float result = _lib.ComputeCircumference(3f);
            Assert.AreEqual(18.8496f, result);
        }

        [TestMethod]
        public void MassIsComputedCorrectly()
        {
            float result = _lib.CalculateMass(80f,"Milano");
            Assert.AreEqual(8.16f, result,0.01f);
        }

    }

    internal class StubPiWebService: IPiWebService
    {
        public float GetPi()
        {
            return 3.1416f;
        }

        public float GetGravity(string location)
        {
            return 9.8f;
        }
    }
}
```

Notice that, in this case, an overload of the `Assert.AreEqual` method was used, which is the overload that accepts a delta between the expected result and the actual result.

Exercise 4 Solution

Another expectation was set to the mock object:

```
using Microsoft.VisualStudio.TestTools.UnitTesting;
using Rhino.Mocks;

namespace CalculatorLib.Test
{

    [TestClass]
    public class MathLibTestWithMock
    {

        private MathLib _lib;
        private MockRepository mocks;
        private IPiWebService mockedWS;

        [TestInitialize]
```

```
public void SetupLib()
{
    mocks = new MockRepository();

    mockedWS = mocks.DynamicMock<IPiWebService>();

}

[TestMethod]
public void CircumferenceIsComputedCorrectly()
{
    Expect.Call(mockedWS.GetPi()).Return(3.1416f);
    _lib = new MathLib(mockedWS);
    mocks.ReplayAll();

    float result = _lib.ComputeCircumference(3f);
    Assert.AreEqual(18.8496f, result);
    mocks.VerifyAll();
}

[TestMethod]
public void MassIsComputedCorrectly()
{
    Expect.Call(mockedWS.GetGravity("Milano")).Return(9.8f);
    _lib = new MathLib(mockedWS);
    mocks.ReplayAll();

    float result = _lib.CalculateMass(80f, "Milano");
    Assert.AreEqual(8.16f, result, 0.01f);
    mocks.VerifyAll();
}
    }
}
```

Notice that the mock is set up in the fixture setup method, and then each test method sets its expectations and then calls the ReplyAll and VerifyAll methods to ensure that an actual call to the Web service was made.

Chapter 9

Exercise 1 Solution

For this exercise, you first need to reference the Rhino Mocks library and then, as you read in the "Testing Routes" section, you need to mock the HttpContext and set the URL you want to test.

```
[TestMethod]
public void Url_with_only_lang_is_mapped_correctly()
{
    MockRepository mocks = new MockRepository();
    //Mock setup
    HttpContextBase mockHttpContext = mocks.DynamicMock<HttpContextBase>();
```

```
        HttpRequestBase mockHttpRequest = mocks.DynamicMock<HttpRequestBase>();

        RouteCollection routes = new RouteCollection();
        MvcApplication.RegisterRoutes(routes);

        using (mocks.Record())
        {
            SetupResult.For(mockHttpContext.Request).Return(mockHttpRequest);
            SetupResult.For(mockHttpRequest.AppRelativeCurrentExecutionFilePath)
                .Return("~/it");
        }

        using (mocks.Playback())
        {
            RouteData routeData = routes.GetRouteData(mockHttpContext);
            Assert.IsNotNull(routeData, "Should have found the route");

            Assert.AreEqual("Home", routeData.Values["Controller"]
                , "Expected a different controller");

            Assert.AreEqual("Index", routeData.Values["action"]
                , "Expected a different action");

            Assert.AreEqual("Home", routeData.Values["pageTitle"]
                , "Expected a different pagetitle");

            Assert.AreEqual("it", routeData.Values["language"]
                , "Expected a different language");
        }
    }
```

Exercise 2 Solution

In the exercise you need to write two tests, one that verifies the it parameter and another for the en one. Both are the same, except for the value of the parameter, so it's better to use a helper method for this:

```
[TestMethod]
public void Index_is_Rendered_with_Italian()
{
    ExecTest("it");
}

[TestMethod]
public void Index_is_Rendered_with_English()
{
    ExecTest("en");
}

private void ExecTest(string language)
{
    // Arrange
    HomeController controller = new HomeController();

    // Act
```

```
ViewResult result = controller.Index("Home", language) as ViewResult;

// Assert
Assert.IsNotNull(result);
Assert.AreEqual("Index", result.ViewName);
}
```

Exercise 3 Solution

This test is the usual test that verifies that the ViewData collection contains the value expected by the test:

```
[TestMethod]
public void Message_is_Correctly_Formatted()
{
    // Arrange
    HomeController controller = new HomeController();

    // Act
    ViewResult result = controller.Index("BookList", "en") as ViewResult;

    // Assert
    Assert.IsNotNull(result);
    Assert.AreEqual("BookList EN", result.ViewData["Message"]);
}
```

Exercise 4 Solution

In this test you have to verify that a RedirectToRouteResult action result is returned and the action that the user is being redirected to is "NotSupported":

```
[TestMethod]
public void Redirect_To_NotSupported_with_French()
{
    // Setup
    HomeController controller = new HomeController();

    // Execute
    RedirectToRouteResult result = controller.Index("Home", "fr")
        as RedirectToRouteResult;

    // Verify
    Assert.IsNotNull(result);
    Assert.AreEqual("NotSupported",result.Values["action"]);
}
```

Exercise 5 Solution

To include the testing of the TempData collection, you need to supply an agnostic TempDataDictionary to the controller:

```
[TestMethod]
public void Redirect_To_NotSupported_with_French()
```

```
    {
        // Setup
        HomeController controller = new HomeController();
        controller.TempData  = new TempDataDictionary();

        // Execute
        RedirectToRouteResult result = controller.Index("Home", "fr")
            as RedirectToRouteResult;

        // Verify
        Assert.IsNotNull(result);
        Assert.AreEqual("NotSupported",result.Values["action"]);
        Assert.AreEqual("fr",controller.TempData["language"]);
    }
```

Chapter 10

Exercise 1 Solution

This exercise has too many possibilities to cover here. The more you practice with replacing WebForms' server controls with ASP.NET MVC functionality, the more easily you will be able to adapt to each scenario.

Exercise 2 Solution

Taking as a starting point the code of the first Try It Out, all you need to do to reduce the code duplication is to extract from the two actions of the HomeController.cs file the code that retrieves the list of climbs and that adds it to the ViewData dictionary.

The code for the HomeController.cs follows. (The lines of code that are different from the ones in the first Try It Out example are highlighted.)

```
namespace Exercise.Controllers
{
    [HandleError]
    public class HomeController : Controller
    {
        public ActionResult Index()
        {
            ViewData["Message"] =
                "Welcome to the climb archive on ASP.NET MVC!";

            var _repository = new ClimbRepository();
            SendClimbListToView(_repository);

            return View();
        }

        public ActionResult About()
        {
```

```
            return View();
        }

        public ActionResult Climb(string name)
        {
            var _repository = new ClimbRepository();

            Climb climb = _repository.GetClimb(name);

            SendClimbListToView(_repository);
            return View(climb);
        }

        private void SendClimbListToView(ClimbRepository _repository)
        {
            var climbs = _repository.GetTopClimbs();
            ViewData["Climbs"] = climbs;
        }
    }
}
```

Exercise 3 Solution

If the list of climbs recurs among your projects, then the HtmlHelper approach is the best suited for this exercise. Starting from the previous solution, you have to adjust three files in order to get the HtmlHelper working.

First is a file named Helpers\ListHelpers.cs. It contains the implementation of the helper:

```
using System.Text;
using System.Web.Mvc;
using Exercise.Models;
using System.Web.Mvc.Html;

namespace Exercise.Helpers
{
    public static class ListHelpers
    {
        public static string RenderList(this HtmlHelper htmlHelper,
            object value)
        {
            ClimbList list = value as ClimbList;
            if (list == null)
                return "";
            StringBuilder builder = new StringBuilder();
            if(list.Count==0)
                return "<div style=\"border: 1px solid red\">"+
                    "No climb to display</div>";
            builder.Append("<div style=\"border: 1px solid red\"><ul>");
            foreach (Climb climb in list)
            {
                builder.AppendFormat("<li>{0}</li>",
                    htmlHelper.ActionLink(climb.Name,
```

```
                              "Climb", new { name = climb.Name }));
            }
            builder.Append("</ul></div>");
            return builder.ToString();
        }
    }
}
```

Notice that the helper makes use of another extension method to get the link for the detail page.

Then you need to change the two views that need the list, replacing the call to the partial view, with one to the newly created helper:

```
<%=Html.RenderList(ViewData["Climbs"]) %>
```

Chapter 11

Exercise 1 Solution

First you have to enable the custom error in the Web.config file:

```
<customErrors mode="On"></customErrors>
```

Then write an action that always fails because of a SQL connection problem, like this one:

```
public ActionResult Index()
{
    ViewData["Message"] = "Welcome to ASP.NET MVC!";

    SqlConnection conn;
    using (conn = new SqlConnection(
        @"data source=.\SQLEXPRESS;Integrated Security=SSPI"))
    {
        conn.Open();
    }
    return View();
}
```

And finally decorate the class with the following attributes:

```
[HandleError (Order = 2)]
[HandleError (Order = 1, View = "DBConnectionError",
    ExceptionType = typeof(SqlException))]
```

To make this work, you have to create a new view named DBConnectionError.aspx in the Shared folder so that all the controllers in your application can redirect to it:

```
<%@ Page Title="" Language="C#" MasterPageFile="~/Views/Shared/Site.Master"
Inherits="System.Web.Mvc.ViewPage" %>

<asp:Content ID="Content1" ContentPlaceHolderID="TitleContent" runat="server">
```

```
        DBConnectionError
</asp:Content>

<asp:Content ID="Content2" ContentPlaceHolderID="MainContent" runat="server">

    <h2>
        Sorry, the database is not available, please retry again later.
    </h2>

</asp:Content>
```

Exercise 2 Solution

The implementation can be made even more complex to take into account many different ways of specifying a list of blocked IPs, but for the purposes of this example, a list of single IPs will be enough.

First you need to write the action:

```
internal class BlockByIPAttribute : ActionFilterAttribute
{
    public string Networks { get; set; }

    public override void OnActionExecuting(
        ActionExecutingContext filterContext)
    {
        string userIP = filterContext.HttpContext.Request.UserHostAddress;
        foreach (string ip in Networks.Split(';'))
        {
            if (userIP.Equals(ip.Trim()))
                filterContext.Result = new ViewResult()
                    {ViewName = "BannedIP"};
        }
    }
}
```

And then you have to mark with the attribute the class declaration:

```
[BlockByIP (Networks ="192.0.0.1; 10.0.1.200; 127.0.0.1")]
public class HomeController : Controller { }
```

And, finally, create the BannedIP.aspx view in the Shared folder so that it can be used by all the controllers of your application:

```
<%@ Page Title="" Language="C#" MasterPageFile="~/Views/Shared/Site.Master"
Inherits="System.Web.Mvc.ViewPage" %>

<asp:Content ID="Content1" ContentPlaceHolderID="TitleContent" runat="server">
    BannedIP
</asp:Content>

<asp:Content ID="Content2" ContentPlaceHolderID="MainContent" runat="server">
    <h2>Your IP is Banned</h2>
</asp:Content>
```

Exercise 3 Solution

Another filter to implement, this time overriding only the `OnActionExecuted` method:

```
internal class MessageFilterAttribute : ActionFilterAttribute
{
    public string Message { get; set; }

    public override void OnActionExecuted(
        ActionExecutedContext filterContext)
    {
        if(!filterContext.Canceled && filterContext.Exception==null)
        {
            ((ViewResult) filterContext.Result).ViewData["Message"] = Message;
        }
    }
}
```

And then, to change the title only if everything goes well and to actually prove it, you have to change the order of execution of the filters, putting the `MessageFilter` before the `BlockByIP` one:

```
[BlockByIP (Order = 2, Networks = "192.0.0.1; 10.0.1.200; 127.0.0.2")]
[MessageFilter (Order = 1, Message = "Modified by the filter")]
```

Chapter 12

Exercise 1 Solution

`JsonResult` is a good option for the return type of action methods in AJAX scenarios in ASP.NET MVC. The usage of this option is pretty simple and consists of two main steps: Replace the return type of the action method with `JsonResult` and return your result in JSON format, and parse the JSON data in your views to render the output.

Here we implement a sample that passes a list of people as a list to `ListItem` objects and use jQuery to render them in a list in the view.

First we need to create the appropriate action method, which is called `GetData` for our example:

```
using System.Collections.Generic;
using System.Web.Mvc;
using System.Web.UI.WebControls;

namespace JsonResultMvc.Controllers
{
    [HandleError]
    public class HomeController : Controller
    {
        public ActionResult Index()
        {
            ViewData["Message"] = "Welcome to ASP.NET MVC!";

            return View();
```

```
        }

    public JsonResult GetData()
    {
        List<ListItem> list = new List<ListItem>() {
            new ListItem() { Text = "Keyvan Nayyeri" },
            new ListItem() { Text = "Simone Chiaretta" },
            new ListItem() { Text = "Scott Guthrie" },
            new ListItem() { Text = "Scott Hanselman" },
            new ListItem() { Text = "Phil Haack" },
            new ListItem() { Text = "Rob Conery" }
        };

        return this.Json(list);
    }
    }
}
```

Here we create a list of `ListItem` objects and just call the `Json` method to serialize the list into the JSON format. This `Json` function is a built-in and handy function to serialize objects to the JSON format.

Now we need to apply the changes in the user interface. First we need to add JavaScript references for the jQuery script to our master or view. Then we need to write jQuery code to load data from the action method and parse the JSON format to deserialize the data:

```
<%@ Page Language="C#" MasterPageFile="~/Views/Shared/Site.Master"
Inherits="System.Web.Mvc.ViewPage" %>

<asp:Content ID="indexTitle" ContentPlaceHolderID="TitleContent" runat="server">
    Home Page
</asp:Content>
<asp:Content ID="indexContent" ContentPlaceHolderID="MainContent" runat="server">
```

```
    <script type="text/javascript">
        $.fn.addItems = function(data) {
            return this.each(function() {
                var list = this;
                $.each(data, function(index, itemData) {
                    var option = new Option(itemData.Text);

                    list.add(option);
                });
            });
        };
        $(function() {
            $('#btnClick').click(function() {
                $.getJSON("/Home/GetData", null, function(data) {
                    $("#itemsList").addItems(data);
                });
            });
        });
    </script>
```

```
    <h2>
```

```
        <%= Html.Encode(ViewData["Message"]) %></h2>
    <button id="btnClick" name="btnClick">
        Click Me</button>
    <br />
    <select id="itemsList" name="itemsList" size="6">
    </select>
</asp:Content>
```

This jQuery code simply calls the GetData action method to get the JSON data, uses getJSON to deserialize the collection, and then adds the items to the list to be displayed to the end-user.

The download package for this appendix contains the full source code of this application where you can see this in action.

Exercise 2 Solution

The main trick in ASP.NET MVC to show the AJAX progress as an animated image is the usage of the LoadingElementId property for the AjaxOptions object.

The logic for the contact form is not of interest here. We build a simple contact form in this exercise, but you can see a more professional contact form with validation options in Chapter 14 of the book.

We start by writing a ContactController with a ContactForm action method that responds to contact form requests:

```
using System.Net.Mail;
using System.Threading;
using System.Web.Mvc;

namespace AjaxProgress.Controllers
{
    public class ContactController : Controller
    {
        public ActionResult ContactForm()
        {
            return View();
        }

        [AcceptVerbs(HttpVerbs.Post)]
        public ActionResult ContactForm(string name,
            string email, string subject, string body)
        {
            Thread.Sleep(2000);

            MailAddress from = new MailAddress(email, name);
            MailAddress to = new MailAddress("keyvan@wrox.com");

            MailMessage mail = new MailMessage(from, to);
            mail.Subject = subject;
            mail.Body = body;

            SmtpClient smtp = new SmtpClient("mail.wrox.com");
```

```
            smtp.DeliveryMethod = SmtpDeliveryMethod.Network;
            smtp.Send(mail);

            return View();
        }
    }
}
```

This is a fairly straightforward code. The second `ContactForm` action method responds to the POST requests to send e-mails. First there is a short thread sleep just to keep the AJAX progress for a few seconds to be able to notice its animation. Then a regular SMTP scenario happens to send an e-mail.

On the user interface side we need to add references for `MicrosoftAjax` and `MicrosoftMvcAjax` script files to our master or view. Then we can build the view based on the AJAX features:

```
<%@ Page Title="" Language="C#" MasterPageFile="~/Views/Shared/Site.Master"
Inherits="System.Web.Mvc.ViewPage" %>

<asp:Content ID="Content1" ContentPlaceHolderID="TitleContent" runat="server">
    Contact
</asp:Content>
<asp:Content ID="Content2" ContentPlaceHolderID="MainContent" runat="server">
    <h2>
        Contact</h2>
    <img id="updating" src="/content/ajax-loader.gif" style="display: none;"
alt="Updating ..." />
    <br />
    <% using (Ajax.BeginForm("ContactForm",
            new AjaxOptions { LoadingElementId = "updating" }))
        { %>
    <div>
        <table>
            <tr>
                <td>
                    Name:
                </td>
                <td>
                    <%= Html.TextBox("name") %>
                </td>
            </tr>
            <tr>
                <td>
                    Email:
                </td>
                <td>
                    <%= Html.TextBox("email") %>
                </td>
            </tr>
            <tr>
                <td>
                    Subject:
                </td>
                <td>
                    <%= Html.TextBox("subject")%>
                </td>
```

```
                    </tr>
                    <tr>
                        <td>
                            Body:
                        </td>
                        <td>
                            <%= Html.TextArea("body") %>
                        </td>
                    </tr>
                    <tr>
                        <td>
                        </td>
                        <td>
                            <input type="submit" value="Send" />
                        </td>
                    </tr>
                </table>
            </div>
            <% } %>
    </asp:Content>
```

We use the `BeginForm` element just like what you saw in Chapter 12, but we use the `AjaxOptions` parameter to apply additional settings.

Here we set the `LoadingElementId` to the id of an HTML image element that refers to the AJAX progress icon, but we use CSS styles to make it visible by default. At runtime ASP.NET MVC makes this image visible when an AJAX interaction happens.

Chapter 13

This chapter doesn't have exercises.

Chapter 14

Exercise 1 Solution

Modify the `Index` action method, and add `Duration`, `Location`, and `VaryByHeader` parameters to cache data based on these parameters:

```
[OutputCache(Duration = 90,
    Location = OutputCacheLocation.Server,
    VaryByParam = "None",
    VaryByHeader = "HTTP_REFERER")]
public ActionResult Index()
{
    ViewData["Message"] = "Caching in ASP.NET MVC";
    ViewData["CurrentTime"] = DateTime.Now.ToString();

    return View();
}
```

Exercise 2 Solution

The solution consists of two parts: modifying the ContactController and modifying the Contact view.

First, modify the Contact action method in ContactController to get a url parameter, then add an if condition to make sure that it is set to a string value and this value is a valid Internet URL (using regular expressions):

```
[AcceptVerbs(HttpVerbs.Post)]
public ActionResult Contact(string name, string email, string url,
    string subject, string body)
{
    // Validate Name
    if (string.IsNullOrEmpty(name))
        ModelState.AddModelError("name", "You must enter your name.");

    // Validate Email
    if (string.IsNullOrEmpty(email))
        ModelState.AddModelError("email", "You must enter your email.");
    else
    {
        Regex regex = new Regex
            (@"\w+([-+.']\w+)*@\w+([-.]\w+)*\.\w+([-.]\w+)*",
            RegexOptions.IgnoreCase);

        if (!regex.IsMatch(email))
            ModelState.AddModelError("email", "You must enter a valid email.");
    }

    // Validate URL
    if (string.IsNullOrEmpty(url))
        ModelState.AddModelError("url", "You must enter your URL.");
    else
    {
        Regex regex = new Regex
            (@"(?<http>(http:[/][/]|www.)([a-z]|[A-Z]|[0-9]|[/.]|[~])*)",
            RegexOptions.IgnoreCase);

        if (!regex.IsMatch(url))
            ModelState.AddModelError("url", "You must enter a valid URL.");
    }

    // Validate Subject
    if (string.IsNullOrEmpty(subject))
        ModelState.AddModelError("subject", "You must enter a subject.");

    // Validate Body
    if (string.IsNullOrEmpty(body))
        ModelState.AddModelError("body", "You must enter the body text.");

    // Send Email
    if (ViewData.ModelState.IsValid)
    {
        MailAddress from = new MailAddress(email, name);
```

```
        MailAddress to = new MailAddress("keyvan@wrox.com");

        MailMessage mail = new MailMessage(from, to);
        mail.Subject = subject;
        mail.Body = body;

        SmtpClient smtp = new SmtpClient("mail.wrox.com");
        smtp.DeliveryMethod = SmtpDeliveryMethod.Network;
        smtp.Send(mail);

        return RedirectToAction("Index", "Home");
    }

    // There is an error, so we display the form with error messages
    return View();
}
```

Now modify the Contact view to display a textbox for the user to enter their URL value:

```
<%@ Page Title="" Language="C#" MasterPageFile="~/Views/Shared/Site.Master"
Inherits="System.Web.Mvc.ViewPage" %>

<asp:Content ID="Content1" ContentPlaceHolderID="TitleContent" runat="server">
    Contact Form
</asp:Content>
<asp:Content ID="Content2" ContentPlaceHolderID="MainContent" runat="server">
    <h2>
        Contact Form</h2>
    <p>
        You can use this form to contact us.
    </p>
    <%= Html.ValidationSummary() %>
    <% using (Html.BeginForm())
        { %>
    <div>
        <table>
            <tr>
                <td>
                    Name:
                </td>
                <td>
                    <%= Html.TextBox("name") %>
                    <%= Html.ValidationMessage("name")%>
                </td>
            </tr>
            <tr>
                <td>
                    Email:
                </td>
                <td>
                    <%= Html.TextBox("email") %>
                    <%= Html.ValidationMessage("email") %>
                </td>
            </tr>
            <tr>
```

```
                <td>
                    URL:
                </td>
                <td>
                    <%= Html.TextBox("url") %>
                    <%= Html.ValidationMessage("url")%>
                </td>
            </tr>
            <tr>
                <td>
                    Subject:
                </td>
                <td>
                    <%= Html.TextBox("subject")%>
                    <%= Html.ValidationMessage("subject")%>
                </td>
            </tr>
            <tr>
                <td>
                    Body:
                </td>
                <td>
                    <%= Html.TextArea("body") %>
                    <%= Html.ValidationMessage("body")%>
                </td>
            </tr>
            <tr>
                <td>
                </td>
                <td>
                    <input type="submit" value="Send" />
                </td>
            </tr>
        </table>
    </div>
    <% } %>
</asp:Content>
```

Chapter 15

Exercise 1 Solution

Modify the ChangePassword action methods, and update their Authorize action filter to use the Users parameter:

```
[Authorize(Users = "keyvan")]
public ActionResult ChangePassword()
{
    ViewData["PasswordLength"] = MembershipService.MinPasswordLength;

    return View();
```

```
    }
```

```
[Authorize(Users = "keyvan")]
[AcceptVerbs(HttpVerbs.Post)]
[System.Diagnostics.CodeAnalysis.SuppressMessage("Microsoft.Design",
"CA1031:DoNotCatchGeneralExceptionTypes",
    Justification = "Exceptions result in password not being changed.")]
public ActionResult ChangePassword(string currentPassword, string newPassword,
string confirmPassword)
{
    ViewData["PasswordLength"] = MembershipService.MinPasswordLength;

    if (!ValidateChangePassword(currentPassword, newPassword, confirmPassword))
    {
        return View();
    }

    try
    {
        if (MembershipService.ChangePassword(User.Identity.Name, currentPassword,
newPassword))
        {
            return RedirectToAction("ChangePasswordSuccess");
        }
        else
        {
            ModelState.AddModelError("_FORM", "The current password is incorrect or
the new password is invalid.");
            return View();
        }
    }
    catch
    {
        ModelState.AddModelError("_FORM", "The current password is incorrect or the
new password is invalid.");
        return View();
    }
}
```

Exercise 2 Solution

Modify the Web.config file, and add an <authorization /> element that restricts access to the change password page for the role:

```
<location path="account/changepassword">
    <system.web>
        <authorization>
            <allow roles="Users"/>
            <deny users="?"/>
        </authorization>
    </system.web>
</location>
```

Chapter 16

Exercise 1 Solution

Many scenarios are possible. One possible scenario could be to add some filtering before the whole pipeline is started. For example, you can write a route handler that checks on a blacklist to prevent spammers from hitting the site. Writing a route handler in this case can be a better solution than writing it as an action filter (as you saw in Chapter 11) because this way you save the resources of the server by stopping spammers even before controllers are hit.

Exercise 2 Solution

For this exercise we decided to use Unity, the Inversion of Control Container developed by the Pattern & Practice group of Microsoft.

The first thing you have to do is download Unity from `http://www.codeplex.com/unity` and reference the core assembly, together with the correct connectors from MvcContrib, inside your ASP.NET MVC Web application. At the end you need to add references to:

❑   `MvcContrib.dll`

❑   `MvcContrib.Unity.dll`

❑   `Microsoft.Practices.Unity.dll`

The code of the controller and model is exactly the same as what you read in the section titled "Using the Controller Factory that Comes with MvcContrib" in Chapter 16 (Listing 16-3 and Listing 16-4). What you implement differently is the initialization and configuration of Unity, which is a bit different than Ninject. And all this initialization lies in the `Global.asax.cs` file, whose code is presented here:

```csharp
public class MvcApplication : System.Web.HttpApplication, IUnityContainerAccessor
{
    private static UnityContainer _container;

    public static IUnityContainer Container
    {
        get { return _container; }
    }

    IUnityContainer IUnityContainerAccessor.Container
    {
        get { return Container; }
    }

    public static void RegisterRoutes(RouteCollection routes)
    {
        routes.IgnoreRoute("{resource}.axd/{*pathInfo}");

        routes.MapRoute(
            "Default",                                      // Route name
            "{controller}/{action}/{id}",                   // URL with parameters
```

499

```
                new { controller = "Home", action = "Index", id = "" } //
        );
    }

    protected void Application_Start()
    {
        InitializeContainer();
        RegisterRoutes(RouteTable.Routes);
    }

    private void InitializeContainer()
    {
        if (_container==null)
        {
            ControllerBuilder.Current
                .SetControllerFactory(typeof(UnityControllerFactory));
            _container = new UnityContainer();
            _container.RegisterType<IPiWebService, PiWebServiceWrapper>();
            _container.RegisterType<MathController>();
        }
    }
}
```

The first highlighted area contains the implementation of the `IUnityContainerAccessor` interface, which is used by MvcContrib to get the reference to the Unity container. The second area contains the `InitializeContainer` method, which is responsible for registering the controller factory for the current Web application and for configuring the IoC Container.

Exercise 3 Solution

This is a very personal decision because mostly it boils down to which syntax you prefer for writing your views.

You might like NVelocity, which comes with the power of the directives that make the code for some looping scenarios cleaner and more elegant then explicitly looping through collection. Or you might prefer the syntax introduced by NHaml, where there are no angle brackets, and where the most used tags (div and span) are inferred by the context.

Or you might fall in love with Spark: conditions and for-loops attributes of HTML elements, so there is no tag soup, just HTML markup. Spark is also the only alternative view engine (as of the versions used for this book) that supports named content placeholders and that comes with an add-on for VisualStudio to make the development experience similar to that of the WebForm view engine experience.

Exercise 4 Solution

Obviously, the possibilities here are limitless. As you explore various implementations, you will continue to build on your knowledge and discover a wealth of tactics and approaches. The important thing is to keep experimenting and building your knowledge.

Exercise 5 Solution

The problem of the code shown in Listing 16-23 is that it doesn't work in a real Web scenario when more users might come from the same IP address. But fixing the problem is pretty easy: All you need is to store a cookie with a unique identifier in the browser of the user, and use that identifier as a key for storing the `TempData` in the cache. Here is the code for the new `CacheTempDataProvider`:

```
public class CacheAndCookieTempDataProvider : ITempDataProvider
{
    private const string keyName = "__TempData";
    private const string cookieName = "__TempDataId";
    public IDictionary<string, object> LoadTempData(
        ControllerContext controllerContext)
    {
        string cacheKey = GetCacheKey(controllerContext.HttpContext);
        Dictionary<string, object> tempData =
            controllerContext.HttpContext.Cache[cacheKey]
            as Dictionary<string, object>;
        if (tempData != null)
        {
            controllerContext.HttpContext.Cache.Remove(keyName);
            return tempData;
        }
        return new Dictionary<string, object>();
    }

    public void SaveTempData(ControllerContext controllerContext,
        IDictionary<string, object> values)
    {
        string cacheKey = GetCacheKey(controllerContext.HttpContext);
        controllerContext.HttpContext.Cache.Insert(cacheKey, values);
    }

    private string GetCacheKey(HttpContextBase httpContext)
    {
        string uniqueIdentifier = GetUniqueIdentifier(httpContext);
        return String.Format("{0}[{1}]", keyName, uniqueIdentifier);
    }

    private string GetUniqueIdentifier(HttpContextBase context)
    {
        var uniqueIdCookie = context.Request.Cookies.Get(cookieName);
        if (uniqueIdCookie == null)
        {
            uniqueIdCookie = new HttpCookie(cookieName);
            uniqueIdCookie.Value = Guid.NewGuid().ToString();
            context.Response.Cookies.Add(uniqueIdCookie);
        }
        return uniqueIdCookie.Value;
    }
}
```

Highlighted are the lines of code that store and retrieve the unique identifier (a Guid) from the cookies collection. All the rest is the same code as in Listing 16-23.

Chapter 17

Exercise 1 Solution

Here we import the exact same template to be able to exhibit all the differences in the rendered HTML code.

Create an ASP.NET WebForms application and import the master page, CSS file, and other user interface elements from the ASP.NET MVC application. You can see the code for the imported template in the download package for this appendix.

Create a folder named `Contact` with a `Default.aspx` page inside it that uses the imported master page. The code for this page is presented here:

```
<%@ Page Language="C#" AutoEventWireup="true" CodeBehind="Default.aspx.cs"
Inherits="ValidationWebForms.Contact.Default" MasterPageFile="~/Site.Master" %>

<asp:Content ID="Content1" ContentPlaceHolderID="TitleContent" runat="server">
    Contact Form
</asp:Content>
<asp:Content ID="Content2" ContentPlaceHolderID="MainContent" runat="server">
    <h2>
        Contact Form</h2>
    <p>
        You can use this form to contact us.
    </p>
    <form id="form1" runat="server">
    <asp:ValidationSummary ID="ValidationSummary1" runat="server" />
    <div>
        <table>
            <tr>
                <td>
                    Name:
                </td>
                <td>
                    <asp:TextBox ID="txtName" runat="server"></asp:TextBox>
                    <asp:RequiredFieldValidator ID="RequiredFieldValidator1"
runat="server" ErrorMessage="You must enter your name."
                        ControlToValidate="txtName" Text="*">
</asp:RequiredFieldValidator>
                </td>
            </tr>
            <tr>
                <td>
                    Email:
                </td>
                <td>
                    <asp:TextBox ID="txtEmail" runat="server"></asp:TextBox>
                    <asp:RequiredFieldValidator ID="RequiredFieldValidator2"
runat="server" ErrorMessage="You must enter your email."
```

```
                    ControlToValidate="txtEmail" Text="*">
</asp:RequiredFieldValidator>
                    <asp:RegularExpressionValidator ID="RegularExpressionValidator1"
runat="server" ErrorMessage="You must enter a valid email."
                    ControlToValidate="txtEmail" Text="*"
ValidationExpression="\w+([-+.']\w+)*@\w+([-.]\w+)*\.\w+([-.]\w+)*">
</asp:RegularExpressionValidator>
                </td>
            </tr>
            <tr>
                <td>
                    Subject:
                </td>
                <td>
                    <asp:TextBox ID="txtSubject" runat="server"></asp:TextBox>
                    <asp:RequiredFieldValidator ID="RequiredFieldValidator3"
runat="server" ErrorMessage="You must enter a subject."
                    ControlToValidate="txtSubject" Text="*">
</asp:RequiredFieldValidator>
                </td>
            </tr>
            <tr>
                <td>
                    Body:
                </td>
                <td>
                    <asp:TextBox ID="txtBody" runat="server"
 TextMode="MultiLine"></asp:TextBox>
                    <asp:RequiredFieldValidator ID="RequiredFieldValidator4"
runat="server" ErrorMessage="You must enter the body text."
                    Text="*" ControlToValidate="txtBody">
</asp:RequiredFieldValidator>
                </td>
            </tr>
            <tr>
                <td>
                </td>
                <td>
                    <asp:Button ID="btnSubmit" runat="server" Text="Send"
OnClick="btnSubmit_Click" />
                </td>
            </tr>
        </table>
    </div>
    </form>
</asp:Content>
```

You see that this code is more complicated than the ASP.NET MVC view code for the contact view. All the HTML helpers are replaced with ASP.NET WebForms server controls and the validation messages are replaced with RequiredFieldValidator and RegularExpressionValidator controls. You also need to set the properties for these controls. Having the right declaration for your server controls, the form validation happens behind the scenes and is managed by ASP.NET.

The code-behind for this page is very simple and just includes the business logic to create and send the e-mail message within the `btnSubmit_Click` event:

```
protected void btnSubmit_Click(object sender, EventArgs e)
{
    MailAddress from = new MailAddress
        (this.txtEmail.Text, this.txtName.Text);
    MailAddress to = new MailAddress("keyvan@wrox.com");

    MailMessage mail = new MailMessage(from, to);
    mail.Subject = this.txtSubject.Text;
    mail.Body = this.txtBody.Text;

    SmtpClient smtp = new SmtpClient("mail.wrox.com");
    smtp.DeliveryMethod = SmtpDeliveryMethod.Network;
    smtp.Send(mail);
}
```

Running this application and checking the HTML source code for the contact page, you should see something like this:

```
<!DOCTYPE html PUBLIC "-//W3C//DTD XHTML 1.0 Strict//EN"
"http://www.w3.org/TR/xhtml1/DTD/xhtml1-strict.dtd">
<html xmlns="http://www.w3.org/1999/xhtml">
<head id="ct100_Head1">
    <title>Contact Form </title>
    <link href="/Content/Site.css" rel="stylesheet" type="text/css" />
</head>
<body>
    <div class="page">
        <div id="header">
            <div id="title">
                <h1>
                    Validation (WebForms)</h1>
            </div>
            <div id="menucontainer">
                <ul id="menu">
                    <li><a href="/">Home</a></li>
                    <li><a href="/contact">Contact</a></li>
                </ul>
            </div>
        </div>
        <div id="main">
            <h2>
                Contact Form</h2>
            <p>
                You can use this form to contact us.
            </p>
            <form name="aspnetForm" method="post" action="default.aspx"
onsubmit="javascript:return WebForm_OnSubmit();"
            id="aspnetForm">
                <div>
                    <input type="hidden" name="__EVENTTARGET" id="__EVENTTARGET"
value="" />
```

```
                <input type="hidden" name="__EVENTARGUMENT" id="__EVENTARGUMENT"
value="" />
                <input type="hidden" name="__VIEWSTATE" id="__VIEWSTATE"
value="/wEPDwUKMTQwNDU0MzA3M2RkQwHR7CeF8tBb5v2vCdRK0qbWsdQ=" />
        </div>

        <script type="text/javascript">
//<![CDATA[
var theForm = document.forms['aspnetForm'];
if (!theForm) {
    theForm = document.aspnetForm;
}
function __doPostBack(eventTarget, eventArgument) {
    if (!theForm.onsubmit || (theForm.onsubmit() != false)) {
        theForm.__EVENTTARGET.value = eventTarget;
        theForm.__EVENTARGUMENT.value = eventArgument;
        theForm.submit();
    }
}
//]]>
        </script>

        <script src="/WebResource.axd?d=7HQfF2LGlWaEfijDO5cW-
Q2&amp;t=633525753830425488"
            type="text/javascript"></script>

        <script src="/WebResource.axd?d=8ewvgf1_WrDKztVS7v-ijiYV4VdebJkEK9Ik_
bBCLmE1&amp;t=633525753830425488"
            type="text/javascript"></script>

        <script type="text/javascript">
//<![CDATA[
function WebForm_OnSubmit() {
if (typeof(ValidatorOnSubmit) == "function" && ValidatorOnSubmit() == false) return
false;
return true;
}
//]]>
        </script>

        <div id="ctl00_MainContent_ValidationSummary1" style="color: Red;
display: none;">
        </div>
        <div>
            <table>
                <tr>
                    <td>
                        Name:
                    </td>
                    <td>
                        <input name="ctl00$MainContent$txtName" type="text"
id="ctl00_MainContent_txtName" />
                        <span id="ctl00_MainContent_RequiredFieldValidator1"
style="color: Red; visibility: hidden;">
```

```
                                    *</span>
                        </td>
                    </tr>
                    <tr>
                        <td>
                            Email:
                        </td>
                        <td>
                            <input name="ctl00$MainContent$txtEmail" type="text"
id="ctl00_MainContent_txtEmail" />
                            <span id="ctl00_MainContent_RequiredFieldValidator2"
style="color: Red; visibility: hidden;">
                                *</span> <span
id="ctl00_MainContent_RegularExpressionValidator1" style="color: Red;
                                visibility: hidden;">*</span>
                        </td>
                    </tr>
                    <tr>
                        <td>
                            Subject:
                        </td>
                        <td>
                            <input name="ctl00$MainContent$txtSubject" type="text"
id="ctl00_MainContent_txtSubject" />
                            <span id="ctl00_MainContent_RequiredFieldValidator3"
style="color: Red; visibility: hidden;">
                                *</span>
                        </td>
                    </tr>
                    <tr>
                        <td>
                            Body:
                        </td>
                        <td>
                            <textarea name="ctl00$MainContent$txtBody" rows="2"
cols="20" id="ctl00_MainContent_txtBody"></textarea>
                            <span id="ctl00_MainContent_RequiredFieldValidator4"
style="color: Red; visibility: hidden;">
                                *</span>
                        </td>
                    </tr>
                    <tr>
                        <td>
                        </td>
                        <td>
                            <input type="submit" name="ctl00$MainContent$btnSubmit"
value="Send" onclick="javascript:WebForm_DoPostBackWithOptions(new WebForm_PostBack
Options(&quot;ctl00$MainContent$btnSubmit&quot;, &quot;&quot;, true, &quot;&quot;,
&quot;&quot;, false, false))"
                            id="ctl00_MainContent_btnSubmit" />
                        </td>
                    </tr>
                </table>
```

```
          </div>

              <script type="text/javascript">
//<![CDATA[
var Page_ValidationSummaries =  new Array(document.getElementById("ctl00_
MainContent_ValidationSummary1"));
var Page_Validators =  new Array(document.getElementById("ctl00_MainContent_
RequiredFieldValidator1"), document.getElementById("ctl00_MainContent_
RequiredFieldValidator2"), document.getElementById("ctl00_MainContent_
RegularExpressionValidator1"), document.getElementById("ctl00_MainContent_
RequiredFieldValidator3"), document.getElementById("ctl00_MainContent_
RequiredFieldValidator4"));
//]]>
          </script>

              <script type="text/javascript">
//<![CDATA[
var ctl00_MainContent_RequiredFieldValidator1 = document.all ? document.all["ctl00_
MainContent_RequiredFieldValidator1"] : document.getElementById("ctl00_MainContent_
RequiredFieldValidator1");
ctl00_MainContent_RequiredFieldValidator1.controltovalidate = "ctl00_MainContent_
txtName";
ctl00_MainContent_RequiredFieldValidator1.errormessage = "You must enter your
name.";
ctl00_MainContent_RequiredFieldValidator1.evaluationfunction =
"RequiredFieldValidatorEvaluateIsValid";
ctl00_MainContent_RequiredFieldValidator1.initialvalue = "";
var ctl00_MainContent_RequiredFieldValidator2 = document.all ? document.all["ctl00_
MainContent_RequiredFieldValidator2"] : document.getElementById("ctl00_MainContent_
RequiredFieldValidator2");
ctl00_MainContent_RequiredFieldValidator2.controltovalidate = "ctl00_MainContent_
txtEmail";
ctl00_MainContent_RequiredFieldValidator2.errormessage = "You must enter your
email.";
ctl00_MainContent_RequiredFieldValidator2.evaluationfunction =
"RequiredFieldValidatorEvaluateIsValid";
ctl00_MainContent_RequiredFieldValidator2.initialvalue = "";
var ctl00_MainContent_RegularExpressionValidator1 = document.all ?
document.all["ctl00_MainContent_RegularExpressionValidator1"] : document.
getElementById("ctl00_MainContent_RegularExpressionValidator1");
ctl00_MainContent_RegularExpressionValidator1.controltovalidate = "ctl00_
MainContent_txtEmail";
ctl00_MainContent_RegularExpressionValidator1.errormessage = "You must enter a
valid email.";
ctl00_MainContent_RegularExpressionValidator1.evaluationfunction =
"RegularExpressionValidatorEvaluateIsValid";
ctl00_MainContent_RegularExpressionValidator1.validationexpression = "\\
w+([-+.\']\\w+)*@\\w+([-.]\\w+)*\\.\\w+([-.]\\w+)*";
var ctl00_MainContent_RequiredFieldValidator3 = document.all ? document.all["ctl00_
MainContent_RequiredFieldValidator3"] : document.getElementById("ctl00_MainContent_
RequiredFieldValidator3");
ctl00_MainContent_RequiredFieldValidator3.controltovalidate = "ctl00_MainContent_
txtSubject";
```

```
ctl00_MainContent_RequiredFieldValidator3.errormessage = "You must enter a
subject.";
ctl00_MainContent_RequiredFieldValidator3.evaluationfunction =
"RequiredFieldValidatorEvaluateIsValid";
ctl00_MainContent_RequiredFieldValidator3.initialvalue = "";
var ctl00_MainContent_RequiredFieldValidator4 = document.all ? document.all["ctl00_
MainContent_RequiredFieldValidator4"] : document.getElementById("ctl00_MainContent_
RequiredFieldValidator4");
ctl00_MainContent_RequiredFieldValidator4.controltovalidate = "ctl00_MainContent_
txtBody";
ctl00_MainContent_RequiredFieldValidator4.errormessage = "You must enter the body
text.";
ctl00_MainContent_RequiredFieldValidator4.evaluationfunction =
"RequiredFieldValidatorEvaluateIsValid";
ctl00_MainContent_RequiredFieldValidator4.initialvalue = "";
//]]>
        </script>

        <div>
            <input type="hidden" name="__EVENTVALIDATION" id="__
EVENTVALIDATION" value="/wEWBgLcnPqgCAKX08/vCwKH+NrJAQLM8a6DDwLNysbkCwL25qnqCBhnOoK
lPayWbiPQuCDdSDLHzs8L" />
        </div>

        <script type="text/javascript">
<!--
var Page_ValidationActive = false;
if (typeof(ValidatorOnLoad) == "function") {
    ValidatorOnLoad();
}

function ValidatorOnSubmit() {
    if (Page_ValidationActive) {
        return ValidatorCommonOnSubmit();
    }
    else {
        return true;
    }
}
// -->
        </script>

    </form>
    <div id="footer">
        Wrox Press © 2009
    </div>
    </div>
    </div>
</body>
</html>
```

No surprise if you couldn't understand what's going on here! Now run the ASP.NET MVC application and check the HTML code for the contact page:

```
<!DOCTYPE html PUBLIC "-//W3C//DTD XHTML 1.0 Strict//EN"
"http://www.w3.org/TR/xhtml1/DTD/xhtml1-strict.dtd">
```

```
<html xmlns="http://www.w3.org/1999/xhtml">
<head>
    <title>Contact Form </title>
    <link href="../Content/Site.css" rel="stylesheet" type="text/css" />
</head>
<body>
    <div class="page">
        <div id="header">
            <div id="title">
                <h1>
                    Validation</h1>
            </div>
            <div id="menucontainer">
                <ul id="menu">
                    <li><a href="/">Home</a></li>
                    <li><a href="/Contact/Contact">Contact</a></li>
                </ul>
            </div>
        </div>
        <div id="main">
            <h2>
                Contact Form</h2>
            <p>
                You can use this form to contact us.
            </p>
            <form action="/Contact/Contact" method="post">
            <div>
                <table>
                    <tr>
                        <td>
                            Name:
                        </td>
                        <td>
                            <input id="name" name="name" type="text" value="" />
                        </td>
                    </tr>
                    <tr>
                        <td>
                            Email:
                        </td>
                        <td>
                            <input id="email" name="email" type="text" value="" />
                        </td>
                    </tr>
                    <tr>
                        <td>
                            Subject:
                        </td>
                        <td>
                            <input id="subject" name="subject" type="text" value=""
/>
                        </td>
                    </tr>
                    <tr>
                        <td>
                            Body:
```

509

```
                                </td>
                                <td>
                                    <textarea cols="20" id="body" name="body" rows="2">
</textarea>
                                </td>
                            </tr>
                            <tr>
                                <td>
                                </td>
                                <td>
                                    <input type="submit" value="Send" />
                                </td>
                            </tr>
                        </table>
                    </div>
                    </form>
                    <div id="footer">
                        Wrox Press © 2009
                    </div>
                </div>
            </div>
        </body>
    </html>
```

You see that this code speaks for itself!

Chapter 18

Exercise 1 Solution

There are two main steps to be taken: updating the CommentForm control to add validation elements, and updating the IndividualPost action method in PostController to add validation logic.

First, update the CommentForm control to add some validation HTML helpers:

```
<%@ Control Language="C#" Inherits="System.Web.Mvc.ViewUserControl" %>
<h3 id="respond">
    Leave a Reply</h3>
<%= Html.ValidationSummary() %>
<% using (Html.BeginForm("IndividualPost", "Post"))
    { %>
<p>
    <label for="AuthorName">
        Name (required)</label><br />
    <%= Html.TextBox("AuthorName", null, new { tabindex = "1" })%>
    <%= Html.ValidationMessage("AuthorName")%>
</p>
<p>
    <label for="AuthorEmail">
        Email Address (required)</label><br />
    <%= Html.TextBox("AuthorEmail", null, new { tabindex = "2" })%>
```

```
            <%= Html.ValidationMessage("AuthorEmail")%>
    </p>
    <p>
        <label for="AuthorUrl">
            Website (required)</label><br />
        <%= Html.TextBox("AuthorUrl", null, new { tabindex = "3" })%>
        <%= Html.ValidationMessage("AuthorUrl")%>
    </p>
    <p>
        <label for="Body">
            Your Message (required)</label><br />
        <%= Html.TextArea("Body", new { rows = "10", cols = "20", tabindex = "4" })%>
        <%= Html.ValidationMessage("Body")%>
    </p>
    <p class="no-border">
        <input class="button" type="submit" value="Publish" tabindex="5" />
    </p>
<% } %>
```

Now update the IndividualPost action method in the PostController that accepts HTTP POST verb requests:

```
[AcceptVerbs(HttpVerbs.Post)]
public ActionResult IndividualPost(int id, Comment comment)
{
    // Validate Name
    if (string.IsNullOrEmpty(comment.AuthorName))
        ModelState.AddModelError("AuthorName",
            "You must enter your name.");

    // Validate Email
    if (string.IsNullOrEmpty(comment.AuthorEmail))
        ModelState.AddModelError("AuthorEmail",
            "You must enter your email.");
    else
    {
        Regex regex = new Regex
            (@"\w+([-+.']\w+)*@\w+([-.]\w+)*\.\w+([-.]\w+)*",
            RegexOptions.IgnoreCase);

        if (!regex.IsMatch(comment.AuthorEmail))
            ModelState.AddModelError("AuthorEmail",
                "You must enter a valid email.");
    }

    // Validate URL
    if (string.IsNullOrEmpty(comment.AuthorUrl))
        ModelState.AddModelError("AuthorUrl",
            "You must enter your URL.");
    else
    {
        Regex regex = new Regex
            (@"(?<http>(http:[/][/]|www.)([a-z]|[A-Z]|[0-9]|[/.]|[~])*)",
```

```
                    RegexOptions.IgnoreCase);

            if (!regex.IsMatch(comment.AuthorUrl))
                ModelState.AddModelError("AuthorUrl",
                    "You must enter a valid URL.");
        }

        // Validate Body
        if (string.IsNullOrEmpty(comment.Body))
            ModelState.AddModelError("Body",
                "You must enter the body text.");

        if (ViewData.ModelState.IsValid)
        {
            comment.PostID = id;
            this._commentRepository.AddComment(comment);
            return RedirectToAction("IndividualPost");
        }
        else
        {
            Post post = this._postRepository.GetPost(id);

            ViewData["Title"] = post.Title;

            ViewData["Categories"] = this._categoryRepository.GetCategories();
            ViewData["Post"] = post;
            ViewData["Comments"] = this._commentRepository.GetComments(id);

            return View();
        }
    }
}
```

The main body of this code is already familiar to you because you've dealt with this validation type in some chapters and exercises in this book. After validating the values of the comment form, the comment can be added to the database, but if this validation fails, we need to load data and show it along with validation errors.

Exercise 2 Solution

You already have learned that mocking is a very good technique in unit testing applications. One of the main reasons to use a Dependency Injection approach in the development of WroxBlog was the ease of mocking and unit testing. Now we're going to unit test WroxBlog with the Rhino Mocks framework and you see how that DI approach is becoming handy.

After creating a unit test project and adding a Rhino Mocks reference to your test project, you need to create three test classes to test `HomeController`, `PostController`, and `CategoryController`. We only test these controllers as the main part of testing and leave some other options such as testing the routing system to you.

First, we start with `HomeController` and create a `HomeControllerTest` class:

```
using System.Web.Mvc;
using Microsoft.VisualStudio.TestTools.UnitTesting;
using Rhino.Mocks;
using WroxBlog.Controllers;
```

```
using WroxBlog.Models;
using WroxBlog.Models.Interfaces;

namespace WroxBlog.Tests
{
    [TestClass()]
    public class HomeControllerTest
    {
        private TestContext testContextInstance;

        public TestContext TestContext
        {
            get
            {
                return testContextInstance;
            }
            set
            {
                testContextInstance = value;
            }
        }

        private MockRepository mocks;

        private IBlogRepository blogMockContext;
        private IPostRepository postMockContext;
        private ICategoryRepository categoryMockContext;

        [TestInitialize]
        public void SetupMocks()
        {
            mocks = new MockRepository();
            blogMockContext = mocks.DynamicMock<IBlogRepository>();
            postMockContext = mocks.DynamicMock<IPostRepository>();
            categoryMockContext = mocks.DynamicMock<ICategoryRepository>();
        }

        [TestMethod()]
        public void AboutTest()
        {
            using (mocks.Record())
            {
                Expect.Call(blogMockContext.GetAboutText()).Return("Test");
            }

            HomeController controller = new HomeController
                (blogMockContext, postMockContext, categoryMockContext);

            using (mocks.Playback())
            {
                ActionResult result = controller.About();
                ViewResult viewResult = result as ViewResult;

                string aboutText = (string)viewResult.ViewData["AboutText"];

                Assert.AreEqual("Test", aboutText);
```

```
            }
    }

            [TestMethod()]
            public void IndexTest()
            {
                CategoryCollection fakeCategories = new CategoryCollection();
                for (int i = 0; i < 5; i++)
                {
                    fakeCategories.Add(new Category() { ID = i });
                }

                PostCollection fakePosts = new PostCollection();
                for (int i = 0; i < 10; i++)
                {
                    fakePosts.Add(new Post() { ID = i });
                }

                using (mocks.Record())
                {
                    Expect.Call(categoryMockContext.GetCategories())
.Return(fakeCategories);
                    Expect.Call(postMockContext.GetRecentPosts(10)).Return(fakePosts);
                }

                HomeController controller = new HomeController
                    (blogMockContext, postMockContext, categoryMockContext);

                using (mocks.Playback())
                {
                    ActionResult result = controller.Index();
                    ViewResult viewResult = result as ViewResult;

                    CategoryCollection categories = viewResult.ViewData["Categories"]
                        as CategoryCollection;
                    Assert.AreEqual(5, categories.Count);

                    PostCollection posts = viewResult.ViewData["Posts"]
                        as PostCollection;
                    Assert.AreEqual(10, posts.Count);
                }
            }
        }
    }
}
```

Here we need to create dynamic mock objects for our repositories. We do this in test initialization in order to be able to apply the objects in both our test methods.

In AboutTest we record our expected value for the GetAboutText function of IBlogRepository and then create an instance of the controller. Inside the mock playback, we get the ActionResult value for the About action method from the controller and compare it with the text value that we had set for GetAboutText.

In `IndexTest` we create fake `CategoryCollection` and `PostCollection` objects and record our expected values for the repository methods involved. Then we create an instance of the `HomeController` and get the `ActionResult` value for the `Index` action method. Here we can compare the values from the view data collection with our expected values.

The next test class is `PostControllerTest`, which tests `PostController`:

```
using System.Web.Mvc;
using Microsoft.VisualStudio.TestTools.UnitTesting;
using Rhino.Mocks;
using WroxBlog.Controllers;
using WroxBlog.Models;
using WroxBlog.Models.Interfaces;

namespace WroxBlog.Tests
{
    [TestClass()]
    public class PostControllerTest
    {
        private TestContext testContextInstance;

        public TestContext TestContext
        {
            get
            {
                return testContextInstance;
            }
            set
            {
                testContextInstance = value;
            }
        }

        private MockRepository mocks;

        private ICategoryRepository categoryMockContext;
        private IPostRepository postMockContext;
        private ICommentRepository commentMockContext;

        [TestInitialize]
        public void SetupMocks()
        {
            mocks = new MockRepository();
            categoryMockContext = mocks.DynamicMock<ICategoryRepository>();
            postMockContext = mocks.DynamicMock<IPostRepository>();
            commentMockContext = mocks.DynamicMock<ICommentRepository>();
        }

        [TestMethod()]
        public void IndividualPostTest()
        {
            CategoryCollection fakeCategories = new CategoryCollection();
            for (int i = 0; i < 5; i++)
```

```
                    {
                        fakeCategories.Add(new Category() { ID = i });
                    }

                    Post fakePost = new Post()
                    {
                        ID = 6,
                        Title = "Test",
                        Body = "This is a test post"
                    };

                    CommentCollection fakeComments = new CommentCollection();
                    for (int i = 0; i < 3; i++)
                    {
                        fakeComments.Add(new Comment()
                        {
                            ID = i
                        });
                    }

                    using (mocks.Record())
                    {
                        Expect.Call(categoryMockContext.GetCategories())
.Return(fakeCategories);
                        Expect.Call(postMockContext.GetPost(6)).Return(fakePost);
                        Expect.Call(commentMockContext.GetComments(6))
.Return(fakeComments);
                    }

                    PostController controller = new PostController
                        (postMockContext, categoryMockContext, commentMockContext);

                    using (mocks.Playback())
                    {
                        ActionResult result = controller.IndividualPost(6);
                        ViewResult viewResult = result as ViewResult;

                        string title = (string)viewResult.ViewData["Title"];
                        Assert.AreEqual("Test", title);

                        CategoryCollection categories = viewResult.ViewData["Categories"]
                            as CategoryCollection;
                        Assert.AreEqual(5, categories.Count);

                        Post post = viewResult.ViewData["Post"] as Post;
                        Assert.AreEqual("This is a test post", post.Body);

                        CommentCollection comments = viewResult.ViewData["Comments"]
                            as CommentCollection;
                        Assert.AreEqual(3, comments.Count);
                    }
                }
            }
        }
    }
```

Like the first test class, here we set up dynamic mock objects for the repository classes in the test initialization. In IndividualPostTest we create fake CategoryCollection, Post, and CommentCollection objects, and we record the expected values for the corresponding service functions. Creating an instance of PostController and getting the ActionResult for the IndividualPost action method, we can compare the values for Title, Categories, Post, and Comments from the view data collection with our expectations.

The last test class is CategoryControllerTest, which tests the CategoryController:

```
using System.Web.Mvc;
using Microsoft.VisualStudio.TestTools.UnitTesting;
using Rhino.Mocks;
using WroxBlog.Controllers;
using WroxBlog.Models;
using WroxBlog.Models.Interfaces;

namespace WroxBlog.Tests
{
    [TestClass()]
    public class CategoryControllerTest
    {
        private TestContext testContextInstance;

        public TestContext TestContext
        {
            get
            {
                return testContextInstance;
            }
            set
            {
                testContextInstance = value;
            }
        }

        private MockRepository mocks;

        private IPostRepository postMockContext;
        private ICategoryRepository categoryMockContext;

        [TestInitialize]
        public void SetupMocks()
        {
            mocks = new MockRepository();
            postMockContext = mocks.DynamicMock<IPostRepository>();
            categoryMockContext = mocks.DynamicMock<ICategoryRepository>();
        }

        [TestMethod()]
        public void CategoryIndexTest()
        {
            string categoryName = "MVC";

            CategoryCollection fakeCategories = new CategoryCollection();
```

```
              for (int i = 0; i < 5; i++)
              {
                  fakeCategories.Add(new Category()
                  {
                      ID = i
                  });
              }

              PostCollection fakePosts = new PostCollection();
              for (int i = 0; i < 10; i++)
              {
                  fakePosts.Add(new Post()
                  {
                      ID = i
                  });
              }

              using (mocks.Record())
              {
                  Expect.Call(categoryMockContext.GetCategories())
.Return(fakeCategories);
                  Expect.Call(postMockContext.GetPostsInCategory(categoryName))
.Return(fakePosts);
              }

              CategoryController controller = new CategoryController
                  (postMockContext, categoryMockContext);

              using (mocks.Playback())
              {
                  ActionResult result = controller.CategoryIndex(categoryName);
                  ViewResult viewResult = result as ViewResult;

                  string title = (string)viewResult.ViewData["Title"];
                  Assert.AreEqual(categoryName, title);

                  CategoryCollection categories = viewResult.ViewData["Categories"]
                      as CategoryCollection;
                  Assert.AreEqual(5, categories.Count);

                  PostCollection posts = viewResult.ViewData["Posts"]
                      as PostCollection;
                  Assert.AreEqual(10, posts.Count);
              }
          }
      }
  }
```

Having discussed the previous two test classes, this should be easy for you to understand. Again, we create dynamic mock objects in the test initialization for the IPostRepository and ICategoryRepository services.

In the `CategoryIndexTest` method we try to test the working of the category controller for a specific category. We create fake `CategoryCollection` and `PostCollection` classes to set the expected returning values for our service functions. Then we compare the view data extracted from the `ActionResult` returned from the `CategoryIndex` action method to make sure that Title, Categories, and Posts are our expected objects.

Note that for better unit testing, more scenarios and cases can be tested in WroxBlog, but we just worked on the core tests that are more common. You can continue this progress with more specific tests.

Chapter 19

This chapter doesn't have exercises.

Index